# THE CHURCH AND FREEMASONRY
## IN BRAZIL, 1872-1875
## A STUDY IN REGALISM

This dissertation was conducted under the direction of Dr. Manoel S. Cardozo, as major professor, and was approved by Dr. Friedrich Engel-Janosi, Dr. J. Manuel Espinosa, and Dr. John Tracy Ellis, as readers.

The Catholic University of America

# THE CHURCH AND FREEMASONRY IN BRAZIL, 1872-1875 A STUDY IN REGALISM

### A DISSERTATION

Submitted to the Faculty of the Graduate School of Arts and Sciences of the Catholic University of America in Partial Fulfillment of the Requirements for the Degree of Doctor of Philosophy

BY

Sister Mary Crescentia Thornton
OF THE
Sisters of Charity of the Blessed Virgin Mary
Clarke College, Dubuque, Iowa

GREENWOOD PRESS, PUBLISHERS
WESTPORT, CONNECTICUT

*The Library of Congress has catalogued this publication as follows:*

---

Library of Congress Cataloging in Publication Data

Thornton, Mary Crescentia, Sister, 1910–
    The Church and Freemasonry in Brazil, 1872–1875.

    Reprint of the ed. published by Catholic University
of America Press, Washington.
    Originally presented as the author's thesis,
Catholic University of America, 1948.
    Bibliography:  p.
    1.  Freemasons and Catholic Church.  2.  Catholic
Church in Brazil.  3.  Church and state in Brazil.
I.  Title.
HS495.T4  1973        366.1'0981        73-2647
ISBN 0–8371–6816–3

---

## TABLE OF CONTENTS

# PREFACE

The Religious Question that arose out of a conflict between the Church and Freemasonry in Brazil in the eighteen seventies had far-reaching consequences in the political as well as in the religious life of the country. The simple narrative of the controversy has frequently been written, but a satisfactory analysis of the underlying forces that produced it, and a complete evaluation of the separate incidents that constitute it, remain to be done. It is the purpose of this study to interpret in the light of contemporary sources the significance of this prolonged and dynamic controversy that contributed indirectly to the downfall of the Brazilian Empire in 1889.[1]

Had relations between the temporal and the spiritual authorities in the empire been uniformly harmonious prior to the crisis of the seventies; had the attitude of the State toward the Church been equitable; had the Church herself been strong and free, the Religious Question, that began as a quarrel between two social groups, would never have developed into a major political issue of sufficient moment to weaken the very empire itself. The Episcopal-Masonic controversy was in reality but the apex of a pyramid of conflicts between the spiritual and the temporal powers; its wide base was laid in the early years of the empire; its super-structure was erected in the reign of Dom Pedro II, through a series of minute and vexatious regulations that regalistic statesmen devised to bring the Church into more complete subservience.

While Freemasonry has in our interpretation been dislodged from its place of primary importance in the Religious Question, it has by no means disappeared from among the factors that contributed to the conflict; neither can it be ignored in a study of the general incompatibility that prevailed in the relations of Church and State in the Brazilian Empire. It must be regarded, however, as the occasion, not the cause, of the grave controversy between Church and State known as the Religious Question. This controversy illustrates the interplay of regalism and Free-

---

[1] The Religious Question is considered as one of three major causes that contributed to the downfall of the Brazilian Empire in 1889. See Percy A. Martin, "Causes of the Collapse of the Brazilian Empire," *The Hispanic American Historical Review*. IV (February, 1921), 4-48.

masonry on the Church in Brazil and reveals the fact that Freemasonry was, in large measure, the tool of regalistic statesmen.

As regards the spelling of, and the use of written accents on, Portuguese words in this study, the reader not familiar with the present state of orthography in Brazil will detect what may appear to him to be inconsistencies. In direct quotations from the Portuguese, such as in titles of books, an attempt has been made to respect the original; in all other instances the rules of orthography in force in Brazil before the recent accord between the Brazilian Academy of Letters and the Lisbon Academy of Sciences became law, have been followed.

To Dr. Manoel S. Cardozo, at whose suggestion this study was begun, I am indebted for valuable criticism throughout its development. I also owe much to Dr. Friedrich Engel-Janosi, Dr. J. Manuel Espinosa, and Dr. John Tracy Ellis for their careful reading of the manuscript, and to Dr. Sisto Rosso, O.F.M., for his assistance in handling Italian sources, as well as for a critical reading of the monograph. I wish to express my gratitude to Heitor Lyra, Brazilian minister to Denmark, who gave helpful suggestions; to Father Cândido Santini, S.J., of the Central Seminary, São Leopoldo, Rio Grande do Sul, Brazil, who supplied me with a copy of his useful monograph on patronage in Brazil; and to Sister Mary Paul, Saint Mary College, Xavier, Kansas, who provided me with letters excerpted from J. Guerin's *Notices biographiques sur Mgr. J. B. Miège*. I acknowledge with deep appreciation the courteous assistance given me by the staffs of the National Archives, Washington, D. C.; the Library of Congress, Washington, D. C., particularly the Hispanic Foundation and the Law Library; the Library of the Pan American Union; The Oliveira Lima Library and the Mullen Library, The Catholic University of America, Washington, D. C.; the Newberry Library, Chicago; and the University of Chicago Library. My sincere gratitude is due, likewise, to the Superiors of my Congregation, who gave me the opportunity to study at The Catholic University of America, and to the sisters, particularly to Sister Mary Philippa, B.V.M., who assisted with the preparation of the manuscript.

SISTER MARY CRESCENTIA, B.V.M.

May 24, 1946

# CHAPTER I

## EUROPEAN BACKGROUNDS OF BRAZILIAN LIBERALISM AND FREEMASONRY

Early in the seventies of the last century two Brazilian bishops contested the right of Freemasons to membership in Brazilian religious associations. The immediate provocation of their action was Masonic propaganda against the Church and especially against the Brazilian episcopacy, occasioned by the fact that Bishop Dom Pedro Maria de Lacerda, of Rio de Janeiro, suspended a priest in March, 1872, for public participation in a Masonic festival. The Holy See had repeatedly condemned the Masonic fraternity in general, but the pontifical decrees condemning Freemasonry had never been promulgated in Brazil because they lacked the *placet*[1] required by the imperial constitution. The contest between the religious associations and the bishops began in Pernambuco when the new bishop of Olinda, Dom Vital Maria Gonçalves de Oliveira, placed a religious brotherhood under interdict because it refused to expel members affiliated with Masonry. Similar action was soon taken by the bishop of Pará, Dom Antônio de Macedo Costa. An appeal made by the brotherhoods caused the imperial government to take action which led to the imprisonment of the bishops and ultimately to the serious embarrassment of the government because of the impasse in which this action had placed it. It is these events in Brazilian history which are known as the Religious Question, and it is this question that fills the history of Brazil during the last years of the empire.

---

[1] The *placet* may be defined as "a faculty which civil rulers impart to a Bull, papal Brief, or other ecclesiastical enactment in order to give it binding force in their respective territories. This faculty is conceded after ecclesiastical laws have been examined and found not derogatory to any right of the civil power and, therefore, suitable for promulgation." This definition assumes the term *placet* to be synonymous with the term *exequatur*. See Salvatore Luzio, "Exequatur," *The Catholic Encyclopedia*, V. 707-708. See also pp. 25-26 below.

1

Various interpretations of the Religious Question have been offered. One explanation is that the Freemasons perpetrated the quarrel to injure Catholicism in Brazil. Advocates of this theory hold that the leaders of Freemasonry surmised that the time was opportune because they would now have the support of the Liberal group, whose members were incensed by the decrees of the Vatican Council (1869-1870), and of the new Republican Party, formally established in 1870, whose adherents wanted to effect the overthrow of the empire. Another plausible interpretation is that the Liberals and the Republicans, through the instrumentality of Freemasonry, attacked the Church, a pillar of the monarchy, to weaken the empire and to prepare the way for the overthrow of the emperor and the establishment of a republican form of government.[2] A third representation alleges that the pope, acting through intermediaries, instigated the quarrel as a testing ground for his recently proclaimed dogma of infallibility.[3] Probably the most popular of all the interpretations is that the bishops of Olinda and Pará, overzealous and misguided as a result of their French training,[4] viewed Brazilian

---

[2] While the Republicans did not initiate the quarrel, there is no doubt that they made use of it in their campaign to discredit the monarchy. See Francisco [Xavier da] Cunha, *Reminiscencias, propaganda contra o imperio na imprensa e na diplomacia* (Rio de Janeiro, 1914), pp. 383-386, 427-428, 435-436, 557-560, 564-566, 567-568, 571-574.

[3] The attitude of Brazilian statesmen toward the dogma of papal infallibility was by no means unique. The Döllinger group in Germany, headed by Johann Josef Ignaz von Döllinger (1799-1890), professor of canon law and church history at the University of Munich, exemplifies one radically adverse reaction to the pronouncement. The attitude of William Gladstone (1809-1898) in England typified another violent reaction. In Brazil the tendency was to see in the policies of Pius IX, especially in his Syllabus of Errors (1864) and in the definition of the dogma of papal infallibility (1870), a secret movement sponsored by an ultramontane element, Jesuitical in source, which planned to make the Church of Pius IX a highly centralized institution that had little in common with the allegedly true Roman Catholic Church referred to in the imperial constitution. See Américo Jacobina Lacombe, "O Aspecto religioso da questão dos bispos," *Verbum* (Rio de Janeiro), I (December, 1944), 334.

[4] Dom Vital Maria Gonçalves de Oliveira took his first year of theology at the Seminary of Olinda; he then enrolled at St. Sulpice in Paris; the following year he entered the Capuchin Order at Versailles; here he remained

Freemasonry as akin to that of the French Grand Orient, and challenged it, without taking the trouble to discover that it was not Masonry of the French type, and was, moreover, in no way harmful to the Church; thus, by their intransigent attitude, they perpetrated a quarrel that could easily have been avoided.

A careful study of the controversy between Freemasonry and the Catholic Church in Brazil has fostered what appears to be the well-founded conclusion that this quarrel, once launched, ceased to be a contest over Freemasonry as such, and became a decisive struggle between the temporal and the spiritual authorities. The controversy must be studied, therefore, not as an isolated conflict, but as the most serious as well as the most spectacular in a series of altercations between the Church and the State from the creation of the Brazilian Empire in 1822 to its overthrow in 1889. As this controversy is explainable in relation to the conflicts that preceded it, so these in turn are more intelligible in the light of the Liberal European ideologies that gave them their distinctive regalistic, Gallican, and Jansenist shades.

## II

It has been said that the nineteenth century was *"par excellence* the century of secularism."[5] Indeed, all the "isms" that the nineteenth century either produced or revitalized may be said to be the result in one way or another of the disarrangement of the hierarchy of order. It is to this hierarchy that Donoso Cortés refers when he writes that the diverse errors of the modern mind falsify the immutable hierarchical order established in things. This order, he says, places the supernatural over the natural,

---

for his novitiate; he completed his studies for the priesthood at the Capuchin house of studies in Toulouse. Dom Antônio de Macedo Costa was trained at St. Sulpice in Paris.

[5] Raymond Corrigan, *The Church in the Nineteenth Century* (Milwaukee, 1938), p. 38. Donald Attwater, *A Catholic Dictionary* (New York, 1943), p. 481, defines secularism: "The teaching that the foundation of morality, duty, and religion is to be sought in nature alone, and that, therefore, the teaching aids and sanctions of supernatural religion and the Church are of no account in human conduct."

and, in consequence of this, faith over reason, grace over free will, Divine Providence over human liberty, Church over State: in a word, God over man.[6]

By 1800 modern man had become autonomous to a degree that even Kantian philosophy could hardly have predicted. The starry heavens above and the moral law within, which had satisfied Kant's mind as proof for the existence of God, had not been sufficient to hold the statesmen of Europe to their moorings in a Christian religion which philosophy had robbed of its rational justification. Man had ruled religion[7] out of world affairs. Religion, it is true, still influenced the lives of men and women, but it did so as a private matter; the great issues of state were settled without calling for its counsels or considering its rights. The world had outgrown religion; society and politics, education and even morality had been emancipated "from the Church that presumed to speak in the name of God."[8] The world of the nineteenth century had, in fine, gone a long way toward the secularization of society; and among the forces that helped to bring about the new order of things was Freemasonry.[9]

We need not concern ourselves with the claims of Freemasonry to great antiquity, because, whatever its antecedents in the medieval or even in the ancient world, it began its great laic cru-

---

[6] Juan Donoso Cortés, *Obras escogidas de Don Juan Donoso Cortés* (Madrid [1932]), II, 294.

[7] The term "religion" is used here in the sense of a revealed body of truths, and implies a divine teaching authority and a visible church organization.

[8] Corrigan, *op. cit.*, p. 38. For a brief summary of philosophical trends, see Fernand Mourret, *L'Église et la Révolution*, Vol. VII of *Histoire générale de l'Église* (Paris, 1914), pp. 24-44.

[9] For a general discussion of Freemasonry see Robert F. Gould, *A Concise History of Freemasonry* (New York, 1924); Hermann Gruber, "Masonry," *Catholic Encyclopedia*, IX, 771-788; Albert G. Mackey, *The Encyclopedia of Freemasonry* (Chicago, 1927); Ernest Nys, *Idées modernes, droit international et franc-maçonnerie* (Bruxelles, 1908); Henry Leonard Stillson (ed.), *History of the Ancient and Honorable Fraternity of Free and Accepted Masons and Concordant Orders* (Boston, 1906); John S. M. Ward, *Freemasonry and the Ancient Gods* (London, 1921); Arthur Edward Waite, *A New Encyclopaedia of Freemasonry* (London, 1921). See also Masonic journals, especially *The New Age Magazine* (Washington, D. C.) and *The American Tyler-Keystone* (Ann Arbor, Michigan).

sade only after the reform of English Freemasonry in 1717.[10]
Its reorganizers, the fathers of its new constitution, viewed modern Masonry as the heir apparent of Christianity, which they
believed was in the last stages of decadence. The English Freemasons did not repudiate Christianity, even though many of
them subscribed to the deistic belief that supernatural religion,
based on revelation and circumscribed by dogma, was destined
to disappear and to be superseded by a religion of humanity
based on science and reason.[11] These Freemasons valued Christianity as a social force which had done a great work in raising
men to their present level of civilization, and which still exercised a great influence over the mass of the people. But the
future, they believed, would belong to men equipped to live in
an atmosphere of scientific self-sufficiency.

These fathers of modern Masonry sought to effect a compromise between medieval Christianity and modern rationalism.
To do this, they would persuade the Christian to treat the established dogmas of Christianity as private opinions, and invite
the rationalist to acknowledge a supreme First Cause, regarded
as the Great Architect of the Universe, which would satisfy both
a social and a scientific need.[12] Masonry, in its apparent determination to be the intermediary between medieval Christian Europe
and modern scientific Europe, set itself to be all things to all

[10] The philosophy of Freemasonry is well described in J. G. Findel, *History
of Freemasonry* (2d rev. ed., London, 1871); Bernard Faÿ, *Revolution and
Freemasonry (1680-1800)* (Boston, 1935), and in a series of articles by
John M. Cooper: "Freemasonry's Two Hundredth Birthday," *The Ecclesiastical Review*, LVI (June, 1917), 590-616, "Freemasonry, State and
Church," *ibid.*, LVII (July, 1917), 43-65, "Freemasonry and Modern
Life," *ibid.*, (August, 1917), 164-184. These articles give a dispassionate
picture of what Freemasonry is in itself and of how it fits into the modern
world pattern. Faÿ's work, while not so accurate in detail as Professor Cooper's, is equally as objective and more comprehensive. Faÿ's purpose is "to show
that before all political revolutions started a great intellectual and moral revolution had been effected" (p. ix).

[11] Faÿ, *op. cit.*, p. 307.

[12] Faÿ, *op. cit.*, p. 310-311; Cooper, "Freemasonry and Modern Life,"
*loc. cit.*, pp. 164-174. Professor Cooper, having just completed a survey of
what Masons themselves have to say about the modern beginnings of their
own society, writes, p. 171: "Weighing all the above facts, we are justified,

men, and in so doing became a powerful bond among men of the rising middle class, and a link between them and the established ruling gentry.[13]

Freemasonry's dream of becoming the "friendly and legal heir of Christianity"[14] did not materialize, but for many years there seemed to be ample justification for its hope. The Enlightenment, which developed in the Christian Europe of the eighteenth century, was in a real sense the natural and logical consequence of the Renaissance and the Reformation. Under its various forms — English Rationalism, French *Philosophie,* and German *Aufklärung* — the Enlightenment was essentially the same in all countries: a spiritual crisis, as Maritain sees it, at the end of which man conceived himself to be the center of his history and the ultimate end of his activity on earth, and arrogated to himself the divine privilege of absolute independence or self-sufficiency.[15] In view of this development, it was natural for the early leaders of Masonry to believe that they were witnessing the end of Christianity. Supernaturalism, they felt, was old-fashioned; naturalism, on the contrary, was popular.

---

it seems, in drawing the following conclusion: Early English Masonry, while not exactly the direct offspring of deism, was largely inspired by contemporary rationalism. Some of its ideas were derived from deistic rationalism, although its sympathies were on the whole inclined more to Christian rationalism. It did not exclude the deists from its ranks, but aimed rather at gathering into one fold, deist, Christian rationalist, and conservative Christian."

[13] Faÿ, *op. cit.,* 312-317. Gustave Bord, *La Franc-Maçonnerie en France des origines à 1815 à* (Paris [1909]), I, 97-101, xv-xvi, xxiii-iv. Bord says that the consequence of this equality was disrespect for authority. He is of the opinion (p. xxiv) that Masonry was influential in the early stages of the French Revolution because of its adherence to the dogma of equality. When the proletariat gained control of the government, the Masonic dogma of equality was no longer heralded, and Freemasonry temporarily ceased to be a powerful force in France. "Masonry," writes Cooper ("Freemasonry, State and Church," *loc. cit.,* p. 48), "participated, especially as a propagandist, in the movement that culminated in the French Revolution, although after 1791-92, when the proletariat gained the ascendancy nearly all the French lodges closed their doors and suspended work."

[14] Faÿ, *op. cit.,* p. 307.

[15] Jacques Maritain, *The Angelic Doctor: the Life and Thought of St. Thomas Aquinas* (New York, 1931), p. 70. See also Maritain, *The Things*

Chief among the tenets of Freemasonry are a belief in progress, a faith in the power of the human mind to arrive at truth, and a conviction that human science is "the foundation of all knowledge, the source of all certitude, even of religious belief."[16] Freemasonry, therefore, was bound to conflict with the Catholic Church, which adheres to dogma, respects the past, and insists on clear-cut distinctions between reason and revelation.[17] Eighteenth century Freemasonry, "the apostle of science and progress and the enemy of tradition," brought about "the complete intellectual upset which characterized that era," and "paved the way for the social and political revolutions of the latter part of that century."[18]

The papacy detected the peril of Masonry almost from the beginning. On April 28, 1738, Pope Clement XII launched his bull *In eminenti apostolatus specula*[19] in which he condemned Freemasonry and forbade Catholics under pain of excommunication to take part in Masonic societies, to favor their increase, or to give them asylum either in their homes or elsewhere. On April 15, 1751, Pope Benedict XIV by his bull *Providas Romanorum Pontificum*[20] renewed the prohibitions of his predecessor and pointed out the consequences to which the rationalistic ideology of these associations would lead.[21]

When the Masonic fraternity realized that the papacy looked

*That Are Not Caesar's* (New York, 1930), p. xxv: "The error of the modern world and the modern mind consists in the claim to ensure the domination of nature by reason while at the same time refusing the domination of reason by supernature."

[16] Faÿ, *op. cit.*, p. 309.

[17] *Ibid.*, pp. 309-310; Manuel B. Grainha, *Histoire de la franc-maçonnerie en Portugal, 1733-1912* (Lisbonne, 1913), p. 220.

[18] Faÿ, *op. cit.*, pp. 309-310; Cooper, "Freemasonry, State and Church," *loc. cit.*, p. 48.

[19] *Bullarum diplomatum et privilegiorum sanctorum Romanorum pontificum* (Taurinorium, 1872), XXIV, 366-367.

[20] *Bullarii Romani continuati: Benedicti XIV pont. opt. max. olim Prosperi Cardinalis de Lambertinis Bullarium* (Pragae, 1886), III, i, 283-286.

[21] Bord, *op. cit.*, 194-195. Cooper, Freemasonry and Modern Life," *loc. cit.*, 174, writes: "The oaths, the secrets, the ritual, and such things, are minor matters; the essential part of Masonry from the Catholic standpoint

upon the Masonic ideology as incompatible with the supernaturalism of Roman Catholicism, and was prepared to warn Catholics against Freemasonry, it began its fight against the Head of
the Catholic Church.[22] So successful was its anti-papal propaganda that many Masons, who believed in the divinity of Christ
and correlatively in the divine institution of Christianity, were
led to view the papacy as the source of evil, and to join in the
cry for a return to the primitive Church.[23] This campaign
against the Holy See won for the Masonic societies a large following among Gallican and Jansenist Catholics, many of whom,
as regalistic statesmen, propagated anti-papal ideas in governmental circles.[24] In the nineteenth century the same ideas were
rampant in Brazil, particularly after the separation of the country from Portugal in 1822, when efforts were made to proclaim
the new freedom in all sections of Brazilian society. In Brazil,

---

is the philosophy." Hermann Hettner, *Geschichte de englischen Literatur*, Vol.
I, *Literaturgeschichte des achtzehnten Jahrhunderts* (Braunschweig, 1894),
p. 216, says: "The Papal See . . . with the keen insight particularly characteristic of it in ecclesiastical and political matters, grasped in the clearest
manner the inmost essence of Freemasonry. The Papacy banned it as early as
1738, and expressly on the ground that the order was based not on ecclesiastical but on purely human foundations; '*affectata quadam contenti honestatis
naturalis specie*,' as the Papal Bull put it."

[22] At this same time, Freemasonry began its defamation of the Society of
Jesus, which by reason of the purpose of its establishment was reckoned by
the enemies of Rome in the post-reformation era as the bulwark of the papacy.
Bord, *op. cit.*, I, 203, says: "À côté de la Papauté un autre corps organisé
attirera des le début les attaques de la maçonnerie. Le jésuites sont puissants;
ils sont riches; ils sont intelligents; ils sont unis. Il faut les détruire . . . .
On forme contre eux l'opinion: dans les loges, dans les salons, dans les sociétés
littéraires, dans les pamphlets, dans la rue."

[23] *Ibid.*, 201: "Contre elle [the papacy], tout d'abord, les maçons ne luttent
pas de front, ils ne l'attaquent pas dans ses dogmas, mais dans sa discipline.
Dans la correspondance des maçons, comme dans celle de Willermoz par ex-
emple, on constate qu'autour de lui on veut revenir à la primitive Église; on
reconnaît la divinité du Christ que avait mis l'humanité dans sa vraie voie.
Mais cet homme pieux, même devot a l'horreur de la Papauté; c'est elle qui a
tout perdu, c'est d'elle que vient tout le mal."

[24] *Ibid.* Bord writes, "Gallicans, jansénistes et parlementaires pensent comme
lui [Willermoz, see note 23] aussi gallicans et jansénistes et parlementaires
encombrent-ils les loges. Ils feront plus tard le clergé constitutionnel." Léon

as in Europe, the alignment of many political leaders and dis-affected Catholics with Masonry against the Holy See was a reality. That is why many Brazilians who avowed themselves Catholics, and who may have looked upon themselves as more Catholic than the pope, were hostile to the Holy See and to the claims of the Roman pontiff. In Brazil as elsewhere, Freemason-ry's propaganda against Rome bore abundant harvest because of schismatic and heretical tendencies fostered, or at least shielded, by statesmen who were nominally Catholic.

The correlation between the new Masonic societies and the new spirit of nationalism is a factor in modern European history. At the time when the fathers of reformed Masonry were draw-ing the blueprint of the new society which in their minds would take the place of the social order based on revealed Christianity, so-called Catholic statesmen in Catholic countries were de-uni-versalizing Catholicism so that they could fit it into the structure of the national state.[25] Inevitably these statesmen were loath to recognize the universality of the spiritual jurisdiction of the papacy,[26] which they considered an infringement upon national sovereignty. Indeed, they exhibited a rather uniform attitude of

---

Séchéé, *Les derniers Jansénistes et leur rôle dans l'histoire de France depuis la ruine de Port-Royal jusqu'à nos jours (1710-1890)* (Paris, 1891), *passim*, draws attention to the anti-papal ideas current among Jansenistic Catholics of eighteenth and nineteenth century France, but remarks that their opposition to the papacy was no more violent than that of nineteenth century Catholic Lib-erals. See pp. 12-14 below.

[25] Emmet J. Hughes, *The Church and the Liberal Society* (Princeton, N. J., 1944), p. 3, says: "The national state signified at once the coalescence of myriad feudal provinces and the disintegration of the quasi-universal Christian society: the capitulation of the medieval dichotomy of *jus divinum* and *jus naturale* to the mundane and militant might of national sovereignty."

[26] The modern struggle to control the papacy goes back to the thirteenth century, when Roman law was first appealed to in an effort to establish the claims of temporal rulers. The most famous example of this period is the attempt of the *regestes* of Philip the Fair to gain control of the Church in France. Their efforts brought forth the famous bulls of Boniface VIII, espe-cially *Clericis laicos* and *Unam sanctam*. The effort to share in the government of the Church took different forms in different countries. In Spain and Portugal, the privileges of patronage assured the sovereigns a voice in the management of the affairs of the Church within their domains. Other sover-

opposition to that jurisdiction. Yet these same statesmen were unwilling to act precipitously, and therefore sought to find legal justification for their usurpation of power in Church matters. They vindicated their acts by referring to the *jus circa sacra* which, they maintained, included the *jus reformandi*, the *jus advocatiae*, and the *jus cavendi*.[27] To these asserted rights, which enhanced the power of the State over the Church and curtailed the exercise of papal jurisdiction within the confines of the State, was added the royal *placet*, or censorship of bulls, letters, and other pontifical acts.

The State, having limited as far as possible the jurisdictional control of the papacy, proposed to dominate the domestic hierarchy through the exercise of special privileges. Some of these privileges originated in papal grants, but they had been extended by the State in the course of time. In many Catholic countries, the State, by a sort of eminent domain, had usurped the property of the Church, compensating her by assuming responsibility for

---

eigns, not enjoying such privileges, tried to attain the same end by controlling the College of Cardinals. During the period of the Avignon residence of the popes, France had an enviable position in this regard. With the break-up of western Christendom at the time of the Reformation, England lost interest in the papacy, and the continental countries tended more and more toward national churches. The Peace of Augsburg (1555) gave birth to the rule, *cujus regio, ejus religio*. The prerogative of supervision tacitly acknowledged, the princes in the German provinces assumed greater and greater control over the affairs of the Church within the limits of their domain. In France, the Gallican Liberties (see pp. 17-18 below) received more and more juridical significance. The Thirty Years' War (1618-1648), which gave new prominence to the problem of the relations between Church and State, inspired Grotius (see p. 16 below) to attempt to systematize the control of the State over the religion of its subjects.

[27] Arturo Carlo Jemolo, "Giurisdizionalismo," *Enciclopedia Italiana*, XVII, 366-367. *Jus reformandi* infers the power of the sovereign to watch over the unity and purity of the faith. *Jus advocatiae* is the alleged right of the State to hear appeals against acts of the ecclesiastical authority. This right will be discussed in some detail later in this chapter under the designation, "Recourse to the Crown." (See p. 24 below). *Jus cavendi* included the rights, which the State claimed, to exercise a preventive control over certain ecclesiastical acts. Nabuco de Araújo's appeal to the *jus cavendi* in justification of the State's prohibition of the admission of novices into religious orders is referred to in Chapter III, p. 96, note 136 below.

the payment of Church officials from the national treasury. But the fact of the transfer of property was often forgot, and statesmen felt that, since Church officials were paid by the State out of state funds, they were civil servants, subject to the same supervision as other state officials.[28]

## III

It is of course true that Freemasonry may be looked upon as an amalgam of characteristics peculiar to the modern world. Beyond Freemasonry lay the great reality — the fact that men were already alienated from the Christian way of life; were enamored of the great Leviathan; were hostile to the claims of the papacy; and were persuaded that the human race was destined in the near future to achieve complete autonomy. Masonry in a sense exploited the trends inherent in modern society; with good reason has Faÿ said that faith in the future of humanity spread in the eighteenth century, not only as an abstract fact, but also as a social force, "through the agency of Freemasonry which at once accepted it and advocated it." Faÿ is also of the opinion that "the great historical importance of modern Freemasonry results from this attitude which it adopted in the eighteenth century and to which it has consistently adhered."[29]

The trends that Freemasonry exploited may be found in Liberalism,[30] the *Weltanschauung* of modern society. Liberalism, in the words of Sardá y Salvany, is "the dogmatic affirmation of the absolute independence of individual and of social rea-

---

[28] Corrigan, *op. cit.*, p. 113. See also Jemolo, "Giurisdizionalismo," *loc. cit.*, pp. 366-367.

[29] Faÿ, *op. cit.*, p. viii. Faÿ adds: "Thus Freemasonry has become the most efficient social power of the civilized world. But it has been a hidden power, difficult to trace, to describe and to define. Consequently most historians have avoided treating it seriously and giving it due credit." See also J. G. Findel, *op. cit.*, pp. 125-126, 135-151, *passim.*

[30] On Liberalism see Guido Ruggiero, *The History of European Liberalism*, trans. by R. G. Collingwood (London, 1927); George J. Weill, *L'éveil des nationalités et le mouvement Libéral 1815-1848* (Paris, 1930). Weill's study considers Liberalism in France. For the philosophical background of economic liberalism, see Élie Halévy, *Le Radicalisme philosophique* (Paris,

son."[31] The Liberal, therefore, substitutes "the naturalistic principle of free examination for the supernatural principle of faith,"[32] and establishes human reason as the criterion of truth. The Liberal ideology was inevitably bound to clash with Catholicism on a philosophical plane, for Catholicism, as Sardá y Salvany says, is "the dogma of the absolute subjection of the individual and social reason to the law of God."[33] So apparent is the antithesis between Catholicism and Liberalism, that, had Liberalism been confined to the speculative realm and not invaded the domain of practical life, no hybrid ideology would have been conceivable.[34] But Liberalism was never purely speculative; in fact, its origin was essentially political, and in its inception Liberalism constituted a movement against political ab-

---

1904). See also Antonin Debidour, *Histoire des rapports de l'église et de l'état en France de 1789 à 1905* (Paris, 1898-1906); Hermann Gruber, "Liberalism," *Catholic Encyclopedia*, IX, 212-214; K. Hilgenreiner, "Liberalismus." *Lexikon für Theologie und Kirche*, VI, 542-546.

[31] Félix Sardá y Salvany, *El Liberalismo es pecado* (Barcelona, 1887), p. 32. Donald Attwater, *op. cit.*, p. 308, defines Liberalism as follows: "A group of errors regarding the relation between Church and State, divine law, ecclesiastical law and various articles of belief. In various forms it contends that all laws are derived from the authority of the State (Absolute Liberalism); or, while granting a juridical authority to the Church, it denies that the Church is in any way supreme or superior to the State and, maintaining that her authority is over consciences only, lays down that she has no external or social authority (Moderate Liberalism); or, granting the Church's independence and supremacy, it lays down that her power should not be pressed."

[32] Sardá y Salvany, *op. cit.*, p. 33.

[33] *Ibid.*, pp. 32-33.

[34] Ruggiero, *op. cit.*, pp. 399-403. In this work, recognized as an excellent study of Liberalism by one of its advocates, we find (pp. 339-340) the following explanation of why the Catholic Church must be hostile to it: ". . . there is a permanent reason for this opposition, independent of all transitory facts, in the authoritarian structure of the Church, as claiming to be invested with power from above, in its doctrine of sin, redemption, and grace, implying the fallen character of human liberty and reason and the need of external aid; and in the function which it claims, of a supernatural mediator between man and God: whereas Liberalism assumes that, without any intermediary, and by his own unaided efforts man is fully able to realize all the values of the spiritual life."

solutism that any champion of true liberty might endorse.[35]
Since the philosophical implications inherent in a movement are
easily overlooked when such a movement sponsors practical
reforms, Catholics were attracted to it.[36] The Church approved
sound political, economic, and social reforms advocated by Catholic Liberals,[37] but when Catholics, carried away by their enthusiasm for Liberal doctrines, either justified unwarranted
means to legitimate ends, or endorsed the philosophy underlying
Liberalism, the Church condemned them.[38] Unfortunately for
the Church in the nineteenth century, Catholics who subscribed
to the more extreme tenets of Liberalism played important rôles

---

[35] It should be remarked that Liberalism, considered as a political theory or
tendency opposed to centralization and absolutism, is not at variance with
either the spirit of the Catholic Church or its teaching. Toward the end of
the eighteenth century, however, the word came to signify a partial or complete emancipation of man from the supernatural, moral, and divine order;
it was these tenets of Liberalism as a philosophy that were condemned by the
Church. Hughes, *op. cit.*, p. 4, writes: "To view Liberalism as an innocuous
political attitude to which most educated and civilized people generously subscribe is to stare unknowingly at a shell drained of its substance . . . . The
completed structure of Liberalism embodies an autonomous, self-sustaining
conception of man's relationship to his God, his universe, his society. In this
sense is Liberalism a faith, and by virtue of this fact has it been forced to fight
other faiths. It has, in particular, fought the Catholic faith."

[36] Useful studies of Catholic Liberalism are: C. Constantin, "Libéralisme
catholique," *Dictionnaire de théologie catholique*, IX, 506-628; Anatole Leroy-Beaulieu, *Les Catholiques libéraux, l'église et le Libéralisme de 1830
à nos jours* (Paris, 1885); and Georges J. Weill, *Histoire du Catholicisme libéral en France 1828-1908* (Paris, 1909).

[37] The expression Catholic Liberalism may have one of two meanings: in
its acceptable sense it connotes a sponsoring of liberal measures which are essentially good and consequently in no way inimical to Catholic doctrine; in its
second sense it implies an endorsement of the philosophy of Liberalism. The
expression Liberal Catholicism, an appellation in which the contradiction is
obvious, is sometimes incorrectly applied to Catholic Liberalism; it is hardly
inaccurate, however, when applied to the attitude of those who in effect subscribe to an alteration of Catholic dogma to permit of the acceptance of the
philosophy of Liberalism.

[38] Félicité Robert de Lamennais (1782-1854) exemplifies those who, in their
enthusiasm for political reform, were not circumspect in choosing means to
desired ends. See Joseph A. G. Hergenröther, *Anti-Janus: An Historico-
Theological Criticism of the Work Entitled "The Pope and the Council" by*

in the political affairs of predominantly Catholic countries; and it was in these countries that the position of the Church was most deftly undermined.[39] These Liberal Catholic statesmen might or might not belong to a Masonic society, but, whether or not they allied themselves formally with the Masonic fraternity, they worked to promote its ends by their very adherence to Liberalism.[40] Many statesmen, and even many ecclesiastics, influenced by the Liberalism of the age, showed a strongly regalistic attitude toward the Church. In countries where a union of Church and State existed, as in Brazil, the age-old policies of regalism received new life and vigor.

---

*Janus*, trans. by J. B. Robertson (Dublin, 1870), pp. xxxvi-xxxviii; Leroy-Beaulieu, *op. cit.*, pp. 89-90. The Italian priest and political philosopher, Vincenzo Gioberti (1801-1852) was an outstanding proponent of Liberalism in its philosophical sense. After the publication of his work, *Il Gesuita Moderno* (Lausanne, 1846-1847), King Carlo Alberto of Piedmont wrote to Pope Pius IX to protest the bad influence that Gioberti's works had on the clergy of Turin. See *Il Gesuita Moderno*, Vol. XII, *Edizione nazionale delle opere edite e inedite di Vincenzo Gioberti* (Milano, 1940), p. xxii. For the religious thought of Gioberti see *ibid.*, pp. 343-347. Tullio Vecchietti, *Il pensiero politico di Vincenzo Gioberti* (Milano [1941]), p. 49, writes: "And of Catholicism it remained in the ultimate analysis nothing but the name: it was in fact civilization becoming reality, civilization in the making. The new Rome, the myth of the new Rome which Gioberti predicted, did not represent but was the personification of the religious urge of mankind and the actualization of his ideal continuously reemphasized: the reconciliation of religion with civilization."

[39] Moderate Catholic Liberals, like Montalembert, who advocated sound political, economic, and social reforms, were frequently misinterpreted by more radical Liberals. When Montalembert's famous dictum "The free Church in the free State" became a shibboleth of Liberalism the expression meant something very different from what Montalembert had in mind when he used it at the Congress of Malines in August, 1863. (See Weill, *Histoire du Catholicisme libéral*, pp. 166-168; Leroy-Beaulieu, *op. cit.*, pp. 186-187, writes: "La fameuse formule que Montalembert eut le regret de se voir dérober par Cavour 'L'Église libre dans l'État libre,' présentée comme la devise ou le mot d'ordre de la secte [of radical Liberals] et interpretée dans un sens manifestement étranger à Montalembert et à ses amis, come si elle comportait la separation de l'Église et de l'État ou la subordination de l'Église au pouvoir civil."

[40] Many Brazilian Liberals were members of the Masonic fraternity. See pp. 220-221 below.

## IV

Regalism may be defined as the inordinate exercise of royal power in Church matters, and the concomitant subordination of Church interests to those of the State. It stems from the rivalry incipient in the fact that authority, both spiritual and temporal, is exercised over the same individual. Theoretically, the institution that directs the spiritual welfare of the individual is acknowledged to be the higher in jurisdiction; in practice, history shows that, as the Church lost her authority over temporal rulers, she lost also her sanctions against these rulers for usurpation of rights which she felt she alone should exercise. The history of the usurpation of Church rights by the State in modern times begins with the quarrel of Boniface VIII and Philip the Fair, attains full growth in the epoch of the Protestant revolt, and reaches maturity in the political theories of Grotius, Hobbes, Bodin, Gouvêa, and Voltaire.

Cândido Mendes de Almeida,[41] who regards regalism as a continuation of the doctrine of Caesaro-papism, says that Philip the Fair is the founder of modern Gallican regalism through his extraordinary pretensions relative to the *jus regalia,* from which originated the name *regalista.*[42] The *regalia* consisted in useful and honorable rights, which the kings of France enjoyed in some churches of that country, but which through abuse were grossly

---

[41] Cândido Mendes de Almeida (1818-1881) is recognized as one of the foremost jurisconsults of nineteenth century Brazil, and his well-known *Direito civil ecclesiastico brasileiro antigo e moderno em suas relações com o direito canonico* (2v., Rio de Janeiro, 1866) ranks among the best studies on civil and ecclesiastical law.

[42] Almeida, *Direito civil ecclesiastico brasileiro,* I, i, xlv; Michel André, *Cours alphabétique et méthodique de droit canon dans ses rapports avec le droit civil ecclésiastique* (Paris, 1853), V, 12-14. André, *op. cit.,* p. 12, gives the following definition of *Régale:* "La régale, en latin *regalia,* est le droit qu'avait autrefois ou que pretendait avoir le roi de jouir des revenus des évêchés vacants dans ses États et de disposer des bénéfices sans charge d'âmes que en dépendaient, jusqu'à ce que le nouvel évêque eut pris possession de l'évêché, prêté le serment de fidélité et satisfait aux autres formalités que étaient requises pour la clôture de la régale."

distorted from their regular purpose.[43] Even though the name derives from the French, the ideology is in no way confined to the French nation. This doctrine, which subordinates religion to politics, the Church to the State, encountered favorable interpreters in Luther, Calvin, and the other reformers of the sixteenth century, as well as in the most celebrated political thinkers of post-Reformation Europe. Buchanan in Scotland, Bacon and Hobbes in England, Bodin in France, Grotius in Holland propagated the same ideas. To Grotius the modern world owes the systematization of the doctrine of the supremacy of the State in matters of religion. Yet in the century before Grotius, António de Gouvêa was popularizing that doctrine in Portugal.[44] It is significant that Gouvêa strongly influenced the political thought and activity of King John III (1522-1557), the monarch under whom Portugal worked out a system of colonial administration for Brazil.[45]

In a letter to Cardinal Farnari, dated June 19, 1852, Donoso Cortés analyzes the modern errors pertaining to the relation between Church and State. He classifies them under four headings: those of the moderate regalist, those of the more ardent regalist, those of the revolutionary, and those of the socialist and communist. The moderate regalist equates the State with the Church in order to sustain his contention that what is of a mixed nature is really of a lay nature and what is of an ecclesiastical nature is really of a mixed nature. Thus the moderate regalist, without going the whole way and saying that the Church is subordinate to the State, gives justification to the royal demand that bulls, apostolic letters, and other acts of the ecclesiastical authority ob-

---

[43] Almeida, *Direito civil ecclesiastico brasileiro*, I, i, xlv (note), writes: "A *Regalia* consistia em certos direitos uteis ou honorificos, de que gosavão os Reys de França em algumas Igrejas daquelle paiz, no tempo da vacancia dos Bispados. Elles percebião as rendas, apresentavão os Beneficios, e ha exemplos de os conferirem directamente. Uma tal prerogativa, arrancada á benevolencia e gratidão da Igreja, dava lugar a odiosos abusos. O XIV Concilio Geral congregado em Lyão em 1274, reconhecendo esses direitos, limitou-os ás Igrejas onde então se achavão estabelecidos, prohibindo alarga-los."

[44] Almeida, *Direito civil ecclesiastico brasileiro*, I, i, xlvi-xlix.

[45] On António de Gouvêa see Diogo Barbosa Machado, "Antonio de Gouvea," *Bibliotheca Lusitana* (Lisboa, 1741), I, 291-296.

tain the royal *placet* in order to have force in the nation. From the same premise, the moderate regalist concludes the right of the State to inspect seminaries and schools, to control Church finance, and to accept complaints of Church members against ecclesiastical censure. The more ardent regalist asserts that the Church is inferior to the State, and therefore that the civil power has the right of revoking any concordat agreed upon with the Supreme Pontiff; of establishing, to all intents and purposes, a national church over which the State rules supreme; of disposing of the goods of the Church; and of regulating her activities by means of decrees and laws passed by the national legislative assembly.[46]

Regalism functioned in Catholic countries with varying degrees of success; in France it had the advantage of being organized in that distinctly French system known as Gallicanism. This system codified all the supposed Liberties enjoyed from time immemorial by the Church in France.[47] These Liberties were formulated for the first time by Bossuet in the "Declaration of the Clergy of France of 1682."[48] Gradually two types of Gallicanism were evolved, a "parliamentary or judicial Galli-

---

[46] Donoso Cortés, *op. cit.*, II, 292-293.

[47] A. Degert, "Gallicanism," *Catholic Encyclopedia*, VI, 352, says: "Most of its partisans regarded Gallicanism rather as a revival of the most ancient traditions of Christianity, a persistence of the common law, which law, according to some (Pithou and Quesnel), was made up of the conciliar decrees of the earliest centuries or, according to others (Marca, Bossuet), of canons of the general and local councils, and the decretals, ancient and modern, which were received in France . . . ." History shows, however, that the French Church was paying unquestioned homage to Roman supremacy in the centuries immediately prior to the fourteenth. As we have observed above, the first glimmering of the modern Gallican ideas appeared in the reign of Philip the Fair (1263-1314). The Gallican theory received new impetus in the last quarter of the fourteenth century with the translation into French of Marsilius of Padua's *Defensor Pacis*. During the Great Schism (1377-1417), Pierre d'Ailly and Jean Gerson sponsored the idea that the General Council is above the Pope and is the sole organ of infallibility. In the reign of Louis XIV, as we shall see presently, modern Gallicanism assumed a very definite form.

[48] The Declaration of 1682 was the work of a group of ecclesiastics and deputies assembled on March 19, 1682, by Louis XIV. The interference of Innocent XI in the design of the French king to extend the *régale* to all the

canism which tended to increase the rights of the State to the prejudice of those of the Church," and an episcopal Gallicanism which "lessened the doctrinal authority of the Pope in favor of that of the bishops."[49] When these Liberties were later enumerated by Guy Coquille and Pierre Pithou, they were eighty-three in number, including the four named by Bossuet. Some of them were quickly copied by sovereigns of other nations where a union of Church and State existed. Among the Gallican Liberties that won general acceptance were: a) the kings of France have the right to assemble councils in their dominions, and to make laws and regulations touching upon ecclesiastical matters; b) papal bulls and letters may not be executed without the *placet* of the king or his officers; and c) it is lawful to have recourse to the crown against ecclesiastical censure.

As we have already said, these theories relative to the rights of the State to supervise the activities of the Church within the royal domain spread rapidly throughout eighteenth century Europe.[50] Quite understandably, the champions of absolute power were quick to give them sturdy protection; yet, ironically enough, it was not the secular statesmen who stood foremost as defenders and propagators of these Gallican tenets, but rather the Jansenists.[51] This fact has led a modern writer to remark that "Jansenism, the most critical heresy the Church faced after

---

churches of his kingdom prompted Louis XIV to call this group together and to ask for the formulation of the Gallican Liberties. The Pope, by Rescript of April 11, 1682, voided and annulled the work done by the assembly. The king retracted in 1693, but the Declaration of 1682 continued to be the symbol of Gallicanism. On the Gallican Liberties see André, *op. cit.*, III, 500-533.

[49] Degert, "Gallicanism," *loc. cit.*, p. 352.

[50] Febronianism in Germany, Josephism in Austria, *Giurisdizionalismo* in several of the Italian States, Regalism in Spain and Portugal, and Erastianism in England were domestic varieties of French Gallicanism.

[51] Jansenism is the name applied to the doctrines derived from the writings of Cornelius Jansen (1585-1638), professor at the University of Louvain and during the last two years of his life bishop of Ypres. Jansen died in the Catholic Church; the controversy connected with his name broke out after his death. The so-called Jansen doctrines were gleaned from a book which the bishop left in manuscript; in it he undertook to present the doctrines of St. Augustine. The errors in his interpretation were concerned chiefly with the

the sixteenth century, was in no small degree a new bottle for the old wine of Gallicanism."[52] The Jansenist group, in the desperation of its quarrel with the Holy See, sought protection from French statesmen, who sheltered it on the pretext that its condemnation by the Holy See had no juridical significance in France, since it had not been acted upon by the whole episcopacy.[53] Catholics tainted with Jansenism were apt to be more zealous in their opposition to the claims of the papacy than were statesmen motivated solely by political considerations.[54]

Conditioned by their own opposition to the Holy See, Jansenist Catholics were susceptible to Masonic propaganda against the papacy. Modern Masonry, it will be recalled, began its campaign against the Head of the Catholic Church when it realized that the papacy had detected its rationalistic character and had begun to warn the faithful against it. So subtle and yet so convincing was this anti-papal propaganda that many a Freemason

---

doctrine of grace. These errors were carried on by an intimate friend of Jansen, the abbot of St. Cyran (1581-1643), who added an extreme type of asceticism to the doctrinal principles previously laid down by Jansen. A priest, Antoine Arnauld, succeeded the abbot of St. Cyran as leader of the Jansenist sect. Arnauld preached and wrote against frequent Communion. In 1696 Paschasius Quesnel succeeded Arnauld as head of the group. After a period of relative calm, the Jansenist controversy raged again following the publication by Quesnel of an edition of the New Testament. In the copious notes or reflections that accompanied this work the heretical opinions of Quesnel were discernible. The Jansenist teachings were condemned by the Holy Office in 1641, and were subsequently condemned by the Holy See in 1642, 1653, 1664, and 1669. Although Louis XIV and Bossuet were the avowed enemies of the Jansenists, Gallican statesmen were their ready defenders. One is justified in saying that the Jansenist spirit, a spirit of defiance and exaggerated asceticism, poisoned the religious life of France long after Jansenism as such had ceased to exist.

[52] Hughes, op. cit., p. 83. See also Joseph de Maistre, De l'église gallicane dans son rapport avec le souverain Pontife (Paris, 1821), p. 18.

[53] Degert, "Gallicanism," loc. cit., p. 356, says: "It was Gallicanism which allowed the Jansenists condemned by popes to elude their sentences on the plea that these had not received the assent of the whole episcopate."

[54] See Léon Séché, Les derniers Jansénistes et leur rôle dans l'histoire de France depuis la ruine de Port-Royal jusqu'à nos jours (1710-1870) (Paris, 1891), and Arturo Carlo Jemolo, "Giansenio," Enciclopedia Italiana, XVI, 970-973. Séché remarks the affinity between Liberal Catholicism and Jansen-

was led to look, not only with disdain, but also with fear on the alleged pretensions of the Holy See. This propaganda, however, did something even more significant than turn Freemasons away from Rome; it attracted disaffected Catholics to Freemasonry.

It is important to an understanding of Church-State relations in the nineteenth century to see why and how modern Masonry as a society became the meeting ground of all those who for any reason repudiated the jurisdiction of the Holy See. The inference to be drawn from what has been said concerning Gallicanism and Jansenism is not that every individual of Gallican or Jansenist tendencies formally enrolled himself in one of the Masonic societies, but that, within or without the precincts of these societies, such men felt kindly disposed toward Freemasonry and looked with benevolent disdain on the papal pronouncements condemning it.

Since the goal of this survey of modern attitudes toward the Church and particularly toward the jurisdictional prerogatives of the papacy is to interpret the Church-State problem in the Empire of Brazil in the nineteenth century, it is well to narrow the study to a consideration of the political import of Gallicanism and Jansenism in Portugal. The statesmen of Brazil, as we shall discover later, derived their ideas largely from France; their institutions, customs, and laws largely from Portugal.

## V

Jansenism came to Portugal in the seventeenth century under the cloak of Gallican regalism, but did not show itself openly

---

ism and stresses the fact that both groups were hostile to the claims of the papacy. Jemolo ("Giansenio," *loc. cit.*, p. 972), referring to a movement sponsored by the intellectuals of the University of Pavia, says: ". . . it is a movement that arose in the university in close connection with the whole spiritual life of the Empire under Joseph II; the doctrines are those of Jansenism, but often re-thought in original form and under a different aspect; . . . the problem of the constitution of the Church, of the reciprocal relations between Pope and bishops, of the relationship between State and Church has for the Pavia group an importance not inferior to that of strictly theological questions."

until after the marquis of Pombal came to power in 1750.[55] As minister under Joseph I (1750-1777), Pombal introduced into Portugal the policies of the enlightened monarchs of the eighteenth century. He was the avowed enemy of the Portuguese nobility, of the Society of Jesus, and of the papacy.[56] In his effort to create in Portugal a despotic form of absolute monarchy, Pombal resorted to Machiavellian tactics and Gallican arguments. In his endeavor to insure the full and unquestioned supremacy of the king, he ordered Portuguese public law to be rewritten. The revised code claimed for the king exalted and independent sovereignty immediately from God, Who endowed His vassal with indisputable wisdom and absolute power.[57]

Soliciting the aid of all forces that would contribute to the establishment of national control over the Church, Pombal welcomed the assistance of Jansenist Catholics. Under his protection they published four famous tracts: *Tentativa theologica,*[58]

---

[55] On José Sebastião de Carvalho e Melo, marquis of Pombal, see John Smith. *Memoirs of the Marquis of Pombal* (2v., London, 1843); João António dos Santos e Silva, *Revista historico-politica de Portugal desde o ministerio do Marques de Pombál até 1842. Precedida d'uma rapida exposição dos factos principaes da revolucão franceza em 1789 até á invasão dos francezes em Portugal* (Coimbra, 1852); J. Lúcio de Azevedo, *O Marquês de Pombal e a sua epoca* (2nd ed., Lisboa, 1922); and Francisco Luiz Gomes, *Le Marquis de Pombal, esquisse de sa vie politique* (Lisbonne, 1869).

[56] Silva, *op. cit.,* p. 85, claims for Pombal the distinction of having influenced Pope Clement XIV against the Jesuits and of having been largely instrumental in persuading the Pope to issue the brief, *Dominus ac redemptor,* which, in 1773, ordered the suppression of the Society of Jesus throughout the world.

[57] Silva, *op. cit.,* pp. 80-85; see also Gomes, *op. cit.,* pp. 372-377.

[58] See Inocêncio Francisco da Silva, *Diccionario bibliographico Portuguez* (Lisboa, 1858), I, 228-229; "[António Pereira de Figueiredo,] *Tentativa theologica, em que pretende mostrar que impedido o recurso á Sé Apostolica, se devolve aos Bispos a faculdade de dispensar nos impedimentos publicos do matrimonio e de prover espiritualmente em todos os mais casos reservados ao Papa, todas as vezes que assim o pedir a publica e urgente necessidade dos subditos. Offerecida aos Senhores Bispos de Portugal* (Lisboa, 1766)." This work, says Silva, went into three editions and was translated into Italian, Latin, French, German, and Spanish. Father Pereira, an Oratorian, was secularized in 1769. See Azevedo, *op. cit.,* p. 286.

*Deducção chronologica,* [59] *Compendio historico da Universidade de Coimbra,*[60] and the *Estatutos*[61] of the great reform of the University of Coimbra in 1772. These tracts enunciated a Portuguese version of the French Jansenist-Gallican doctrine. Through them, Cândido Mendes de Almeida points out, the Portuguese Jansenists sought to establish the doctrine of State over Church not only in Portugal but also in her dominions.[62]

In this period privileges and so-called liberties tended to coalesce. We find, for example, the right of patronage,[63] an

---

[59] Lúcio de Azevedo, *op. cit.,* p. 288, quotes Theiner, *Histoire du pontificat de Clément XIV* (Paris, 1852) as saying of the *Deducção chronologica:* "Obra porventura a mais importante de quantas se teem publicado contra os jesuitas." Lúcio de Azevedo himself writes, *ibid.,* p. 291: "A impressão produzida pela *Deducção chronologica* foi enorme. Em França e Hespanha os adversarios dos jesuitas acolheram-na com jubilo de facil explicação." See also Mário Brandão e M. Lopes de Almeida, *A Universidade de Coimbra* (Coimbra, 1937), ii, 72.

[60] Brandão and Almeida, *op. cit.,* pp. 71-72; *ibid.,* p. 72, note 1, give the complete title of this work: "Compendio/Historico do Estado/ da Universidade/ de/ Coimbra/ no tempo da invasão dos denominados/ Jesuitas/e/ dos estragos/ feitos nas siencias/ e nos professores, e directores/ que a regiam pelas maquinações/ e publicações/ dos novos estatutos por elles fabricados./ Lisboa/ Na Regia officina Typographica/Anno MDCCLXXI/Por ordem de Sua Magestade."

[61] *Ibid.,* p. 85, note 2, gives the complete title: "Estatutos/ da/ Universidade/ de Coimbra/ compilados debaixo da immendiata/ e suprema inspecção/ de El Rei D. José I./ Nosso Senhor/ pela Junta/ de Providencia Literaria/ creada pelo mesmo Senhor/ para/a restauração/ das Sciencias, e Artes Liberaes/ nestes Reinos, e todos seus Dominios/ ultimamente roborados/por Sua Magestade/ na sua lei de 28 de Agosto/ deste presente Anno de 1772./ Lisboa/ na Regia Officina Typografica/ Anno MDCCLXXIII./ De Ordem de Sua Magestade./"

[62] Almeida, *Direito civil ecclesiastico brasileiro,* I, i, liii. See also Lúcio de Azevedo, *op. cit.,* p. 286. Azevedo says: ". . . a autonomia religiosa da nação era, póde-se dizer, completa, e o ministro omnipotente, em tudo a ella respectivo, suggeria, intervinha e dispunha."

[63] On the right of patronage, see Johannes Baptist Sägmüller, "Patron and Patronage," *The Catholic Encyclopedia,* XI, 560-562: F. Lucii Ferraris, "Juspatronatus," *Bibliotheca canonica iuridica moralis theologica nec non ascetica polemica rubricistica historica* (Roma, 1888-1890), IV, 662-699; Fortunato de Almeida, *História da igreja em Portugal* (Coimbra, 1910-1922), especially Vol. III, Part I; Cândido Mendes de Almeida, *Direito civil ecclesiastico brasileiro,* I, i, ccxxxix-ccclvii; and Cândido Santini, *De regio*

honorable and ancient privilege of the kings of Portugal,[64] reiterated in a new and extreme form and interpreted to include such liberties as the royal *placet* and the right of recourse to the crown, which had no juridical foundation. Ignoring the testimony of numerous papal bulls, the most regalistic among the jurisconsults of eighteenth century Portugal attempted to show that the right of patronage was inherent in sovereignty, the right or title having been acquired not through papal grant, but through usage from time immemorial.[65] Although this ultra-regalistic doctrine did not have very wide approbation, and even at the time it was enunciated was not given widespread credence, it had important consequences in subsequent years, both in Portugal and in Brazil.[66]

---

*iure Patronatus in Brasilia* (Pôrto Alegre, 1934).

[64] Sägmüller, "Patron and Patronage." *loc. cit.*, p. 560: Fortunato de Almeida, *História da igreja em Portugal*, I, 219-226; Almeida, *Direito civil ecclesiastico brasileiro*, I, i, ccxxxix-ccclxvii. Sägmüller defines the right of patronage (*jus patronatus*) as "a determined sum of rights and obligations entailed upon a definite person, the patron, especially in connection with the assignment and administration of a benefice, not in virtue of his hierarchical position, but by the legally regulated grant of the Church, out of gratitude towards her benefactor." The Portuguese sovereigns came originally to enjoy the right of patronage as a result of their work as defenders of Christendom against the Mohammedans. Kings and nobles built churches and monasteries in the land won from the Moors, and over these the Holy See granted to the benefactors special patronage privileges. Frequently the lay patron overstepped the limits of the patronage right, and the papacy had to correct the abuses. In the course of the thirteenth century a number of papal bulls were issued to correct these evils. New adjustments had to be made between the Portuguese sovereigns and the Holy See when Portugal began to extend her domain beyond her geographical boundaries. In these programs of expansion, the Order of Christ, founded in 1317 by King Diniz, played a prominent rôle. Martin V, by a bull, the text of which has been lost, granted to Prince Henry (1394-1460), as grand master of the Order of Christ, special patronage privileges. These privileges were reiterated by Pope Calixtus III through the bull *Inter Caetera* (1456), and additional privileges and powers were given to the prior major of the Order of Christ by subsequent Pontiffs. See pp. 60-62 below.

[65] Almeida, *Direito civil ecclesiastico brasileiro*, I, i, ccxlvii, says that Pereira de Castro in his *Manu Regia* (cap. 22 and 63), "descobre ensanchas para sustentar que o Padroado Regio das Igrejas não precisa de Bullas para manter-se, basta aos Reys a prescripção immemorial."

[66] See pp. 65-66, 67 note below.

No less threatening to the independent action of the Church was the alleged right of rulers to hear complaints filed by recalcitrant members against the penalties inflicted by the Church. This right of recourse to the crown[67] was nothing more nor less than an expedient which the temporal power laid hold upon to influence, dominate, and subordinate the ecclesiastical power in its decisions, on the pretext that to the temporal sovereign belongs the duty to protect his subjects from all oppression and violence, even such violence as may be alleged against the Church.[68] It meant that the Church was not free to discipline those of her members who violated her laws. The application of sanctions hung in the balance, while the temporal power made the final decisions concerning their justice and equity. Such restrictions could mean nothing but servitude for the Church; yet the most extravagant defender of the right of recourse considered it as a right inseparable from sovereignty itself.[69]

The Church never approved of this interference on the part of governments,[70] but the success of her opposition varied with the temper of the government in question. In Portugal, as elsewhere, the gravity of the evil differed with the times and the ruler. Toward the end of the seventeenth century, legislation governing recourse showed some deference to Rome, but such civility was gradually discontinued. In the eighteenth century,

---

[67] Marquês de São Vicente, *Considerações relativas ao beneplacito, e recurso á corôa em materias do culto* (Rio de Janeiro, 1873), p. 33, gives the following descriptive definition of the right of recourse: "O recurso á Corôa é um meio especial do direito publico, pelo qual se invoca a alta jurisdicção politica, a fim de que faça cessar o abuso da autoridade ecclesiastica, a aggressão contra as prerogativas ou leis do Estado, contra os direitos dos subditos delle, ou contra a disposição dos canones recebidos. E' tambem reciprocamente o meio de fazer cessar o abuso da autoridade temporal contra os direitos da igreja, ou contra os direitos dos ministros della em relação ao culto." The Marquês de São Vicente was a moderate regalist.

[68] Almeida, *Direito civil ecclesiastico brasileiro*, I, iii, 1263-1264; André, "Appel comme d'abus," *loc. cit.*, I, 184-191.

[69] *Ibid.*, I, iii, 1263-1264.

[70] André, "Placet," *loc. cit.*, IV, 391-394. André, in giving the history of the *placet*, stresses the fact that the alleged claim of sovereigns to this privilege was repeatedly repudiated by the Holy See.

especially during the reign of Joseph I and the ministry of the marquis of Pombal, when the doctrines of Jansenist-Gallicanism dominated government circles, the right of recourse was given great prominence.[71]

The royal *placet*, or the right of government censorship of all ecclesiastical bulls, letters, and other documents, which, like the right of recourse, was included among the Liberties of the Gallican Church enumerated by Pithou, resembles the right of recourse more than the right of patronage, in so far as neither the recourse nor the *placet* was founded on even the vaguest papal authorization.[72] Bulls and letters established the right of patronage in Portugal and in Spain,[73] but no such documents secured the other two. At most, they rested on the implicit permission of the Holy See, inferred from its having tolerated them and having signed concordats with nations that persisted in using them.[74]

## VI

We have shown briefly the development of modern regalism in Portugal, and have laid special stress on the juridical devices which statesmen used to control the activities of the Church within the royal domains. By extending their legitimate right of patronage to include such liberties as the right of recourse to

---

[71] Almeida, *Direito civil ecclesiastico brasileiro*, I, iii, 1269-1270; Paschalis Josephi Mellii Freirii [Pascual José de Melo Freire], *Institutionum juris civilis Lusitani* (Lisboa, 1809). Melo Freire, an ultra-regalist, was deeply impressed with the *alvará* of January 18, 1765, which increased the effectiveness of the right of recourse by making the appeal to the crown more direct. He discusses the *alvará* at length under "De jure principis circa sacra," in Liv. I, iii, 1270, of his cited work. Referring to this section, Almeida says (I, iii, 1269) : "Todo este titulo he digno de ler-se porque nelle se acha condensada a quinta essencia do Regalismo do seculo XVIII."

[72] Almeida, *Direito civil ecclesiastico brasileiro*, I, i, ccxlvi (note), says that Pereira de Castro in *Manu Regis* (cap. 62) gives notices of bulls authorizing the kings of Portugal to use the *placet*. André, *op. cit.*, IV, 394, discusses papal condemnation of this alleged right.

[73] See p. 9, note 26 above.

[74] André, "Placet," *loc. cit.*, IV, 391-394; *ibid.*, "Appel comme d'abus," I, 184-191. The right of recourse has different names in different countries; it is called *appel comme d'abus* in France.

the crown and the right of royal *placet*, rulers in Portugal brought the Church into almost complete subjection to the State. All these so-called liberties[75] will be claimed by statesmen in the Brazilian Empire in the nineteenth century. The tendency with Brazilian political leaders will be to unite French and Portuguese pretensions and to be, if possible, more imperious than the statesmen of either of the other two countries in their demands on the Holy See. Yet it is not so much the excessive character of these demands which impresses one, as the equanimity with which the generality of statesmen acquiesced in the regalistic demands of some of their leaders. In the Brazilian parliament, as in all popular assemblies, the majority were individually neutral, but they were swayed to the right or the left by their more passionate colleagues.

When we seek an explanation for the indifferent attitude of most of the Brazilian statesmen toward the rights of the Church and particularly those of the papacy, we find it partly in Portuguese and French customs and ideologies, and partly in the anti-papal propaganda of Freemasonry. The attitudes of nineteenth century Brazilian party leaders were the product of inherited leanings toward Jansenist-Gallican regalism and of environmental influences traceable to Masonry. A brief study of the development of Freemasonry in Brazil is essential to a clear understanding of the relations between Church and State in the Empire. Similarly, an examination of conditions that prevailed within the Brazilian Church will help to explain why the union of the spiritual and civil powers, established by the imperial constitution, came to signify, not a co-operation between two related but distinct authorities, but a subordination of Church to State.

---

[75] Patronage, as we have shown (see p. 23, note 64 above) is a right granted by the Church; it is a liberty only in the extreme form in which it was practiced by eighteenth and nineteenth century rulers in Portugal and by nineteenth century political leaders in Brazil.

# CHAPTER II

## LIBERALISM AND FREEMASONRY IN BRAZIL

According to Mário Melo, one of its foremost Brazilian historians, Masonry came to Brazil in the declining years of the eighteenth century.[1] The learned botanist, Manuel de Arruda Câmara (1752-1810), a native of Goiana (Pernambuco), returned from Europe, "where his spirit had been formed,"[2] and settled in Itambié (Pernambuco) where he founded the celebrated Areópago. This secret society, says Melo, was "a sort of Masonic lodge obeying the same precepts as our institution, but having political activity as its principal end."[3] Arruda Câmara had been educated at the University of Coimbra and the University of Montpellier. He was a close friend of D'Alembert and the disciple of Condorcet, and during his residence in France (1787-1798) participated actively in the revolutionary movement. Enamoured of the philosophy of the French Revolution, he returned to Brazil with the intention of freeing the country from Portuguese control and of establishing a republic, probably under French auspices.[4]

---

[1] Mário Melo, *A Maçonaria no Brazil, prioridade de Pernambuco* (Recife, 1909), p. 9. Bartolomeu de Almeida, "A Maçonaria no Brasil," *A Ordem,* XII (March and April, 1933), 236-241, is of the opinion that Masonry existed in Brazil from the middle of the eighteenth century. He believes that the fraternity had a part in the expulsion of the Jesuits (1757), and he is certain that the *Inconfidência Mineira* (1789) was instigated by Masonry. This opinion is also held by Aires da Mata Machado Filho, *Arraial do Tijuco Cidade de Diamantina* (Rio de Janeiro, 1944), p. 58. On Masonry in the *Inconfidência Mineira,* see p. 30, note 12.

[2] Melo, *A Maçonaria no Brazil,* p. 9.

[3] See also Sérgio da Costa, *As Quatro coroas de D. Pedro I* (2d. ed. rev., Rio de Janeiro [1940]), p. 39.

[4] Francisco Muniz Tavares, *Historia da Revolução de Pernambuco em 1817,* revised and annotated by Manoel de Oliveira Lima (3d ed., Recife, 1917), p. 45. Lima writes: "Arruda Câmara (1752-1810), egresso carmelita secularizado por um breve pontificio, alumno da Universidade de Coimbra e medico pela faculdade de Montpellier, foi sempre um exaltado partidario das idéas

The Areópago was frequented by prominent persons, both lay and ecclesiastic, from the provinces of Pernambuco and Paraíba.[5] Among them were Antônio Carlos Ribeiro de Andrada, youngest of the three brothers who figured so prominently in the official circles of the First Empire; Francisco de Paula Cavalcanti de Albuquerque, a leader in the revolutionary movement of 1801; Father Miguel Joaquim de Almeida, professor at the seminary of Olinda and prominent Masonic propagandist; Father João Ribeiro Pessoa, professor at the seminary of Olinda and one of the moving spirits of the Revolution of 1817; and the Carmelite friar, Joaquim do Amor Divino Caneca, one of the Masonic heroes of the Revolution of 1824.[6] The allegedly patriotic conspiracy of 1801 was plotted in the Areópago, and consisted in a plan to form Pernambuco into a republic under the protection of Napoleon. This abortive conspiracy destroyed the Areópago, but not before the Masonic spirit had been firmly established in other secret societies.[7] Foremost among these was the Academia do Paraíso (*i.e.*, Academy of Paradise) founded in Pernambuco by Father Ribeiro Pessoa, who had been initiated into Masonry in 1807 in Lisbon, where he had gone for further study after attending the seminary of Olinda.[8] The Academia do Paraíso was to play an important rôle in the Pernambucan Revolt of 1817. This latter attempt to establish an independent republic in northern Brazil ostensibly

francezas." Hereafter Lima's annotations to Tavares' *Historia da Revolução de Pernambuco em 1817* will be cited as Lima, "Annotações." See also Lídia Besouchet, *José Ma. Paranhos, Vizconde Do Río Branco, ensayo histórico-biográfico* (Buenos Aires, 1944), pp. 205-206.

[5] Melo, *A Maçonaria no Brazil*, p. 9.

[6] *Ibid.*

[7] *Ibid.* See also Mário Melo, *A Maçonaria e a Revolução Republicana de 1817* (Recife, 1912), pp. 7-17. Mário Melo, *Frei Caneca* (Recife, 1933), p. 5, says of these early secret societies which were frequently called academies: "Essas academias eram sociedades secretas, espécie de maçonaria política, onde se exaltava o nacionalismo e onde se fazia o juramento de trabalhar pela emancipação da pátria. Recebiam adeptos de todas as vilas para maior eficácia na propaganda."

[8] Melo, *A Maçonaria no Brazil*, p. 10; Lima "Annotações", p. 45, writes: "Desejando ordenar-se, entrou para o seminario de Olinda, onde leccionou

grew out of general dissatisfaction with the officials imposed on the captaincy of Pernambuco by the royal government,[9] but fundamentally it was another movement toward independence and political liberalism sponsored by the Masonic fraternity.[10] Of similar origin was the Revolution of 1824 which attempted to throw off the yoke of the imperial government and to establish, under the so-called Confederation of the Equator, an inde-

antes e depois de ir a Lisboa aperfeiçoar-se nos estudos frequentando o Collegio dos Nobres, e entrar para o sacerdocio."

[9] As early as 1815, Prince John recognized that in certain sections of Brazil, notably in Pernambuco, influential groups were growing restive under the colonial status that prevailed in Brazil in spite of the fact that Rio de Janeiro was now the seat of the imperial government. In an effort to win back the allegiance of these groups, the prince regent had in that year elevated Brazil to the rank of kingdom, a constituent part of the United Kingdom of Portugal, Brazil, and Algarves. This failed to satisfy the patriots of Pernambuco. Discontent gave way to open rebellion after the prince regent, toward whom the Pernambucan leaders were ill-disposed, became King John VI, in 1816, on the death of his mother, Queen Maria I. Under the aegis of Freemasonry the patriots of Pernambuco were developing plans for an insurrection, when early in 1817 they were betrayed to government officials. They were obliged to begin their insurrection prematurely (March 6, 1817), and consequently were ill-prepared to resist the disciplined troops sent against them. The movement collapsed on May 20, 1817. A splendid eye-witness account of the Pernambucan Revolution of 1817 is found in L. F. de Tollenare, *Notas Dominicaes tomadas durantes uma residencia em Portugal e no Brasil nos annos de 1816, 1817, e 1818, parte relativa a Pernambuco traduzida do manuscripto Francez inedito por Alfredo de Carvalho com um prefacio de M. de Oliveira Lima* (Recife, 1905), pp. 175-226. The author is not sympathetic with the movement, but is interested in its leaders, their ideologies and objectives, and in the general reaction of the people.

[10] Melo, *A Maçonaria e a Revolução Republicana de 1817*, p. 7, says: "A idéa de governo republicano no Brasil, depois do exemplo que a França nos deu, foi sempre inspiração da maçonaria." See also Tavares, *op. cit.* In the introduction, p. iv, Oliveira Lima writes: "A revolução de 6 Março teve o seu chronista, que d'ella foi actor—o doutor, depois monsenhor Muniz Tavares (1793-1876), um dos muitos sacerdotes que, empolgados pelas idéas liberaes, prepararam o rompimento entre colonia e metropole por meio do advento do regimen democratico. Recommendado de Arruda Câmara, o sabio naturalista, discipulo do padre João Ribeiro, o eximio patriota, foi cappellão da agonia do hospital do Paraiso e secretario da sua administração, o que importa em dizer que foi membro notorio da respectiva academia, á qual pertence em boa parte

pendent republic for northern Brazil.[11]

While Pernambuco appears to have been the earliest shrine of Masonry in Brazil, the activities of the society were by no means confined to that province.[12] Manuel Joaquim de Meneses says that in the last years of the colonial régime Masonic lodges existed which were more or less regular, particularly in the captaincies of Rio de Janeiro, Baía, and Pernambuco. Of these, some were installed under the auspices of the Grand Orient of Portugal, others under the Grand Orient of France, and some independently.[13] When Brother Francisco José de Araújo arrived in 1803 with authority from the Grand Orient of Portu-

---

a propaganda local dos principios gerados pela philosophia do seculo XVIII e applicados nas revoluções americana e franceza."

[11] The Revolution of 1824 was a republican movement originating in Pernambuco in protest against the emperor's having dissolved the Constitutional Convention in November, 1823 (see p. 56, note 2 below). When word reached the province in July, 1824, that the new constitution, drawn up under Dom Pedro's supervision and promulgated by him on March 25, 1824, divided sovereignty between the Crown and parliament, the patriots issued a proclamation denouncing the emperor as a traitor who planned to allow the Portuguese in Brazil to rule the empire. They called upon the northern provinces to throw off his authority and to join in the formation of the "Confederation of the Equator." Uprisings occurred in Paraíba, Rio Grande do Norte, and Ceará, and some republican sentiment was expressed in Maranhão, but in general the people were indifferent to the movement, which was easily suppressed early in 1825. A brief account of the revolution and an indication of the part Masonry played is to be found in Melo, *Frei Caneca*.

[12] Melo, *A Maçonaria no Brazil*, p. 11, says that it is suspected that the *Inconfidência Mineira* was instigated by Masonry, but that there is no positive evidence. According to Melo, the known Freemason was Dr. José Alves Maciel, the major spirit of the *sonho de poetas*. Tiradentes, who is usually glorified as the hero of the conspiracy, was simply the messenger of Maciel. It is not absolutely clear that the fraternity of the conspirators was a secret society, like the Areópago, that aimed at the establishment of the Republic of Pernambuco in 1801, and the Masonic academies and lodges that had the same idea in 1817 and 1824. For another interpretation of the *Inconfidência Mineira*, see Lúcio José dos Santos, *A Inconfidencia Mineira, papel de Tiradentes na Inconfidencia Mineira* (São Paulo, 1927). Santos writes, p. 90: "Tiradentes e quasi todos os conjurados eram maçons. A conjuração foi dirigida pela maçonaria . . . . Mas, em todo o processo da Inconfidencia nenhum vestigio se encontra de acção propriamente maçonica."

[13] Manuel Joaquim de Meneses, *Exposição historica da maçonaria no Brasil*

gal, the four lodges of Rio de Janeiro, Reunião, Filantropia, Constância, and Emancipação, were affiliated with Portuguese Masonry. After the coming of the Portuguese court in 1808, these lodges continued their work, in spite of the disapproval of the regent, Prince John. The hostility of the regent was not shared by all members of the court, many of whom joined a newly formed lodge which bore the name "John of Bragança."[14]

In 1815 an independent lodge, established in Rio de Janeiro under the title Comércio e Artes, delayed its incorporation into the Portuguese Grand Orient because its members aspired to the establishment of a supreme Masonic organization in Brazil.[15] The advance of Freemasonry in Brazil encountered more or less opposition, depending on the attitudes of the royal government and of the captains-general in the various provinces.[16] The Pernambucan Revolution of 1817 led to a persecution of Masonic societies by the government under the direction of Antônio de Vila Nova Portugal, and to the promulgation in 1818 of a law proscribing secret societies. Freemasonry, to all intents and purposes, had to suspend its activities; yet, as Meneses assures us, "the zealous Masonry of our Brethren was not sleeping."[17] Actually the plans for independence were germinating during this period of governmental suppression.[18]

The demand for constitutional government in Portugal in 1820[19] gave Brazilian Freemasons occasion to launch their crusade for fuller participation in the government. Perceiving that the Portuguese projects relating to governmental reform, which supposedly included Brazilian interests, were more reactionary

---

particularmente na provincia do Rio de Janeiro en relação com a independencia e integridade do imperio (Rio de Janeiro, 1857), p. 9. For a brief history of Brazilian Freemasonry see Astréa: Almanak Maçonico para 5847 (Rio de Janeiro, 1847). See also Costa, op. cit., pp. 38-41.

[14] Meneses, op. cit., pp. 9-10. Prince John was violently opposed to all secret societies; for this reason, historians reject Meneses' assertion (p. 9) that he knew of the establishment of this lodge.

[15] Meneses, Exposição historica da maçonaria no Brasil, p. 10.

[16] Ibid.

[17] Ibid.

[18] Ibid.

[19] See pp. 55-56.

than liberal in character, the Masonic fraternities of Brazil opened their campaign for independence. The patriots, recognizing the need of being united in order to carry through efficiently their plan for independence, reorganized the Comércio e Artes lodge. With the increase in membership through the initiation of a large number of men who favored independence for Brazil, the society was divided on May 28, 1822, into three lodges, Comércio e Artes, União e Tranquilidade, and Esperança de Niterói. A Brazilian Grand Orient was thus created, and the patriarch of Brazilian independence, José Bonifácio de Andrada e Silva, was chosen grand master.[20] French, English, and American Masonry immediately extended recognition to the Brazilian fraternity.[21]

Prior to the declaration of Brazilian independence on September 7, 1822, Dom Pedro, made regent of Brazil by his father in 1821, was eager to become a Freemason. His minister, José Bonifácio, tried to dissuade him;[22] nevertheless, influenced by Gonçalves Lédo, one of the foremost figures in the independence movement, the prince regent was initiated in the summer of 1822 into the Comércio e Artes lodge, under the name of Guatimozin. Shortly after his initiation, the prince was given all the degrees and created grand master of the Brazilian Grand Orient.[23] At this same time, there existed in Rio de Janeiro

---

[20] *Ibid.*, pp. 30-31. See also Antônio de Meneses Vasconcelos de Drummond, "Annotações de A. M. V. de Drummond á sua biographia publicada em 1836 na *Biographie Universelle et Portative des Contemporains*," *Anais da Biblioteca Nacional do Rio de Janeiro*, XIII (1890), ii, 43.

[21] Lúcio José dos Santos, "A Maçonaria no Brasil," *A Ordem*, VIII (July, 1932), 17; Meneses, *op. cit.*, p. 30; Costa, *op. cit.*, pp. 41-42.

[22] Drummond, "Annotações," *loc. cit.*, p. 44, writes: "José Bonifácio resistio quanto poude á vontade do principe de entrar para a Maçonaria mas nem os rogos nem a razão puderão demover este moço impetuoso do seu projecto. José Bonifácio cedeu e elle mesmo o conduzio para aquillo que a sua razão e a sua experiencia não permittião de consentir. Estes desejos do principe lhe erão nutridos por certas pessoas que procuravão por todos os meios ampararem-se delle para o diminar. Já tinhão visto malogrados outras tentativas, e presumião serem mais felizes n'esta que se envolvia em um mysterio do qual o principe não poderia sahir livremente. Sua Alteza exultou com a sua entrada na Maçonaria, que foi para elle uma grande novidade."

[23] *Ibid.*, p. 45. Meneses, *op. cit.*, pp. 36-37. Francisco Adolfo de Varn-

another secret society, officially known as the Nobres Cavalheiros de Santa Cruz, but popularly called the Apostolado, which was also working to promote independence. Some individuals held membership in both these societies. Nevertheless, the two groups tended to drift apart and to reflect the rivalries between the two political factions, the one headed by José Bonifácio, who was staunchly monarchial in his views; the other, by Gonçalves Lédo, who tended toward a republican position.[24] Although the Grand Orient vowed fidelity to the prince regent and initiated intense propaganda for independence, a strong republican sentiment prevailed in the Masonic lodges; it was for this reason that José Bonifácio veered to the Apostolado.[25]

Shortly after the establishment of independence, which was first proclaimed in the Grand Orient on August 20, 1822, Dom Pedro, under the influence of José Bonifácio, suspended all Masonic activity. In an order of October 27, 1822, Dom Pedro announced that by right of his dual authority as chief of State and as chief of Freemasonry he prohibited further Masonic assemblies.[26] Nevertheless, in spite of governmental suppression, the fraternity continued its work in secret.[27] As the despotism

hagen, *História da independência do Brasil* (Rio de Janeiro [1940]), pp. 195, says that Dom Pedro was admitted to Masonry on August 2, 1822, but the notes added to Varnhagen's *História* by the Baron of Rio Branco (*ibid.*, note 54) state that Pedro was admitted July 13, 1822, and became grand master three days later. Melo, *A Maçonaria no Brazil*, p. 17, note 16, says that Pedro was made grand master on October 4, 1822. Rio Branco's notes to Varnhagen's *História* will hereafter be cited as (Notes of R. B.).

[24] There is a difference of opinion among writers as to when and why the Apostolado was created. For a discussion of the different views see Melo, "*A Maçonaria no Brazil*"; Drummond, "Annotaçoes," *loc. cit.*; Costa, *op. cit.*, pp. 43-58; and "Projecto de constituição no 'Apostolado' e sua auctoria," *Re vista do Instituto Histórico e Geográfico Brasileiro*, LXXVII (1914) ii, 3-19.

[25] See Varnhagen, *op. cit.*, p. 186, note 36: "O que ha de certo é que no Grande Oriente Maçônico, installado em 28 de Maio, era preponderante o partido de Lédo, rival de José Bonifácio, e que no *Apostolado*, criado ao quasi mesmo tempo, era onipotente José Bonifácio" (Notes of R. B.).

[26] Meneses, *op. cit.*, pp. 60-61; Lúcio José dos Santos, "A Maçonaria no Brasil," *loc. cit.*, p. 17.

[27] Melo, *A Maçonaria no Brazil*, p. 24, writes: "Perseguidos assim, sem ponto certo de reunião, sem garantia para funcionar em parte alguma, os

of the young emperor increased and as he grew more unpopular, the Freemasons, assisted by other forces and factors in operation at the time, succeeded in creating opposition sufficient to force his abdication on April 7, 1831.[28] After being suppressed for nine years, the Grand Orient was re-established and José Bonifácio was re-elected grand master.[29]

It is not difficult to account for the respected place that Freemasonry held in the Brazilian Empire. The most honored founders of that Empire were its leaders, and the avowed objective of the earliest Masonic lodges was the establishment of independence. The fraternity was consequently respected by many people as the symbol of national freedom. After independence was established, many of the lodges were transformed into philanthropic societies which contributed materially to the support of religion and participated actively in religious and charitable undertakings. Conceivably the generality of Brazilians might have believed that these activities constituted the whole of Masonry, and, accordingly, that Brazilian Freemasonry had nothing in common with the Masonic fraternities of Europe. Intellectual leaders could not, however, have been ignorant of the fundamental character of Masonry, much less of the fact that during the early decades of the Second Empire a strongly radical wing was forming within the ranks of the Brazilian fraternity.[30] An explanation for the indifference of the ecclesiastical and Catholic lay leaders of Brazil to the dangers for both Church

---

maçons mais firmes ás suas crenças determinavam com antecedencia a caza de um irmão qualquer discréto, confabulavam, tomavam suas rezoluções e deste modo, a Maçonaria continuava a ser uma potencia oculta, dominando como outróra."

[28] *Ibid.* Melo writes: "Dessas confabulações [secret meetings], si é que não eram debaixo de todos os preceitos do ritual, quaze sempre prezididas ou assistidas por Jozé Bonifácio e padre Diogo Antonio Feijó, nasceram as bazes da reação contra a dinastia, idéa que teve o aplauzo de quaze toda a população do Rio de Janeiro, motivando o 7 de Abril de 1831, quando Pedro I, reunciou o trôno do Brazil em favor do seu filho, para quem nomeava tutor, José Bonifacio de Andrade e Silva, 1.° grão mestre da Maçonaria e um dos obreiros de mais influencia em todo o imperio."

[29] *Ibid.*, p. 25.

[30] See pp. 193, 219-220 below.

and monarchy inherent in Masonry is to be found in the prevalence of heterodox ideologies during the early days of the Empire. At the time the Empire was established, the clergy constituted one of the best educated classes in Brazil; correlatively, they represented a large part of the intellectual élite most influenced by the philosophies current in Europe during the eighteenth and nineteenth centuries. An investigation into the intellectual training of the Brazilian clergy of the early decades of the nineteenth century will help to explain why many of its members were blind to the consequences of the usurpation of spiritual authority by the imperial government, and why many of them were captivated by Freemasonry.

## II

The spirit of regalism which characterized the union of Church and State in the Empire of Brazil may be traced to doctrines, notably those of Gallicanism and Jansenism, which the marquis of Pombal (1750-1777) fostered in Portugal so that he might the more successfully carry out what seemed to be his plan of founding a national church, with bishops, theologians, and religious orders under the direction of the State.[31] These doctrines were disseminated through the University of Coimbra, whose schools, especially those of medicine, mathematics, canon and civil law, theology, and philosophy, were thoroughly reorganized in 1772, with orientation strongly in the direction of

---

[31] Oscar Mendes, "O Liberalismo no Brasil sob o ponto de vista catholico," *A Ordem*, XI (January, 1932), 34. Eugênio Vilhena de Morais, "O Patriotismo e o clero no Brasil," *Revista do Instituto Histórico e Geográfico Brasileiro*, XCIX (1926), 146, cites Father Gonzaga de Azevedo (*O Jesuita*, II, 132), who gives the following estimate of the Pombaline reforms: "O Marquez de Pombal desquiciou o organismo social portuguez e arrancou-o de suas bases estaveis. Suppoz que podia fundar uma igreja nacional independente de Roma, um quasi anglicanismo (como lhe chamou o cardeal Pacca) com bispos, theologos e conventos ás suas ordens. De facto, só conseguiu derrancar o catolicismo que deixou entre nós mal ferido, com um clero cobarde; e com os estabelecimentos e todos os machinismos de formação ecclesiastica embaraçados em seus movimentos organicos, enfeudados para sempre ao Estado."

the natural sciences.[32] Since this university was a unique center of culture for Brazilian students, the doctrines which Pombal sought to spread by means of it were absorbed by many young men from Brazil.[33] Mendes says that

> Pombal made regalism the principal weapon with which he fought his invincible rival, the Company of Jesus, and it was by the door opened wide by Regalism that Liberalism penetrated in Brazil, to begin its secular work of the emasculation of our intelligence and of our soul.[34]

He initiated what Batista Pereira calls the Pombalization of the clergy, a systematic indoctrination of clerical students with libertine ideas and false doctrines which made some priests ready accomplices in the Pombaline scheme of establishing in Portugal

---

[32] Mário Brandão and M. Lopes de Almeida, *A Universidade de Coimbra, Esbôço da sua História* (Coimbra, 1937), ii, 107: "O espirito que informava a reforma provinha dum empirismo sistemático que caracterizava a ideologia orientadora dos modeladores dos estatutos."

[33] Antônio Batista Pereira, *A Formação Espiritual do Brasil* (São Paulo, 1930), p. 109, writes: "Como se operou a influencia pombalina no espirito brasileiro? Por meio da creação de um clero cesarista, de um clero jansenista, pelo regimen *ad hoc* instaurado pelo branco reformador da Universidade de Coimbra." Tristão de Ataide [pseud. for Alceu Amoroso Lima], "Formação do Brasil," *Estudos*, 5th Series (Rio de Janeiro, 1933), p. 240, writes: "Foi [Pombal] ele que envenenou as fontes da nossa vida espiritual, corrompendo de enciclopedismo o ensino em Coimbra a contaminando o espirito brasileiro por meio de 'um clero quasi todo ceptico e regalista!' " See also Morais, "O Patriotismo e o clero," *loc. cit.*, p. 124: "Concentrado todo o ensino superior em Coimbra, da sua Universidade dependeu naturalmente toda a nossa cultura superior, tanto civil como ecclesiastica, até 1827, anno da creação das nossas Academias de Direito."

[34] "Pombal fez do regalismo a arma principal com que guerreou a sua invencivel rival, a Companhia de Jesus. E foi pela porta escancarada pelo regalismo que o liberalismo penetrou no Brasil, para começar a sua obtra secular de emasculador da nossa inteligencia e da nossa alma." Mendes, "O liberalismo no Brasil," *loc. cit.*, p. 34. Later he writes (*ibid.*, p. 35) : "Foi esse homem que, sob o disfarce de combater os jesuitas, moveu á Igreja guerra surda, inoculando-lhe destruidor veneno em ponto vital, isto é, deturpando a mente do clero."

and her colonies a Liberal Catholicism, inimical to the papacy.[35] These doctrines and ideas were insured a more direct and efficient penetration into Brazil with the establishment in 1800 of the seminary of Olinda by Bishop Dom José Joaquim da Cunha de Azeredo Coutinho.[36] This seminary, located in the old *colégio* of the Jesuits, which had been one of the important centers of learning in colonial Brazil, was to be a nursery of Liberalism and free thought.[37] Bishop Azeredo Coutinho had been educated at the University of Coimbra, where his kinsman, the staunchly Jansenist Dom Francisco de Lemos de Faria Pereira Coutinho, functioned as Pombal's principal assistant in instituting curricular reform.[38] Thoroughly imbued as he was with Liberal ideas, Bishop Azeredo Coutinho, whom Oliveira

---

[35] Pereira, *op. cit.*, p. 109.

[36] Dom José Joaquim da Cunha de Azeredo Coutinho was born in Campos in the captaincy of Rio de Janeiro on September 8, 1783; went to the University of Coimbra in 1775; was elected bishop of Olinda (Pernambuco), November 21, 1794; was consecrated January 25, 1796; took possession of his see by proxy on August 6, 1798, and formally on January 1, 1799. In February, 1800, he founded the seminary of Olinda. He was transferred to the see of Elvas (Portugal) in 1806. Bishop Dom José was elected to act as a Brazilian delegate to the Constituent Assembly in Lisbon in 1821. He arrived at the meeting on September 10, but illness prevented him from participating. He died on September 12. See J. da C. Barbosa, "D. José Joaquim da Cunha de Azeredo Coutinho," *Revista do Instituto Histórico e Geográfico Brasileiro*, I (1839), 349-352; *ibid.*, VII (1845), 106-115; Sebastião de Vasconcelos Galvão, "D. José Joaquim da Cunha Azeredo Coutinho," *Diccionario chorographico, historico e estatistico de Pernambuco* (Rio de Janeiro, 1908), I, 427-429.

[37] Mendes, "O liberalismo no Brasil," *loc. cit.*, pp. 35-36; Tollenare, *op. cit.*, pp. 167-168; Tavares, *op. cit.*, pp. lxxix-lxxx. Lima, "Annotações," p. 36, writes: "O seminario realmente transformou as condições do ensino e com este as condições intellectuaes da capitania, porque constituio, alem de um viveiro de sacerdotes, uma eschola secundaria leiga, aliás a unica, ministrando, como se vê do seu programma, educação theologica e tambem instrucção civil em bellas lettras e n'algumas sciencias . . . . Admittiam-se portano n'ella estudantes que se não destinavam ás ordens sacras, mas que queriam fazer suas humanidades ou mesmo cursar mathematicas."

[38] Brandão and Almeida, *op. cit.*, ii, 82-84. Dom Francisco de Lemos was made rector of the University in May, 1770. He and his brother, Dr. João Pereira Ramos de Azeredo Coutinho, played prominent rôles in the Pombaline reforms. Mendes, "O Liberalismo no Brasil," *loc. cit.*, p. 35, describes Dom

Lima calls "a spiritual son of the University of Coimbra,"[39] was indifferent to the orthodoxy of the ideas disseminated in the classroom by the professors. The Masonic chronicler of the Pernambucan Revolution of 1817, Muniz Tavares, writes that the bishop's "thoughts were not circumscribed by the rigid circle of old-fashioned ideas; with discernment he had selected eminent professors whom he brought with him from Portugal."[40] Many of these professors were ardent followers of Descartes, and had introduced Cartesian philosophy into the University of Coimbra in the intellectual renovation that followed the expulsion of the Jesuits.[41] Seminarians trained at Olinda were not always taught to discern truth from error, as the Church understood that distinction; neither were they imbued with a high regard for the sacred character of the priesthood. They were, on the contrary, thoroughly indoctrinated with Liberal ideas, even in religion, and many of them left the seminary to become engrossed in politics and in revolutionary conspiracies.[42] Even if a spirit of patriotism, says Mendes, prompts men to honor those priests who, eager to effect the liberation of their country, heroically suffered in the cause of freedom, their weakness as priests cannot be overlooked. We cannot but agree with Oliveira Lima, Mendes adds, when he says that "priests who were thus politicians could not be

---

Francisco de Lemos: "A auxiliá-lo nessa obra diabolica [Pombalization of the clergy], teve ele [Pombal], como principal aliado, o brasileiro D. Francisco de Lemos de Faria Pereira Coutinho, jansenista rubro, a quem, pela sua ação funesta sobre o clero, o cardeal Pacca chamava de 'lobo rapiante.' " See Bartolomeo Pacca, *Notizie sul Portogallo con una breve relazione della nunziatura di Lisbona dall'anno 1795 fino all'anno 1802* (2d ed., Velletri, 1836), p. 35.

[39] Lima, "Annotações," p. 33. See also Morais, "O Patriotismo e o clero no Brasil," *loc. cit.*, p. 124.

[40] Tavares, *op. cit.*, p. lxxix.

[41] Mendes, "O liberalismo no Brasil," *loc. cit.*, pp. 35-36; Manuel de Oliveira Lima, *Pernambuco seu desenvolvimento historico* (Leipzig, 1895), p. 216. For a full account of the changes that were made in the University of Coimbra, see Brandão and Almeida, *op. cit.*, ii, 63-120; Tavares, *op. cit.*, p. lxxix.

[42] Lima, "Annotações," *loc. cit.*, p. 35. "A independencia brazileira foi mais directamente ainda servida no seu preparo pelo seminario que em Pernambuco fundou Azeredo Coutinho .... Sendo o prelado mação ... não é

priests of canonically exemplary lives."[43]

The fact that priests did not hesitate to belong to Freemasonry has been used by the defenders of the Brazilian fraternity, who undertake to prove that Freemasonry was, until the Religious Question of the seventies, nothing more than a patriotic and charitable organization. Actually, the affiliation of ecclesiastics in no way attests to the non-religious character of Freemasonry; it only proves that the ecclesiastics who joined its ranks subscribed to Liberal doctrines inimical to Catholic principles. Vilhena de Morais denies that these priests could have belonged to Masonry without knowing that it was condemned by the Church and without knowing the reasons for its condemnation.

> That there might have been among the laity a vast number of deluded persons, there does not remain the least shadow of doubt. The same, however, could not be maintained in relation to the members of the clergy who were affiliated to the lodges, whose position in the sight of the Church they had the strict obligation of knowing.[44]

While it would seemingly be impossible for priests to be ignorant of the existence of papal pronouncements against Masonry, the Jansenist and Liberal training prevalent in the seminaries would make it relatively easy for them to convince themselves that these papal sanctions were not operative in Brazil.[45] Imbued as they were with the doctrines of Liberalistic regalism,

---

pouco plausivel suppor que o seminario se converteria n'um ninho de idéas liberaes, e idéas liberaes eram idéas subversivas, contribuindo decididamente tal nucleo intellectual para a organização das academias secretas." See also Mendes, "O liberalismo no Brasil," loc. cit., p. 36; Morais, loc. cit., p. 124.

[43] Lima, "Annotações," loc. cit., p. 42; Mendes, "O liberalismo no Brasil," loc. cit., p. 37.

[44] "Que houvesse entre leigos grandiosissimo numero de iludidos, não resta a menor sombra de duvida. O mesmo, porém, já não se poderia afirmar em relação aos membros do clero, filiados ás lojas, cuja situação em face da Igreja tinham estricta obrigação de conhecer." Eugênio Vilhena de Morais, O gabinete Caxias e amnistia dos bispos (Rio de Janeiro, 1930), p. 34.

[45] Jansenism and Liberal Catholicism had many points in common; notable among these was their common hostility to the papacy. Léon Séché, Les derniers Jansénistes et leur rôle dans l'histoire de France depuis la ruine de Port-Royal jusqu'à nos jour (1710-1870) (Paris, 1891), III, 245-246,

they would find ready justification for Masonic hostility toward the papacy. It is incontestably true that it was the better educated among the clergy of Brazil who allowed the Church in the empire to be preyed upon by regalism and Masonry. Regalism aimed at drawing the Brazilian Church from communion with Rome, while Masonry conspired to enervate the clergy and to undermine the faith of the laity through the substitution of religious pageantry for solid Catholic worship. Yet what seemed to be an overpowering coalition destined to destroy the Catholic faith of Brazil contained within itself the elements of its own destruction. Regalists among Brazilian statesmen thought that they could use Masonry as a political tool without subscribing to Masonic hostility to revealed religion. They were to discover that while individual members and even whole lodges might be free from such hostility, the fraternity as an international society would always be inimical to Catholicism, and hostile elements within the nation would eventually force the government into an open contest on the subject of religion.

The fact must not be overlooked that the majority of priests who joined Freemasonry would never have been attracted to it had they not been previously indoctrinated with certain Liberal principles. The Liberalism they adopted did not confine itself to securing civil and political liberty, but invaded the spheres of discipline and order. As Mendes says, "under the pompous labels of liberty of thought, liberty of word and of the press, liberty of beliefs and of cults, [Liberalism] recognizes the strange right of doing evil, of subverting order, of scandalizing, of poisoning, of corroding the social organism."[46]

---

writes: ". . . je me suis attaché surtout à faire ressortir, dans le récit des événements qui se sont déroulés de 1830 à 1870, les points de contact, d'affinité, de parenté, que j'avais remarqués entre le catholicisme libéral et le Jansénisme doctrinal des grands jours." Of the two groups, Séché considers the Liberal the more hostile to the papacy. (See *ibid.*, p. 248.)

[46] ". . . sob os rótulos pomposos de liberdade de pensmento, liberdade de palavra e de imprensa, liberdade de crenças e de cultos, reconhece o estranho direito de fazer o mal, de subverter a ordem, de escandalizar, de envenenar, de corroer o organismo social." Mendes, "O Liberalismo no Brasil," *loc. cit.*, p. 33.

"Priests," writes Oliveira Lima, "formed the most educated class of the country, and for this very reason the most vehement love of liberty was sheltered among them."[47] This fact is attested by travelers in Brazil in the early nineteenth century. Tollenare observes that he found among Brazilian ecclesiastics a remarkable familiarity with the doctrines of the French Revolution, and the most profound veneration for French philosophies of the eighteenth century.[48] Of Father João Ribeiro, whom he calls the protagonist of the Pernambucan Revolution of 1817, Tollenare says: "Carried away by the reading of the works of Condorcet, he expressed the highest confidence in the progress of the human spirit; his imagination advanced more quickly than his century and above all was far ahead of the attitudes [indole] of his countrymen."[49] The German scientists, Spix and Martius, who visited Brazil in the years 1817-1820, remark that the study of philosophy — which had formerly been taught "according to an ancient system" — had taken a new turn since Kantian philosophy had been made accessible to the Brazilian student. "It surprised us very agreeably," they write, "to find the terms and ideas of the German school transplanted to the soil of America."[50] Although in many cases distorted, these philosophies had nevertheless directed some of the thought of the Brazilian clergy.

Many of the men responsible for introducing modern European philosophies into Brazil were men of good morals and of superior intellectual attainment, but, intrigued by novel ideas of freedom and progress, they did not examine the full import of some of the doctrines to which they subscribed. Notable among Brazilian ecclesiastics who accepted Liberal doctrines uncritically were three Brazilian prelates, all of whom were at one time affiliated with Masonry.[51] Bishop Azeredo Coutinho

---

[47] Lima, *Pernambuco seu desenvolvimento historico*, p. 241.

[48] Tollenare, *op. cit.*, pp. 32, 121.

[49] *Ibid.*, p. 189.

[50] Johann Baptist von Spix and Carl Friedrich Philipp von Martius, *Reise in Brasilien auf Befehl Sr. Majestät Maximilian Joseph I Königs von Baiern in den Jahren 1817 bis 1820* (München, 1823-1831), I, 209.

[51] Four Brazilian bishops are listed by Melo, *A Maçonaria e a Revolução*

(1743-1821), the founder of the seminary of Olinda,[52] is described by Mendes as a man of virtue, learning, and strong character, but as one who entertained Liberal opinions, without due consideration of their consequences.[53] The same may be said of Dom José Caetano da Silva Coutinho (1767-1833), bishop of Rio de Janeiro,[54] a Portuguese by birth but recognized as a Brazilian citizen, since he was in Brazil when independence was proclaimed. This prelate had been educated at the University of Coimbra, and had brought to Rio de Janeiro the philosophical ideas popular at Lisbon. Bishop Dom José Caetano played a prominent part in the political life of the First Empire, serving as president of the Constitutional Convention of 1823[55] and later as president of the Senate. He is described by an Anglican clergyman traveling in Brazil at the time as "a man of very liberal opinions, perfectly and sincerely tolerant of every sect, while he is warmly attached to his own."[56] The same traveler remarks on the erudition and refinement of this prelate, and observes that

---

*Republicana de 1817,* pp. 26, 35. Dom Sebastião Pinto do Rêgo (1802-1868) was made bishop of São Paulo in 1861. He does not have the same national importance as the other three prelates. Melo (*ibid.,* p. 26, note) records him as having said: "Jezus Cristo instituiu a caridade. A maçonaria apoderou-se dela e constituiu-a sua mestra. E' sob os seus auspícios que não morre a sua esperança e se robustece a sua fé. Bendita seja esta irmã da igreja na virtude." This is typical of the eulogistic sentiments with which Brazilian ecclesiastics honored Freemasonry. For other examples see *ibid.,* pp. 24-26, note 31.

[52] See pp. 37-38 above. Azeredo Coutinho was in Brazil less than eight years.

[53] Mendes, "O Liberalismo no Brasil," *loc. cit.,* p. 36.

[54] Dom José Caetano was elected on November 4, 1805, his appointment was confirmed by Pius VII in 1806, and he took possession of the see of Rio de Janeiro on April 28, 1808. See José de Sousa Azevedo Pizarro e Araújo, *Memorias historicas do Rio de Janeiro* (Rio de Janeiro, 1820) II, v, 267-268; Inocêncio Francisco da Silva, *Diccionario biblographico Portuguez,* IV (Lisboa, 1893), 285-286; Luiz Gonçalves dos Santos, *Memorias para servir á historia do Reino do Brasil* (Lisboa, 1825), I, 70-71.

[55] See p. 56, note 2, below.

[56] R. Walsh, *Notices of Brazil in 1828 and 1829* (London, 1830), I, 368.

"he is a man of strict observance and blameless life himself, and exceedingly temperate in his habits."[57]

The third of the Liberal bishops, Dom Manuel do Monte Rodrigues de Araújo (1798-1863), count of Irajá and bishop of Rio de Janeiro, was to have the greatest personal influence.[58] He was trained in the seminary of Olinda where he was later professor of theology for seventeen years. Two of his works, *Compendio de Theologia*[59] and *Elementos de Direito Ecclesiastico*,[60] had tremendous influence in Brazil. The first of these, adopted in all the seminaries of the empire, is described by the bibliographer, Sacramento Blake, as a work that "is without a doubt the one that was most in conformity with our customs."[61] The author, according to Blake, had been instructed "like all priests of the period" in a theology saturated with Jansenism "which among condemned heresies is considered a subtle poison that invades doctrine without its being felt."[62] The *Compendio de Theologia* was examined by the Sacred Congregation of the Index, was discovered to be Jansenist, and was ordered corrected. Dom Manuel showed himself obedient to the Holy See in this matter, and the errors did not appear in subsequent editions.[63] The significant thing in this instance is that such doctrines could be held and taught by a man who professed to be and who gave evidence of being in good faith. The explanation must be that

---

[57] *Ibid.*, pp. 368- 369. Dom José Caetano appears to have had only a sociological interest in religion. If he had considered the Church he purported to serve as a divine institution, he could not have countenanced the introduction of any other religion into a country which was entirely Catholic.

[58] See J. C. Fernandes Pinheiro, "Dom Manoel do Monte Rodrigues de Araújo," *Revista do Instituto Histórico e Geográfico Brasileiro*, XXVII (1867), ii, 194-217.

[59] *Compendio de Theologia moral para uso do Seminario de Olinda* (2 v., Pernambuco, 1837).

[60] *Elementos de Direito Ecclesiastico publico e particular, em relação á disciplina geral da egreja, e com applicação aos usos da egreja do Brasil* (3 v., Rio de Janeiro, 1859).

[61] Sacramento Blake, *Diccionario bibliographico brazileiro*, VI (Rio de Janeiro, 1899), 165.

[62] *Ibid.*

[63] *Ibid.*

in his own training he had absorbed these doctrines and was now without malice disseminating them.[64] In like manner his *Elementos de Direito Ecclesiastico* was discovered to be strongly Jansenist and regalistic in its interpretation of the relation between Church and State. In its delineation of the rights of the State in ecclesiastical matters it subscribed to many principles of Gallicanism.[65] This work was brought to the attention of the Sacred Congregation of the Index two years after the bishop's death, when it was condemned.

Like so many Brazilians, Bishop Dom Manuel was attracted to Masonry because he saw it as the exponent of Brazilian nationalism and because it appeared to be a society consecrated to the Liberal principles which his education had led him to admire. He did not hesitate, however, to repudiate Freemasonry when he discovered it was inimical to the Church. In 1847 he wrote a pastoral letter urging Catholics affiliated with Masonry to leave the fraternity, and to abjure whatever error against faith and morals [*bons costumes*] they had adhered to or professed as Masons.[66] Throughout his episcopacy, Dom Manuel was the champion of ecclesiastical discipline;[67] nevertheless, his early

---

[64] Morais, "O Patriotismo e o clero," *loc. cit.*, p. 122, says of priests trained in the Gallican-Jansenist tradition: "A cultura, porém, que recebiam esses padres a disseminavam depois, por toda a parte, generosamente."

[65] Blake, *op. cit.*, VI 167. In spite of the fact that this work was placed on the Index in 1869, it was constantly appealed to by the imperial government to justify its alleged rights of imperial *placet* and of recourse to the Crown at the time of the Episcopal-Masonic controversy.

[66] Pedro Maria de Lacerda, *Carta pastoral do Bispo de S. Sebastião do Rio de Janeiro publicando as letras apostolicas do Summo Pontifice e Santo Padre Pio IX de 19 de maio de 1783 sobre a absolvição dos Maçons* (Rio de Janeiro, 1873), p. 4, writes: "Aos confessores que houverem de absolver aos maçons recommendamos que leião no Apostolo de 4 de Maio de anno corrente, e na nossa Pastoral ahi publicada, a carta que nosso antecessor o Exm. Sr. D. Manoel do Monte Rodrigues de Araujo, Conde de Irajá, escreveu em data de 18 de Outubro de 1847, ácerca de desfazer-se o maçon dos livros, papeis, insignias, etc., que tiver da sociedade, e de abjurar quaesquer erros contra a fé e bons costumes a que tenha adherido ou professado na maçonaria."

[67] Before he was made bishop, while he was serving in the Chamber of Deputies, Dom Manuel supported ecclesiastical discipline against Diogo Antônio Feijó in the celibacy question, even though he was of Feijó's party. See

leanings toward Liberal Catholicism and his affiliation with Freemasonry strengthened the position of those who believed that the Church should be subject to the State and who maintained that Brazilian Freemasonry was in no way hostile to the Church. In a discourse in the Chamber of Deputies on May 24, 1873, Alencar Araripe, a delegate from Pernambuco, asserted that one is in good company in Masonry, since not only notable statesmen have belonged to the Brazilian fraternity, but also three bishops: Dom José Joaquim; Dom Manuel, count of Irajá; and Dom José Caetano.[68]

## III

In his endeavors to nationalize the Church of Brazil, Pombal contributed not only to the intellectual prostitution of the clergy but also to its moral deterioration. The expulsion of the Jesuits from Brazil was incontestably one of the foremost contributing causes of this deterioration. Foreign travelers in Brazil in the nineteenth century remark it;[69] the hostility of Freemasons to the return of the Jesuits as seminary professors points to it;[70] and contemporary Brazilian historians accept it.[71] The decadence followed also from having bishoprics unoccupied for extended periods, and from maintaining the diocesan clergy in such a state of penury that the dignity of the priestly vocation was diminished. Since Pombal desired to have the Church within the Portuguese Empire directly under the control of the king, he tried to have as little recourse as possible to the Holy See. This

---

Pinheiro, "D. Manoel do Monte Rodrigues de Araújo," *loc. cit.*, pp. 202-204. In like manner, in 1861 he stood firm against the current agitation for civil marriage (*ibid.*, pp. 222-226). This movement was largely Masonic in origin.

[68] *Anais da Câmara dos Deputados, 1873* (Rio de Janeiro, 1873), I, 163.

[69] Spix and Martius, *op. cit.*, I, 223, "Das Studium der Theologie ward hier früherhin durch die Jesuiten sehr befördert, aus deren Collegium mehrere ausgezeichnete Männer hervorgingen." George Gardner, *Travels in the Interior of Brazil* (2d ed., London, 1849), pp. 61-62.

[70] See pp. 221-223 below.

[71] Morais, "O patriotismo e o clero no Brasil," *loc. cit.*, pp. 121-123; Pereira, *op. cit.*, pp. 68-69, 85-87.

created an anomalous situation. The State might lay claim to full jurisdiction over the Church, but, unless it wanted to become openly schismatic, it could not maintain unlimited jurisdiction, for all hierarchical appointments had to be confirmed by the Holy See. Frequently Pombal left episcopal sees vacant for years rather than appeal to Rome for confirmation of an appointment.[72] In Brazil the evils that followed from this policy were manifold. Religious discipline among the diocesan clergy broke down; religious instruction of the laity was neglected; and admission to holy orders came to be in many instances sacrilegious, since the candidate had neither vocation nor training for the priesthood.[73] In this period the custom developed among families of demanding that the least intelligent son be ordained. " 'You are going to be a priest!' " writes Pereira, "was a common and offensive expression, reproaching with intellectual shortsightedness the individual addressed."[74]

During the Pombaline régime (1750-1777), the appropriation of ecclesiastical tithes for other than religious purposes contributed to the demoralization of the Brazilian diocesan clergy. Shortly after the discovery of Brazil in 1500, the king[75] appropriated all the tithes levied there, but assumed the responsibility of providing for the support of public worship and of paying stipends for the adequate support of the clergy.[76] When the stipulation was made, it was a necessary expedient because the country was exceedingly poor and the population so small that the tithes were not sufficient to maintain the Church. Later, when the wealth and population of Brazil increased, the stipends

---

[72] Morais, "O patriotismo e o clero no Brasil," *loc. cit.*, p. 124. And when the sees were finally filled, the candidate was sure to be an ecclesiastic trained to accept the Pombaline system. Frequently in these instances the Holy See accepted the proposed candidate to prevent a greater evil.

[73] Pereira, *op. cit.*, p. 111, writes: "O governador do bispado de Marianna em menos de sete mezes ordenou oitenta a quatro pretendentes." See also Morais, "O patriotismo e o clero no Brasil," *loc. cit.*, p. 122.

[74] Pereira, *op. cit.*, p. 113.

[75] The king received the ecclesiastical tithes as grand master of the Order of Christ. (See p. 61 below).

[76] See p. 60, note 13, below.

were not increased. By the end of the eighteenth century, bishops and priests were living in a state of penury, while the Portuguese government was collecting enormous sums in tithes.[77] This financial arrangement stimulated among the clergy a violent hostility to Portuguese rule, and became one of the major contributing factors in drawing priests into the vanguard of the revolutionary movements of the early nineteenth century. Penury was a common bond uniting the intellectually superior among the clergy with the intellectually inferior.[78] Since the most inadequate diocesan seminaries seem to have been equipped to disseminate the new philosophical trends of eighteenth century Europe, even priests of the less well-educated group were familiar with the doctrines of the French Revolution and with the Liberal principles of the period.[79] "Notwithstanding the humble ranks from which the clergy are raised, and the insufficient means of education afforded them," writes a traveler in Brazil in the early nineteenth century, "they have already felt the effects of that influx of light and knowledge, which an inter-

---

[77] For a full study of tithes see Oscar de Oliveira, S.J., *Os dizimos eclesásticos do Brasil nos períodos da Colônia e do Império* (Juiz de Fóra, 1940); See also John Armitage, *The History of Brazil* (London, 1836), I, 6-8; Walsh, *op. cit.*, I, 358-360. When describing the Brazilian situation, Walsh compares it with the current situation in England; "From the increase of population and produce, the tithes amount to an enormous sum, while the stationary stipend of two hundred dollars is a comparative trifle, and insufficient to procure the common comforts of life, so that the state of the clergy in Brazil is, generally speaking, a state of poverty . . . . Nor are these dignitaries of the church [archbishops and bishops] more amply provided for . . . . Such of them as I had the pleasure to know and visit, appeared to me to live with great moderation and simplicity; and, so far from abounding in superfluities, did not seem to me to enjoy even what, in England, would be considered necessaries to men of their rank in life." Tollenare, *op. cit.*, pp. 123-124, describes the situation in similar terms. For a discussion of tithes, see pp. 60-62.

[78] Melo, *Frei Caneca*, p. 5, writes: "Os conventos eram, ao tempo, os únicos educandarios, para os ricos e para os pobres. E somente depois de passarem pelos conventos iam os filhos de ricos para Coimbra." Among the religious orders, the Carmelites and the Benedictines of Olinda were notably wealthy and intellectually alert. See Tollenare, *op. cit.*, pp. 32-33, 121.

[79] Spix and Martius, *op. cit.*, I, 106; Tollenare, *op. cit.*, pp. 32-33, 121.

course with strangers and free institutions, has spread through the country."[80] An impoverished Liberal clergy quite logically took a leading part in the independence movement, and with equal consistency strengthened the revolutionary element in Masonry, a society whose Liberalistic philosophy and whose secret character made it an indispensable tool to those who proposed to unite in a movement of rebellion. Oliveira Lima says that the Pernambucan Revolution of 1817 was a revolution of priests,[81] and Mendes remarks that "this strange marriage of priests and Masons continued even in the struggle for independence and in the subsequent revolts of [18]24[82] and [18]42[83]."

While many of its more radical members joined in the uprisings that followed the establishment of both the First and the Second Empires, the primary political activity of the Brazilian clergy after the Second Empire was established was not that of fomenting revolutionary movements, but of shaping imperial policies through membership in the national legislative assembly. Apparently forgetting that the Church in colonial Brazil had been degraded through the evils of royal patronage and largely removed from direct papal jurisdiction, the majority of the priest-deputies supported ultra-regalistic measures designed to bring the Church under the complete domination of the State. The Jansenist attitude toward the papacy which these ecclesiastics had acquired in their seminary training made them eager to curtail the rights of the Holy See in the Brazilian Church; at the

---

[80] Walsh, *op. cit.*, I, 366-367. The author is writing of the years 1828-1829, but what he says is applicable to Brazil at the end of the eighteenth century. Although works coming into Brazil had ostensibly to be approved by a censor, it was easy to evade this regulation. See Tollenare, *op. cit.*, p. 121. Lima, "Annotações," p. 38, remarks that after 1808 foreign books came freely into Brazil.

[81] Lima, "Annotações," p. 41. Melo, *A Maçonaria e a Revolução Republicana de 1817*, pp. 68-70, note 80, lists the names of more than sixty ecclesiastics who participated in this revolution.

[82] On the Revolution of 1824 see p. 30, note 11, above. Morais, "O Patriotismo e o clero," *loc. cit.*, p. 130, says that not less than twenty-four priests participated in the revolt.

[83] "Esse conúbio esdruxulo de padres e maçons continou ainda na lutas pela independencia e nas subsequentes revoltas de 24 e 42." Mendes, "O Liberalis-

same time, their implicit faith in representative institutions made them believe that the Church could still operate as a free institution even though it was subject to civil authority. While ecclesiastics in the national assembly were furthering the interests of the State at the expense of the freedom of the Church, the diocesan clergy were neglecting their sacerdotal duties and were permitting parochial direction to pass to the control of the religious brotherhoods.[84] These religious associations, which were composed entirely of the laity and which very early developed into centers of Masonic activity, became the nucleus around which religious activity revolved.[85] The results were a steady

---

mo no Brasil," *loc. cit.*, p. 37. In 1842 an abortive Liberal Revolution occurred in São Paulo and in Minas Gerais. It began in protest against the allegedly reactionary laws of the cabinet of 1841 and against the dissolution of the Chamber of Deputies to which a great Liberal majority had been elected in 1840. Dom Pedro II dissolved the cabinet at the request of the ministry which claimed that the election of 1840 was invalid because of the violence and the irregular voting tactics that had been resorted to. Among notable persons to participate in the uprising was Diogo Antônio Feijó (see pp. 68-76 below). See Aluísio de Almeida, *A revolução liberal de 1842* (Rio de Janeiro, 1944). Manuel de Oliveira Lima, *O Imperio Brazileiro 1822-1889* (São Paulo [1927], p. 30, writes: "O manifesto paulista de Feijó é um documento notavel pelas idéas, si bem que de linguagem violenta."

[84] D. P. Kidder and J. C. Fletcher, *Brazil and the Brazilians* (Philadelphia, 1857), pp. 107-108, give the following description of the Brazilian brotherhoods: "These fraternities are not unlike the beneficial societies of England and the United States, though on a more extended scale . . . . They have a style of dress approaching the clerical in appearance, which is worn on holidays, with some distinguishing mark by which each association is known. A liberal entrance-fee and an annual subscription is required of all the members, each of whom is entitled to support from the general fund in sickness and in poverty, and also to a funeral of ceremony when dead. The brotherhoods contribute to the erection and support of churches, provide for the sick, bury the dead, and support [sic] masses for souls. In short, next after the State, they are the most efficient auxiliaries for the support of the religious establishment of the country. Many of them, in the lapse of years, have become rich by the receipt of donations and legacies, and membership in such is highly prized." See also Manoel S. Cardozo, "The Lay Brotherhoods of Colonial Bahia," *The Catholic Historical Review*. xxxiii (April, 1947), 12-30.

[85] See Charles d'Ursel, *Sud-Amérique* (Paris, 1879), pp. 35-37, for a description of the popular religious festival. Ursel remarks that the brotherhood sponsoring the particular ceremonial he describes was made up, as were most

decline in solid Catholic life and worship and a concomitant increase in superficial religious activity.

In view of conditions that prevailed when independence was established, it is not difficult to comprehend how the Church, both in her ministers and in her faithful, came to that state of decadence which characterized her throughout the period of the empire.[86] Outstanding members of the clergy, who should have been spiritual leaders, were far more preoccupied with the affairs of State than with their priestly obligations. Obsessed by the current ideas of progress, they aligned themselves with regalistic nationalists against the right of the papacy to regulate the Church within the State. They joined the vanguard in the promotion of state policies whose inevitable consequences were the subjection of Church to State, and the weakening of the spiritual as well as the social force of the Church within the nation.[87] As in similar instances in history when churchmen served the State at the expense of what they owed the Church, the clergy of Brazil lost the exalted and esteemed position which it had previously held.[88] Father Júlio Maria, in his splendid historical

---

of the brotherhoods of Brazil, of men who were also affiliated with Freemasonry. Walsh, *op. cit.*, I, 364-365, discusses the nature of the brotherhoods and their importance in the Brazilian church. Joseph Burnichon, *Le Brésil d'aujourd'hui* (Paris, 1910), p. 204, writes: "Les fêtes, non pas précisément les fêtes d'Église qui passent souvent inaperçues, mais les fêtes particulières, locales, des confréries ou des patrons, sont solemnisées avec grand éclat . . . ."

[86] The work of the Church in Brazil during the colonial era up to the last half of the eighteenth century (the Pombal era) was highly commendable. See José Luiz Alves, "Os Claustros e o clero no Brasil," *Revista do Instituto Histórico e Geográfico Brasileiro*, LVII (1894), ii, 1-257; Father Júlio Maria, "A Religião, ordens religiosas, instituições pias e beneficentes no Brazil," *Livro do Centenario: 1500-1900* (Rio de Janeiro, 1900), I, ii, 5-63; Serafim Leite, *História da Companhia de Jesus no Brasil* (Lisboa-Rio de Janeiro, 1938-19——) ; Morais, "O Patriotismo e o clero," *loc. cit.*, pp. 114-124. For a traveler's comment, see Gardner, *op. cit.*, pp. 61-62.

[87] Father Júlio Maria, "A Religião," *loc. cit.*, pp. 85-86; Manuel Tavares Cavalcanti, "Relações entre o estado e a igreja," *Revista do Instituto Histórico e Geográfico Brasileiro*, tomo especial, VI (1922), 304-305; Morais, "O patriotismo do clero," *loc. cit.*, pp. 123-124; 145-147.

[88] F. Badaró, *L'Église au Brésil pendant l'empire et pendant la république*

survey of the Church in Brazil, points out a certain retributive justice in the degradation which members of the clergy suffered at the hands of secular officials:

> It was just . . . that the clergy should gradually lose that very prestige which it enjoyed in the eyes of the people and which it used against the Church. It was just that *regalism* itself, satisfied in all its aspirations, should throw aside the instrument which it had used on so many and on such solemn occasions to combat the Holy See and even to slander the Holy Father, more than once treated by the clergy in parliament as an arbitrary, capricious, usurping, and hypocritical person . . . . It was just that the episcopacy and clergy, both in agreement in raising, on the ruins of the liberty of the Church, the triumphant bust of Caesarism, should fall in Brazil into that lamentable moral prostration, whose last degree was its complete social nullification.[89]

Their enthusiastic acceptance of State supervision of ecclesiastical affairs shows how unaware Brazilian bishops and priests were of the danger in this policy. The State occupied itself with the creation of dioceses, the reorganization of seminaries, the establishment of faculties of theology, while the foremost clergymen fought for the alleged rights of the State against Rome.[90] The Brazilian Church had little to hope for from such state-con-

---

(Rome, 1895), p. 36, writes: "L'élément clérical avait trahi sa mission, et, par une conséquence naturelle, était tombé dans une prostration mortelle."

[89] "Era justo, porém, que o clero fosse perdendo esse mesmo prestigio, de que gozava aos olhos do povo, e de que se serviu contra a Egraja. Era justo que o proprio *regalismo*, satisfeito em todas as suas aspirações, atirasse para um lado o instrumento de que se tinha servido, em tantas e tão solemnes occasiões, para combater a Sancta Sé, e até injuriar o Sancto Padre, mais de uma vez tractado pelo clero, no parlamento, de arbitrario, de caprichoso, usurpado e hypocrita . . . . Era justo que o espicopado e o clero, concordes ambos em elevar sobre as ruinas da liberdade da Egreja o busto triumphante do cesarismo, caíssem no Brasil nessa lamentavel prostração moral, cujo ultimo gráo foi a sua completa nullificação social." Father Júlio Maria, "A Religião," *loc. cit.*, p. 86.

[90] *Ibid.*, pp. 69-71.

trolled seminaries; Brazilian Freemasonry, on the other hand, had little to fear.[91] The debilitated clergy contented itself with a superficial fulfillment of its sacerdotal functions. As Father Júlio Maria says,

> If we compare the small and sickly progress of the Brazilian Church in such a long period of time, with the rapid and prodigious development of that [Church] in the United States in one third of the same time, we cannot fail to attribute the causes to two phenomena: in the United States, to the intrepidity of the episcopacy, to the activity of the clergy, to the freedom which the Church enjoys; in Brazil, to Gallicanism, to regalism, and to the servitude of the Church in a régime of false union.[92]

Travelers in Brazil in the nineteenth century do not speak untruly when they describe the degenerate state of the Church.[93] Their criticism is not any more severe than that of Brazilians who have investigated the situation and analyzed the needs of

---

[91] The determination of Brazilian bishops to regain control of the seminaries was one of the fundamental causes underlying the Episcopal-Masonic controversy of the seventies. See pp. 221-223 below.

[92] "Si comparamos o pequeno e rachitico desenvolvimento, em tão large espaço de tempo, da Egreja brasileira com o rapido e prodigioso desenvolvimento da dos Estados-Unidos num terço do mesmo prazo, não podemos deixar de attribuir as causas dos dous phenomenos nos Estados-Unidos á intrepidez do episcopado, á actividade do clero, á liberdade de que gosa a Egreja; no Brasil, ao gallicanismo, ao regalismo, e á servidão da Egreja num regimen de falsa união." Father Júlio Maria, "A Religião," *loc. cit.*, p. 87.

[93] As typical accounts and characteristic evaluations of the Church see Professor and Mrs. Louis Agassiz, *A Journey in Brazil* (Boston, 1868), pp. 495-497; Thomas Ewbank, *Life in Brazil* (New York, 1856), *passim;* Kidder and Fletcher, *op. cit., passim;* Henry Koster, *Travels in Brazil* (London, 1816), *passim;* William Scully, *Brazil; Its Provinces and Chief Cities; the Manners and Customs of the People* (London, 1866), pp. 8-9; Tollenare, *op. cit., passim;* Spix and Martius, *op. cit.,* I, *passim;* Walsh, *op. cit.,* I, 358-382. Of all these accounts, Walsh's is the most optimistic on the state of religion; he says that despite gaudy devotion to saints there is a fundamental piety among Brazilian people. Sully, *op. cit.,* p. 8, says: ". . . though the religious feelings of the people have been in a great measure shocked and undermined, the attachment of many to the creed of their forefathers is undeniable."

the Catholic faithful during the era of the empire. Father Júlio Maria writes:

> The principal need of the Brazilian parishes is the teaching of doctrine . . . . In the parishes, the majority of the faithful does not have a clear idea of what it believes and practices; it does not know the value of the sacrifice of the mass; it does not know what is the value of a Sacrament; it does not discern the parts of penance; it literally knows only the decalogue.[94]

What these travelers failed to distinguish was that the corrupt practices of the Brazilian Church had their source in regalistic and Jansenist theories. In the empire of Brazil the jurisdiction of the Holy See was so effectively curtailed that the Church was scarcely more than a bureau of the government. Bishop Macedo Costa in the collective pastoral of 1890[95] describes the situation accurately when he says that "among us, the oppression exercised

[94] "A principal necessidade das parochias brasileiras é a doutrinação . . . . Nas parochias, a maioria dos feis não tem idéa clara do que crê e practica, não conhece o valor do sacrificio da missa; não sabe o que é um sacramento; não discerne as partes da penitencia; não conhece sinão litteralmente o Decalogo . . . ." Father Júlio Maria, "A Religião," loc. cit., p. 88.

[95] Pastoral collectiva do episcopado, de 19 de marco de 1890, quoted in João Dornas Filho, O padroado e a igreja brasileira (São Paulo [1938]), pp. 286-293. This pastoral letter, which was written by Macedo Costa following the separation of Church and State after the establishment of the Republic, is a careful exposition of the attitude of the Church toward the separation of the two powers. The Church approves, not of a separation which is tantamount to a divorce between things temporal and things spiritual, but of a separation that allows both powers to operate freely, yet permits of their cooperation in furthering the spiritual and temporal interests of the citizens. Macedo Costa writes (ibid., p. 290): "Em nome da ordem social, em nome da paz publica, em nome da concordia dos cidadãos, em nome dos direitos da consciencia, repellimos os catholicos a separação da Igreja do Estado; exigimos a união entre os dous poderes . . . . Mas, notae bem, não queremos, não podemos querer essa união de incorporação e de absorpção, como tem tentado realizal-a certo ferrenho regalismo monarchico ou republicano—união detestavel, em que o regimen das almas constitue um ramo da administração publica com o seu ministerio de cultos preposto aos interesses religiosos." Pereira, op. cit., pp. 126-129, points out that it was through the efforts of Rui Barbosa that the freedom of the Church was insured in the postivistic republic established in

by the State in the name of a supposed patronage, was one of the principal causes of the weakening of our Church, of her almost complete atrophy."[96]

---

Brazil in 1889. In his youth, Rui Barbosa was very hostile to the Church (see p. 226 below) but as a mature man he returned to the faith and became one of its most ardent defenders.

[96] Dornas, *op. cit.*, p. 289.

# CHAPTER III

## CHURCH AND STATE IN BRAZIL, 1822-1872

The invasion of Portugal by the armies of Napoleon drove the Portuguese sovereigns out of Lisbon on November 29, 1807, and necessitated the transfer of the Portuguese court to Rio de Janeiro. This transfer was in effect the first step in an evolutionary process whereby Brazil would achieve her independence. Prince John, who was acting as regent for his mother, the incapacitated Queen Mary I, was in Brazil only a short time when he recognized the stagnating effects produced on Brazilian social and economic life by colonial restrictions, and began to legislate for their gradual abolition. When, on December 16, 1815, Brazil was proclaimed a co-ordinate part of the new United Kingdom of Portugal, Brazil, and Algarves, a second step toward independence had been achieved. In the following year Queen Mary I died, and the regent became King John VI. Prosperity in Brazil varied during the next few years. The Brazilians liked having the king in Brazil, but resented the heavy taxes which the upkeep of the royal court entailed. In Portugal, meanwhile, things were not going well. The council of regency which John had established in 1807 and which had been exercising nominal rule since that time was overthrown by a revolutionary movement in August, 1820. The *de facto* government adopted provisionally a constitution modeled on the Spanish Constitution of 1812, and called a meeting of the *Côrtes*. This *Côrtes* invited John to return to Portugal and also invited the Brazilians to send delegates to a constituent assembly. When King John, realizing that it was not safe to remain longer away from Portugal, sailed for Lisbon with his court on April 24, 1821, a third step toward Brazilian independence was taken.

At a time when uprisings and revolts in various provinces disturbed conditions within Brazil and showed the imminent need for changes in government, delegates elected to participate in the constituent assembly at Lisbon left for Portugal. Before they had been long in attendance at the assembly, the Brazilian delegates realized that the meeting was dominated by a group of politicians determined to reduce Brazil to her former status of colony. Brazilian patriots, on being apprised of the intentions of the majority in the Lisbon assembly, resolved to work more openly toward complete independence for Brazil. After a period of indecision, Dom Pedro, who had been left as regent of Brazil when the royal family returned to Portugal, acquiesced in the demand of Brazilian statesmen that he remain as monarch of the independent nation. The *Grito de Ipiranga*, Brazil's declaration of independence of September 7, 1822, was the answer of the Brazilians to the Portuguese demand that Brazil revert to colonial status. On October 12, 1822, Dom Pedro was declared emperor.[1] The proclamation of independence announced the establishment of the empire, but before national autonomy could be insured a twofold task had to be accomplished: the empire must be recognized by other powers, and its own internal affairs must be put in order. The first part of the program, while vitally important to the history of Brazil, has place in this survey only in so far as it includes recognition of the empire by the Holy See. The second, that of establishing an orderly government, inevitably presented many complex problems, but only one of them, involving the relations between Church and State, will be discussed.

## II

A few months after the promulgation of the constitution of 1824,[2] the emperor, Dom Pedro I, sent to Rome a special min-

---

[1] On the independence movement see John Armitage, *The History of Brazil* (London, 1836) ; Manuel de Oliveira Lima, *O movimento da independência, 1821-1822* (São Paulo, 1922) ; Francisco Adolfo de Varnhagen, *História da independência do Brasil* (Rio de Janeiro [1940]) ; F. Renaut, "L'Émancipation du Brésil," *Revue d'Histoire Diplomatique*, XXXII (1918), 541-599; ———, "L'Organisation constitutionelle du Brésil, les débuts de la politique personnelle de Dom Pedro," *ibid.*, XXXIV (1919), 39-89; ———, "Le Brésil et l'Europe," *ibid.*, XXXVI (1922), 50-95.

[2] The constitutional convention which Dom Pedro I, before being proclaimed emperor, had promised to call, was formally opened on May 3, 1823. Men-

ister, Monsignor Francisco Correia Vidigal, to negotiate with the Holy See for the recognition of Brazilian independence,[3] and to solicit at the same time certain favors from the Holy Father. For reasons which will later be made clear, the Brazilian government was particularly eager that the Supreme Pontiff transfer to the Brazilian emperor the grand masterships of the three military orders, of Christ, of Aviz, and of Santiago. The Brazilian minister was in Rome two years before he achieved the desired recognition of the new empire of Brazil,[4] and an additional four months before he persuaded the Holy Father to transfer the

---

tion has already been made of the fact that nineteen ecclesiastics were members, and that one of them, Dom José Caetano, bishop of Rio de Janeiro, was chosen its president. Among the outstanding laymen who were delegates were the three Andrada brothers. While the convention was at work, the antipathy of its more influential members toward Portuguese residents of Brazil began to be expressed in violent speeches. This opposition toward the Portuguese together with the manifest leaning of delegates toward the principles of the French Revolution were, according to Oliveira Lima, the two basic reasons why Dom Pedro opposed the assembly. On November 12, 1823, the emperor employed soldiers to evict the delegates forcibly from the convention hall. Having dissolved the constitutional convention, Pedro appointed a commission of ten to draw up another constitution, this time under his direction. This document, which was to remain for sixty-five years the fundamental law of the empire, was approved by the municipal councils and promulgated on March 25, 1824. In the constitution of 1824, says Oliveira Lima, Pedro achieved two objectives which the members of the Constitutional convention had opposed: 1) Pedro wanted to share sovereignty with parliament (viz., moderative power); the members of the convention had wanted sovereignty to reside exclusively in parliament; 2) Pedro wanted a constitution prepared under his direction and submitted to the town councils for their approval and sanction; the convention wanted to impose a constitution on the emperor. See Manuel de Oliveira Lima, O imperio brazileiro, 1822-1889 (São Paulo, 1927), pp. 11-17; John Armitage, op. cit., I, 116-157. For a discussion of Dom Pedro's support of the Portuguese residents of Brazil see Alan K. Manchester, "The Paradoxical Pedro, First Emperor of Brazil," The Hispanic American Historical Review, XII (1932), 176-196.

[3] Instrucções de Vidigal, Rio de Janeiro, August 28, 1824, in Ministério das Relações Exteriores, Archivo diplomatico da independencia (Rio de Janeiro, 1922), III, 300-310. Monsignor Vidigal's first letter from Rome is dated January 15, 1825. (Vidigal to Carvalho e Melo, ibid., p. 321.) Hereafter this work will be cited as Archivo diplomatico.

[4] João Dornas Filho, O padroado e a igreja brasileira (São Paulo [1938]),

grand masterships to the new emperor.[5] The delay was caused, the Brazilian minister believed, not by the unreasonableness of the Brazilian demands, but by the fact that he was not able to allay the fears aroused in the Supreme Pontiff by the menacing threats of the Holy Alliance.[6]

The successful diplomacy of the Holy Alliance in delaying the establishment of harmonious relations between the newly-created Brazilian empire and the papacy is but one incident in the larger story of the part played by the European powers in shaping the destinies of the new nations of Ibero-America. Yet there is substantial reason for believing that fear of the Holy Alliance was not the primary reason why the Holy See hesitated to recognize the new Brazilian empire. Cândido Mendes de Almeida believes that, while the Holy See would be reluctant to recognize as an autonomous nation a state which had not gained the recognition of its mother country, the real cause of the delay was traceable to certain principles in the Brazilian constitution which were out of harmony with strict orthodoxy.[7] Some of the clauses of the

---

p. 42. "Dois annos esteve monsenhor Vidigal em Roma," writes Dornas, "sem ao menos poder entregar á Sua Santidade as suas credenciaes . . . . Finalmente, a 23 da janeiro de 1827 eram a independencia e o Imperio do Brasil reconhecidos pela Santa Sé, alçando Vidigal nesse mesmo dia as armas do Brasil á porta da legação."

[5] *Ibid.*, p. 43. Oscar de Oliveira, *Os dizimos eclesiásticos do Brasil nos períodos da Colônia e do Império* (Juiz de Fóra, 1940), p. 91, says that on August 8, 1826, Msgr. Vidigal wrote to the minister of foreign affairs that such rights and privileges had been "transferred and conveyed" (*transfundidos e passados*) to the founder of the Brazilian nation and to his successors. However, the bull *Praeclara Portugalliae*, which actually conferred these rights and privileges, was not issued until May 15, 1827. See *ibid.*, p. 92.

[6] Vidigal to Carvalho e Melo, January 15, 1825, *Archivo diplomatico*, III, 321-322; Vicente A. da Costa to Carvalho e Melo, January 16, 1825, *ibid.*, pp. 322-327.

[7] Cândido Mendes de Almeida, *Direito civil ecclesiastico brasileiro, antigo e moderno em suas relações com o direito canonico* (Rio de Janeiro, 1866), I, i, cclxii-cclxiii, writes: ". . . he inexplicavel a demora que houve em levar por diante os desejos do Governo Imperial, a não ser pelo descommunal de suas pretenções, e certos principios encontrados na Constituição de um Povo Catholico em desharmonia com a sua orthodoxia." See also F. Badaró, *L'Église au Brésil pendant l'empire et pendant la république* (Rome, 1895), p. 9.

constitution[8] gave the Holy Father reason to believe that the new imperial government, although professing to be Catholic, was not wholehearted in its loyalty to the Holy See. This distrust, adds Almeida, was well-founded, judging from occurrences in the empire, especially in the decade of 1827-1837, and was confirmed by the content of the instructions given to Monsignor Vidigal by the imperial minister of foreign affairs.[9]

The Brazilian minister to the Holy See was told that the result of his conferences with the Holy Father ought to be a concordat which would determine the manner of regulating affairs between the two authorities. Those which appertained to the emperor in his quality of sovereign protector of the Church in Brazil should be distinguished from those which must be regulated by an agreement between the two contracting parties: Church and State.[10] In all matters relative to the Church, the imperial government recommended that its minister proceed with much discretion and judgment. He was warned that the court of Rome liked very much to meddle in the affairs of the State in matters of jurisdiction and to obtain the greatest advantages in pecuniary matters.[11] The imperial constitution gave to the emperor the right of patronage in the Brazilian Church, but the minister was to treat specially with the Holy Father concerning those patronage rights which accrued to the grand master of the Order of Christ. The emperor asked that the Holy See transfer to him and his descendants the grand masterships of the military orders with their respective privileges.[12] He sought particularly the grand mastership of the Order of Christ, because to it per-

---

[8] Almeida, op. cit., I, i, cclxiii, note, calls attention to the fact that among the powers of the emperor enumerated in the constitution (article 102) were included the right of ecclesiastical patronage and the right to concede or deny permission (i.e., placet) for the publication of ecclesiastical documents within the empire. Since the Holy See regarded ecclesiastical patronage as a privilege which it alone could confer (see p. 23 above), and since it never sanctioned the placet (see p. 24n above), quite understandably the Holy Father looked with misgiving on these clauses of the Brazilian constitution.

[9] Ibid., cclxiii.

[10] "Instrucções de Vidigal," sec. 12, Archivo diplomatico, III, 304.

[11] Ibid., sec. 10.

[12] Ibid., sec. 14.

tained the patronage of minor benefices in connection with which
he would have the right to collect the ecclesiastical tithes.[13]

Mention has already been made of the place of the Order of
Christ in the overseas expansion in Portugal.[14] It will, nevertheless, be conducive to a better understanding of the right of patronage to review briefly the privileges conferred by the Holy
See on this military order, and to distinguish the two types of
patronage, royal and ecclesiastic, enjoyed by the Portuguese sovereigns. By the bull *Inter Caetera quae* of March 13, 1456,
Pope Calixtus III conceded to the great prior of the Order of
Christ ordinary episcopal jurisdiction as prelate *nullius dioecesis*
in all the overseas lands conquered or to be conquered.[15] This
bull, besides conceding spiritual jurisdiction to the Order of
Christ, reaffirmed the bull *Romanus Pontifex,* dated January 8,
1455, by which Nicholas V confirmed the temporal dominion
of the Portuguese kings in territories conquered beyond the seas.
The bull *Aeterni Regis clementis* of June 21, 1481, issued by
Sixtus IV, reaffirmed what had been granted by the bull *Inter
Caetera quae* relative to the spiritual jurisdiction of the Order of
Christ and the temporal jurisdiction of the Portuguese sover-
eigns. Later, Leo X, by the bull *Praecelsae devotionis* of November 3, 1514, confirmed the temporalities of the Portuguese kings

---

[13] The ecclesiastical tithe is defined by Father Oliveira (*op. cit.*, p. 17) as
a tenth part or another determined portion of the fruits or other profits licitly
acquired, which, by ecclesiastical precepts, ought to be paid in tribute for the
subsidy of the divine cult and the sustenance of ministers of the Church who
administer the sacraments to the faithful and perform for them other spiritual
functions. Throughout the colonial period the kings of Portugal received
the ecclesiastical tithes as grand masters of the Order of Christ. *Ibid.*, 51-52.
See also p. 47, note 77, above.

[14] See p. 23, note 64, above.

[15] Oliveira, *op. cit.*, pp. 35-36. Pope Calixtus III said that he granted these
privileges to the Order of Christ on petition of King Afonso and Prince
Henry, who asked that the spirituality [*espiritualidade*] of the ultramarine
territories conquered from the Saracens, both present and future, be given to
the Order of Christ. All of the bulls cited in this section are given in the
original and in translation in Frances G. Davenport, *European Treaties Bearing on the History of the United States and Its Dependencies to 1648* (Washington, D. C., 1917), pp. 9-26, 27-32, 49-55, 112-117.

in the overseas territories, acquired or to be acquired.[16]

To the great prior of the Order of Christ belonged the spiritual jurisdiction in these territories[17] and also the patronage of all minor benefices. By the bull *Dum fidei* of June 7, 1514, Leo X, subjecting still to the Order of Christ the patronage of all benefices *nullius dioecesis*, possessed or to be possessed in the colonial territories, granted to King Emmanuel, as grand master of the Order of Christ[18], and to his successors the patronage of all minor benefices which until then had belonged to the great prior.[19] Five days later, June 12, 1514, by the bull *Pro excellenti*, Pope Leo X created the diocese of Funchal in Madeira and

---

[16] Oliveira, *op. cit.*, p. 36, note 9, "Mendes de Almeida e outros afirmam que a jurisdição da O. de Cristo nas terras ultramarinas foi confirmada pelas bulas de Nicolau V e Calixto III (Cf. Tomo I, Parte ii, pag. 364, nota).—E' falso, porém que Nicolau V tenha concedido tal graça à O. de Cristo. A bula *Dum diversa nobis* de Nicolau V simplesmente concede ao rei de Portugal a faculdade de subjugar os Sarracenos e outros infiéis, para que estes possam abraçar a fé católica; ao mesmo tempo concede graças espirituais aos fiéis que de qualquer modo os auxiliarem em tais pelejas. A bula *Romanus Pontifex* desse mesmo Papa confirma o dominio temporal dos reis nas terras de conquistas, atuais ou futuras, e concede jurisdição espiritual a todos os sacerdotes que os reis enviarem a essas terras. Portanto só as bulas de Calixto III e de Xisto IV falam de jurisdição espiritual da O. de Cristo nas terras de conquistas portuguêsas." Father Oliveira cites various historians, including Varnhagen, Galanti, Fleiuss, Handelmann, and Rocha Pita, who have misconstrued the bulls granting spiritual jurisdiction to the Order of Christ. These historians are inclined to see a temporal jurisdiction where none exists. Father Oliveira concludes: "Não sabemos como estes autores chegaram a estas conclusões. A' O. de Cristo as duas bulas já citadas dão sómente a espiritualidade daquelas terras; os reis tinham sôbre as mesmas o dominio temporal."

[17] As prelate *nullius dioecesis*.

[18] Oliveira, *op. cit.*, p. 48, note 45: "D. Manuel, Duque de Beja, depois rei de Portugal, foi eleito Grão Mestre da O. de Cristo em 1483. Desde então cessou o Grão-mestrado de ser eletivo, pois o sucessor deste, D. João III, foi deputado Grão-Mestre *ad vitam* pela S. Sé, pela bula *Eximiae devotionis affectus*, de 19 de Março de 1523. A 30 de Dez. de 1551 ficou *in perpetuum* anexo à corôa, pela bula *Praeclara charissimi*." This last bull assigned the masterships of the other two orders, Santiago and Aviz, in perpetuity to the Portuguese crown. *Ibid.*, p. 49.

[19] These minor benefices were parochial and applied to those ecclesiastics who were directly concerned with administering to the spiritual needs of the faithful.

included within its jurisdiction the territory of Brazil. Thus it came about that, in Brazil, the Portuguese king possessed a double patronage: one secular, the patronage of the episcopal benefice of the diocese of Funchal, which accrued to the king as king; and one ecclesiastical, the patronage of minor benefices which accrued to the king as grand master of the Order of Christ.[20]

From this brief exposition, it becomes apparent why the emperor of Brazil was eager not only to gain the recognition of the Holy See but also to secure the transfer of the grand mastership of the Order of Christ, which would give him patronage of the minor benefices[21] and, as a corollary of this patronage, the right of collecting the ecclesiastical tithes.[22] The Brazilian minister was urged in his instructions to secure a continuation of the privileges which were exercised up to this time by the monarchs of Portugal and which were now due to His Imperial Majesty as sovereign and as grand master of the Order of

---

[20] Oliveira, *op. cit.*, pp. 48-49. In the bull *Super specula* of February 25, 1551, which created the first diocese in Brazil proper, this double patronage is formally designated. In the creation of subsequent dioceses, the patronage of the Order of Christ, *i.e.*, *infra episcopais*, is implicitly contained in the documents of erection but is not explicitly stated.

[21] The minor benefices were supported by the ecclesiastical tithes. The major benefices [*beneficios episcopais*], which included archbishoprics, bishoprics, canonries, and all cathedral dignities, were in theory supported by the king, but actually they were financed out of the ecclesiastical tithes. Oliveira, *op. cit.*, p. 109, says: "Os dízimos do Brasil Colonial, que foram abundantíssimos, como já o mostrámos, os reis os arrecadavam, confundindo-os com as rendas civis. Por isto ainda que nas bulas se diga que os benefícios sejam dotados çom as rendas civís, de fato eram *todos* eles dotados com as rendas dos dízimos da O. de Cristo."

[22] Oliveira, *op. cit.*, pp. 79-83. Father Oliveira proves that the ecclesiastical tithes always belonged to the Order of Christ; were never secularized by the Holy See, even though the kings of Portugal, by concession of the Holy See, received sometimes *as kings* the tithes or part of them. All during the colonial period, the kings received as grand masters of the Order of Christ, the tithes of Brazil. See *ibid.*, pp. 51-52. Father Oliveira says (pp. 108-109): "A O. de Cristo conservou em todo tempo do Brasil Colonial o seu padroado para os benefícios infra-episcopais, como de sobra prova o Pe. Santini [*De Regio Jure Patronatus in Brasilia* (Pôrto Alegre, 1934)] (No Brasil Império manteve os mesmos privilégios). Portanto deveria dotar os seus benefícios, pois

Christ.[23] The government referred to the necessity of effecting the transfer of the title of grand master to the emperor and his descendants "in order to continue the practice of the rights which are inherent in it" that His Imperial Majesty might receive the "tithes of all the Churches in its possession . . . ."[24] The pecuniary urgency which prompted the imperial government to seek the transfer of the grand mastership of the Order of Christ is revealed in the instructions. Apparently to impress the minister with the importance of obtaining this ecclesiastical patronage, he was reminded of the fact "that the Bishops and Curates of Brazil do not receive the tithes but only stipends, and that in the present circumstances the State is not able to do without so great a revenue. . . ."[25] Badaró probably does not err when he says that "the question of money dominated entirely the spirit of the imperial régime, whose purpose appears to be the policy of war on the treasury of the Church in order to weaken it, or rather, to subdue it by famine."[26] He seems correct, too, in his

---

*PATRONUM FACIUNT DOS, AEDIFICATIO, FUNDUS.* E as rendas de que dispunha no Brasil para estas dotações eram precisamente os dízimos que o reis arrecadavam.

"E a prova mais evidente é que depois da nossa emancipação política, o nosso primeiro imperador pedia à S. Sé a dignidade de Grão-Mestre das Ordens Militares, com os seus respectivos privilégios. Ora, ao Grão-Mestrado da O. de Cristo, em particular, pertencia então o padroado dos benefícios menores, para cuja dotação percebia os dízimos eclesiásticos."

[23] "Instrucções de Vidigal," sec. 14, *Archivo diplomatico,* III, 304. "A respeito dos Benefícios Curados e tudo o mais que a este respeito se acha estabelecido tratará V.I. de obter que continue a praticar-se como até agora, em virtude dos Direitos que a S. M. Imperial deve competir na qualidade de Soberano e de Grão-Mestre da Ordem de Cristo, refundindo-se em nova Bulla todos os Direitos que até aqui exercia o Soberano de Portugal na referida qualidade." Oliveira (*op. cit.,* p. 109, note 22) remarks on the mistaken notion which the author of these instructions had relative to ecclesiastical rights of the king. "Não só os benefícios curados, mas *TODOS* os benefícios eclesiásticos pertenciam aos reis, como tais ou como Grão-Mestres da O. de Cristo . . . . E', pois, de estranhar que o redator destas *Instruções* ignorasse isto."

[24] "Instrucções, de Vidigal," sec. 15, *Archivo diplomatico,* III, 304-305.
[25] *Ibid.,* sec. 17, p. 305.
[26] Badaró, *op. cit.,* p. 6. "Instrucções de Vidigal," sec. 27, *Archivo diplomatico,* III, 308, refers to the nuncio apostolic. In section 31, *ibid.,* p. 309),

observation that imperial statesmen had established the Catholic religion as the religion of the State so that they might dictate the laws of the Church.[27]

Cândido Mendes de Almeida says that it was the first session of the national legislature (1826-1829) that caused the most serious damage to the Church and made the greatest encroachment on the rights of the Holy See.[28] The assertion is substantiated by other historians. Magalhães remarks that regalistic and Liberal ideas were common not only among counselors of the emperor, but also among members of the Brazilian parliament, notably among the twenty-two ecclesiastics who had been elected deputies. If such ecclesiastics, he continues, as Dom Romualdo Antônio de Seixas, Dom Marcos Antônio de Sousa, Dom José Caetano da Silva Coutinho, Monsignor Francisco Correia Vidigal, and Father Antônio Vieira da Soledade were moderate regalists, Diogo Antônio Feijó, Miguel José Reinaut, Canon Januário da Cunha Barbosa, Monsignor José de Sousa Azevedo Pizarro e Araújo, Antônio da Rocha Franco, José Custódio Dias, and José Bento Leite Ferreira de Melo were ultra-regalists, distinguished for their vehement defense of the prerogatives of the State against the rights claimed by the Holy See. It was the secular clergy, Magalhães concludes, who, by deed or by lack of prestige, helped Dom Pedro I most in establishing the preëminence of the temporal over the spiritual.[29] Badaró says that at this time there was scarcely a priest or a religious who was not contaminated by Jansenism and who was not convinced of the supremacy of the

---

the minister is urged to secure a reduction of papal fees on the pretext that Brazilian subjects should not pay tribute to a foreign sovereign.

[27] Badaró, *op. cit.*, p. 7.

[28] Almeida, *op. cit.*, I, i, cccxlii.

[29] Basílio de Magalhães, *Estudos de história do Brasil* (São Paulo, 1940), pp. 91-92. Later Magalhães makes it clear that, while Dom Romualdo Antônio de Seixas was moderately regalistic, he was not hostile to the Holy See. Magalhães writes (p. 102, note), "Do número desses levitas acomodatícios [Magalhães is here speaking of the twenty-three ecclesiastics who were members of the National Legislature in 1834-1837] deve ser excluído d. Romualdo Antônio de Seixas . . . ."

State over the Church.[30] In view of the Liberal and Jansenist ideologies with which the candidates for the priesthood were imbued, and to which attention has already been called,[31] there is no cause for surprise in the discovery that ecclesiastics gave notable support to the State in its efforts to curtail the rights of the Church, and particularly the jurisdiction of the Holy See. Neither is it surprising to discover that the more radical members of the first session of the national legislature were affiliated with Freemasonry.[32] Badaró remarks that priests friendly to Rome had no hope of election.[33] The attitudes of this ultra-regalistic group were given full expression in the shaping of civil policy relative to ecclesiastical affairs, largely because from it were chosen the members of the ecclesiastical commission to which was assigned all matters relative to the Church. On the recommendations of this commission, the Chamber of Deputies as a whole depended for its information on all ecclesiastical measures.

The regalistic view of the ecclesiastical commission[34] is well illustrated in the report it made to the Chamber of Deputies, advising the Chamber to reject the bull *Praeclara Portugalliae* of May 15, 1827, in which Leo XII transferred the grand masterships of the three military orders to the emperor of Brazil, and conceded to the crown of Brazil the same rights that had been granted to Portugal by Leo X and Julius III in 1514 and

---

[30] Badaró, *op. cit.*, p. 29.

[31] See pp. 37-45 above.

[32] See Almeida, *Direito civil ecclesiastico brasileiro*, I, i, ccxlii, note; Badaró, *op. cit.*, p. 36. Father Júlio Maria, "A Religião, ordens religiosas, instituições pias e beneficentes no Brazil," *Livro do Centenario: 1500-1900* (Rio de Janeiro, 1900), I, ii, 86, remarks that the priests most antagonistic to the Holy See were those affiliated with Freemasonry: Diogo Antônio Feijó, Miguel José Reinaut, Monsignor Pizarro e Araújo, Canon Januário da Cunha Barbosa, Antônio da Rocha Franco, José Custódio Dias, and José Bento Leite Ferreira de Melo.

[33] Badaró, *op. cit.*, p. 37.

[34] The ecclesiastical commission at this time was composed of the following deputies: Limpo de Abreu, Bernardo de Vasconcelos, Diogo Feijó, Campos Vergueiro, José Clemente Pereira, Lúcio Soares Teixeira de Gouvêa, Antônio da Rocha França, and Miguel José Reinaut. *Anais da Câmara*, 1826, I, i-vi.

1550, respectively.[35] The commission reasoned that the Order of Christ had been granted the right of patronage over churches in territories which it had "conquered" from the infidel or which it had "constructed" or "endowed" in newly acquired lands, but that in Brazil the Order of Christ had done none of these things; hence the Church of Brazil had never belonged to the patronage of the Order of Christ. Consequently, the commission argued, the kings of Portugal exercised in Brazil the right of patronage, not as grand masters of the Order of Christ, but as kings. Patronage was, therefore, inherent in sovereignty, and belonged to the emperor of Brazil through the unanimous proclamation of the people and the fundamental law of the land. The commission's conclusion was that the papal bull was of no importance, since it had for its end the confirmation of rights which the emperor already held by worthier titles.[36]

While Brazilian statesmen could say with truth that the right of patronage had originally been granted over churches in lands which the Order of Christ had "conquered" from the infidel or which it had "constructed" or "endowed"[37] in newly acquired

---

[35] Anais da Câmara, 1827, V, 127; see also Oliveira, op. cit., pp. 91-92.

[36] Anais da Câmara, 1827, V, 128-129. Commenting on the report of the ecclesiastical commission on the bull Praeclara Portugalliae, Father Oliveira says (op. cit., p. 100) : "Concedendo Leão XII ao nosso primeiro Imperador a dignidade de Grão-Mestre das Ordens de Cristo, Santiago e Aviz, pela bula Praeclara Portugalliae . . . foi esta apresentada à Assembléa Geral para o beneplácito. A Câmara dos Deputados composta de vários membros em extremo regalistas . . . . aprovava o parecer da Comissão que afrontosamente rejeitava a bula por ser ela 'ofensiva à Constituição do Império,' 'ociosa,' até 'injusta,' e que os privilégios que a S. Sé pretendia conceder ao Imperador eram 'essencialmente inerentes à Soberania do atual Imperador do Brasil e Seus Successores . . . .' " See also Almeida, op. cit., I, i, cclxxviii; Badaró, op. cit., pp. 11-21. These ideas were probably gathered from the book by Dom José Joaquim da Cunha de Azeredo Coutinho, Alegasaõ juridica, Na qual se mostra, que saõ do Padroado da Coroa, e naõ da Ordem Militar de Cristo, as Igreja, Dignidades, e Beneficios dos Bispados do Cabo de Bojador para o Sul, em que se compreendem os Bispados de Cabo Verde, S. Thomé, Angola, Brazil, India, até á China (Lisboa, 1804).

[37] These conditions were laid down by the Council of Trent. See H. J. Schroeder, Canons and Decrees of the Council of Trent (St. Louis, 1941), pp. 113, 241-243, 387, 508-510.

lands, they probably knew that, as prerogatives of the Portuguese crown applicable to Brazil, all rights of patronage over minor benefices were held by the Portuguese king as grand master of the Order of Christ. They must have known, moreover, that all rights of patronage were held by specific grants from the Holy See; none was inherent in sovereignty.[38] Patronage of major benefices, it will be recalled, had been given to the king as king; patronage of the minor benefices had been conceded to him in his capacity of grand master of the Order of Christ.[39]

Refusal to accept the bull *Praeclara Portugalliae* was one in a series of rebuffs offered to the Holy See by the Chamber of Deputies, whose leaders treated the Holy Father with contempt in the very first session, and designated him simply as the bishop of Rome.[40] Monsignor Vidigal had secured the nomination of a nuncio apostolic to Brazil, but the Chamber of Deputies rejected the appointment on the pretext that it had been made on condition of the nuncio's having certain prerogatives detrimental to the independence of the Brazilian government.[41] When the bull *Sollicita Catholici gregis cura* (July 15, 1826), erecting the dioceses of Goiaz and Mato-Grosso, was submitted to the legislature, only that part was approved which referred to the ex-

---

[38] See pp. 22-23 above.

[39] Viveiros de Castro, *Accordams e votos (Commentados)* (Rio de Janeiro, 1925), p. 391, says: "Considerando que o Padroado não é um direito majestatico, e como tal nunca foi considerado, nem mesmo pelos civilistas portuguezes mais eivados das theorias regalistas como Cabedo, Mello Freire, Almeida e Souza, e outros; nem é inherente á soberania nacional como sustentaram no Imperio os estadistas que queriam dar arrhas do seu espirito voltairiano; é um instituto que a Igreja fundou no interesse do seu serviço e sem prejuizo da sua liberdade; é o direito, se não totalmente espiritual, *quasi espiritual*, como dizem os canonistas, ou *temporal com espiritualidade annexa*, como pensam muitos jurisconsultos reinicolas." Castro acknowledges his indebtedness to Cândido Mendes de Almeida for facts incorporated into the above observation; he seems, however, to have missed Almeida's reference to Pereira de Castro who, in his *Manu Regia*, claims that patronage is not derived from papal grants but belongs to the king by right of immemorial usage. See p. 23, note 65, above.

[40] Badaró, *op. cit.*, p. 9. Almeida, *op. cit.*, I, i, cclxxviii.

[41] *Anais da Câmara*, 1827, III, 123-141. See Badaró, *op. cit.*, p. 7; Dornas, *op. cit.*, p. 43.

tension and limits of the new dioceses.[42] Moreover, a law was
passed that ordered the provisions of the Council of Trent put
into effect. The fact that these provisions had been part of the
civil law of Brazil as well as of canon law for three centuries
was ignored.[43]

### III

The opposition to the Holy See which was evident during
the reign of Dom Pedro I (1822-1831) assumed new proportions during the period of the Regency (1831-1840).[44] The
efforts of statesmen to wrest ecclesiastical jurisdiction from the
Holy See and to center it directly in the Brazilian episcopacy
now became almost fanatical. An explanation for this new bit-
terness is to be found in the personality and the influence of the
priest-statesman, Father Diogo Antônio Feijó, who throughout
the greater part of the period was the leader of the ultra-regalistic
faction.

Diogo Feijó was born in São Paulo in 1784. The identity
of his parents is unknown, but the supposition is that his father
was a priest. The stigma of illegitimacy impressed itself irre-
vocably on the mind of the boy, and influenced markedly his
moral and intellectual development.[45] After he had completed
his studies and had been ordained, Feijó, in 1818, disposed of
all his possessions and went to Itú to join the Fathers of Our
Lady of Patronage [*Padres do Patrocínio*], an unofficial re-

---

[42] *Anais da Câmara*, 1827, III, 123-141. Rafael M. Galanti, *Compendio
de historia do Brazil* (São Paulo, 1910), IV, 208, says that the parliament
"recusou conceder o subsidio que a Curia Romana reclamava como necessario
para manter uma Nunciatura Apostolica perante o throno imperial." In 1827
the bull *Romanorum pontificum vigilantia* freed the dioceses of Pará and
Maranhão from the see of Lisbon and declared them suffragans of the archbishop of Baía. See Magalhães, *op. cit.*, p. 93.

[43] Badaró, *op. cit.*, p. 10.

[44] Dom Pedro I abdicated in April, 1831, leaving his son, a child not yet
six years of age, as his successor. A temporary committee of regency functioned
until June, 1831, when a regular one of three members was established. In
1834, an amendment known as the *Ato Adicional* was added to the constitution; it provided, among other things, for a single regent.

[45] Among the best biographies of Feijó are Eugênio Egas, *Diogo Antonio
Feijó* (São Paulo, 1912) and Octávio Tarquínio de Sousa, *Diogo Antônio
Feijó* (Rio de Janeiro, 1942). Of these two works that of Sousa is the more
disinterested.

ligious community.[46] Tarquínio de Sousa says that Feijó removed to Itú to fulfill as perfectly as possible his priestly vocation. He wished to exercise the ecclesiastical ministry, not indifferently or lamentably, as was commonly done by priests in Brazil, but with genuine fervor, in the sincere desire of preserving purity of life and of attaining moral perfection.[47] The same author is of the opinion that Feijó thought that, by living with the Fathers of Our Lady of Patronage and by following their practices of rigorous asceticism, he would build his life on merit and cause his illegitimate birth to be overlooked.[48] Since it was difficult for a child born out of wedlock to be admitted to the priesthood, Feijó experienced personally, early in his career, the penalties deriving from the moral laxity of his parents. This explains in part his later opposition to clerical celibacy, and indicates the urges that gave strong motivation to his own irreproachable moral conduct.[49]

---

[46] Sousa, op. cit., p. 25. See also J. C. Fernandes Pinheiro, "Os Padres do Patrocinio ou o Porto Real de Itú," Revista do Instituto Histórico e Geográfico Brasileiro, XXXIII (1870, ii, 137-148. The society was started by Jesuino de Monte Carmelo, a pious layman who, after the death of his wife, joined the Third Order of Our Lady of Mount Carmel and devoted his life to prayer and penance. His home became the domicile of an unofficial religious group which took its name from a nearby church built by Jesuino de Monte Carmelo and dedicated to Our Lady of Patronage. Among the first members of the society were Jesuino's two sons, Fathers Elias and Simão, a nephew, Father João Paulo Xavier, and a protégé, Father Manuel da Silveira. This group was joined by other priests and laymen, some of whom remained continually in the community, while others, who seem not to have been actually members, were frequent visitors. Among the members were Feijó and Antônio Joaquim de Melo, later bishop of São Paulo.

[47] Sousa, op. cit., pp. 25-28.

[48] Ibid., pp. 27-28. The author thus describes Feijó's attraction to the Fathers at Itú: "Grande em verdade fora a sedução! Sentira-se preso a esses homens, a esses padres que sabiam ser padres, que não se relaxavam em costumes faceis, tendo amasias, atirando ao mundo filhos que carregariam por toda a vida a vergonha de sua origem. Eram padres de verdade, vivendo segundo o Evangelho. E assim quis viver o padre Diogo Antônio Feijó, inclinado por feitio pessoal a estremar-se, a definir-se inteira e corajosamente, numa atitude cujo avesso seria muitas vezes uma excessiva simplificação das cousas, uma certa falta de finura para perceber que nem tudo é simples, nem tudo é facil."

[49] Ibid., p. 13.

In spite of the purity of intention which motivated the Fathers of Our Lady of Patronage, they seem to have inclined toward a Jansenist type of asceticism. This tendency appears to have developed from over-eagerness to attain perfection, coupled with a misconception of the spiritual life obtained from books on asceticism imprudently chosen and badly comprehended.[50] Into this already dangerous atmosphere, Feijó introduced an element of Kantian philosophy, acquired while working out the courses in rational and moral philosophy which he taught at Itú.[51] Had the times been different, Feijó might have remained a Father of Our Lady of Patronage all his life, and if he were remembered at all today it would be as one who "by intellectual libertinism" had been on the point of "sinking into heresy."[52] The era was one of great political ferment, however, and Feijó was stirred by the spirit of the times. The urge to participate in the political activities of his country was soon to take precedence over the urge toward contemplation and spiritual perfection. Tarquínio de Sousa assures us that it was the unrest of the times, not lack of fervor, that took Feijó away from Itú.[53]

In Brazil toward the end of 1821 repercussions of the efforts of Portuguese patriots to introduce constitutionalism into the mother country[54] brought Feijó to the political phases of his career. The house of the Fathers of Our Lady of Patronage developed into a center of political activity, with Feijó taking a leading part in the discussions.[55] In 1822 he was elected delegate to the Lisbon Constituent Assembly. With this assignment, Father Feijó was launched as a public figure. In Lisbon he soon became aware of the reactionary character of the assembly, and he withdrew to return to Brazil and took part in the movement

---

[50] Pinheiro, "Os Padres do Patrocinio," *loc. cit.,* p. 141. In mentioning the Jansenist and Gallican influences, Pinheiro refers to the *Tentativa Theologica* (see p. 21 above).

[51] Sousa, *op. cit.,* p. 30; Pinheiro, "Os Padres do Patrocinio," *loc. cit.,* p. 141.

[52] Sousa, *op. cit.,* p. 30.

[53] *Ibid.,* pp. 31-32, 55-56.

[54] See p. 55 above.

[55] Sousa, *op. cit.,* p. 31.

for independence. After the break with Portugal, he was elected delegate to the constitutional convention assembled by Dom Pedro I, in 1823.[56] He was a member of the Chamber of Deputies from 1826 to 1832, and held during the Regency the portfolio of Justice from July 1831 to August 1832. From October 1835, to September 1837, he was sole regent of the empire, and from July 1833, until his death in 1843, he was a member of the Senate.[57]

Father Feijó probably acted from conviction, yet the fact cannot be overlooked that some of his actions played havoc with the rights of the Church in Brazil. Cavalcanti, in an article treating of relations between Church and State, gives the following estimate of the work of Feijó toward the creation of a national Church:

> It was reserved to the great figure of the Regency, Father Diogo Antônio Feijó, to reach the extreme limits of the pretensions of the temporal power. From 1831 as Minister of Justice and then as Regent, his acts are in manifest and declared rebellion against the aspirations of the Papacy to the supreme exercise of ecclesiastical authority. It belonged to him to consider and to treat openly the bishops and priests as functionaries of the State, and he endeavored to free them from obedience to the Roman hierarchy except in matters purely spiritual. The Empire owes him this conquest which later statesmen only consolidated. Archbishops and bishops thus appointed did not hesitate in assenting to the precepts of the civil government, and in this fashion the institutions of patronage and the *placet* were validated.[58]

---

[56] It will be recalled that Father Feijó joined José Bonifácio to effect the overthrow of Dom Pedro I, which had been decided upon by their Masonic affiliates.

[57] Mention has already been made of the fact that Father Feijó was implicated in the Liberal uprising of 1842. See p. 49n above.

[58] "Estava reservado ao grande vulto da regencia, o padre Diogo Antonio Feijó attingir ás raias extremas das pretensões do poder temporal. Desde 1831 como ministro da Justiça e em seguida como regente, os seus actos são de manifesta e declarada rebeldia contra as aspirações do Papado ao exercicio

Feijó deplored the prevalence of immorality among the clergy, and he was convinced that the evil could be eradicated only by permitting ecclesiastics to marry. On October 10, 1827, when Ferreira França introduced the question of celibacy in the Chamber of Deputies, Feijó began at once to advocate clerical marriage. He enunciated the following four theses: 1) the temporal power has the right to dispense the impediments to matrimony; 2) history shows that celibacy was not always a clerical requirement; 3) prohibiting the marriage of priests brings untold evils to society; and 4) the general legislative assembly of Brazil has the right and the obligation to oppose clerical celibacy.[59] In great detail he enlarged upon these four points, giving what seemed to many hearers a substantial argument for his position.[60] He maintained that celibacy was not possible for all ecclesiastics, and that as long as the Church maintained a law of celibacy, universal in its application, there would be grave moral evils in the Church. Brazil, he asserted, bore witness to this fact. Feijó reminded the members of the Chamber that they, as the protectors and defenders of religion, must eradicate the scandal of clerical immorality to avert the ruin of the social order. He demanded that the imperial government negotiate a concordat with

supremo da autoridade ecclesiástica. Coube-lhe considerar e tratar abertamente os bispos e parochos funccionarios do Estado e procurou desligal-os da obediencia a hierarchia romana, excepto em materia puramente espiritual. A elle deve o Imperio esta conquista que os estadistas posteriores apenas consolidaram. Archbispos e bispos assim nomeados não tiveram duvida em assentir aos preceitos do governo civil e deste modo se validaram as instituições do padroado e beneplacito." Manuel Tavares Cavalcanti, "Relações entre o Estado e a Igreja," *Revista do Instituto Histórico e Geográfico Brasileiro*, tomo especial, VI (1922), 306-307.

[59] *Anais da Câmara*, 1827, V, 116.

[60] The debate which followed Feijó's speech gives evidence of the favor with which his remarks were received by some members of the Chamber. See *Anais da Câmara*, 1827, V, 116-119. Many deputies, however, were not persuaded by Feijó's eloquence. Most of his arguments were subsequently refuted by Father Luis Gonçalves dos Santos and Frei Antônio Dias. See Sousa, *op. cit.*, p. 84. A good exposé of his asserted historical proofs is to be found in the anonymous pamphlet entitled *Causa da religião e disciplina ecclesiastica do celibato clerical defendida da inconstitucional tentativa do Padre Diogo Antonio Feijó* (Rio de Janeiro, 1828).

the Holy See that would establish the right of the State to re-
solve all marriage cases and to determine what constitutes an
impediment to marriage. Feijó maintained that the Brazilian
government must persuade the Holy See to acknowledge that the
law of celibacy was purely disciplinary, and could, without
hazard to ecclesiastical prerogatives, be dealt with by the Church
of each individual country.[61]

After finishing his discourse, Feijó asked leave to have his
remarks printed. Dom Romualdo de Seixas, archbishop of Baía,
opposed the granting of this request. He pointed out that when
Luther commenced his reform, he began immediately to advocate
clerical marriage, and that Erasmus had sardonically observed
that the giving in marriage had made Luther's reform a comedy.
In spite of the archbishop's protest, however, the majority voted
in favor of publication.[62] Periodically during the next seven
years, the question of celibacy was reopened on the floor of the
Chamber. Each time the opposition was successful in defeating
the issue, yet Feijó continued to sponsor the anti-celibacy project
and to challenge the right of the Holy See to regulate matters
of discipline for the universal Church.[63]

In 1833 Feijó submitted the same question to the provincial
assembly of São Paulo and invited that body to consult the
bishop of the diocese, Dom Antônio Joaquim de Abreu Pereira,
on how well celibacy was observed. The bishop admitted, when
questioned, that it was not observed in his diocese, and agreed
that the abolition of the law would serve religion and the
State.[64] The movement against the canonical precept of celibacy

---

[61] *Anais da Câmara*, 1827, V, 116-119.

[62] *Ibid.*, p. 120.

[63] One of the hardest fought battles in the Chamber occurred on May 25,
1832, and concerned the right of the state to regulate impediments to marriage. Father Soares da Rocha and Antônio Pereira Rebouças fought the measure; Feijó, Carreiro da Cunha, Antônio Maria de Moura, Costa Ferreira, Ferreira e Melo, and Maia supported it. See *Anais da Câmara*, 1832, I, 41-45.
No vote was taken. When the measure came up again in July of the same year,
it was blocked by a speech delivered by Dom Romualdo. [João] Pandiá
Calógeras, *Da Regencia á quéda de Rozas* (São Paulo, 1933), p. 128.

[64] Feijó went to São Paulo on July 30, 1832, to arouse interest in his
anti-celibacy project. He secured immediate support from the bishop of São

could not be ignored by the Holy See. On February 18, 1834, the papal chargé in Brazil, Scipione Fabbrini, wrote in part to the minister of foreign affairs:

> The 'Correio Oficial' has just announced that the Provincial Council of São Paulo made the following resolutions: 1) that the bishops in their dioceses have the same rights as the Holy Father in the whole Catholic Church; 2) that the law of celibacy is simply disciplinary. Conclusion: the bishops are able to dispense the disciplinary canons of the General Councils in their dioceses, and to permit marriage of the clergy in their dioceses.
>
> I understand that the Bishop of São Paulo and the General Council submitted this affair to the judgment of the Government, and I, as the delegate of the Holy See, take the liberty of addressing this confidential letter to Your Excellency in order to know the opinion of the Government respecting the matter.[65]

The answer of the imperial minister, Aureliano de Sousa e Oliveira Coutinho, to Monsignor Fabbrini was far from reassuring:

---

Paulo. Calógeras, *op. cit.*, pp. 126-127, says: "Idéas jansenistas, processos regalistas levados ao exaggero, gallicanismo em toda a linha, taes parece serem os moveis da propaganda e da acção de grande parte do clero inferior, saturado de leituras que iam da Encyclopedia ás obras revolucionarias publicadas em França, e que tanto concorreram para as mudanças politicas de 1830 e de 1848. No proprio episcopado, não seria excepção unica o bispo de S. Paulo, a admittir o casamento dos padres." See also Dornas, *op. cit.*, pp. 68-69.

[65] "Le *Correio Oficial* vient de publier que le Conseil Provincial de S.-Paulo veut prendre les mesures suivantes: 1) Les évêques dans leurs diocèses ont les mêmes droits que le Saint-Père dans toute l'Église Catholique; 2) La loi du célibat est simplement disciplinaire. Conclusion: Les évêques pourront dispenser dans leurs diocèses les canons disciplinaires des Conciles Généraux; ils peuvent permettre le mariage au clergé de leurs diocèses. On m'a dit que l'évêque de S.-Paulo et le Conseil Provincial viennent de soumettre cette affaire au jugement du gouvernement, et moi, comme délégué du Saint-Siège, je prends la liberté d'adresser à Votre Excellence cette lettre confidentielle, pour avoir l'avis du gouvernement à ce sujet. Je reste, Excellence, avec le doux espoir d'obtenir une réponse qui tranquillisera le coeur du Saint-Père. Je profite de l'occasion pour renouveller à Votre Excellence l'assurance de ma haute considération." Magalhães, *op. cit.*, pp. 98-99.

In response to the note of the 18th of this month, in which you manifest the desire to know the thought of the Government on the question of celibacy of the clergy discussed in São Paulo, I have the honor of telling you in all frankness that the Government of His Majesty is convinced that the celibacy of the priests constitutes a point of discipline which Sovereigns, in their States, are able to alter at will, to the benefit of their subjects. The Government knows that the celibacy of the clergy in Brazil does not exist in fact, and this state of affairs encourages public immorality enormously. It should, therefore, take measures which are energetic and appropriate to the circumstances. And as the matter is very serious, the Government will not make known publicly its opinion, but will convey it to the Chamber of Deputies with which it desires to be always in accord, and in the hope that it will find a remedy to heal the evil that causes so much damage to the Church.[66]

When the ecclesiastical commission made its report to the Chamber of Deputies on July 26, 1834, the position of the Church on clerical celibacy was assailed.[67] The report caused Dom Romualdo de Seixas, archbishop of Baía, to observe that nothing was saved, not even the encyclical of Gregory XVI, the definitions of the Council of Trent, or the canons. Everything, in fact, that favored the discipline of celibacy was attacked.[68]

---

[66] "Em reposta á nota de 18 deste mez na qual manifestaes o desejo de conhecer o pensamento do Governo sobre a questão do celibato dos padres agitado em S. Paulo, tenho a honra de vos dizer com toda a franqueza que o Governo de Sua Magestade está convencido de que o celibato dos padres constitue um ponto de disciplina que os Soberanos, em seus Estados, podem alterar á vontade, em beneficio de seus subditos. O Governo sabe que o celibato do clero no Brazil não existe de facto, e esse estado de coisas favorece enormemente a immoralidade publica. Deve, por isso, tomar medidas energicas e apropriadas ás circustancias. E como o negocio é muito serio, o Governo não fará conhecer publicamente o seu pensamento, mas enviará á Camara dos Deputados com aquelle desejo de marchar sempre de accordo e na esperança de que ella encontrará um remedio para sanar o mal que tanto damno causa á Igreja." Ibid., p. 70.

[67] Anais da Câmara, 1834, II, 144-147.

[68] D. Romualdo Antônio de Seixas, Memorias do Marquez de Santa Cruz, Arcebispo da Bahia (Rio de Janeiro, 1861), p. 84.

Yet in spite of the abundance of argument with which its advocates fortified the anti-celibacy project, it failed to win the support of a majority of the members of the Chamber of Deputies. Such clerics as Canon Luiz Gonçalves dos Santos and the Carmelite, Father Peres, defended with striking brilliance the cause of ecclesiastical discipline. These highly gifted priests won a majority of the deputies to the support of celibacy[69] and defeated their ecclesiastical colleagues, who were among the most acrimonious defenders of the arguments opposing it.

The question of celibacy as a legislative issue was terminated in 1834, but the germ of the controversy was carried over into another issue which threatened to be even more serious in its consequences. The Holy See was to experience the full import of the regalistic temper of the Brazilian government when it refused to approve the appointment of Father Antônio de Moura as bishop of Rio de Janeiro. On April 30, 1833, the anti-celibacy faction had nominated Father Moura[70] for the office which had been left vacant by the death of the court chaplain, Dom José Caetano da Silva Coutinho.[71]

In support of its rejection of the Brazilian candidate, the Roman curia listed a number of impediments and objections: 1) Father Moura suffered from epilepsy; 2) there was reason to believe that he was an illegitimate son; and 3) it was well-known that he had been one of the important supporters of the marriage project.[72] Of all the reasons listed by the Holy

---

[69] *Ibid.*, p. 85.

[70] Circular letter of Oct. 6, 1835, of the secretary of the Sacred Congregation for Extraordinary Ecclesiastical Affairs. Rubrica 251, Segretaria di stato, Vatican Archive. Magalhães, *op. cit.*, p. 100, note, gives the following biographical data on Father Moura: "Nascido em Sabará (Minas-Gerais), recebeu ordens sacras no Brasil e conquistou a láurea de bacharel pela universidade de Coimbra. Regressando á pátria, foi nomeado, em 1828, lente de Direito Eclesiástico do curso jurídico de São Paulo, onde depois passou a reger a cadeira de Processo Civil e Criminal. Eleito representante de Minas-Gerais para a 2ª e 3ª legislaturas, da assembléia geral (1830-1833 e 1834-1837), chegou a presidir a Câmara dos Deputados, onde se salientou entre os jansenistas mais ardorosos."

[71] See pp. 42-43 above.

[72] Dornas, *op. cit.*, p. 73; Tarquínio de Sousa, *op. cit.*, pp. 231-232.

See, the one that most incensed the Gallican element in the Brazilian parliament was the implication that Moura was unworthy of the office because he had advocated anti-celibacy measures. An impasse was inevitable since this hindrance was the one least likely to be dispensed by the Roman curia: it involved not a physical defect, but an attitude toward ecclesiastical discipline which, if countenanced by Rome, might work havoc within the Church of Brazil.[73] Luiz Moutinho de Lima Álvares da Silva, the Brazilian envoy to Rome, tried to impress upon the Brazilian minister of foreign affairs the reasonableness of the papal position, and to convince him that the Holy Father was eager to maintain cordial relations with Brazil, but obviously could not accept a man of Moura's convictions. The Regency, however, "seemed determined from the beginning to make this a trial of strength between the civil and ecclesiastical powers, and to see how far it would be possible to make the latter sacrifice its scruples, and even its principles, to the desire of preserving good understanding with the former."[74]

Rather than admit its position to be untenable, the imperial government recalled Álvares da Silva from Rome and appointed José Joaquim da Rocha in his place. The new minister succeeded no better than his predecessor. When he sent word to his government that His Holiness would confirm the nomination of Father Moura if the latter would retract in writing all that he had formerly held against sound doctrine, the situation became acute.[75] Antônio de Meneses Vasconcelos de Drummond replaced Rocha, whose last despatch was answered by Aureliano de Sousa e Oliveira Coutinho with the following comment: "Your predecessor should not have agreed with what His Holi-

---

Sousa does not mention epilepsy, but implies that Moura drank to excess.

[73] Tarquínio de Sousa, op. cit., p. 232.

[74] "Authority of the Holy See in South America," The Dublin Review, V (July, 1838), 240. Pandiá Calógeras, op. cit., p. 135, says that Moutinho wrote in September and again in October of 1833 of the impossibility of changing the attitude of the Holy Father.

[75] Reflexões imparciaes sobre a falla do trono e as respostas das camaras legislativas de 1836, na parte relativa ao bispo eleito d'esta diocese e á Santa Sé Apostolica (Rio de Janeiro, 1837), pp. 19-20. Hereafter this work will

ness proposed to him relative to the matter of the confirmation of the bishop-elect of Rio de Janeiro inasmuch as that matter was the concern of the Imperial Government and not of the bishop, whose doctrines are not condemned by the Constitution of the Country."[76]

That the government, in proposing Father Moura for the see of Rio de Janeiro, was making a test case of its authority cannot be denied. It is known that the bishop-elect, asked by the government whether or not he had repudiated his former stand on doctrine, after he was requested to do so by the Holy Father, replied that he had retracted nothing.[77] It may be inferred that such a repudiation would have made Father Moura unacceptable to the imperial government. The next move of the imperial ministry was an even more open avowal of what seemed to be its determination to sponsor for church offices men who had shown themselves more regalistic than Catholic. Such was the case of Father Feijó who was at this time nominated to the see of Mariana (Minas-Gerais). At almost the same time, this ardent champion of the rights of the State against those of the Church was elected sole regent of the empire,[78] and nothing more was heard of his nomination to the episcopacy. Egas says that Feijó would not allow his nomination to be presented to Rome because he did not wish to subject himself to an authority to which he did not subscribe.[79] Tarquínio de Sousa remarks that Feijó ordered his nomination to the bishopric of Mariana pigeonholed.[80]

When the Holy See continued to refuse to confirm Moura's nomination, Manuel Alves Branco, the minister of foreign af-

be cited as *Reflexões imparciaes.*

[76] Calógeras, *op. cit.,* p. 137.

[77] *Reflexões imparciaes,* p. 20.

[78] Tarquínio de Sousa, *op. cit.,* p. 233, writes: "No mesmo dia 9 de outubro de 1835, em que, doente de cama, recebera o convite da Assembléa para tomar posse do logar de Regente, chegara ás suas mãos um oficio do ministro da Justiça Aureliano Coutinho, comunicando-lhe que fora nomeado bispo de Mariana." See also Egas, *op. cit.,* I, 42-43.

[79] Egas, *op. cit.,* I, 42-43.

[80] Tarquínio de Sousa, *op. cit.,* p. 235.

fairs, made the following report to the Chamber of Deputies:

> The Holy Father has not yet ordered the issuance of the Bulls of confirmation for the appointment which the Regency made in the name of His Majesty, the Emperor, of Dr. Antônio Maria de Moura as Bishop of the Diocese of Rio de Janeiro. The Imperial Government, having shown the liveliest and sincerest desires of treating the Holy See with all due politeness and respect, is fully convinced that His Holiness, considering the serious consequences that the refusal of the said Bulls will bring with it, will not fail to yield to the energetic representations which our Minister has lately made to him and to the recent measures of the Government.[81]

Despite the diplomatic representations and the measures adopted by the government, the pope replied, as before, that it was out of his power to approve the candidate for the diocese of Rio de Janeiro.[82]

This pronouncement of the Sovereign Pontiff was communicated to the Brazilian parliament by Feijó in the Speech from the Throne of 1836, and the following points relative to the ecclesiastical controversy were presented to the consideration of the legislature:[83]

---

[81] "Ainda não forão mandadas expedir pelo Santo Padre as Bullas de confirmação á nomeação, que fez a Regencia, em Nome do S. M. o Imperador, do Doutor Antonio Maria de Moura para Bispo da Diocese do Rio de Janeiro. O Governo Imperial, tendo mostrado os mais vivos e sinceros desejos de tratar com toda a devida polidez, e respeito a Santa Sé, está bem persuadido, que Sua Santidade, considerando as serias consequencias, que trará com sigo a recusação das ditas Bullas, não deixará de condescender com as representações energicas que o nosso Ministro lhe tem ultimamente feito, e ultimas providencias do Governo." *Relatorio da Repartição dos Negocios Estrangeiros apresentado á Assembléa Geral Legislativa na sessão ordinaria de 1835, pelo respectivo Ministro e Secretario de Estado Manoel Alves Branco* (Rio de Janeiro, 1835), p. 12.

[82] *Reflexões imparciaes*, p. 24.

[83] While Father Feijó, the new regent, had not initiated the cause of Father Moura in Rome, he shared the opinions of Branco and other ministers relative to the claims of the Holy See. See Sousa, *op. cit.*, pp. 231-236.

I cannot . . . conceal from you [the fact] that His Holiness, after two years of reciprocal explanations, resolved not to accept the imperial presentation of the bishop-elect of this diocese. The government has law and justice on its side, but His Holiness obeys his conscience. After this decision, the government considered itself exonerated from using condescension with the Holy See, without being wanting however in the respect and obedience due to the Head of the Universal Church.

It lies in your hands [addressing the Chamber] to free the Brazilian Catholic from the difficulty, and in many instances, the impossibility of begging solutions at such a distance, that should not be refused him within the Empire. So holy is our religion, so well calculated the system of ecclesiastical government, that, being compatible with every sort of civil government, its discipline may be modified for the interests of the State, without ever compromising the essential part of the same religion. Notwithstanding this collision with the Holy Father, our friendly relations continue with the Court of Rome.[84]

Although Feijó was at this time popular in government circles, both houses declined to participate in the controversy. Such clauses in Feijó's speech as "its discipline may be modified for the interests of the State" recalled the recent controversy on celibacy, and gave further proof that the same regalistic philos-

---

[84] "Não posso comtudo occultar-vos, que Sua Santidade, depois de dous annos de explicaçãoes reciprocas, resolveu não aceitar a apresentação imperial do bispo eleito desta diocese. O governo tem de seu lado a lei e a justiça, mas Sua Santidade obedece á sua consciencia. Depois desta decisão julgou-se o governo desonerado de ter condescendencias com a Santa Sé, sem comtudo faltar jámais ao respeito e obediencia ao chefe da Igreja Universal.

"Em vossas mãos está livrar o catholico brazileiro da difficuldade e muitas vezes impossibilidade de mendigar tão longe recursos, que lhe não devem ser negados dentro do Imperio. É tão santa a nossa religião; tão bem calculado o systema do governo ecclesiastico, que sendo compativel com toda a casta de governo civil, póde sua disciplina ser modificada pelo interesse do Estado, sem jámais comprometter o essencial da mesma religião. Não obstante esta collisão com o Santo Padre, nossas relações amigaveis continuam com a Côrte de Roma." *Fallas do Throno desde o Anno de 1823 até o Anno de 1872* (Rio de Janeiro, 1872), p. 248. See also *Anais da Câmara*, 1836, I, 13.

ophy was dominant in high places. Yet the Chamber, adopting a more sober attitude, replied in part to the regent's speech as follows:

> The Chamber laments . . . the state of collision with His Holiness in which the Imperial Government now finds itself; and hopes that without detriment to the prerogatives of the Crown, and without compromising national interests, the same Government will avoid altering our relations with the Head of the Universal Church; and therefore considers that for the present it should not take any other measure.[85]

The reply of the Senate is no less explicit:

> It is painful to the Senate to know that the delicate conscience of His Holiness does not allow him to confirm the presentation of the Bishop for this diocese. Still the assurance which your Imperial Majesty gives of the continuance of amicable relations with the Court of Rome, the respect and obedience which Your Imperial Majesty protests (as was to be expected) to the Holy Father, as visible Head of the Universal Church, give the Senate well-grounded hopes that the prudence and wisdom of Your Imperial Majesty will yet find delicate means which, without impairing the Dignity of the Nation, will conciliate this misunderstanding. The Senate thus does not consider itself called upon to propose at present efficacious measures to maintain the decorum and rights of Your Imperial Majesty's Throne.[86]

---

[85] "Lamenta porém a camara a collisão em que está o governo imperial com Sua Santidade; e espera que, sem quebra das regalias da corôa e sem compromettimento dos interesses nacionaes, o mesmo governo conseguirá evitar que se alterem as nossas relações com o chefe de igreja universal; e por isto entende que por agora, não lhe cumpre tomar alguma outra medida." *Anais da Câmara*, 1836, I, 33. See also *ibid.*, pp. 42, 47.

[86] "É doloroso para o Senado saber que a melindrosa consciencia de Sua Santidade lhe não consente confirmar a apresentação do Bispo para esta Diocese. Todavia, a certeza que V. M. dá de que continuão as relações amigaveis com a Côrte de Roma, o respeito e obediencia que V. M. I. protesta (como era de esperar) ao Santo Padre, como Chefe visivel da Igreja Universal, dão ao Senado bem fundadas esperanças de que a prudencia e a sabedoria de V. M. I.

No information relative to the government's negotiation with the Holy Father had been given to the legislature, other than the rather vague annual reports of the minister of foreign affairs which asserted each time that the Supreme Pontiff had not yet ratified the nomination of Father Moura.[87] Certain deputies seem to have become suspicious that relations with the Holy See were not as friendly as the regent and his ministers would have them infer. The suspicion led to long discussions in the Chamber of Deputies as to the diplomatic procedure which had evoked the pope's rejection of the Brazilian representation. Bernardo de Vasconcelos asserted in the Chamber of Deputies on May 9, 1836, that the note presented to the Supreme Pontiff by the Brazilian minister to the papal court was a copy and a parody of the ultimatum which Lord Strangford, in the name of the British government, had issued on August 11, 1823, to the sultan of Constantinople.[88] Limpo de Abreu, who was then minister of justice, answered that such a comparison was fantastic,[89] but others averred later that Vasconcelos had been correctly informed.[90] It was discovered further that the "energetic representations" of the Brazilian minister to which the regent had

---

ainda acharão suaves meios que, sem mingoa da Dignidade da Nação, conciliarão esta disconcordancia, dispensando-se assim o Senado de propor, por agora, medidas efficazes para sustentar o decóro e direitos do Trono de V. M. Imperial." *Reflexões imparciaes,* p. 67.

[87] In the report of Aureliano de Sousa e Oliveira Coutinho, minister of foreign affairs in 1834, the first account of the negotiation with the Holy See was given to the Brazilian government: "Tendo sido nomeado o Dr. Antonio Maria de Moura, Bispo da Diocese do Rio de Janeiro, por motivos occorentes, tem-se procrastinado a expedição das Bullas na fórma do estilo; mas o Governo Imperial espera, que á vista de novas instrucções enviadas ao seu Agente em Roma, ellas serão em breve expedidas como cumpre á Dignidade do Imperio, e aos proprios interesses da Curia Romana." *Relatorio da Repartição dos Negocios Estrangeiros apresentado á Assembléa Geral Legislativa na sessão ordinaria de 1834, pelo respectivo Ministro e Secretario de Estado Aureliano de Souza e Oliveira Coutinho* (Rio de Janeiro, 1834), p. 15. The report of the minister of foreign affairs for 1835 has already been cited. See p. 79 above.

[88] *Anais da Câmara,* 1836, I, 34.

[89] *Ibid.,* p. 44.

[90] *Reflexões imparciaes,* pp. 22-23. Dom Romualdo de Seixas says in his

referred in his Speech from the Throne were in reality an ultimatum: ". . . either you [Holy Father] will confirm within thirty
days the bishop of Rio de Janeiro or Brazil will separate from
the Roman communion."[91]

In 1837, an anonymous author published in Rio de Janeiro
a stringent indictment of the policy of the ministry. The essay,
entitled *Reflexões imparciaes sobre a falla do trono e as respostas
das camaras legislativas de 1836 na parte relativa ao bispo eleito
d'esta diocese e a sé apostolica,* put the Vatican-Brazilian diplomatic situation in a new perspective; it reviewed the controversy
and published an exact copy of the Strangford-Brazilian notes.
This publication evoked from the legislative chambers a severe
condemnation of the foreign policy of the Regency, and elicited
from the press a public censure of those ministers who had perpetrated what was in its opinion an outrage against the Holy
Father.

When, on May 19, 1837, the debate in the Chamber of Deputies turned to the foreign policy of the ministry, Honório Hermeto Carneiro Leão challenged the foreign office's proposal to
exchange the ministers at Rome and Lisbon:

> After having made public to the people of the court
> [*i.e.*, Rio de Janeiro] a note to the Holy See from our
> ex-minister in Rome of a nature to discredit us in the
> courts of Europe, it was certainly not the occasion to
> promote this diplomat to [the rank of] envoy ex-
> traordinary and minister plenipotentiary at a court
> where the ex-minister [*i.e.*, of foreign affairs] says
> there are great interests to sustain, and with which we
> are tied in very close relations.[92]

Limpo de Abreu, who had on a previous occasion denied the

---

*Memorias* (p. 97) that it was the internuncio, Monsignor Fabbrini, who detected the plagiarism. He discovered the Lord Strangford note of August 11,
1823, to the Sublime Porte in Henri Augusto Meisel, *Cours de Style diplomatique* (Paris, 1826), II, 191-201. See also Viscount Strangford to The
Reis Effendi, August 11, 1823, *British and Foreign State Papers, 1822-1823*
(London, 1850), 859-864.

[91] Seixas, *op. cit.*, p. 97.

[92] "Depois de se ter manifestado perante o publico da côrte, uma nota do

alleged plagiarism by Brazil of the Strangford note, defended the promotion of the Brazilian minister at Rome, Antônio de Meneses Vasconcelos de Drummond. The similarity between the two notes was probably a coincidence, Abreu maintained, and was not a sufficient cause for depriving the minister of his diplomatic promotion.[93] Miguel Calmon du Pin e Almeida[94] refused to allow this defense of the Brazilian minister to pass unchallenged:

> The worthy deputy [Carneiro Leão], to whom I have already referred, speaking of our envoy who addressed to the Holy See a note almost like the one which Lord Strangford addressed to the Ottoman Porte, asked the reason why the same diplomat had been removed to Lisbon. I venture to explain that to him. He was removed, I mean, promoted, for the very reason that he had treated the Holy Father as the Grand Turk had been treated. I cannot persuade myself that that diplomat, an able man, and as such I know him, would have made so vile a plagiarism, and have insulted the Head of the Church, without being put up to it by the Government; and that same conjecture is found supported by the promotion and great consideration given by the same Government to the said diplomat. I characterized the plagiarism as vile, because if the style of the English ambassador suited the representative of the civilization and power of Europe in addressing himself to the Sultan of Constantinople, certainly the same style (even more exacerbated, or still more insulting in some sentences) did not become the representative of a Christian people addressing the Supreme Pontiff . . . . Gentlemen, the history of that note is shameful to Brazil. I understand that, when the Roman Curia received it, the Holy Father, justly affected, ordered it to be com-

---

nosso ex-ministro em Roma á Santa Sé, capaz de nos desacreditar nas côrtes da Europa, não era certamente occasião de promover a este diplomata para enviado estraordinario, e ministro plenipotenciario junto a uma côrte, onde o Sr. ex-ministro diz que ha grandes interesses a sustentar, e com a qual estamos ligados em relações muito estreitas." *Anais da Câmara*, 1837, I, 90.

[93] *Ibid.*, pp. 91-92.

[94] Later Marquis of Abrantes.

municated to the diplomatic corps resident in Rome, which, if not the most influential, is at least the most diplomatic court in Europe, and so much so that it merited from Voltaire himself the reputation of refinement. The diplomatic corps expressed to His Holiness the feelings of pain that the unbecoming character of the note had produced in its members; and I understand, likewise, that even the Hanoverian minister (who indirectly represents his Britannic Majesty), was quite expressive in presenting his condolence in view of the behavior of our diplomat. The position of the latter became untenable in Rome, he found himself isolated . . . ."[95]

The persuasiveness of Calmon's speech is attested by the number of deputies who were drawn to the side of the opposition, and who joined Bernardo de Vasconcelos, Honório Hermeto, and others in decrying the dictatorial policies of the Regency.[96]

---

[95] "O nobre deputado, a quem já me referi, fallando do nosso diplomata, que dirigira á Santa Sé uma nota quasi igual á que lord Strangford dirigira á Porta Ottomana, perguntou porque raz[ã]o fôra o mesmo diplomata removido para Lisbôa. Atrevo-me a explicar-lhe isso. Foi removido, não digo bem, foi promovido, por isso mesmo que havia tratado o Santo Padre, como fôra tratado o Grão Turco. Não me persuado que aquelle diplomata, homem habil, e que como tal o conheço, fizesse um plagiato asqueroso, e insultasse ao chefe da igreja, sem que fosse insuflado pelo governo; e essa mesma conjectura acha-se abonada pelo promoção e maior consideração dada pelo mesmo governor ao dito diplomata. Qualifiquei de asqueroso o plagiato, porque se o estyle do embaixador inglez cabia ao representante da civilisação e do poder europêo dirindo-se ao sultão de Constantinopla, de lerto o mesmo estylo (e até exacerbado, ou ainda mais insolente em alguns periodos), não cabia ao representante de um povo christão dirigindo-se ao summo pontifice . . . . Senhores, a historia dessa nota é vergonhosa para o Brasil. Consta-me que quando a curia romana a recebêra, o Santo Padre, justamente sensibilisado, a mandára communicar ao corpo diplomatico residente em Roma, que se não é a côrte mais influente, é de certo a mais diplomatica da Europa, e tal que merecêra do proprio Voltaire o conceito de atilada. O corpo diplomatico exprimio a Sua Santidade os sentimentos da magua que o descomedido theor daquella nota havia produzido em seus membros; e consta-me até que o ministro de Hanover (que indirectamente representa a S. M. Britannica) fôra assás expressivo em sua condolencia á vista do proredimento do nosso diplomata. A posição deste ficou falseada em Roma, elle achou-se isolado . . . ." Anais da Câmara, 1837, I, 94.

[96] Vasconcelos asserted in the Chamber of Deputies that the Brazilian gov-

Public opinion was equally vocal in condemning the insults offered by the imperial ministry to the Holy See. The liberal paper, *O Sete d'Abril,* published in Rio, in its issue of May 27, 1837, republished in Portuguese the celebrated notes under the caption "For Sr. Limpo d'Abreu." In the same issue the diplomatic crisis with the papal court was reviewed, the policy of the Brazilian government censured, and the position of the Sovereign Pontiff sustained.

The *Jornal dos Debates* of Rio de Janeiro carried a long article on May 20, 1837, condemning the reappearance in the ministry of the former minister of foreign affairs, Manuel Alves Branco, and repudiating the papal policy which this minister had sanctioned. The article's leading paragraph reads:

> The reappearance of Sr. Manuel Alves Branco in the Ministry, while yet are pending the negotiations with the court of Rome in which he most grievously compromised the dignity of the Brazilian name, appears to us a fact as impolitic as it is contrary to the interests of the nation. The note of September 23, 1835, addressed to the Holy See by Sr. Alves Branco, at that time Secretary of State for Foreign Affairs, is the subject of eternal disgrace for the Government of Brazil . . . . That note, in addition to being a wretched and ridiculous plagiarism, wounds in an indecent and brutal manner the dignity of the Head of the Universal Church, the venerable pastor of the Catholic Flock.[97]

---

ernment was not conducted on a parliamentary basis, for if it were the ministers would be responsible to parliament. Feijó, he maintained, was involved in all the acts of the ministry, and exercised more authority than did Dom Pedro I in the last years of his reign. See *Anais da Câmara,* 1836, I, 60, 192. It must not be overlooked that Vasconcelos was the political opponent of Feijó.

[97] "A re-aparição do Sr. Manoel Alves Branco no Ministerio, quando existem ainda pendentes com a côrte de Roma as negociações em que elle comprometteo da maneira a mais grave a dignidade do nome Brasileiro, parece-nos um facto tão impolitico como contrario aos interesses da nação. A nota de 23 de Setembro de 1835 dirigida à Santa Sé pelo Sr. Alves Branco, então Secretario d'Estado dos Negocios Estrangeiros é materia de um eterno desdouro para

The article gives the two notes, and concludes by placing the blame on the imperial ministry which either prepared the Brazilian note or sanctioned it when it was prepared by the minister in Rome.

Regarding the religious crisis, even those who admired Feijó now found it impossible to defend his ministers or the Gallicanism to which he showed himself committed.[98] Dom Romualdo de Seixas observed in his memoirs that he believed that Feijó had a predilection for schism and heresy; that there was a hump of anarchy in his cerebral convolutions.[99] Feijó retired from public life on September 19, 1837; while the religious issue alone did not ruin his political career, it was a contributing factor. In July, 1838, he addressed a letter to the president of the council, Bernardo de Vasconcelos, renouncing the see of Mariana to which he had been nominated in 1835. In this letter Feijó acknowledged that he had written against certain points of ecclesiastical discipline, and had argued against these same points in the Chamber of Deputies. He wished now to retract all that could, directly or indirectly, have offended against ecclesiastical discipline. Even though he were convinced, wrote Feijó, that what he had advocated was for the good of the Church, he would retract because he desired above all to be a true and obedient son of the Church. He might have erred, he acknowledged, in spite of his good intentions; hence, if any scandal was given by his discourses or writings, he wished it to be eradicated by his open declaration.[100] When Moura publicly renounced the see of Rio de Janeiro in the fall of 1838,[101] and when the ap-

---

o Govêrno do Brasil . . . . Essa nota além de constituir um miseravel e ridiculo plagiato, fere de um modo indecente e brutal a dignidade do chefe da Igreja Universal, o venerando Pastor da Grei Catholica."

[98] Modern biographers are agreed that the religious controversy was one of the major contributing factors in the downfall of Feijó.

[99] Seixas, op. cit., p. 100.

[100] This letter, published in the Observador Paulistano, September 4, 1838, is quoted by Calógeras, op. cit., pp. 158-159.

[101] Moura's renunciation of the see of Rio de Janeiro, dated October 1, 1838, and addressed to Minister Bernardo de Vasconcelos, was published in the Aurora Fluminense, May 31, 1839. This letter is also quoted by Calógeras, op. cit., pp. 159-161.

pointment of Manuel de Monte Rodrigues de Araújo[102] to the office was promptly confirmed by the Holy See, the contest between the imperial government and the Supreme Pontiff was peacefully terminated.

Nowhere is the attitude of imperial statesmen toward the Roman Pontiff better illustrated than in the nomination of Father Moura to the see of Rio de Janeiro and of Father Feijó to the see of Mariana. Brazilian ministers[103] knew that Rome could not countenance the anti-celibacy project that Feijó, Moura, and other members of the ecclesiastical commission had sponsored. The imperial ministers must have realized that any ecclesiastic who had favored the project would be *persona non grata* to the Vatican. There is a striking parallel between this struggle of the period of the Regency and the Episcopal-Masonic controversy of the seventies, which is the pivotal issue to be reviewed in the present study. In the former contest, imperial statesmen aligned themselves directly against the Holy See; in the latter, they fought the orthodoxy of two of their own prelates. In both instances the endeavor was fundamentally the same: an attempt to repudiate the supremacy of Rome over the Church in Brazil.

## IV

When Feijó resigned as regent, the office was provisionally assumed by the minister of the interior (*ministro do império*), Pedro de Araújo Lima who, in April, 1838, was formally elected regent. With a full understanding of his duties to the dynasty and to the Brazilian people, Araújo Lima, who later received the title of marquis of Olinda, adhered strictly to the duties of a constitutional executive. He promptly carried out the requirements of parliamentary government, and organized a cabinet with Bernardo de Vasconcelos, the Conservative leader of the Chamber of Deputies, at its head. The new Conservative ministry found itself bitterly opposed by the Liberals, who took ad-

---

[102] See pp. 43-45 above.

[103] In all efforts of the imperial government to control the Church, the imperial ministers were more hostile to the papacy than were the majority of the members of the legislative chambers.

vantage of uprisings in various parts of the empire to discredit the government and to popularize the notion that the Regency possessed neither the prestige nor the authority necessary to bring the provincial revolts to an end.[104] As early as 1839, Feijó, together with many other Liberals in parliament, had decided that the best way to end internal disorder would be to effect the immediate coronation of the young emperor. Since Dom Pedro II had not reached the age required by the constitution for the proclamation of his majority,[105] three conditions had to be favorable if such action was to be initiated with hope of success: Dom Pedro had to be willing, public opinion had to be favorable, and parliament had to endorse the action. The boy-emperor and the people supported the move, but the Conservative majority in parliament favored either a change in the constitutional requirement or a deferment of the coronation until Pedro had reached the age prescribed by the constitution. The Liberals in parliament demanded that the question be put to a vote. When they were defeated by only two votes in the Senate, and, when agitation continued in the Chamber, the Conservative government determined, in order to prevent further agitation, to prorogue parliament. At this juncture, Dom Pedro, who was at this time at São Cristóvão palace, was asked his opinion. Pedro's reply, "Quero já," forced the Conservatives to accede to the demands of the Liberals. The parliamentary revolution had been successful; Dom Pedro II was proclaimed emperor by the general assembly on July 23, 1840.

The statesmen who advised the new emperor felt toward the Church much as Feijó did.[106] They upheld the doctrine that the

---

[104] A civil war known as *Guerra dos Farrapos* had been going on in Rio Grande do Sul since 1835, and, by 1839, it had extended as far north as the province of Santa Catarina, where an ephemeral republic was established. During the years 1839-1840, the province of Maranhão was the theater of an extensive uprising known as the *Balaiada*.

[105] Dom Pedro would be eighteen, the age required by the constitution for the proclamation of his majority, on December 2, 1843.

[106] Prominent among the advisers of the young emperor was José Antônio Pimenta Bueno, later Marquis of São Vicente, whose *Considerações relativas ao beneplacito, recurso á corôa em materias do culto* (Rio de Janeiro, 1873) is an excellent exposition of the regalist's position.

State had the right to supervise all religious activities. They looked upon the nomination of bishops and the assigning of ecclesiastical benefices as exclusive rights of national sovereignty, and were willing to allow to the Holy See only the faculty of confirmation. They held that no pontifical act could be enforced in the empire unless it received the imperial *placet*, and they maintained that church members could have recourse to the crown against ecclesiastical censures. The number of decrees, laws, resolutions, and regulations adopted by the imperial government as a means of invading the domain of the spiritual authority bears witness to the thoroughness with which regalistic theories were carried into practice.[107]

The emperor, who personally subscribed to the tenets of Liberalism, favored a strict supervision of the Church, and especially of the members of the hierarchy, by the State. The ideas of Dom Pedro II on the subject of religion cannot be perfectly formulated, yet some notion of them can be gleaned from the notes he jotted in the margin of E. de Pressense's *Les Origines*,[108] and from his own curious autobiographical sketch, *Fé de ofício*.[109] From his marginal notes on *Les Origines*, it can be inferred that Dom Pedro II subscribed to the evolutionary theories in fashion at the time. Joaquim Nabuco says that for Dom Pedro religion was a subjective, highly personal thing. He depended directly on God, the Creator, Whose works he, as a scientist, admired profoundly. The emperor, the same author continues, was in matters of religion an emancipated spirit, who organized his own creed, conciliating dogma with scientific hy-

---

[107] Magalhães, *op. cit.*, p. 104, writes: "O rol de tais atos, inserto no 'Manual Eclesiástico,' enche nada menos de 150 páginas (341-491)."

[108] Edmond Dehault de Pressense, *Les Origines le problème de la connaissance, le problème cosmologique, le problème anthropologique, l'origine de la morale et de la religion* (Paris, 1883). In a commemorative address given before the Brazilian Historical and Geographical Institute on October 10, 1890, Manuel Francisco Correia discussed the marginal notes which Dom Pedro had written in his copy of *Les Origines*. The emperor himself had presented this copy to Correia on May 6, 1864. The address was published in the *Revista do Instituto Histórico e Geográfico brasileiro*, LV (1892), ii, 1-13.

[109] Published by the Viscount of Taunay in Rio de Janeiro in 1891.

potheses. He was a limited Catholic who paid conventional deference to the externals of religion while maintaining interior freedom.[110] Pedro subscribed to Cavour's version of Montalembert's ideal of a free church in a free state,[111] but he believed that this could not be achieved until the people of Brazil were educated to accept a Liberal Catholicism; in the meantime, the State must maintain strict supervision over the spiritual authority. In this supervision, Pedro accepted so completely the regalist view that he considered any attempt on the part of ecclesiastical authority to throw off the yoke of civil domination not only as an attack on the civil authority, but also as a personal affront.

Although Dom Pedro II manifested interest neither in the regeneration of the clergy nor in the need for solid religious instruction of the laity, he showed himself eager to advance the external prestige of the Church in the empire. Three new dioceses were created between 1848 and 1853, one in Rio Grande do Sul, a second in Diamantina (Minas-Gerais), and a third in Ceará.[112] In 1847 Pedro considered obtaining a cardinal for the Church in Brazil.[113] The idea of establishing a Brazilian cardinalate was not new; the first steps toward it had been taken in 1830, and the arrangements with the Holy See had at that time been successfully expedited. In a letter dated August 16, 1833, the imperial minister in Rome, Luis Moutinho de Lima Álvares e Silva, announced that Pope Gregory XVI was deliberating the creation of a cardinalate in Brazil.[114] The committee of justice of the Council of State was favorable to the

---

[110] Joaquim Nabuco, *Um estadista do imperio, Nabuco de Araujo, sua vida, suas opiniões, sua época* (Rio de Janeiro, 1898-1899), III, 389-391, note 1.

[111] See p. 14, note 39, above.

[112] Magalhães, *op. cit.*, p. 105. *Relatorio da repartição dos negocios estrangeiros apresentado á assembléa geral legislativa na primeira sessão da decima primeira legislatura pelo respectivo ministro e secretario de estado Conselheiro Antonio Coelho de Sá e Albuquerque* (Rio de Janeiro, 1861), pp. 45-46.

[113] "Direito do Brasil á apresentação de candidato ao cardinalato: Consulta de 6 de março de 1847 da secção de justiça do conselho de estado," transcript, Miscellaneous Papers, Oliveira Lima Library, The Catholic University of America.

[114] *Ibid.* See also Magalhães, *op. cit.*, p. 106.

creation of this new ecclesiastical office which, it said, not only
would contribute to the "splendor of the throne," but also
would give to the emperor additional ways of rewarding the
services that Brazilian ecclesiastics rendered to the State and to
the Church.[115] At that time, however, Pedro I decided "for
economic and other reasons" not to accept the cardinalate for
Brazil.[116] Similarly Pedro II, after exhibiting lively interest in
the appointment of a Brazilian cardinal, decided against the creation of one. He appears to have foregone the privilege, not because he realized that a Brazilian cardinal would be unable to
participate in papal elections, nor because he wished to avoid the
increased expenditure that the office would place on the national
treasury, but because he desired to keep away from the subtleties
of the Roman curia.[117] This, incidentally, was the basic reason
why the government of the First Empire had rejected the offer
both of a cardinal and of a nuncio.[118] It should be remarked
that while Dom Pedro II was primarily interested in augmenting
the external prestige of the Church in the empire, and made
all his hierarchical appointments with this in view, the scrupu-
lous care with which he selected worthy men for the episcopacy
was to have a salutary effect on the spiritual life of Brazil. In
fact, it was bishops whom the emperor had chosen who were to
free the Church from the domination of the State.

Before these energetic prelates began their contest with the civil

---

[115] "Direito do Brasil," *doc. cit.*

[116] *Ibid.* See also Magalhães, *op. cit.*, p. 106. The report of the committee
of justice mentions only economic reasons; Magalhães writes ". . . . para
motivos de economia e outras razões."

[117] [Francisco Régis de] Oliveira [minister to Spain, to João Artur de
Sousa Correia, minister to the Holy See], March 5, 1847. Sousa Correia
Papers, Oliveira Lima Library, The Catholic University of America. The
additional information in the citation was found in Raúl Adalberto de Campos,
*Relações diplomaticas do Brasil contendo os nomes dos representantes diplo-
maticos do Brasil no estrangeiro . . . de 1808 a 1908* (Rio de Janeiro, 1913),
pp. 69, 104. The letter does not state explicitly the reason for not establishing the cardinalate. Magalhães, *op. cit.*, p. 106, writes ". . . 'para evitar
subtilezas, de que se prevalece constantemente a curia romana,' . . . ." Magalhães does not give the source of the quotation.

[118] "Direito do Brasil," *doc. cit.*

power over the right of the Church to operate as a free institution, ultra-regalists in the imperial government were almost successful in their efforts to establish in Brazil a national church that was scarcely more than a department of state. The steps toward this complete domination were systematic. The bishops and priests were proclaimed state officials;[119] ecclesiastical tithes having been diverted into government channels,[120] the Church depended on the State for financial support. Soon the belief was current that since ecclesiastics were state officials, paid out of state funds, they were subject in all matters to the State. The position of churchmen determined in this fashion, it was easy to argue that the government should require a bishop to obtain permission from the civil authority to go beyond the confines of his diocese; that it should make regulations for canons and other cathedral dignitaries; and that it should supervise seminaries and approve textbooks of theology.[121] The right to regulate ecclesiastical matters was extended even to provincial officials who, by the provisions of the amendment to the constitution known as the *Ato Adicional* (1834), were given the authority to fix the limits of dioceses and to pass laws for quasi-religious associations.[122]

While the diocesan clergy was being brought more and more under the supervision of the civil authority, the regular clergy was not exempt from government interference. In the instructions to Monsignor Vidigal of August 28, 1824, was included a demand that the Supreme Pontiff free Brazilian orders and congregations from foreign generals and prohibit men belonging to foreign religious communities from entering Brazil.[123] The request was rejected by the Supreme Pontiff because he main-

---

[119] Magalhães, *op. cit.*, p. 98, writes: "Em 1831, os bispos e párocos foram declarados funcionários civis e tratados como tais pelos agentes do poder executivo—doutrina que teve mais claro assento no Ato Adicional [1834]."

[120] See p. 63 above.

[121] See Dom Antônio de Macedo Costa, "Pastoral colectiva," quoted in Dornas, *op. cit.*, pp. 286-293.

[122] *Collecção das leis do imperio do Brasil de 1834, Parte I* (Rio de Janeiro, 1866), pp. 15-22.

[123] "Instrucções de Vidigal," *Archivo diplomatico*, III, 308-309.

tained that petitions for separation must come from the orders and congregations themselves. Later, some Brazilian communities petitioned for separation, and their requests were granted by the Holy See.[124] During the same period, certain religious communities were suppressed by the imperial government. Notable among them were the Mercenarians of Pará, the Oratorians of Perambuco, the discalced Carmelites of Baía, Sergipe, and Pernambuco, and the Capuchins of Pernambuco.[125] Permission to suppress the Mercenarians was solicited from the Holy See and granted on condition that the estates be applied to the foundation and support of a hospital and an orphanage. These stipulations were set aside by the imperial government, which took all the lands, slaves, and cattle, and fulfilled none of the conditions laid down by the Holy See.[126] During the First Empire and the Regency, numerous measures designed to curtail the rights of religious orders and congregations were introduced into the national legislature. On September 26, 1827, a law was passed restricting the right of mortmain,[127] and on December 9, 1830, another measure was enacted prohibiting religious orders without the consent of the government.[128] In 1831 Feijó proposed to the papal chargé, Scipione Fabbrini, that he institute a reform of religious communities. This movement was abortive, as were similar movements in 1835 and 1840. In 1832 a law imposed on religious orders and congregations the obligation of paying tithes on the produce of all communal lands.[129] In 1834 a measure was introduced that provided for incorporating into the national patrimony the estates of the Benedictine order throughout the empire. The government, the measure stipulated, would give each monk a pension and a slave; each religious, according to the project, could be secularized and could reside wherever he

[124] Father Júlio Maria, "A Religião," *loc. cit.*, p. 76.

[125] Magalhães, *op. cit.*, p. 95.

[126] Badaró, *L'Église au Brésil*, pp. 52-53.

[127] Magalhães, *op. cit.*, p. 94.

[128] F. Badaró, *Les Couvents au Brésil* (Florence, 1897), p. 34.

[129] Father Júlio Maria, "A Religião," *loc. cit.*, p. 77.

pleased.[130] This measure failed to pass the Senate, but the belief remained strong in governmental circles that wealthy communities should be dispossessed for what was considered to be the common good. In 1843 the military orders of Christ, of Santiago, and of Aviz were secularized.[131]

The precedents established by the First Empire and the Regency were closely followed by the Second Empire, whose policy of curtailing the freedom of religious communities culminated with the famous circular of José Nabuco de Araújo. On May 19, 1855, Nabuco, minister of justice, signed a circular that suspended the right of any convent or monastery of the empire to receive novices until a concordat that the government was going to propose to the Holy See was concluded.[132] Some orders tried to evade this restriction by sending candidates to Rome for novitiate training with the intention of having them return to Brazil after they had been admitted to vows. The imperial government issued an *aviso* on October 27, 1870, prohibiting the repatriation of these religious.[133] Nabuco's plan was not confined to refusing admission to novices, but included also an elaborate series of reforms dealing with the suppression of some religious orders, the reorganization of others, and the conversion of the wealth of some orders into funds for seminaries and for the settlement of the public debt.[134] In 1858, the monastic reforms proposed by Nabuco were included in the draft of a concordat offered to the Holy See by Carvalho Moreira, later baron of Penêdo. The Supreme Pontiff held that the question of the suppression of convents and the question of the conversion of religious wealth were matters to be resolved by briefs. Monsignor Falcinelli was sent to Brazil to investigate the situation,

[130] Badaró, *L'Église au Brésil*, pp. 59-60; Magalhães, *op. cit.*, pp. 96-97. Badaró, *Les Couvents au Brésil*, pp. 55-56, says that the Holy See favored the reform of the Benedictines, but the reform it suggested was rejected by the Chamber of Deputies.

[131] Magalhães, *op. cit.*, p. 105.

[132] Nabuco, *Um estadista*, I, 315. This concordat was never negotiated.

[133] *Ibid.*, I, 315-318; Badaró, *Les Couvents*, pp. 56-57.

[134] Dornas, *op. cit.*, p. 26, note 1, writes,. ". . . João Alfredo [de Oliveira], por aviso de 27 de outubro de 1870, observava aos geraes de todos os conventos:

but he failed to secure a settlement of the problem of religious orders. Nabuco placed responsibility for the failure of the negotiations on the imperial government's lack of a constructive plan of reform. The negotiations were declared terminated by imperial resolution of December 4, 1858.[135] Since the Nabuco reform was never completed,[136] a clause of the circular of 1855, intended to be provisional, continued in effect. Novitiates were not re-established in Brazil until after the separation of Church and State in 1890.

The problem of religious orders was a grave one in Brazil. The imperial government could justly say that many orders needed to be reformed; this assertion was corroborated by Brazilian bishops.[137] Badaró, in his study of the convents of Brazil, criticized severely the laxity that had crept into religious communities; yet, while acknowledging that the orders needed reform, Badaró maintains that the imperial government was interested, not in reforming the orders, but in gaining possession of their wealth.[138] An Anglican clergyman who visited Brazil in

---

" 'O governo imperial sabe de fonte official que frei João de Santa Gertrudes, do Rio de Janeiro, apresentou-se em Roma acompanhado de tres jovens brasileiros . . . . que entraram como noviços na Ordem dos Benedictinos. O governo imperial não pode e nem deseja impedir que os subditos brasileiros se passem ao estrangeiro para fazer profissão nas Ordens Religiosas que existem; mas devo observar a Vossa Paternidade Reverendissima que a permissão para admissão de noviços nas Ordens Religiosas do Imperio está suspensa pelo aviso de 19 de maio de 1855 e seria contravir a essa determinação si fosse permittido aos brasileiros que professem em Ordens Religiosas estrangeiras de fazer parte das communidades existentes no Brasil. Sua Magestade o Imperador ordena, assim, que mesmo os brasileiros que fizerem profissão em Roma não poderão, voltando ao Imperio, fazer parte das Ordens que aqui existem'."

[135] Nabuco, Um estadista, I, 318-320; Badaró, Les Couvents, pp. 59-60.

[136] On June 28, 1870, a resolution was passed to convert religious wealth into security for the internal debt. Nabuco, Um estadista, I, 321. For debate on this measure see Anais do Senado, 1870, I, 190-205. When his proposal to curtail admission into religious orders was assailed in the Senate, Nabuco defended it by saying that he had always considered as included in the jus cavendi, which the State exercised over the Church, such matters as the admission of novices into religious communities. Anais do Senado, I, 194.

[137] Nabuco, Um estadista, I, 308-313; D. Romualdo Antônio de Seixas, op. cit., pp. 170-171.

[138] Badaró, Les Couvents, pp. 60-61, comments: "Il n'est pas question ici

1828-1829 seems to have reached the same conclusion:

> . . . the wealthy orders are just now in imminent danger; from the very reputation of their wealth, the present feeling of the country is not in their favour, and they seem to be held in the same estimation, as they were in France, at the commencement of the revolution. It is therefore generally spoken of, as a thing just and necessary, that their property should be applied to the necessities of the state. The chamber of deputies have already passed a vote to that effect, and it is imagined, that many persons about the throne are equally disposed to the measure, in the hope of annexing some of the confiscated lands to their own estates, as is notoriously the case in every reformation, particularly in our own.[139]

The evils inherent in the Brazilian Church, and the captiousness of governmental policy relative to ecclesiastical affairs bear witness to the fact that union of Church and State in Brazil was not practicable. Before a genuine reform could be instituted, the Church would have to free herself from the domination of the State. In order to achieve this freedom, episcopal leaders had to challenge those members of the government who were using the union of Church and State in Brazil as a means of regulating the spiritual authority. The efforts of the Brazilian episcopacy to rescue the Church from civil control were to be climaxed in the Episcopal-Masonic controversy.

That this controversy did not come sooner is traceable in large part to the fact that at the very time Brazilian bishops

---

de discuter le mérite de l'acte du Ministre Nabuco à l'égard du noviciat. Je crois même que parmi les hommes de son époque ce ministre faisait exception, étant, au fond, de très bonne foi. En tout cas, la mesure qu'il prit, restant incomplète, servit parfaitement les vues des franc-maçons, qui, les portes des couvents fermées, et plusieurs lois de restriction de la libre disposition des biens votées, attendaient tranquillement la mort du dernier moine pour faire passer à l'État toutes leurs propriétés." Badaró adds, p. 61, "Mais les moines ont vécu longtemps; les échafaudages de l'Empire sont tombés, et les couvents sont debout."

[139] R. Walsh, *Notices of Brazil in 1828-1829* (London, 1830), I, 360-361.

were beginning an ecclesiastical reform,[140] the attention of Brazilian statesmen was deflected from the Church by impending political crises. During the entire span of the Second Empire the question of slavery was a problem of major importance. Foreign countries, especially England, were constantly bringing pressure to bear on the imperial government to force Brazilian nationals to discontinue the slave traffic.[141] In the empire itself, an anti-slavery faction had become steadily more articulate, and, through alignment with the republican faction, this anti-slavery group had become a genuine threat to the monarchy. Even more immediate than the slavery issue in turning the attention of imperial statesmen from the ecclesiastical reforms was the diplomatic impasse involving Brazil, Argentina, Uruguay, and Paraguay, which terminated in the Paraguayan war (1864-1870).[142] Internal and external problems occupied the attention of imperial regalists during the very interval when conscientious bishops[143] were quietly beginning a seminary reform that was destined to have far-reaching effects. The efforts of Brazilian bishops to wrest ecclesiastical jurisdiction from the State was not, however, overlooked by regalists among imperial statesmen. Once the political situation was eased, a clash between Church and State was inevitable.

---

[140] See pp. 163-177 below.

[141] On slavery and the slave trade, see: Lawrence F. Hill, *Diplomatic Relations between Brazil and the United States* (Durham, N. C., 1932), pp. 110-145; ————, "Abolition of the Slave Trade in Brazil," *The Hispanic American Historical Review*, XI (1931), 169-197; Percy A. Martin, "Slavery and Abolition in Brazil," *ibid.*, XIII (1933), 151-196; Perdigão Malheiro, *A escravidão no Brasil* (Rio de Janeiro, 1866-1867).

[142] On the Paraguayan war, see L. Schneider, *A guerra da triplice aliança (Imperio do Brazil, Republica Argentina e Republica Oriental do Uruguay) Contra o governo da Republica do Paraguay (1864-1870) com cartas e planos.* Trans. by Manuel Tomaz Alves Nogueira (2 v., Rio de Janeiro, 1875-1876).

[143] Unwittingly Pedro II had prepared the way for ecclesiastical reform by nominating for episcopal offices men whose superior attainments he believed would promote the external prestige of the Church and redound to the glory of the empire.

# CHAPTER IV

FREEMASONRY AND THE RELIGIOUS LAY BROTHERHOODS

The incident which inaugurated the Episcopal-Masonic controversy was in itself of negligible importance. Yet because of the intimate connection between Church and State in Brazil, and because of the incompatible elements which were united in the political and social fabric of the nation, it was destined to give rise to a grave national crisis. On September 28, 1871, the new Conservative ministry,[1] headed by José da Silva Paranhos, viscount of Rio Branco,[2] sponsored an emancipation law, the outstanding clause of which was the provision that all children born of slave mothers were to be free.[3] The law won general approbation and, as an expression of this wholehearted approval,

---

[1] Organized on March 7, 1871.

[2] José da Silva Paranhos was raised to the peerage in 1870. While classified as conservative, Rio Branco showed himself on many occasions to be decededly liberal. The best biographies of Rio Branco are: Barão do Rio Branco, *Biographia de José Maria da Silva Paranhos* (2d. ed., Rio de Janeiro, 1945); Alfredo de Escragnolle, Visconde of Taunay, *O Visconde do Rio Branco* (2d. ed., São Paulo [1930]); Lídia Besouchet, *José Ma. Paranhos, Vizconde Do Río Branco* (Buenos Aires, 1944); Rozendo Muniz Barreto, *Elogio historico de José Maria da Silva Paranhos, Visconde do Rio Branco* (Rio de Janeiro, 1884); P. S. [pseud. for Quintino Bocaiuva], *J. M. da Silva Paranhos, Os nossos homens, retratos politicos e literarios* (Rio de Janeiro, 1864); and Luis de Alvarenga Peixoto, *Apontamentos para a historia. O Visconde do Rio Branco* (Rio de Janeiro, 1871).

[3] This emancipation law (*Lei Rio Branco*), initiated by Rio Branco and popularly called *Ventre Livre* (*i.e.*, Free Womb), was based on a proposal drafted in August, 1868, by Nabuco de Araújo at the request of the prime minister, Zacarias de Góis e Vasconcelos. Nabuco's measure was a companion piece to the legislation of Eusébio de Queiroz, which had, in 1850, abolished the slave traffic. Undoubtedly this second measure would have become law much earlier had not the government been preoccupied with the Paraguayan War (1864-1870). The emperor, Dom Pedro II, and all the leading statesmen of the empire realized that slavery should be abolished, but opinion differed as to how emancipation should be achieved.

the Masonic lodges of Rio de Janeiro held a reception on March 3, 1872, in honor of the prime minister, the viscount of Rio Branco, who was also grand master of one of the two Masonic grand lodges.[4] On this occasion, Father Almeida Martins, a Freemason, delivered a discourse that was later published with his signature in the metropolitan papers.[5] His bishop, Dom Pedro Maria de Lacerda, called Martins to account for his participation in the Masonic celebration, and ordered him to abjure Freemasonry. When the priest refused, the bishop, invoking bulls which condemned Freemasonry but which had never been promulgated in Brazil, suspended his right to preach and to hear confessions.[6] Father Martins threatened to appeal to the Council of State. At the same time, the Masonic press of Rio de Janeiro protested energetically against the action of the bishop. This was the beginning of the most violent ideological campaign ever launched in Brazil.[7]

The Masonic order decided immediately to make the cause of the disaffected priest its own. The grand lodge, Vale do Lavradio, assembled on April 16, 1872, under the presidency of the viscount of Rio Branco, adopted resolutions to defend the attacked brother, and to maintain Masonic authority which it thought was challenged by Catholicism. At this time the old epithet, "ultramontanist," was revived to characterize all Catholics who supported Rome against the alleged rights of the State. At the suggestion of Rio Branco, the Masonic press began an attack on the episcopacy.[8] Finally, an invitation was extended

---

[4] In Rio de Janeiro at this time there were two grand lodges, the Vale do Lavradio, whose grand master was the viscount of Rio Branco, and the Vale dos Beneditinos, at whose head was Councilor Joaquim de Saldanha Marinho.

[5] Basílio de Magalhães, *Estudos de história do Brasil* (São Paulo, 1940), p. 118. Augusto Olímpio Viveiros de Castro, "Contribuções para a biographia de Pedro II, Parte Iª," *Revista do Instituto Histórico e Geográfico Brasileiro*, tomo especial (1925), 477. This work will hereafter be cited as Castro.

[6] Eurico [pseud. for Francisco Ramos Paz], *O Ponto negro—Considerações a proposito do recente acto do bispo do Rio de Janeiro* (Rio de Janeiro, 1872), pp. 18-20. Castro, p. 477; Besouchet, *op. cit.*, p. 231.

[7] Besouchet, *op. cit.*, p. 231.

[8] Castro, p. 477, note 1, writes: "Em discurso pronunciado no Senado, o visconde do Rio Branco declinou a responsabilidade da violentissima cam-

to all Freemasons of Brazil to join the fraternity in its battle against the Church.[9]

The bishop of Rio de Janeiro made no retaliation despite the attacks of Freemasonry. In fact, he failed to take action even to punish a priest, who, despite the bishop's express prohibition, celebrated a Mass at the request of a Masonic lodge. The newspapers had announced that the Mass would be celebrated in a church overflowing with people, "in spite of the wrath of the ultramontanes, in spite of the prohibitions of the bishop." "This," declared the Masonic newspapers, "is the ultimatum of the Masonry of Rio de Janeiro to Bishop Lacerda."[10] The bishop of Rio de Janeiro, notwithstanding the fact that he later

---

panha movida contra a Egreja Catholica, dizendo que elle aconselhára a polemica pela imprensa, mas com moderação. Não foi feliz o nosso grande estadista nesta explicação: homen publico traquejado, conhecendo bem os nossos habitos, elle sabia perfeitamente que as discussões pela imprensa nunca se mantêm no terreno elevado dos principios, descendo logo ás personalidades, descambando sem demora para o terreno inglorio dos doestos e insultos soezes."

[9] Prior to the inauguration of the Episcopal-Masonic controversy, there had been a rift between the two grand lodges of Rio de Janeiro. Brazilian Masonry in general was disunited. The division between the Vale do Lavradio and the Vale dos Beneditinos is alluded to in the resolutions taken in the general assembly referred to above: "Antes, porém, de officialmente serem tomadas providencias do ir. . . . S ∴ M ∴ [Joaquim de Saldanha Marinho] foi visitar a este e manifestou-lhe as mais vivas demonstrações de sympathia, declarando-lhe que na questão vigente não havia divergencia de Cir.: mas uma onda immensa que se levantava contra o ultramontanismo (O Catholicismo romano)." Quoted by Castro, p. 479. The Vale dos Beneditinos held a general session on April 27 and formulated resolutions similar to those drawn up eleven days earlier by the Vale do Lavradio. Both sets of resolutions were published in the B ∴ do Lav ∴ and are quoted by Castro, pp. 478-479. Joaquim Nabuco, O Partido ultramontano suas invasões, seus orgãos e seu futuro, artigos publicados na Reforma (Rio de Janeiro, 1873), p. 58, writes: "A maçonaria brasileira achava-se dividida, tinha perdido sua unidade, estava em guerra intestina, quando, em vez de deixar os dous lados dilacerarem-se inteiramente e devorararem-se um ao outro, o bispo do Rio de Janeiro quiz introduzir a união na Ordem, excommungando-a. Foi preciso que a divisão fosse muito profunda para a familia dividida resistir a esse incentivo de conciliação. Mas o germen está lançado, e por fim a necessidade de uma defensa commum trará a união."

[10] Castro, p. 479.

showed courage in his defense of the bishop of Olinda,[11] displayed marked hesitancy in his early handling of the Masonic situation, and Dom Antônio de Macedo Costa, bishop of Pará, condemns him for his withdrawal from his original stand against Masonry.[12] The likelihood is that Lacerda's change of front was traceable to the advice of the internuncio, Domenico Sanguigni, for the man, a personal friend of the viscount of Rio Branco, consistently supported the government.[13] That Lacerda acted in conformity with the wishes of the imperial government may be attested by the fact that in 1888 it gave him the title of count of Santa Fé.[14]

## II

In the campaign launched in Rio de Janeiro against ultramontanism, a young Capuchin priest, Vital Maria Gonçalves de Oliveira, who had been appointed but not yet consecrated bishop of Olinda, was violently attacked. A Masonic pamphlet, *Ponto Negro,* which appeared in the capital shortly after Vital was consecrated, assailed the bishop, accusing him of favoring the Jesuits.[15] This challenge to Dom Vital was a prelude to the

---

[11] *Representação que a S.M. o Imperador dirige o bispo de S. Sebastião do Rio-de-Janeiro sobre a prisão e processo do exmo. e revmo. sr. bispo de Olinda* [dated February 18, 1874] (Rio de Janeiro, 1874). See Magalhães, *op. cit.,* p. 130.

[12] [Dom] Antônio de Macedo Costa, *A questão religiosa perante a Santa Sé, ou a Missão Especial em Roma em 1873, á luz dos documentos publicados e ineditos* (Maranhão, 1886), p. 148.

[13] Besouchet, *op. cit.,* p. 233, having just referred to the fact that Sanguigni was a personal friend of the Viscount of Rio Branco, observes: ". . . mientras 'los obispos' se hallaban en prisión, Monseñor Sanguigni, concede por un prescripto, en nombre de Su Santidad Pío IX la gracia del oratorio privado al Vizconde de Río Branco, ¡Gran Maestre de la Masonería!" Castro, p. 480, writes: "Este não acudiu ao repto, apesar de ter sido quem primeiro atirou a luva, procedimento este que seria inexplicavel, si não houvesse vehementes presumpções de que elle agiu sob a influencia do internuncio do papa, monsenhor d. Domingos Sanguigni, que, acima de tudo, queria manter as melhores relações com o Govêrno."

[14] Cf. Magalhães, *op. cit.,* p. 119.

[15] Eurico, *op. cit.,* pp. 8-9.

more serious phase of the Episcopal-Masonic controversy. Attention should be called, however, to the fact that the controversy was already under way when Vital assumed an uncompromising position relative to Catholics affiliated with Freemasonry.[16] Vital was consecrated bishop in São Paulo on March 17, 1872, arrived in Recife, the seat of his own diocese, on May 20, and took formal charge of the See on May 24.[17] Probably to try the new bishop, the Masonic press of Recife announced on June 27 that two days later, on the feast of SS. Peter and Paul, the Masonic lodge of Recife would commemorate the anniversary of its founding by having a Mass celebrated in St. Peter's Church. All members of the fraternity were invited to attend.[18] Vital left his opponents in no doubt as to his stand on the matter. He promptly issued a circular, *Reservadíssima*, in which he ordered the clergy not to participate in any ceremony announced as Masonic. He was obeyed; no Mass was celebrated.[19]

In reprisal, the Masonic societies published the names of the clergy and of the lay persons, members of Catholic confraternities and brotherhoods, who were affiliated with Freemasonry.[20] Bishop Dom Vital thereupon ordered all clerics to abjure Ma-

---

[16] Castro, p. 479, says, "É . . . . incontestavel que muito antes de d. Vital tomar posse da diocese de Olinda, já a Maçonaria havia mobilizado as suas fôrças, formado o plano de campanha, e iniciado as operações de guerra, não se limitando á *defensiva*, ao contrario, manifestando o seu espirito aggressivo, mesmo quando o bispo, supposto aggressor, não deu mais signaes de vida, apesar das mais insolentes provocações da imprensa maçonica."

[17] Fr. Fidélis M. de Primério, *Capuchinhos em terras de Santa Cruz nos séculos XVII, XVIII, e XIX* ([São Paulo], 1942), p. 326. "No Seminário [São Paulo] recebeu o aviso do Ministro do Império, communicando-lhe que o imperador por decreto de 21 de maio de 1871, o havia escolhido para bispo de Olinda, e aguardava seu consentimento para aprensentá-lo ao Sumo Pontífice."

[18] Magalhães, *op. cit.*, p. 121; Rafael M. Galanti, *Compendio da historia do Brasil* (São Paulo, 1910), V. 33; Júlio Maria, "A Religião, ordens religiosas, instituições pias e beneficentes no Brazil," *Livro do Centenario: 1500-1900* (Rio de Janeiro, 1900), I, ii, 91-92.

[19] Antônio Manuel dos Reis, *O Bispo de Olinda perante a história* (new ed., edited by Félix de Olivola, Recife, 1940-1944), I, 125.

[20] Magalhães, *op. cit.*, pp. 121-122.

sonry, and all brotherhoods[21] to expel members who refused to
abandon it. When the brotherhoods showed no inclination to
comply with his wishes, Vital ordered the pastors of the parishes
of Recife to exhort the Masonic members of the brotherhoods to
sever connections with Freemasonry. If any member of these
religious associations refused to abjure Masonry, he was to be
expelled, "because," said the bishop, "from such institutions are
excluded the excommunicated."[22] The Brotherhood of Our
Lady of Solitude (*Irmandade de Nossa Senhora da Soledade*)
adamantly refused to expel its Masonic members.[23] After three
formal admonitions and three refusals, the bishop suspended the
rebellious brotherhood on January 5, 1873. At this time the
prelate made clear the nature of the penalty: members of the
brotherhood were not to appear at religious functions as a cor-
porate religious society, nor was the brotherhood to receive new
members. These restrictions were extended to all brotherhoods
that failed to comply with the injunction of the bishop. The
prelate likewise placed under interdict some chapels of brotherhoods that were exclusively Masonic. He was careful to an-
nounce that all these penalties would immediately cease when
the Masonic members of the respective brotherhood abjured
Freemasonry or the brotherhood expelled such members as were
unwilling to abjure. In order to avoid all complications with
the government, Bishop Dom Vital declared that the suspension
of the brotherhoods referred only to the spiritual or religious
side of the societies.[24]

---

[21] Both brotherhoods and confraternities were involved in the controversy
with the bishops over the Masonic affiliations of members, but since these
types of religious associations did not differ essentially, the term brotherhood
will be used throughout the general discussion.

[22] Castro, p. 480.

[23] *Ibid.* Castro says that after Bishop D. Vital published his circular,
*Reservadíssima*, the Brotherhood of Our Lady of Solitude, which was domi-
ciled in the same section of the city as the episcopal palace, but which was
dominated by Freemasons, retaliated by electing as purveyor [*provedor*] Aires
Gama, who was a high official in one of the Masonic lodges and also editor
of *Verdade*, a Masonic organ in which had been published articles attacking
the Virgin Mother.

[24] *Ibid.*

Since the Brotherhood of Our Lady of Solitude did not appeal to the government against the action of the bishop, nothing more is heard of it in connection with this controversy.[25] Another association which came under the bishop's displeasure, the Brotherhood of the Most Holy Sacrament (*Irmandade do Santíssimo Sacramento*), did, however, make such an appeal. As a result, the issue between it and the local ordinary ceased to be a simple problem of religious discipline; it became the occasion of a serious quarrel between Church and State. Before surveying the case of this brotherhood, two matters need to be discussed: the nature of the brotherhoods, and the character of the religious policy of Pope Pius IX. Explanation of the former is essential to an understanding of the place of the brotherhood in the religious and political life of nineteenth century Brazil; and exposition of the latter is indispensable to an interpretation of the attitudes of imperial statesmen toward the actions of the bishop.

The brotherhoods, which had existed in Brazil from colonial days, were quasi-religious organizations made up of laymen. All religious acts, such as official participation of members in religious functions, sharing in the religious privileges accruing to members, and wearing the religious insignia, were subject to episcopal approval, while such matters as incorporation and property were under the supervision of the government. While it was recognized that the brotherhood was fundamentally a religious organization, yet because of its dual character the charter or fundamental law of the corporation had to be approved, both by the spiritual and by the temporal authorities.[26] Besides designating

---

[25] On recourse to the crown see p. 116, note 53, below.

[26] *Collecção das leis do Imperio do Brasil de 1828, Parte I* (Rio de Janeiro, 1878), pp. 47-50. The law of September 22, 1828, reads: "Dom Pedro, por Graça de Deus . . .: Fazemos saber a todos os nossos subditos que a Assembléa Geral decretou, e Nós queremos a Lei seguinte: Art. 1—Ficam extinctos os Tribunaes das Mesas do Desembargo do Paço e da Consciencia e Ordens. Art. 2—Os negocios, que eram da competencia de ambos os Tribunaes extinctos, e que ficam subsistindo serão expedidos pelas autoridades, e maneira seguintes: Sec. II Ao Governo compete expedir, pelas Secretarias de Estado, a que pertencer, e na conformidade das leis, o seguinte: . . . Confirmar os com-

the aims of the society and stipulating the regulations which governed its organization, the charter that gave legal status to each brotherhood stated that no change could be made in the fundamental law without the concurrence of both authorities.[27] It likewise stated that, since the brotherhoods were primarily religious in aim, a person under ecclesiastical censure was excluded from membership.

Practically every parish of Brazil had its religious brotherhoods, which took formal part in all religious ceremonies and festivals.[28] Each brotherhood had its special patron, and the patronal feasts were celebrated each year with pomp.[29] The religious associations had so infiltrated the religious life of Brazil that almost every feast of the liturgical year was a festival day for one or other of them. The result was that, in the minds of many critics, the externals of religion had come to have more meaning for the people than the fundamentals. This unfortunate situation was aggravated by the fact that parish priests were remiss in providing either methodical or adequate religious in-

---

promissos de irmandades, depois de approvados pelos Prelados na parte religiosa."

[27] The *Ato Adicional* (Lei N. 16) of August 12, 1834, assigned the supervision of the religious brotherhoods to the legislative assembly of the respective province. See *Collecção das leis do Imperio do Brasil de 1834, Parte I* (Rio de Janeiro, 1866), art. 10, S. 10, p. 18; and Joaquim Pires Machado Portela, *Constituição politica do imperio do Brazil confrontadas com outras constituições* (Rio de Janeiro, 1876), p. 190. See also *Collecção das leis do Imperio do Brasil de 1860* (Rio de Janeiro, 1860), Decree No. 2711 of December 19, 1860, chap. IX, art. 33, p. 1134-1135.

[28] See Besouchet, *op. cit.*, pp. 236-237, for an estimate of the number of brotherhoods in Recife. The author gives in addition the number of festivals which were not celebrated during the time the respective brotherhoods and their churches were under interdict.

[29] *Ibid.*, p. 192. The author, in speaking of the opposition of Brazilian Catholics to the action of the two bishops in support of Rome, says, ". . . el catolicsmo brasileño encontró la mejor base para su propaganda en esas hermandades religiosas, dotadas de costosas iglesias con lujosos ornamentos, históricas reliquias de santos, imágenes coloniales. Sin las hermandades, nuestro catolicismo hubiera sido incoloro, sin ninguna raíz ni expresión popular. Los santos cubiertos de atavíos, los ropajes de colores brillantes, las fiestas pintorescas, el esplendor de nuestra Iglesia, todo provenía de esas hermandades; era imposible disociarlas en la mentalidad popular."

struction for their parishioners. So many members of the clergy were more interested in power, wealth, and pleasure than in their pastoral duties that religious education of the laity had practically disappeared in Brazil. In the cities, festivals were the core of religious activity; panegyric sermons, the substitute for homiletic instruction. In the smaller towns the same evils prevailed, augmented if anything by the unabashed moral laxity of many priests and religious. A religiously-inclined people, the Brazilians had sought fulfillment for their pious yearnings in elaborate festival observances. Gradually pageantry had been substituted for solid Catholic doctrine and worship, and the religious association for personal spiritual activity. Father Júlio Maria, in his survey of the Church during the Empire, emphasizes again and again the need that existed for religious instruction, and the fact that this need was not met. Criticism was leveled against the Church, he says, because false devotion, which was in no way implemented to regenerate souls or improve morals, had taken the place of genuine Catholic worship.[30]

Besides the overemphasis on external observance that characterized the religious activities of the brotherhoods, a second factor contributed to the part they were to play in undermining the religious life of Brazil. These religious associations had become the centers of Masonic activity, and members wore indiscriminately the religious insignia of their brotherhood and the Masonic regalia of their lodge. Many Brazilians came to regard Freemasonry as the "auxiliary arm of the Church."[31] It is important to remember, writes Lídia Besouchet, that by means of the brotherhoods "was established the bridge of communication between the Catholic religion of the people and Masonry, the spiritual organization of the élite."[32]

One more factor must be examined before a survey can be

[30] Father Júlio Maria, "A Religião," loc. cit., pp. 87-89.

[31] Besouchet, op. cit., p. 185, writes: "Para juzgar 'la cuestión religiosa,' también debemos buscar nuevos elementos: estaba tan profundamente arraigado en la conciencia liberal que la masonería era un complemento, un arma auxiliar de la Iglesia, que al principio la actitud de los obispos fué considerada absurda e incomprensible . . ."

[32] Ibid., p. 192.

presented of the Episcopal-Masonic controversy: the policy of the Vatican, launched in the second half of the nineteenth century.[33] Pope Pius IX (1846-1878), successor to Gregory XVI, was hailed on his election as a liberal-minded statesman under whom the Church would endorse modern progress.[34] Before long, however, men were to discover that the new pontiff, while deeply interested in the welfare of humanity, was the uncompromising enemy of all modern trends bearing such labels as Liberal, Progressive, and Modern. The definition of the dogma of the Immaculate Conception in 1854 aroused the opposition of many Liberal Catholics in Brazil, who found the pronouncement objectionable, not only in itself but also because it represented a public avowal of the right of the Holy See to legislate for the whole Catholic world. Ten years later, in 1864, Pope Pius IX issued the *Syllabus of Errors*, to which was appended the encyclical *Quanta Cura*, anathematizing Freemasonry.[35] In the *Syllabus*, eighty errors were listed, among them some of the most cherished tenets of the modern Liberal.[36] In the course of

---

[33] The expression "new policy of the Vatican" has been used to designate the measures by which Pope Pius IX attempted to counteract the influence of secularism which swept over Europe in the nineteenth century. The previous pontificate had not followed a different policy; on the contrary, Pope Gregory XVI (1831-1846) had showed grave concern for the errors of the age, and issued on August 15, 1832, the encyclical *Mirari Vos*, which struck at an "ugly conspiracy against clerical celibacy," unrestrained "freedom of conscience," other errors all more or less associated with the tenets of Liberalism. For the encyclical *Mirari Vos*, see *Acta ex iis decerpta-quae apud Sanctam Sedem geruntur in compendium opportune redacta* (Romae, 1868), IV, 336-345. This work will hereafter be cited as *Acta Sanctae Sedis*.

[34] On Pope Pius IX, see Josef Schmidlin, *Papstgeschichte der Neuesten Zeit* (München, 1934), II, 8-330; A. Pougeois, *Histoire de Pie IX et de son pontificat* (6 vols., Paris, 1877-1886); Charles Sylvain, *Histoire de Pie IX le Grand et de son pontificat* (3d. ed., Paris, 1883). For a summary of the pronouncements of Pius IX, see Henricus Denzinger, *Enchiridion Symbolorum difinitionum et declarationum de Rebus Fidei et Morum* (Friburgi, 1937), pp. 455-511. This work will hereafter be cited as Denzinger.

[35] For the bull *Quanto Cura*, see *Acta Sanctae Sedis*, III, 160-167.

[36] For the *Syllabus*, see Denzinger, pp. 482-490. An excellent analysis of it is to be found in Robert Hull, *The Syllabus of Errors of Pius IX* (Huntington, Indiana, 1926). The *Syllabus* contained under ten headings a sum-

the next decade, the Supreme Pontiff called a general council to meet at the Vatican on December 8, 1869. At this general council, the first since the Council of Trent (1545-1563), the condemnations of the *Syllabus* were supplemented by the reiteration and further clarification of Catholic doctrine. The prediction of anticlerical Liberals that the *Syllabus* was the last challenge of the dying papacy to the modern world was controverted by the definition of the dogma of papal infallibility, the culminating achievement of the Vatican Council.[37]

In Brazil, as elsewhere, hostility to the policies of Pius IX was manifest in government circles.[38] In an effort to counteract

---

mary of eighty errors. It designated in each instance the papal announcement by which the error had been previously condemned. Despite the importuning of Liberal Catholics and the threats of the enemies of the Church, the Holy Father unflinchingly maintained that no part of the doctrine of Christ may be sacrificed as a concession to the spirit or demands of an age.

[37] On the Vatican Council, see Theodore Granderath, *Histoire du Concile du Vatican depuis sa première annonce jusqu'à sa prorogation d'après les documents authentiques édité par Le P. Conrad Kirch, S.J. et traduit de l'allemand par des religieux de la même Compagnie* (3 v., Bruxelles, 1907-1913); Cuthbert Butler, *The Vatican Council* (New York, 1930); Denzinger, pp. 491-508. The Vatican Council was never formally closed. On the day following the proclamation of the dogma of infallibility, France declared war on Prussia, and many French and German bishops had to return to their respective countries. Later, the invasion of Rome by Italian troops made further meetings impossible. On October 20, 1870, therefore, Pius IX indefinitely suspended its sessions. The Freemasons called a Masonic anticouncil to meet at Naples on December 8, 1869, to offset the influence of the Vatican Council. Raymond Corrigan, *The Church in the Nineteenth Century* (Milwaukee, 1938), p. 187, writes: "The purpose of this sham Council, namely to 'proclaim the great principles of universal human right,' may not have been diabolic in its inspiration. But among the Freemasons who organized it there were men who had given expression to a satanic hatred of God. The best argument with which to exonerate the devil lies in the utterly ridiculous antics of th Naples assembly. With all his experience in human affairs, the devil should be too wise to be held responsible for all the three days' fiasco at Naples. Still, Masonry was an undeniable force in the politico-irreligious world immediately before and after 1870. And the Naples meeting does throw some light upon the attitude of Freemasons toward the Vatican Council."

[38] The disapproval of political leaders like Gladstone and Bismarck had its counterpart in Brazil, where statesmen like Rui Barbosa, Joaquim de Saldanha

the centripetal influence of the papacy, imperial statesmen passed laws to implement further the right of recourse to the crown[39] and initiated measures requiring the civil registration of births and deaths, the recognition of civil marriage, and the secularization of cemeteries. All these measures were prompted by what today seems to have been an absurd desire to reinsure national autonomy against the alleged aggressions of the Holy See. A form of exalted nationalism spurred imperial statesmen to defend uncompromisingly the authority of the State against what it imputed to be the fanaticism of the Roman curia.[40] But if the policies of Pope Pius IX were regarded by regalistic statesmen as a threat to national autonomy, they came as a challenge to Brazilian prelates who viewed with dismay the religious policies sponsored by the imperial government.

---

Marinho, Benedito Otôni, and Joaquim Nabuco were voluble in their recriminations. See Rui Barbosa, *O Papa e o concilio por Janus, versão e introdução de Ruy Barbosa* (2d. ed., São Paulo, 1930) ; ———————, "A Igreja e o Estado," *Novos discursos e conferencias colligidos e revistos por Homero Pires* (São Paulo, 1933), pp. 7-64 [this address was given originally in the Grande Oriente Unido do Brasil on July 21, 1876] ; Joaquim Nabuco, *O partido ultramontano, suas invasões, seus orgãos e seu futuro* (Rio de Janeiro, 1873). For the views of a moderate regalist, see the life of José Nabuco de Araújo by his son, Joaquim Nabuco, *Um Estadista do imperio Nabuco de Araujo, sua vida, suas opiniões, sua época* (Rio de Janeiro, [1898-1899]), III, 369-370. For a favorable explanation of the work of the Council see Dom Antônio de Macedo Costa, *Carta pastoral do excellentissimo e reverendissimo Bispo do Pará publicando as constituições dogmaticas do sacrosancto concilio geral do Vaticano* (São Luiz do Maranhão, 1871).

[39] For the views of a moderate regalist on the right of recourse to the crown, see Marquês de São Vicente, *Considerações relativas ao Beneplacito, e Recurso á Coroa em Materias do culto* (Rio de Janeiro, 1873), pp. 33-61. For a refutation of these views see Ernesto Adolfo de Freitas, *Considerações sobre o opusculo publicado no Rio de Janeiro com o titulo de Considerações relativas ao beneplacito, a recurso á coroa em materias do culto pelo Conselheiro d'Estado Marquez de S. Vicente* (Lisboa, 1874).

[40] Besouchet, *op. cit.*, pp. 184-186. The author concludes her estimate of the repercussions in Brazil to the activities of Pius IX with the following observation: "El sentimiento que los llevaba a obrar con tamaña intransigencia era el de la conciencia del papel que representaba el Estado y de su autoridad, contra la que se levantaba el fantismo de los representantes de la Curía Romana. Era una especie de sentimiento nacionalista exaltado, y tanto parece haber sido

### III

Mention has already been made both of the interdict leveled against the Brotherhood of the Most Holy Sacrament and of the petition of the brotherhood to the crown. It has also been suggested that the recourse of this brotherhood to the emperor occasioned a serious quarrel between Church and State. To understand why the imperial government allowed itself to be drawn into a quarrel between two social forces, *i.e.*, Freemasonry and Roman Catholicism, and to determine why it took the stand that it did, it will be necessary to study each of the three factors in the controversy: the brotherhoods, the Church, and the imperial government.

On December 28, 1872, Dom Vital gave orders to Canon Antônio Marques de Castilho, vicar of the parish of St. Anthony of Recife, to exhort Dr. Costa Ribeiro, a Mason and a member of the Brotherhood of the Most Holy Sacrament, to abjure Masonry, and to proceed in like manner against "each and every Mason in the Brotherhood." His letter of December 28, 1872, to the vicar is as follows:

> Since it has come to our attention that Dr. Antônio José da Costa Ribeiro, notoriously known as a Mason, is a member of the Brotherhood of the Most Holy Sacrament of the Mother Church [*Matriz*], and since the pain of major excommunication laid by various Popes rests upon those initiated in Masonry, we command that Your Reverence without loss of time direct yourself to the Judge of that Brotherhood and order him in our name to exhort the said brother charitably

---

éste el factor preponderante que las cuestiones que en la misma época se plantean con otros países (especialmente con Inglaterra) son también producto de ese deseo de demonstrar al mundo que el Brasil era un país independiente, soberano en sus atribuciones, autónomo en sus deliberaciones. Don Pedro II y sus colaboradores deseaban demostrar que si el Brasil se equivocaba, lo hacía por su cuenta y se mantenía independiente en la defensa de sus derechos aunque no siempre fueran legítimos. La era del romanticismo 'indianista' y 'negrista' es el símbolo de este chauvinismo, de esta embriagués nacionalista." For a confirmation of Besouchet's estimate, see p. 147 below, where the views of José Nabuco de Araújo are surveyed.

and instantly to abjure this sect condemned by the Church. If, unhappily, he does not wish to retract, let him be immediately expelled from the membership of the Brotherhood, inasmuch as excommunicated persons are excluded from such institutions. Let the same procedure be carried out with each and every Mason who might by chance be a member of any Brotherhood existing in the parish of Your Reverence. We await the communication that our orders were fulfilled.[41]

The governing board of the brotherhood was promptly convoked to consider the bishop's order as delivered by the vicar. In its reply to the vicar, the board maintained that it was not able to comply with the wishes of the bishop because its charter did not authorize expulsion of a member for the reason he had cited.[42] In view of this response, Dom Vital addressed a second letter to Canon Antônio Marques de Castilho, on January 9, 1873, in which he directed him to impress upon the brotherhood the necessity of reconsidering the matter:

From the letter of Your Reverence, dated the 8th day of the current month, we see with great sorrow that some members of the Brotherhood of the Most Holy

---

[41] "Constando-nos que o Sr. Dr. Antonio José da Costa Ribeiro, notoriamente conhecido por Maçon, é membro da Irmandade do Santissimo Sacramento dessa matriz, e pesando sobre os iniciados na maçonaria pena de excommunhão maior lançada por differentes Papas, mandamos que V. Revm. sem perda de tempo, dirija-se ao Juiz daquella Irmandade e ordene-lhe em nosso nome que exhorte caridosa e instantemente o dito irmão a abjurar essa seita condemnada pela Igreja. Si por infelicidade este não quizer retractar-se seja immediatamente expulso do gremio da Irmandade, porquanto de taes instituições são excluidos os excommungados. Da mesma sorte se proceda com todo e qualquer Maçon, por ventura membro de qualquer Irmandade existente na freguesia de V. Revm. Aguardamos a communiçação de que as nossas ordens foram cumpridas." *Relatorio apresentado á Assembléa Geral na terceira sessão da decima quinta legislatura pelo Ministro e Secretario d'Estado dos Negocios do Imperio, Dr. João Alfredo Corrêa de Oliveira* (Rio de Janeiro, 1874), appendix D, p. 17. This work will hereafter be cited as *Relatório do Ministério dos Negócios do Império, 1874.*

[42] *Ibid.*

Sacrament of that Mother Church [of St. Anthony], who have the misfortune of being affiliated with Masonry, do not wish, in spite of charitable requests, to abjure, and that the said Brotherhood is resolved not to expel them from its membership, as it should.

We witness with grief and astonishment, we deplore profoundly such flagrant disobedience to the laws of Holy Church, especially when it is perpetrated by men who say they are her submissive sons, and who aspire to the privileges and prerogatives of Catholics.

We are sorry in the extreme that those poor entangled sheep show themselves deaf to the paternal admonitions of their humble pastor. Before applying the penalties designated by the sacred canons for such cases, Your Reverence will make a last effort and exert all means at your disposal to lead those errant children and brethren to the arms of Holy Mother Church.

If this final attempt should be without profit, Your Reverence will be so kind as to communicate with us without delay.[43]

When the vicar transmitted the contents of this second letter to the brotherhood, he advised it to appoint a commission to meet with the ordinary and discuss the problem. The vicar felt that such a procedure would result in an understanding satis-

---

[43] "Pelo officio de V. Revm., em data de 8 do corrente, vemos com grande pesar nosso que alguns membros da Irmandade do Santissimo Sacramento dessa matriz, que tem a desdita de ser filiados á Maçonaria, a despeito de caridosas instancias, não querem abjurar, nem a dita Irmandade está resolvida a expellil--os do seu gremio, como devéra.

"Testemunhamos com dor e pasmo, deploramos profundamente tão flagrante desobediencia ás leis da Santa Igreja, maxime sendo ella perpetrada por homens que se dizem seus filhos submissos, e que aspiram aos fóros e áas regalias de catholicos.

"Sentimos em extremo que essas pobres ovelhas tresmalhadas se mostrem surdas ás paternas admoestações de seu humilde pastor. Antes de applicarmos as penas para casos taes comminadas pelos sagrados canones, tente V. Revm. o ultimo esforço, e envide todos os meios ao seu alcance para conduzir esses nossos filhos e irmãos extraviados aos braços da Santa Madre Igreja.

"Se improficua fôr esta ultima tentativa, queira V. Revm. communicar-nos sem demora." Ibid., pp. 17-18.

factory to both parties.[44] The brotherhood appears not to have received this second communication until January 12. Whether Vital knew of this delay is not known; likely he assumed that since the communication was directed to a parish within the same city as his residence, it would reach the brotherhood more promptly. Whatever the circumstances, the bishop, not hearing from the vicar of St. Anthony parish by January 13, directed a third communication to him. This one assumed the tone of an ultimatum:

> We recommend to Your Reverence that you demand from the Brotherhoods of the Most Holy Sacrament and of the Souls [in Purgatory][45] of your parish the reply to the letter which we directed to Your Reverence on the 9th of the current month, with the understanding that if, in the period of four days from this date they do not respond, we shall consider the answer [to be] in the negative.[46]

On January 19, Galdino Antônio Alves Ferreira, judge of the Brotherhood of the Most Holy Sacrament, sent an effusive response to the vicar of the parish.[47] While protesting fidelity to the Catholic religion and deep respect and love for the bishop, it showed no evidence of a change in the position of the brotherhood relative to members affiliated with Freemasonry. When the bishop received no word from the brotherhood within the limit of the time set for the answer, he carried out his decision "to consider its answer [to be] in the negative" and leveled the sentence of interdict upon the association. This sentence, together

---

44 *Ibid.*, p. 18.

45 This brotherhood is mentioned only in this one communication. It did not appeal to the Crown; hence it is not mentioned again in the course of the controversy.

46 "Recommendamos a V. Revm. que exija das Irmandades do Santissimo Sacramento e das Almas de sua freguesia, a resposta ao officio que a V. Revm. dirigimos em data de 9 do corrente, na intelligencia de que, si no praso de 4 dias contados desta data, não responderem, consideraremos a dita resposta pela negativa." *Relatório de Ministério dos Negócios do Império,* 1874, p. 18.

47 For this letter see Document I, Appendix, pp. 252-254.

with a letter of the vicar in which the nature of the interdict was explained, was submitted to the brotherhood.[48] According to the report of the ministry of the interior, the governing board received these official communications a few hours after it had despatched its letter to the vicar.[49] That the brotherhood was under censure only on its religious side is stressed in the instruction that accompanied the sentence of interdict:

> . . . I declare that the Brotherhood is interdicted only in the religious part, [the members] not being able to appear in any religious acts with insignia that show them to be members [of the Brotherhood], as for example, accompanying the Most Holy Sacrament, taking part in festivals and meetings in the garb of the Brotherhood, nor even collecting alms, vested with cape or garb, etc., the Brotherhood remaining, however, in the full enjoyment of its rights in the temporal part and in the administration of the goods of the same Brotherhood.[50]

The governing board petitioned the bishop to reconsider his sanction. It recalled to his attention its assertion that the broth-

---

[48] *Relatório do Ministério dos Negócios do Império, 1874*, p. 19. "Sentença de interdicto—D. Frei Vital Maria Gonçalves de Oliveira, por mercê de Deus e da Santa Sé Apostolica, Bispo da Diocese de Olinda.—Recusando a Irmandade do Santissimo Sacramento da matriz de Santo Antonio desta cidade, apezar de nossas paternaes admoestações, expulsar do seu gremio alguns membros, que não querem de modo algum abjurar a Maçonaria, Sociedade já muitas vezes condemnada pela Igreja de Jesus Christo, nós, legitimo Pastor desta Diocese, em cumprimento do nosso dever, e em virtude da nossa Autoridade Episcopal, lançamos pena de interdicto sobre a mencionada Irmandade, E declaramos formalmente que a dita pena permanecerá em pleno vigor até á retractação ou eliminação daquelles irmãos que por infelicidade são filiados á Maçonaria. "Dada em nosso Palacio Episcopal da Soledade aos 16 de janeiro de 1873. —Vital, Bispo Diocesano."

[49] *Ibid.*

[50] ". . . declaro que a Irmandade só fica interdicta na parte religiosa, não podendo comparecer a acto algum religioso com signaes que indiquem serem irmãos, como por exemplo acompanhar o Santissimo, assistir ás festividades e reuniões com opas, nem mesmo mandar tirar esmolas, vestido com capa ou opa, etc., ficando porém a Irmandade no pleno gôzo de seus direitos na parte temporal, e administração dos bens da mesma Irmandade." *Ibid.*

erhood was not able to eliminate members for the reason cited, because the charter, approved by both the bishop and the imperial government, did not provide for expulsion on such a charge.[51] Vital replied that he would "very willingly and with promptitude" raise the penalty of interdict as soon as the Masonic brothers either abjured Masonry or were eliminated from the association.[52] Thereupon the brotherhood appealed to the crown.[53] On February 10, a copy of the petition was presented to the president of the province of Pernambuco,[54] Henrique Pereira de Lucena, to be submitted to the imperial minister of justice. The provincial president, by letter of February 18, summoned the bishop to answer the charge made against him by the brotherhood.[55] The prelate replied on February 20:

> Omitting any observation on the innumerable inaccuracies contained in the said petition, I limit myself to saying to Your Excellency that such recourse is condemned by various dispositions of the Church.[56]

On March 4, 1873, José Pereira da Costa Mota, procurator

---

[51] *Ibid.*, pp. 19-20.

[52] *Ibid.*, p. 20.

[53] *Ibid.* The brotherhood held that its petition was authorized by sections 1 and 3 of decree No. 1911 of March 28, 1857. See *Collecção das leis do imperio do Brasil de 1857* (Rio de Janeiro, 1857), pp. 103-105. "Decreto No. 1.911 28 de Marco de 1857. Regula a competencia, interposição, effeitos e fórma do julgamento dos Recursos á corôa. Hei por bem, Usando da autoridade que Me confere O Artigo cento e dous paragrapho doze da Constituição, Decretar o seguinte: Art 1º Dá-se Recurso á Corôa: S. 1ª.—Por usurpação de jurisdicção e poder temporal. S. 2ª.—Por qualquer censura contra empregados civeis em razão de seu Officio. S. 3ª.—Por notoria violencia no exercicio da jurisdicção e poder espiritual, postergando-se o direito natural, ou os Canones recebidos na Igreja Brazileira."

[54] *Ibid.*, pp. 104-105. "Art. 3—He só competente para conhecer dos recursos á Corôa o Conselho d'Estado. Todavia nos casos do Artigo primeiro paragraphos 1 e 2 podem os Presidentes das Provincias decidir provisoriamente as questões suscitadas como decidem os conflictos de jurisdicção."

[55] *Relatório do Ministério dos Negócios do Império, 1874*, p. 20.

[56] "Omittindo qualquer observação sobre as innumeras inexactidões contidas na dita petição, limito-me a dizer a V. Ex. que semelhante recurso é condemnado por varias disposições da Igreja." *Ibid.*, pp. 20-21.

of the crown, wrote to Lucena that in his opinion the bishop had violated the law and that the petition should be submitted to the Council of State.[57]

The prelate's letter of February 20 could not have come as a surprise either to the brotherhood or to the president of the province, since it was not only in keeping with the uncompromising attitude taken by Dom Vital in dealing with the brotherhood, but also in harmony with the tenor of his pastoral "against the snares and machinations of Masonry," issued February 2, 1873, Feast of the Purification.[58] In his pastoral letter the bishop asserted that it was an incontestable fact that for some years there had been disseminated in various parts of the Empire an anti-Catholic propaganda which amounted to a systematic persecution of the Church. He declared that the attack against the Catholic religion was the more pernicious because it was subtly disguised. Masonic societies, he said, were behind that propaganda and that persecution of the Church. In Masonic literature, the Church,[59] the Supreme Pontiff,[60] Catholic dog-

---

[57] *Ibid.*, p. 22. The procurator asserted that the bishop had violated article 1, sections 1 and 3 of the decree 1911 of March, 1857. See note 53 above.

[58] D. Fr. Vital Maria Gonçalves de Oliveira, *Carta Pastoral do Bispo de Olinda premunindo os seus diocesanos contra as ciladas e maquinações da Maçonaria* (Recife, 1873). This work will hereafter be cited, Dom Vital, *Carta Pastoral do Bispo de Olinda*.

[59] *Verdade* [Masonic publication in Pernambuco], January 15, 1873, quoted in *ibid.*, p. 4, referred to the Church as a "Cadaver putrido já decompondo-se em deleterias exhalações!"

[60] *Familia Universal* [organ of the Universal Society of Masons], n. 3, col. 6, quoted in *ibid.*, p. 5. In this work, according to Dom Vital, the pope is referred to as "o sultão da infallibilidade." *Verdade*, no. 7, cited in *ibid.*, p. 32, denied the dogma of infallibility. [In his pastoral, Vital does not give the date of either of these issues.]

mas,[61] and bishops,[62] were assailed.[63] Masonry, Vital continued, while ostensibly devoting itself to philanthropic works, strove at the same time to undermine the Roman Catholic religion, the state religion of Brazil, by profaning its mysteries, denying its dogmas, and encouraging insubordination to its laws. If the episcopacy undertook to execute its duty of protecting the people committed to its care, of fulfilling the precepts laid down by the head of the Church, or of putting into operation ecclesiastical discipline authorized by him, Masonry changed its rôle from that of persecutor to that of innocent victim, and cried loudly against intolerance, Jesuitism, and ultramontanism. The bishop declared that Masonry "moves heaven, sea and earth; puts into activity all its mysterious springs and develops all its means of action to the end of hindering what it calls episcopal preponderance, absolutism, despotism, and fanaticism, and imposes silence

---

[61] *Bibliotheca maçon*, I (1864), 94, quoted in *ibid.*, p. 5. Freemasons ridiculed fundamental dogmas of the Catholic religion, which they called "fanatismo e superstição." The same Masonic work (p. 50, quoted in *ibid.*, p. 29) said that the Holy Trinity "é um invento sacerdotal; e os padres teem sido forçados a reconhecer a unidade de Deus, posto que apparentemente seja composta de tres essencias differentes." The doctrine of grace was attacked in *Familia Universal*, n. 4, cited in *ibid.*, p. 32; the eternity of the punishment of hell, in *Verdade*, n. 14, *ibid.*; the divinity of Christ, in *Verdade*, n. 1, cited in *ibid.*, p. 31.

[62] *Verdade* of January 18, 1873, quoted in *ibid.*, p. 5, called the bishops "lobos e pastores Satanicos." *Bibliotheca maçon*, I [1864], 109, cited in *ibid.*, p. 31, maintained that "o Catholicismo ensinado pelo Vigario de Jesus Christo e pelos Bispos não é o verdadeiro; que só a maçonaria conserva intacto o deposito da fé; que só ella cultiva cuidadosamente a arvore evangelica e conserva estreme o verdadeiro Catholicismo despido do materialismo e da idolatria."

[63] The Masonic attacks on Catholic dogma and discipline recall remarks made by Pinto de Campos in a parliamentary discourse in the Chamber of Deputies, July 15, 1873. See Monsignor Joaquim Pinto de Campos, *Discurso pronunciado na sessão de 15 de julho de 1873 por . . . deputado á Assembléa Geral pelo 5º districto eleitoral da Provincia de Pernambuco* (Rio de Janeiro, 1873), p. 18: "Se ella [Masonry] se diz sinceramente inoffensiva ás leis da Igreja, não consinta que em seu nome e sob sua responsabilidade se preguem na imprença principios tão subversivos da ordem social Christã. Se se responde que a parte sensata da maçonaria repelle esses escriptos, então deve ella apresentar-se francamente contra elles, afastando de si toda a responsabilidade moral."

on imprudent and temerarious prelates."[64] The bishops, Vital maintained, would with God's help continue to defend the cause of the Church and be the champions of the Supreme Pontiff. He then listed the bulls, encyclicals, and allocutions issued by the various popes in condemnation of Freemasonry,[65] and gave a summary of the charges launched against Masonry in some of these pronouncements.

To substantiate further his contention that a person affiliated with Freemasonry could not be considered a loyal son of the Church, Vital called attention to Masonic contempt for Catholic doctrine, giving examples from Masonic manuals, histories, and periodicals.[66] He considered erroneous the allegation that Brazilian Masonry differed from European Masonry, and the corollary that Brazilian Masonry was in no way harmful to Catholicism, and had never incurred ecclesiastical censure.[67] Vital asserted

---

[64] ". . . move céo, mar e terra; põe em actividade todas as suas molas mysteriosas e desenvolve todos os seus meios de acção, a fim de oppor uma remora ao que ella chama *prepotencia, absolutismo, despotismo e fanatismo* episcopal, e força ao silencio os Prelados *imprudentes e temerarios.*" Dom Vital, *op. cit.*, p. 6.

[65] *Ibid.*, p. 9. The following papal pronouncements against Masonry are cited: Clemente XII, *In Eminenti* [1738]; Benedict XIV, *Providas* [*Romanorum Pontificum* (1751)]; Pius VII, *Ecclesiam a Jesu Christo;* Leo XII, *Quo graviora* (March 13, 1826); Pius IX, *Qui pluribus* (Nov. 9, 1846); *Quibus quantisque* (April 20, 1849); *Noscitis et nobiscum* (Dec. 8, 1849); *Singulari quadam* (Dec. 9, 1854); *Quanto conficiamur moerore* (August 10, 1863); *Apostolicae Sedis* (Oct. 12, 1869).

[66] The bishop quoted, besides the Masonic works mentioned: *Revista maçonica* (January, 1848); *Historia geral da Maçonaria Manifesto de 1865;* [Jean-Giullaume] Gyr, [*La Franc-maçonnerie dans sa véritable signification, où son organisation, son but et son histoire par Eduard Emil Eckert, . . . trad. de l'allemand, disposé dans un nouvel order et considérablement augmenté de documents authentiques sur la franc-maçonnerie belge et française par l'abbé Gyr* (Liége, 1854)]; *Le monde maçonique* (May, 1855); and *Pelicano* (n. 35).

[67] Vital cited many proofs of the affiliation between Brazilian and European Freemasonry. He called attention (*op. cit.*, p. 22), to the following statement in the Masonic pamphlet *Ponto Negro* (see p. 100, note 6, above), pp. 16-17: "A maçonaria brasileira é representante das mesmas maximas que acima indicamos e que são as de todas as suas co-irmãs do universo. Os principios expressos em sua constituição filiam-se áquelles." The same pamphlet, the

that "the most superficial study is sufficient to convince any un-prejudiced mind that Masonry in Brazil, in Europe, as well as in any other part of the world is one and the same dark association, with identical tendencies, using the same means in order to attain the very same end."[68] He pointed out that what he said applied to Masonry *in se;* he acknowledged that there were many Free-masons who were not hostile to the Church, but he qualified, ".... this is in spite of their being Masons; it is because they are not *good and true Masons;* it is because they deviate from the principles of Masonry."[69]

In his pastoral, the prelate also spoke of the royal *placet.* He characterized it as "the principal redoubt where Freemasons for-tify themselves, endeavoring to escape the anathemas fulminated by the Holy See against secret societies ...."[70] These rebellious sons of Rome, he asserted, "stir the cold ashes of Jansenism, of Febronianism, of Gallicanism, and from them disinter the *placet.*"[71] He declared without qualification that the doctrine of the right of royal *placet* is heretical. He showed, however, that even if one were to grant its validity, still the bulls against Freemasonry would apply: 1) because the bulls against Masonry issued by Clement XII and Benedict XIV[72] were promulgated in Portugal and her colonies at a time when the *placet* was not exercised;[73] 2) because even those who upheld the right of royal

---

bishop pointed out, acknowledged that the Grand Orient of France had de-manded the elimination of slavery in Brazil as a condition of its recognition of Brazilian Freemasonry. The bishop referred likewise to a discourse offered in the Masonic lodge Conciliação (*Discurso na noite de 17 de Agosto de 1867,* quoted in *ibid.,* pp. 21-22) in which the speaker said: "Espalhados por toda a superficie da terra fazemos uma só communidade, temos a mesma origem, sabe-mos os mesmos mysterios, caminhamos pelo mesmo caminho, e tendemos aos mesmos fins, sujeitos sempre á mesma regra e dirigidos pelo mesmo espirito."

[68] *Ibid.,* p. 17.
[69] *Ibid.,* p. 17.
[70] *Ibid.,* p. 23.
[71] *Ibid.*
[72] See p. 7 above.
[73] Dom Vital, *op. cit.,* p. 38, n. 1. "O placet revogado por D. João II em 1487 só reviveu com Pombal em 1765; e neste intervallo foram publicadas as Bullas acima citadas, uma de 27 de Abril de 1738 e a outra de 18 de Março de 1751."

*placet* admitted that it did not apply to ecclesiastical censures; and 3) because by the allocution of September 25, 1865, Pius IX forbade all Christians of whatever country to enter Masonry, "and declared formally that those who think that the anathema fulminated against this sect *does not have value in countries where it* [Masonry] is tolerated by the civil authority labor under the gravest error."[74] The bishop charged further that Masonry was forbidden by the law of the empire which prohibited secret societies.[75]

There was no alternative, the prelate concluded; the Catholic affiliates of Masonry would have to abjure the society. Thereupon he laid down conditions to apply to all Catholics of his diocese:

1. By virtue of Our Episcopal Authority and in the fulfillment of our divine mission, we condemn and reprove the errors, heresies, and blasphemies which the impious press has spread in the midst of our dear Flock, especially a paper entitled — *Verdade* [Truth] — a Masonic organ, whose reading and subscription we prohibit *sub gravi* to all our much beloved brethren and children in Jesus Christ.

2. Let the Reverend Pastors exhaust all the resources of charity and exert all efforts to the end of enlightening and separating from the Masonic society those who have the unhappiness of belonging to it. But if the latter, in spite of charitable and repeated admonitions, should persist in their criminal obstinacy, let them be eliminated from the midst of the religious Brotherhoods and Confraternities; and let them suffer the consequences of major excommunication which they incur *ipso facto*.[76]

---

[74] ". . . e declarou formalmente que laboram em gravissimo erro os que pensam que o anathema fulminado contra essa seita *não tem valor nos paizes*, onde ella é tolerada pela autoridade civil . . ." *Ibid.*, p. 38.

[75] *Ibid.*, p. 39. Dom Vital refers to the law of October 20, 1823. On laws relative to secret societies, see p. 160, note 16, below.

[76] "1. Em virtude de Nossa Autoridade Episcopal e em desempenho da nossa missão divina, condemnamos e reprovamos os erros, heresias, e blasphemias que tem assoalhado no seio de nosso Rebanho querido a imprensa impia, especial-

This pastoral, a clear statement of Bishop Dom Vital's position relative to Freemasonry and an outright condemnation of the right of royal *placet*, had tremendous repercussions in governmental circles. It will become apparent that imperial statesmen were more influenced by the bishop's pastoral letter and his other pronouncements than by the recourse of the Brotherhood of the Most Holy Sacrament. The recourse was to a large degree the occasion, not the motivation of the subsequent action. In effect, when the president of the province of Pernambuco submitted the recourse to the imperial government, an inevitable crisis between Church and State moved from the smaller circle of the province to the larger circle of the empire.

---

mente um papel intitulado—*Verdade*—orgão maçonico, cuja leitura e assignatura prohibimos sub gravi a todos os nossos irmãos e filhos muito amados em Jesus Christo.

"2. Esgotem os Rvm. Parochos todos os recursos da caridade e envidem todos os esforços no intuito de esclarecer e arredar da sociedade maçonica aquelles que teem a infelicidade de ser nella iniciados. Mas se estes, á despeito de caridosas e repetidas admoestações permanecerem em sua criminosa obstinação, sejam eliminados do seio das Irmandades e Confrarias religiosas, e soffram as consequencias da excommunhão maior em que incorreram *ipso facto*."

# CHAPTER V

## THE IMPERIAL GOVERNMENT AND THE CONFLICT OVER FREEMASONRY

The Brotherhood of the Most Holy Sacrament, in its communication to the bishop, contended that Freemasonry was not condemned in Brazil, since the pontifical acts that anathematized it had never received the imperial *placet*. Catholics affiliated with Masonry were not, in its eyes, under excommunication; hence there was no basis for their expulsion from religious associations. This reasoning threw the burden of proof on the two authorities involved in the supervision of the brotherhood. As we have seen, the position of the spiritual authority was stated by Bishop Dom Vital in his pastoral of February 2, 1873, in which he maintained that Masonry in Brazil was under ecclesiastical censure, and was, moreover, condemned by the imperial law which prohibited secret societies. On the side of the temporal authority, therefore, rested the necessity either of disproving the bishop's assertions and thus sustaining the position of the brotherhood, or of acknowledging the truth of his assertions and forthwith demanding that the brotherhood obey the command of the ordinary.

Anyone following the case would expect the recourse presented by the brotherhood to have confined itself to the facts of the matter: that the bishop had ordered expelled a member who was affiliated with Masonry; that the brotherhood had failed to comply with the order because its charter did not provide for the expulsion of a member on such a charge; and that Vital, rejecting the reason given by the brotherhood and taking its failure to comply with his second order within the time allotted as a refusal to obey, had placed it under interdict. Actually, the brotherhood made its appeal the occasion not only of a long accusation against Dom Vital, but also of a revealing exposition of its philosophy.

Addressing itself to the emperor against the interdict of the bishop, the brotherhood asserted that "to judge by the facts," it could be affirmed that "excessive zeal for the doctrines of the Holy Roman Curia," and lack of understanding of the rights of the State, rights which apparently did not merit from the prelate "the least attention,"[1] prompted him to proceed against the Brotherhood of the Most Holy Sacrament of St. Anthony's parish in Recife. The bishop, the recourse continued, had created an alarm in society which might disturb public order and result in expelling from the Church a large number of the faithful. His acts indicated "the resurrection of ideas in great fashion during the Middle Ages, whose splendor was much augmented by ardent fire, [and] black prisons where it was vainly intended to incarcerate the forces of the spirit and the impulses of liberty."[2]

Articles in Catholic journals, the recourse said, had further aroused the apprehension of the people of Recife as to changes in public order that the bishop planned to provoke. According to the brotherhood, the clergy of the diocese held that the bishop had ascendancy over civil authority; that the civil laws ought not to be obeyed; and that supervision of the State in matters of religion, as insured by the right of royal *placet*, was condemned by the Church. "Teaching in this manner, surrounded by Jesuits and a blind and obedient clergy, certainly the Bishop

---

[1] *Relatório apresentado á Assembléa Geral na terceira sessão da decima quinta legislatura pelo Ministro e Secretario d'Estato dos Negocios do Imperio, Dr. João Alfredo Corrêa de Oliveira* (Rio de Janeiro, 1874), appendix D, "Requerimento da Irmandade do SS Sacramento da freguezia de Santo Antonio do Recife," p. 1. This work will hereafter be cited as *Relatório do Ministério dos Negócios do Império, 1874.*

[2] *Ibid.* "Assim, vai o Bispo produzindo um alarma na sociedade, com o qual póde trazer alteração na ordem publica, e expellir do seio da Igreja crescido numero de ovelhas, que veem transpirar de seus actos a resurreição das idéas tanto em voga na idade média, cujo brilho . . . se augmentava com o ardente fogo, negros carceres onde se pretendeu vãmente encarcerar os impetos do espirito e os impulsos da liberdade." The recourse continues, p. 2: "Esta pretenção exagerada do clero produziu tão terriveis scenas, que basta compulsar as paginas da historia da França, Hespanha e Portugal, para de horror se confranger o coração e não lastimar os esforços que devemos empregar contra sua anachronica volta, cuja existencia seria um escarneo e acommettimento impossivel, sómente capaz de originar lucta e conflictos no Estado."

of this diocese will have dominated within a little while all this society, or will have given occasion to grave conflicts that will bring to the State disorder, which ought to be avoided and prevented at all times."[3]

The recourse gave a description of the agitation in Recife when it was noised abroad that the bishop would forbid his priests to give spiritual aid to sick Catholics who refused to abjure their Masonic affiliations.[4] The residents of the provincial capital feared that the bishop was determined to act even more vigorously. In this, continued the recourse, they were not mistaken, as may be seen by the bishop's action in ordering the Brotherhood of the Most Holy Sacrament to expel Dr. Ribeiro "because he belonged to Masonry and was subject to major excommunication unless he abjured."[5] The recourse spoke of what had happened between the ordinary and the brotherhood up to the refusal of Vital to reconsider its case, and added:

> The petitioner [*i.e.*, the brotherhood] now solicits justice and protection from Your Imperial Majesty in accordance with Decree No. 1911 of March 28, 1857, article 1, sections 1 and 3.[6] It is proved that His Excellency ordered the expulsion of Dr. Antônio José da Costa Ribeiro from the Brotherhood, but the charter, the law which regulates the acts of the petitioner, nowhere authorize the dismissal of the brothers for such a motive; wherefore, speaking respectfully, the Bishop's order is against the law and criminal; wherefore the resistance to this criminal determination is a right expressly guaranteed in the Criminal Code, article 14, section 5,[7] and in the Political Constitution,

---

[3] *Ibid.*, p. 1.

[4] *Ibid.*, p. 2.

[5] *Ibid.*

[6] See p. 116, note 53, above.

[7] José Antônio de Araújo Filgueiras Júnior, *Codigo criminal do Imperio do Brasil annotado com os actos dos poderes legislativo, executivo, e judiciario que tem alterado e interpretado suas disposições desde que foi publicado, e com o calculo das penas em todas as suas applicações* (2d ed., Rio de Janeiro 1876), pp. 15-16. Art. 14. "Será o crime justificavel, e não terá lugar a punição delle . . . Sec. 5—Quando fôr feito em resistencia á execução de ordens illegaes, não se exedendo os meios necessarios para impedi-la."

article 179, section 1. But I am the Spiritual Head, His Excellency will say, and I have absolute power over any of the petitioner's charters, which I may alter and order revoked upon or without request, as it may please me (a thought already expressed in the writings cited); therefore my order should be faithfully executed. But the deficiency of that reasoning on which His Excellency bases his case is manifest.[8].

Having stated its position, the brotherhood proceeded to defend it. All persons resident in Brazil, the recourse stated, were bound by law; hence the exaggerated pretensions of the ordinary could not be sustained, nor could he lay claim to absolute power. Furthermore, the bishop might not alter the charter of the brotherhood without consulting the members, because the right of proposing alterations and modifications belonged to them. Moreover, when the spiritual aspect of the brotherhood was under consideration, not the ordinary but the judge of chapels had primacy of jurisdiction.[9] "It is therefore evident," according to the recourse, "that His Excellency usurped temporal

---

[8] "Neste intuito vem a recorrente solicitar justiça e protecção de v. m. imperial, firmado no decreto n. 1.911, de 28 de Março de 1857, artigo 1º ss. Iª e 3ª. Está provado que s. exa. revma. mandou expulsar da Irmandade o dr. Antonio José da Costa Ribeiro, mas o compromisso, lei reguladora dos actos da recorrente, não auctoriza em parte alguma a eliminação dos irmãos por tal motivo; logo, respeitosamente fallando, a órdem do bispo é contra a lei, e criminosa; logo a resistencia a esta criminosa determinação é um direito garantido expressamente no Codigo Criminal, artigo 14, s. 5ª, e Constituição Politica, artigo 179, s. 1ª. Mas, dira s. exa., sou chefe espiritual, e tenho o poder absoluto sobre todo o compromisso da recorrente, ao qual posso alterar, e mandar revogar, com ou sem proposta, como aprouver (pensamento ja emittido nos escriptos citados); portanto a minha ordem deve ser fielmente executada. Mas, a improcedencia desse raciocinio em que s. exa. se firma, é manifesta." *Relatório do Ministério dos Negócios do Império, 1874*, p. 2.

[9] *Ibid.*, p. 3. The recourse reads: "Ainda S. Exa., dominado pelo mais exagerado ultramontanismo, não considerou que, mandar eliminar um irmão da recorrente, por ser Maçon, além da não ser admittido pelo Compromisso, sua lei reguladora, era acto contrario á parte espiritual, que, por conseguinte, quér a recorrente obedecesse, quér resistisse, como fez, e é do seu dever, commetteu S. Ex. o excesso de jurisdicção temporal, chamando a si a de eliminar irmãos, que somente pertence á recorrente, com recurso para o temporal, ou o Juizo de Capellas, superior, nesta parte, da recorrente."

jurisdiction; that His Excellency issued orders against the law; that in consequence his sentence [*i.e.*, interdict] is null and unjust."[10]

In regard to the charges made by Vital against Dr. Costa Ribeiro, the recourse asserted that the laws of the Roman curia required the *placet* of the government before they could be executed in the empire. The *placet,* it added, was "a privilege of national sovereignty and a guarantee of public order against the invasions of Rome."[11] Since the bulls appealed to by the prelate had not received the *placet,* the brotherhood maintained, they were without value in the empire. With reference to the legality of secret societies, its petition alleged that the bishop was wrong in asserting that Freemasonry was condemned by the imperial law forbidding all secret societies.[12] The brotherhood appealed to article 34 of decree 2,711 of December 19, 1860, which gave legal existence to secret societies "that by their nature may not be deemed criminal."[13]

The recourse touched upon the nature of the interdict and the conditions accompanying its imposition. It protested that the bishop, while imposing the interdict on the Brotherhood of the Most Holy Sacrament, had not penalized other brotherhoods or required the expulsion of their members.[14] "Let it not be said

---

[10] *Ibid.*

[11] *Ibid.*

[12] See Dom Vital, *Carta Pastoral do Bispo de Olinda* (Recife, 1873), February 2, 1873, p. 39. "E' fóra de duvida, Irmãos e Filhos dilectissimos, que a maçonaria brasileira é uma sociedade secreta, em communhão com a da Europa, intrinsecamente má, inimiga da Religião Catholica, Apostolica, Romana; e por consequencia condemnada, não só pela Igreja, senão tambem pelas leis que nos regem, como bem se deprehende da Carta de Lei de 20 de Outubro do anno de 1823, segundo da nossa Independencia e do Imperio."

[13] *Relatório do Ministério dos Negócios do Império, 1874*, p. 3.

[14] *Ibid.*, p. 4. The recourse refers also to the case of Father Almeida Martins. "Si passa a recorrente dos actos de S. Ex. aos dos outros Bispos, vê que nem na Europa, nem no Brazil, houve algum Bispo que se lembrasse de fazer effectivas as Bullas contra a Maçonaria, e declarar sujeitos a excommunhão maior todos, a cada um dos Maçons. E ha bem pouco o Bispo da Côrte, tendo certeza de que o Padre Almeida Martins era Maçon, dirigiu-se a elle, e depois de algumas exhortações, suspendou-o unicamente da prédica e confissão; o que certamente é muito menos do que declarar excommungado, e

that the penalty is spiritual," the recourse continued, "and that Your Imperial Majesty is not qualified to render it void, because penalties and censures themselves, however spiritual they may be, are subject to the supervision of the State . . ."[15]

The recourse closed with an appeal to the emperor against the despotism of a foreign authority which bishops upheld at the expense of natural, civil, and canon law. The brotherhood expressed the hope that His Imperial Majesty would condescend to give attention to the appeal, and would declare "null, invalid, and without effect the sentence of the interdict."[16] In this manner, it declared, His Imperial Majesty "will encourage the belief that in this country reign liberty and progress, incompatible with the spirit and execution of bulls which have no longer any reason for being."[17]

Before entering officially into the controversy between the Brotherhood of the Most Holy Sacrament of Recife and Bishop Dom Vital, the imperial government tried to persuade the latter to recede from his position. On February 15, 1873, the minister of the interior, Councilor João Alfredo Corrêa de Oliveira, who was a kinsman of the bishop, wrote him a persuasive and friendly letter.

> Your Excellency will permit that I speak to you with the frankness which we owe to ourselves as friends and which the circumstances demand.
>
> I am much disturbed by the Masonic question and unhappily I see that the action of time has not modified it.
>
> I fear that the manifestations of resistance to the resolution which Your Excellency took may continue and may perturb public order in that province. I fear also that Your Excellency may be led by logic to extend to all the Brotherhoods the action which you

---

mandar eliminar de uma Irmandade, onde se têm beneficos espirituaes e temporaes."

[15] *Ibid.*
[16] *Ibid.*
[17] *Ibid.*

have already taken in the case of many of them, and when this happens, God knows what will be the result.

I foresee that Your Excellency will have against you almost all the people of Recife, encouraged by the adherences that are beginning to come from other provinces, and aroused to other means of opposition.

I respect the motives of conscience that Your Excellency has in order to carry out the actions that have raised so much furor, and I have the firmest desire of not finding myself in disagreement with Your Excellency, in measures which may be asked of me, and which I may have to take, but my position is most difficult, inasmuch as according to our law, bulls which do not receive the *placet* cannot be executed in the Empire.

I have heard the opinion of persons of integrity, of respected bishops and priests; they acknowledge that Your Excellency is acting in accordance with canon law, but they feel that the application could be different and even dispensed.

The newspapers have said that I am a Mason, and they do not speak the truth, because though I was initiated fifteen years ago, I appeared at only three or four sessions, and immediately thereafter I did what appears to me sufficient to tranquillize my conscience as a Catholic. I am not therefore suspect when I believe, as nearly everybody believes, that Masonry among us is innocent and even beneficial in certain respects.

Now societies which fall in this category, and which as a matter of fact include in their membership the most notable and influential people of the country, might well be dispensed from rigorous treatment, which rigor, without profiting religion, brings danger of effrontery and violence. These societies exist in all Catholic nations; they are tolerated by the State, and left in peace by the bishops in spite of the prohibition of the Church.

Our Constitution permits all religions with their domestic and private cults. Societies composed of foreigners are organized here, with religious ends different from ours, with the authorization of the civil power, and function freely.

When this happens, I do not see how the Government could prohibit Masonic societies, which are made up of Catholics, and which do not have ends that are contrary to the religion of the Empire, and even if this were true, work behind closed doors.

What Your Excellency says respecting the Brotherhoods is in part true, but since to the civil power belongs the right to legislate concerning their organization, and since they are governed by charters in which the two powers, temporal and spiritual, have some say, nearly all the persons whom I have consulted doubt, and many deny, that the act of Your Excellency, in demanding the elimination of the Masonic members, is legitimate.

The Imperial Government has not yet taken a stand; I have avoided doing it in regard to Your Excellency because of the great consideration which you deserve, and which I owe to the ecclesiastical authority; but I do not know how long I shall be able to avoid the intervention which is solicited, and which may be urgent and indispensable through circumstances.

In these conditions, and filled with true affliction, I come to beg Your Excellency to consider ways of not pushing the question and of moderating the opposition, until through the passage of time, through reflection, or by means of more opportune measures, the obligation of the government to avoid dangers to public order may cease, and Your Excellency may be offered opportunity of obtaining peacefully from your sheep, by means of the moral authority of the Church, the acceptance of your counsels and determinations. Time is a great remedy, and what in certain circumstances arouses general resistance and clamor, in others is done with great facility, with one act only, with one word.

I speak to Your Excellency as an obedient son, as a devoted friend; and believe in my purest sentiments; it is driven by them that I address to you the unalter-

able supplication of this letter, and I entrust its effi-
cacy to the prudence and patriotism of Your Excellency.[18]

The graciousness that characterized this letter from the imperial minister was reflected in Vital's reply, written in Recife,
February 27, 1873. The young prelate, however, impressed
upon the imperial minister that as a bishop he could not adopt
the temporizing policy proposed in the letter. In the face of the
challenge of Freemasonry, Dom Vital believed that silence on his
part would be detrimental to the interests of the Church.

> I hasten to respond to the letter of Your Excellency
> dated the 15th of the current month. Thanking Your
> Excellency from the bottom of my heart for the
> frankness and courtesy with which Your Excellency
> was kind enough to write to me, I beg leave of Your
> Excellency to present to you, with equal sincerity and
> openness of heart, some brief reflections, mostly with
> the end in view of making plain to Your Excellency
> my sentiments rather than to plead the cause itself.

> Never did I remain in doubt over the obstacles and
> serious difficulties in which the Masonic question was
> going to place Your Excellency. I understood them
> and measured them, as soon as I realized the circum-
> stance that Your Excellency, being a Catholic, was a
> member of a Ministry whose president is the grand
> master of one of the Masonic groups of the Empire.
> Beforehand, I felt profoundly and vividly the trials
> which Your Excellency would experience. But what
> to do in the face of duty?

> Since I arrived here, Excellency, Masonry has of-
> fered me a terrible dilemma: either to accept the fight,
> fulfilling the duties of a Catholic bishop and passing
> for *imprudent, precipitous, and rash*, which is very
> consistent with my years; or else to close my eyes to
> everything, compromise my conscience, resign myself
> to being a negligent, pusillanimous, and culpable bish-
> op (this was confessed by the Masons themselves).

---

[18] For the original of this letter see Appendix B, pp. 258-259.

I had inevitably to admit one of the two principles, and thereby direct the course of my Episcopacy.

As long as it was possible, without culpability before God, I declined to declare myself. But finally I saw myself in the hard necessity of making a choice, and I did not hesitate in choosing the first part of the dilemma, as was my obligation.

Even if I were an octogenarian bishop, having only a few days of life, I would not betray the duties of my mission; much less would I do it now when I probably still have a long pilgrimage to make.

What a terrible perspective, Excellency, that of a long Episcopacy, inglorious and criminal before God, even though glorious in the eyes of men through condescension and laxity!

Besides, I am certain that Your Excellency, in countersigning the decree of my nomination, was persuaded that the chosen one would be a Catholic bishop, who would comply with his duties, without which, certainly, you would not have done it.

If Masonry had contented itself with working in its lodges *behind closed doors*, as Your Excellency says, nothing would have happened. But, in order to provoke the diocesan prelate, it founded a periodical; it began to attack, to insult, and to deny the dogmas of our Holy Religion, as I prove in my Pastoral of February 2, with irrefragable documents; it showed itself with its vizor up, publishing the names of its adepts, taking the Church to task, and forming in the bosom of the Brotherhoods governing boards in the Masonic fashion.

I did not disturb the Masons in their work shops, Excellency, I did not leave the confines of the Church, of which I am head. I do not dispute directly with the Masons but rather with the Brotherhoods. I do not aim at exterminating Masonry; unhappily not even monarchs themselves are able to do it today; only God. I wish only that the Brotherhoods achieve the end for which they were created. Meanwhile, it appears to me that Masonry ought to be a little more consistent. Seeing that it does not recognize the authority of the Church, let it shout much even against the Church, but leave her alone, leave her to those who are proud of being her obedient children.

It is true, Excellency, that the Brotherhoods are ruled by charters approved by the two powers, temporal and spiritual; however, what confers on them [their] religious character is only the sanction of the latter, without which, as all well know, they are not more than mere civil societies. And, Your Excellency will pardon me the frankness of saying to you that, in the religious side, the temporal power is not a competent judge.

I beg leave not to say anything to Your Excellency about the opinion of *bishops and priests* who judge the *application* of the bulls condemning Masonry *dispensable.*

In spite of the denial of the *placet,* Masonry is really condemned among us for many reasons, which I shall be able to explain on another occasion, if Your Excellency should then consider it convenient. For the time being, I limit myself to saying to Your Excellency that in the Allocution of September 25, 1865, the Holy Father declared Masonry formally condemned *even in countries in which it is tolerated by the secular authority.* And this is enough for the Catholic.

Masonry, Excellency, has moved heaven and earth, it has made protests and appeals, it has finally invoked all means to deprive me of my office [*desauctorar-me*]. I, on the contrary, even though I have received many acts of adherence, with the signatures of thousands of lay people, and have the best people of this city in my favor, until the present have kept silent, confident of the justice of the cause that I defend and of the religious sentiments of Your Excellency. But I am beginning to see that this silence is prejudicial to the cause of the Church.

The letter of Your Excellency allows me to perceive, unless I have not comprehended it duly, that if I continue in the resolution taken, perhaps the decision of the Imperial Government might be unfavorable to me.

It is difficult for me to believe, Excellency, that the same hand that, so short a time ago, signed the decree of my nomination, may now write the sentence of my degradation. Still, if such happens, I entreat Your Excellency earnestly as a good friend, to write instead my decree of imprisonment and of ostracism, because the support lent to Masonry by the Imperial Government, not making me yield in any manner, shall infallibly occasion lamentable conflicts.

Your Excellency understands that this question is one of life or death for the Brazilian Church; it behooves me rather to support [it] with the greatest sacrifices than to relax. I shall proceed always with much calmness, prudence, and leisure; however, to yield or not to go forward is impossible. I do not see the middle way. If Your Excellency foresees that you are not able to support me, and that my resistance is going to give place to sad scenes, let us silence the tempest while there is time. And for that I know only one means: let the Imperial Government ask the Holy See to send me to my convent as soon as possible. However, this measure little helps the Government. If I were a politician or older in years, I would say that serious disturbances of the public order are imminent in almost all of Brazil, and are inevitable, in spite of the greatest prudence; the reason I keep to myself in order to say it to Your Excellency personally when I shall have occasion.

I ask Your Excellency not to be surprised at my excessive frankness. On the present occasion, I do not write to His Excellency, the Minister of the Empire, I write *confidentially* to a friend, and to a friend one tells the whole truth, without dissimulation. In a question of this range and magnitude, all frankness between friends is not too much.

I am not discouraged; on the contrary, after divine help, I expect much of the friendship and of the religious sentiments of Your Excellency.[19]

From these letters it is apparent that both men regretted the impending controversy between Church and State; yet as rep-

---

[19] For the original of this letter see Appendix B, pp. 259-262.

resentatives of the spiritual and temporal interests of the empire, neither saw his way clear to withdraw. The imperial government felt that it could not allow the prelate to disregard its supervisory capacity relative to the religion of the State, for it regarded such a concession as tantamount to acknowledging the absolute authority of the Roman Pontiff. The bishop, challenged by Masonry, could not ignore its threat to the Catholic Church in Brazil, and could not permit Freemasons to continue to claim the privileges of Roman Catholics. As the American minister to Brazil said in a report to the secretary of state: "No sooner . . . had the State entered the field than positions were taken by it and the church from which neither could retire consistently and without loss of power."[20]

When he realized that he had failed to move Dom Vital, the imperial minister turned to the internuncio, Archbishop Domenico Sanguigni, who was an intimate friend of his as well as of the prime minister, the viscount of Rio Branco. He persuaded Sanguigni to write to the bishop of Olinda. In his letter from Petrópolis, dated February 11, 1873, the internuncio showed the stand he might be expected to take in the approaching conflict between Church and State in Brazil.

> After my letter in reply to the most esteemed one of Your Excellency of January 1st last, relative to the bomb which you caused to explode, it was most agreeable to me to see that matters took a better course. The favorable behavior of the Clergy, and of all those who maintain in their conscience the principles of religion and of justice, is comforting indeed.
>
> Even so, much prudence, a very great deal of moderation and patience is still required, inasmuch as the matter in itself is delicate and all hell contrives with the whole world to maneuver against good.
>
> Here we have worked and do work with all diligence. Besides His Excellency, the Minister, there are quite a number of deputies and of important persons

---

[20] National Archives, Department of State, Purrington to Fish, No. 288. September 30, 1875.

interested in the matter. All this, however, greatly needs the help of divine Providence.

With this said, an idea comes to me, which I pass on to you in the hope that you, through your great penetration, will find it convenient, and for this reason, you will not fail to adopt it. Here is the idea.

The measure we speak about has already had its execution, produced its effects, and the brothers (Masons) have directed complaints and reclamations to the Chambers.

What now appears to me useful is that Your Excellency select some place you know best in your diocese, and, taking in your company some trusted priests, go there in order to make and to begin the pastoral visitation. The Most Reverend Vicar General, who is already experienced, could remain in charge of the government of the diocese.

This resolution would have three advantages: 1. You would fulfill a part of your episcopal duty; 2. You would be received, I am certain, in veritable triumph, and this fact would increase all of your moral force; 3. You would allow the enemies and the incredulous to be consumed among themselves, and cool off in the void.

When Your Excellency should find inconvenience in the nearness of Lent, hearing in mind the law of Residence, I hereby grant you the competent authorization and dispensation, being able to return to your cathedral to perform the functions of Holy Week. And in the event of your verifying the utility and profit of this diversion, you could continue the visitation once more.

I also foresaw another obstacle, the necessity of taking with you some money on the occasion of the visitation, not only to succor the poor, but also for other extraordinary occurrences. And since I had a long conference with His Excellency, the Minister, on this matter, I find myself in the position of giving you assurance that *he is also ready to help you with money.*

This is my thought, and these are the measures
which facilitate it with all convenience and decorum,
and I hope that you will adopt it without much delay.[21]

Dom Vital's reply,[22] marked "confidential," is deferential and
courteous.

I hasten to reply to the fine letter of Your Excellency dated the 11th of the current month.

I do not find the words in which to thank you for
the interest Your Excellency has taken in this question which is vital for the Brazilian Church, whose
future, if impiety should now take the palm, will be
deplorable and most sad.

Excellency. I pondered and weighed much the idea
which Your Excellency had the kindness to communicate to me in regard to the pastoral visitation, and I
found it in fact excellent, but unachievable at the present time. [if] Your Excellency will permit me to say
so with candor. Its execution in the present circumstances would produce an effect diametrically opposed
to what Your Excellency proposes. The enemies of
the Church, Excellency, have tried to have me go
away from here, even though it might be only to
Olinda, in order to claim victory. It is just what they
want.

From the reading of the letter of Your Excellency,
I gathered that Your Excellency supposes me without
moral support. No, Excellency, there is no such thing.
Happily I have on my side a large party composed of
the best people, in the capital as out of it. Acts of
adherence with thousands of signatures arrive every

---

[21] For the original of this letter see Appendix B, pp. 262-263.

[22] Castro, p. 488, writes: "A reposta de D. Vital foi em tudo digna de um
Brasileiro e de um Franciscano: apparentando não ter percebido o insulto,
recusou altivamente o dinheiro para o seu uso pessoal, porque como pobre
Capuchinho com pouco se contentava, e os seus parochianos não lhe deixariam
fazer um real de despesa; mas mandou pedir ao ministro que applicasse essa
quantia, que lhe era destinada ao acabamento e mobiliamento do Seminario
pequeno."

day from lay people; I go out every day, travel over the most populous and most frequented streets of the city, and, thanks be to God, have not yet received the slightest insult; on the contrary, everyone greets me. I would remain without moral force if I were to give in now. It seems to me that news arrives there much adulterated. What can one do about it? Many of those who through justice and charity should help the prelate are the ones who seek to embarrass and to compromise him more. It is hard to believe; yet it is the pure truth, Excellency.

I am entirely aware of the necessity of a pastoral visitation in the diocese. And I believe, Excellency, that, after the reform and after the foundation of the two Seminaries, it is the idea that preoccupies me most. But I am obliged to defer it until August:

1. because I am taking care of the minor Seminary, whose interests cannot dispense with my presence; 2. because the Theological Seminary is about to be opened, and, having made some changes, I ought to be present in order to see how things run; 3. because not all of the brotherhoods have replied and because their manner of working varies at each moment, not only does my presence in the capital become absolutely necessary, but much attention on my part is required as well.

For these reasons I regret very much not being able to utilize the faculties which Your Excellency was kind enough to grant me, and I thank you exceedingly for the pecuniary assistance which you offered me on behalf of the Minister of the Empire.

Even though, Excellency, I had to leave now on a visitation, I would dispense with it; because, having made a vow of poverty, I have accustomed myself to distribute to the poor in the manner of the poor what is not absolutely necessary to me. A Capuchin, I content myself with little, and my people would not allow me to make the least expenditure. Still, since His Excellency, the Minister, finds himself so well disposed towards the Church of Jesus Christ and towards this unfortunate diocese, Your Excellency will have the kindness of asking him the favor of applying the amount which he had set aside for me to the finishing and furnishing of the minor Seminary, which has the greatest need, and of supporting my action: this is the greatest service which he can give my diocese and the Church.

Now another thing.

The Masons here, Excellency, have danced with pleasure ever since the steamer of the 22nd arrived; because, they say, the Imperial Government gave them a favorable verdict, and Your Excellency and the Minister of the Empire reprimanded me. They say further that a well-informed person (they even give a name which we both know) communicated to them from the Court that Your Excellency, in accordance with the Minister, wants to oblige me to give in.

Poor things! How they deceive themselves.

They are ignorant of the fact that Your Excellency, besides being the most worthy delegate of the immortal Pius IX, who condemned Masonry so many times, made me swear before my confirmation that I had never been a Mason, that I always condemned the heretical Masonic doctrines, and that against them I would guard the sheep confided to my vigilance.

They are convinced that Your Excellency not only disapproved my action, but even reprimanded me bitterly.

Leave them in their sweet illusion. And I shall go my way, traveling with prudence and leisure as Your Excellency recommends, but at the same time disposed to die a thousand times, if it were possible, rather than give up a single one [of my flock], unless the vicar of Jesus Christ commands me, which is neither probable nor even admissible.

Imploring pardon from Your Excellency for not being able at the present time to put into practice the good counsel of Your Excellency, I ask you to deign to remember in your prayers one who has much need of them . . . .[23]

---

[23] For the original of this letter see Appendix B, pp. 263-265.

The position taken by the bishop of Olinda against the brotherhoods with Freemasons among their members, aroused the bishop of Pará, Dom Antônio de Macedo Costa,[24] to take a similar stand. On the Feast of the Annunciation (March 25), 1873, Dom Antônio issued a pastoral to the clergy and laity of his diocese, in which he considered Masonry under its moral, religious, and social aspects.[25] This pastoral was open in its condemnation of Freemasonry, and since it substantiated all claims with full documentation, there could be little doubt that it would provoke a whirlwind of opposition. The bishop knew the reaction that would follow upon his pronouncement; indeed, he called attention in his letter to the fact that the former bishop of Pará, Dom Romualdo de Sousa Coelho, had incurred the violent opposition of the Masons when he attempted to warn his people against them.[26] Dom Antônio condemned the Masonic journal *Pelicano*, and prohibited the faithful from reading it. He laid down a number of regulations regarding the participation of former Masons in certain religious functions and the conferring of certain sacraments on them. He closed his pastoral with an ultimatum to the brotherhoods:

> Only Masons who declare in writing that they no longer wish to belong to Masonry shall continue to be members of the confraternities and brotherhoods. If, after charitable admonition by our Reverend Vicar General and formal summons, there shall be any con-

---

[24] The bishop of Pará, Dom Antônio de Macedo Costa, was recognized as one of the foremost intellectual leaders of his time. See Castro, pp. 480-481.

[25] D. Antônio de Macedo Costa, *A Maçonaria em opposição á moral, á Igreja e ao estado pastoral de S. Exc. Revm. o Sr. D. Antonio de Macedo Costa, Bispo do Pará* (Recife, 1875).

[26] *Ibid.*, p. 69. D. Antônio says that Dom Romualdo "teve a insigne honra de ser, em seus velhos dias, perseguido, ameaçado e ultrajado pela Maçonaria . . ." The prelate gives the following citation (*ibid.*, note 130) to corroborate his assertion that the efforts of his predecessor to fight Masonry were violently opposed: "O orgão da Maçonaria no Pará ousou collocar o Sr. D. Romualdo entre *os jesuitas petroleiros da humanidade, que arrastaram a sociedade á scenas lutuosas de 1835 por Pastoraes incendiarias e doutrinas subversivas da ordem publica.* Veja-se *Pelicano*, artigo edictorial, n° 65."

fraternity, which we do not presume, that revolts against the order of the Diocesan Prelate, and refuses to obey, it shall be notified that all of its religious functions are suspended until full compliance with Our Order; the Chapel or Church that may be under the jurisdiction of the said confraternity remaining interdicted as long as its [the confraternity's] rebellion shall continue.[27]

When the vicar general, Monsignor Sebastião Borges de Castilho, followed the bishop's instructions and admonished the brotherhoods among whose members were affiliates of Masonry, some of these associations refused to submit. Accordingly five religious associations were suspended.[28] Dom Antônio found himself in a situation identical with that of Dom Vital. One of the dissident brotherhoods interposed a recourse to the crown; the decision of the imperial government in this case was the same as for the Brotherhood of the Most Holy Sacrament of Recife,[29] and therefore what is said of one diocese can be applied with equal accuracy to the other.

When the recourse of the Brotherhood of the Most Holy

---

[27] "Só continuarão a fazer parte das confrarias e irmandades os maçons que declararem por escipto não quererem mais pertencer á Maçonaria. Se depois de caridosa admoestação feita pelo nosso Rvd.Vigario Geral, e formal intimação houver alguma confraria, o que não presumimos, que se revolte contra a ordem do Prelado Diocesano, e recuse obedecer, ser-lhe-ha notificada suspensão de todas suas funcções religiosas, até inteiro cumprimento da Nossa Ordem; ficando interdicta a Capella ou Igreja que estiver debaixo da administração da dita confraria emquanto permanecer a sua rebellião." Ibid., p. 72.

[28] Ordem Terceira de Nossa Senhora do Carmo, Ordem Terceira de S. Francisco, Irmandades do Senhor dos Navegantes, Irmandades [do Senhor Bom Jesus] dos Passos, and Irmandade do S. S. Sacramento de Sant'Ana. See Castro, p. 481.

[29] Relatório do Ministério dos Negócios do Império, 1874, pp. 95-102, "Consulta da Secção dos Negocios do Imperio do Conselho d'estado sobre o recurso á Corôa interposto pela Mesa regedora da veneravel Ordem terceira de Nossa Senhora do Monte do Carmo da capital da provincia do Pará, contra o acto do respectivo Prelado diocesano, que a impediu de exercer suas funcções religiosas." For the report of the committee on the Recourses of other brotherhoods see ibid., pp. 102-104, 104-109. For the decisions of the Council of State see ibid., pp. 109-113.

Sacrament of Recife[30] was presented to the imperial government, the emperor, acting through the minister of state, João Alfredo Corrêa de Oliveira, ordered the committee on internal affairs (*Secção dos Negócios do Império*) of the Council of State to investigate the matter.[31] This committee performed a three-fold task: it solved preliminary technical problems concerning the validity of admitting the recourse; it investigated the soundness of the brotherhood's claims; and it determined whether or not the recourse of the brotherhood should be accepted.[32]

The technical problems were three in number. First, the law provided that a recourse to the crown should be made within ten days after the alleged violation of rights occurred. Actually, twenty days had expired since the bishop had interdicted the brotherhood. In spite of this technical flaw, the committee, after appealing to legal authorities, accepted the recourse. The primary reason cited for waiving the ten-day stipulation was that there was no time limit against abuse. The members of the committee concurred in the decision that the brotherhood had been the victim of abuse; therefore, its delayed recourse was pronounced valid. Secondly, imperial law decreed that to be valid recourse had to be signed by the attorney for the Council of State, but the one in question did not bear this signature. In resolving this difficulty, the committee thought that the omission should be treated as a simple irregularity which the government could overlook if it chose, precedent having already been established for such procedure, provided that this decision was not detrimental to the rights of either party.[33] Finally, the law stipulated that in the event of an alleged instance of notorious vio-

---

[30] It will be recalled that the brotherhood had claimed the right to interpose a recourse to the crown on the basis of decree No. 1.911 of March 28, 1857. The brotherhood alleged that Dom Vital had violated art. 1, sec. 1 and 3. See p. 125 above.

[31] The committee was composed of the following members of the Council of State: the viscount of Bom Retiro, the marquis of Sapucaí, and the viscount of Sousa Franco.

[32] The deliberations of the committee are given in full in *Relatório do Ministério dos Negócios do Império, 1874*, pp. 17-39, under date of May, 1873.

[33] *Relatório do Ministério dos Negócios do Império, 1874*, p. 23.

lence in the exercise of spiritual jurisdiction, the victim of such violence had to apply for redress to the competent ecclesiastical superior, if there was such a person.[34] While admitting that the metropolitan of Brazil, the archbishop of Baía, was Dom Vital's superior, the committee agreed that this technicality could be dispensed in the present instance because in the case of ecclesiastical censures the archbishop could lift only a penalty which he himself had placed; hence his competence in this instance was in doubt. Furthermore, the very seriousness of this particular situation, according to the members of the committee, made a governmental investigation imperative.[35]

In determining the merits of the recourse, the committee established the following principles: 1) No papal bull could be executed in Brazil unless it had received the imperial *placet*. But the bulls which excommunicated Freemasons had never received the imperial *placet*; therefore, the bishop, in applying the penalty of excommunication to the members of Masonic societies, acted in excess of his jurisdiction; hence his act, according to Brazilian law, was without effect. 2) Since the brotherhoods had a dual character, they depended exclusively on the bishop only in their religious aspect; after the approval of their charters, they were in everything else subject to the temporal power, which, through the judge of chapels, exercised the right of inspection. The bishop, therefore, in ordering the exclusion of brothers for a cause not established in the charter, invaded the temporal power; he gave an illegal command which the broth-

---

[34] *Collecção das leis do Imperio do Brasil de 1857*, XVIII (Rio de Janeiro, 1857), i, 104. "Decreto n. 1.911 de Março de 1857: Art. 7—Não será porém admittido o Recurso á Corôa, no caso do Art. 1 paragrapho 3, se não quando não houver ou não for provido o Recurso, que competir para o Superior ecclesiastico." For art. 1 see p. 116, note 53, above.

[35] *Relatório do Ministério dos Negócios do Império, 1874*, p. 24. ". . . além de que, no tocante a censuras, os Metropolitanos só podem absolver as que lhes são reservadas, e neste caso a sua competencia seria posta em duvida, domina o presente recurso a circumstancia mui poderosa de se acharem os factos praticados pelo Rev. Bispo da Sé de Olinda contra a Irmandade, por tal fórma ligados entre si, que o Governo Imperial, tendo de tomar conhecimento de um, não póde deixar de entender ao mesmo tempo com o outro, e de providenciar sobre ambos, si achar procedente o recurso."

erhood ought not to obey. 3) The bishop, in denying the legitimacy of the *placet*, and in "declaring it monstrous, an heretical, false, and pernicious doctrine,"[36] was insubordinate to the law of the State; hence his procedure deserved to be disapproved, to avoid establishing a precedent.

The committee arrived at these conclusions: 1) The bulls anathematizing Freemasonry and excommunicating the members of Masonic societies could not be applied in Brazil because they had never received the required imperial *placet*. Even if this formality could be dispensed with, the order of the bishop would be invalid, because Masonry could not be construed to be a religious society. Neither could it be shown to be in any way conspiring against the Catholic religion. The bishop, therefore, went beyond the established limits of his authority in the pastoral,[37] and in his action after the pastoral was issued.[38] 2) Since the organic constitutions of religious societies in Brazil were within the competence of the civil power, and came under the supervision of the diocesan prelate only as regards the approval and the supervision of the religious part, it was not within the jurisdiction of the bishop of Olinda to order the brotherhood to expel any member because he belonged to Freemasonry. This being the case, the bishop could not cite disobedience on the part of the brotherhood as a reason for placing it under interdict. He could not, moreover, comprehend the whole corporation within the interdict. By going beyond his jurisdiction, the bishop invaded the jurisdiction of the temporal power. 3) The prelate exceeded likewise the limits of his authority when, in his pastoral of February 2, he condemned the doctrine of the

---

[36] *Ibid.*, p. 35.

[37] The pastoral letter issued by Dom Vital was among the documents appended to the recourse of the Brotherhood of the Most Holy Sacrament. See *Relatório . . . 1874*, pp. 3-16; *Collecção . . . 1857*, p. 105; decree no. 1911 of March 28, 1857, art. 21: "O Recurso será instruido com os documentos e inquirições que a Autoridade, o Juiz Ecclesiastico, Procurador da Coroa, Presidente de Provincia, e Ministro da Justiça acharem convenientes para a decisão da questão."

[38] This refers to Bishop Dom Vital's repudiation of the right of recourse. See p. 116 above.

*placet*, which had been recognized even prior to independence, and which after independence was confirmed by the imperial constitution. He likewise overstepped his authority in his letter of February 20, 1873, when he attacked the legitimacy of recourse to the crown. The right of recourse, rooted in laws existent from the remotest times of the Portuguese monarchy, was always applicable in Brazil, and was formally recognized after independence. 4) The committee maintained, finally, that since these acts of the bishop had been fully proved, and since they were covered by paragraphs 1 and 3 of article 1 of decree 1.911 of March 28, 1857, the crown should give attention to the recourse.

Before taking action against the prelate, the emperor ordered the entire Council of State[39] to consider the report of the committee. Besides giving its opinion on the four conclusions reached by the committee, the Council had an additional problem to solve. In the event that it concurred in the decision of the committee, and in the event that the bishop refused to comply with its order to raise the interdict, what action would it take against him?[40] The viscount of Abaeté, who opened the discussion,

---

[39] The Council met on June 3, 1873, at the Palace of São Cristóvão. Its deliberations and decisions are given in full in the *Relatório* . . . *1874*, pp. 40-63, "Consulta do conselho d'Estado pleno sobre o recurso . . ."

[40] *Collecção* . . . . *de 1857*, XVIII, i, 103-105; decree 1911 of March 28, 1857. Art. 24: "Se não obstante, o Juiz ou Autoridade Ecclesiastica não quizer cumprir a Imperial Resolução, será ella como sentença judicial pelo Juiz de Direito da Comarca, que procederá como determinão os Artigos 13 e 14 do Decreto de 19 de Fevereiro de 1838 o qual só nesta parte fica em vigor." "Artigos do Regulamento Nº 10 de 19 de Fevereiro de 1838, aos quaes se refere o Decreto nº 1.911 de 28 de Março de 1857." Art. 13— "Cabe nos limites de jurisdicção dos Juizes de Direito, a respeito do cumprimento das sentenças mencionadas, declarar na fórma dellas, sem algum effeito as censuras, e penas Ecclesiasticas que tiverem sido impostas aos recorrentes, prohibindo e obstando a que a pretexto dellas se lhes faça qualquer violencia, ou cause prejuizo pessoal ou real; mettendo-os de posse de quaesquer direitos e prerogativas, ou redditos, de que houverem sido privados; e procedendo e responsabilisando na fórma da Lei os desobedientes, e que recursarem a execução." Art. 14—"No caso de serem precisas as providencias do Juiz de Direito, na fórma do Artigo antecedente, além das intimações que se fizeram

disagreed with the first conclusion of the committee. He contended that pontifical acts condemning Freemasonry were applicable in Brazil when they had not received the imperial *placet*. A contrary opinion, he maintained, would be founded on the doctrine of an unlimited right of imperial *placet*; such a doctrine was the product of Protestantism and tended, as in England, toward the inauguration of the spiritual supremacy of the monarch. Abaeté was of the opinion that the constitutional clause authorizing the right of imperial *placet*[41] was subordinate to the constitutional clause establishing Roman Catholicism as the religion of the empire.[42] The *placet*, he concluded, could not comprehend the conciliar and pontifical acts that referred to dogmas or to discipline, neither could the refusal of the imperial government to approve such acts exempt the faithful from obedience to them. According to the precepts of the Catholic religion, these matters belong to the Church. Correlatively, then, in conformity with the precepts of the Constitution that established Roman Catholicism as the religion of the empire, these matters were under the jurisdiction of the Church and could be handled only by her. The viscount of Abaeté believed that the temporal power, by the very act of prohibiting secret societies in Portugal and in Brazil, and of declaring them criminal, granted tacit approval to the pontifical bulls condemning Masonic societies, which are secret.[43] Abaeté's argument was not acceptable to most members of the Council.

The *placet*, declared the marquis of São Vicente, who was next to speak, was indispensable both to the independence of the State and to the maintenance of law and public security. He repudiated the arguments of Abaeté. Brazil, he asserted, was not obliged to abrogate the prerogative of sovereignty in order to be Roman Catholic. The viscount of Jaguari and the viscount of Niterói held that the *placet* was limited to temporal interests, hence not applicable to ecclesiastical censures. The remaining

---

aos Juizes e Autoridades Ecclesiasticas, se annunciará tudo por Editaes nos lugares publicos da Comarca." *Ibid.*, p. 106.

[41] Article 102, section 14.

[42] Article 5.

[43] *Relatório do Ministério dos Negócios do Império, 1874*, pp. 40-41.

eight members of the Council upheld without qualification the right of imperial *placet.* Nabuco de Araújo observed that the words of the constitution — the Holy Roman Catholic Apostolic religion *will continue* to be that of the empire — precluded any of the new papal and conciliar pronouncements.[44] "If the *jus cavendi*," he observed, "was heretofore necessary in order to guarantee the rights of the State as regards the invasions of the Church into the temporal domains, today it is more than ever necessary after the *Syllabus* and after the Vatican Council which declared the infallibility of the pope."[45]

Regarding the second conclusion of the committee's report, the viscount of Abaeté agreed that Masonry in Brazil did not constitute a religion; it was, he said, atheistic. He rejected the statement that Masonic societies did not conspire against the Catholic religion. The committee, said the councilor, apparently believed that the Masonic Societies might justly be condemned by pontifical bulls, should it be proved that they did conspire against the Catholic religion. The viscount of Sousa Franco challenged Abaeté's statement that Masonic societies were atheistic,[46] but even if they were, the bishop, he maintained, could not act against the Masonic members of the brotherhoods without invading the sphere of the temporal authority. Sousa Franco disapproved also of the dogma of infallibility and condemned unlimited obedience to the Church in ecclesiastical matters. "No councilor of state, no bishop, and no Brazilian," he added, "is able to subject himself to obedience, direct or indirect,

---

[44] *Ibid.,* p. 49. "O art. 5 da Constituição do Imperio não diz que a Religião catholica apostolica romana será a Religião do Estado, mas que - continuará a ser a Religião do Estado. Esta palavra - continuará - mostra bem que a Religião do Estado seria como até ahi era, isto é, como era a Religião lusitana ao tempo da Constituição, isto é, a Religião catholica com seus dogmas, com os canones recebidos, com as leis portuguezas respectivas."

[45] *Ibid.*

[46] *Ibid.,* p. 46. Sousa Franco said that a Mason could be a good Catholic, but he added: "Não o digo por conhecimento proprio actual, porque, desde que deixei a Academia de Olinda em 1835, nunca mais entrei em loja maçonica nem fiz em nem-uma visita publica ou particular. O meu tempo tem-me sido preciso para outras occupações, e não me tem chegado para frequentar sociedades."

to the Supreme Pontiff without violating Article 1 of the Constitution of the Empire,[47] and without incurring in some degree the penalties of Articles 79, 80, or 81[48] of the criminal code."[49] The viscount of Jaguari said that he was convinced that Freemasons in Brazil were not conspiring against the Catholic religion; he had known many Freemasons who were estimable men, but he added, "we are not dealing with persons, we are dealing with the institution, and it has been condemned by the Supreme Pontiffs."[50] This condemnation, Jaguari held, was enough for Catholics. A person cannot be a member of the Church, he added, without recognizing the supremacy of the Sovereign Pontiff. "Neither should it be said," he contended, "that by this, liberty of conscience is offended. Anyone is permitted to be and to cease to be a Catholic when he chooses, but it is not licit for him to be a Catholic in his own way; he must be one in accordance with the prescriptions of the Church."[51] The other councilors agreed with the committee that Freemasonry was not conspiring against the Catholic religion and that the bishop had no right to order the brotherhood to dismiss a member because he was a Freemason.

The councilors turned next to a consideration of whether or not the bishop in denying the legitimacy of the imperial *placet* and of recourse to the crown had been insubordinate to the civil authority. Abaeté, Muritiba, and Jaguari held that this consideration was irrelevant. The bishop had denied the legitimacy

---

[47] *Constituição politica do imperio do Brazil*, article 1. "O imperio do Brasil he a associação politica de todos os Cidadãos Brasileiros. Elles formão huma Nação livre, e independente, que não admitte com qualquer outro laço algum de união, ou federação, que se opponha á sua Independencia."

[48] Filgueiras, *op. cit.*, pp. 78-79. Art. 79—"Reconhecer, o que for cidadão brasileiro, superior fóra do Imperio, prestando-lhe effectiva obediencia." Art. 80—"Si este crime fôr commettido por corporação será esta dissolvida; e si os seus membros se tornarem a reunir debaixo da mesma, ou de diversa denominação, com a mesma ou diversas regras." Art. 81—"Recorrer á autoridade estrangeira residente dentro ou fóra do Imperio, sem legitima licença, para impetração de graças espirituaes, distincções ou privilegios na jerarchia ecclesiastica, ou para autorização de qualquer acto religioso."

[49] *Relatório do Ministério dos Negócios do Império, 1874*, p. 47.

[50] *Ibid.*, p. 57.

[51] *Ibid.*

of these imperial prerogatives in his pastoral of February 2, which had no connection with the complaint of the brotherhood, the matter now under discussion. The remaining members of the Council accepted the conclusion of the committee that the bishop was challenging imperial prerogatives when he denied the validity of the *placet* and of the recourse to the crown, and should be made answerable for his assertions even though they were not directly connected with the petition which was under consideration.

The Council next discussed whether or not the recourse of the brotherhoods should be accepted and what should be done if the crown did accept it and the bishop refused compliance. Logical to the end, the viscount of Abaeté said that since he had rejected the first three conclusions of the committee, he could not support this final proposition, that the crown give attention to the recourse. He added, however, that he would advocate coercive measures if, once the recourse was accepted, the bishop refused compliance. The marquis of São Vicente believed that the recourse should be accepted. As to what ought to be done in the event that the bishop proved recalcitrant, São Vicente was not sure; circumstances would have to be considered. He would favor the old penalties of forfeiture of citizenship and, if necessary, deportation, but since these penalties were no longer in force, he presumed that the prelate would have to be turned over to a competent tribunal. The viscount of Sousa Franco favored a defense of the brotherhood by the crown. Should the bishop refuse to comply with the decision of the crown, he maintained that Dom Vital, as a public official, would incur the penalties of articles 129, 139, and 146 of the criminal code.[52]

---

[52] Filgueiras, *op. cit.*, pp. 139-140, 154, 159. Art. 129—"Serão julgados prevaricadores os empregados publicos que, por affeição, odio ou contemplação ou para promover interesse pessoal seu: Sec. 1—Julgarem ou procederem contra a literal disposição da lei. Sec. 2—Infringirem qualquer lei ou regulamento." Art. 139—"Exceder aos limites das funcções proprias do emprego." Art. 146—"Haver para si, directa ou indirectamente, ou por algum acto simulado, em todo ou em parte, propriedade ou effeito, de cuja administração, disposição ou guarda deva intervir em razão de officio; ou entrar em alguma especulação de lucro ou interesse relativamente á dita propriedade ou effeito."

If, in this instance, the State triumphed over the Jesuitical pretensions of Rome, declared Sousa Franco, public tranquility would be insured. "If, on the contrary," he added, "the Jesuitical influence should dominate, and Brazil should have the unhappiness of being governed by a will other than that of the Nation, I declare that I would prefer to renounce all my public offices."[53]

The remaining members of the Council of State, while accepting the premise that the State had a right to supervise the Church, were more moderate in their views. They rejected the opinion that Vital would incur some penalties of the criminal code if he repudiated the decision of the crown relative to the brotherhood. Nabuco de Araújo agreed that the recourse should be accepted, but argued that the Supreme Tribunal of Justice was not competent to deal with a problem of disobedience. He held that deportation of the bishop, until he recognized the laws and powers of the state, was preferable in this case, "which is more political than criminal."[54] He advocated this position:

1) Because the criminal proceedings will be bound to affect seriously the dignity and moral force of the Episcopacy;

2) Because the courts of justice will hesitate before the question of conscience that had motivated the conflict, and that question of conscience will be with difficulty elevated to the category of crime.

3) Because the presence of the Bishop will give occasion to new conflicts, fomenting religious war;

4) Because the two powers, temporal and spiritual, are distinct and independent, expulsion from the country will be analogous with the custom followed by one sovereignty toward the representative of another, when the representative's presence becomes incompatible with public order.

5) Because no other measure occurs [to mind] that is

---

[53] *Relatório do Ministério dos Negócios do Império, 1874*, p. 48.
[54] *Ibid.*, p. 49.

more efficacious and more in accordance with the demands of public order, if the Bishop should insist on not recognizing the institutions of the country and the Powers of the State.[55]

The viscount of Muritiba, without committing himself on whether or not the recourse should be accepted, said that if it was accepted and if coercion was necessary, then article 24 of the decree of March 28, 1857, and articles 13 and 14 of the decree of February 19, 1838, must be complied with.[56] Muritiba advised that the crown be satisfied with the provisions of these decrees, and not demand more forceful measures, "whose result would be the decline of respect for the Pastors of the Church."[57] He disagreed with those who held that if the bishop refused to raise the interdict he ought to be tried for violation of article 96 of the criminal code.[58] Bishops and other ecclesiastics should answer for their civil crimes, continued the councilor, but the procedure of Dom Vital could never be regarded as a violation of article 96 or of any other article of the criminal code. Muritiba asserted that "the resistance of the Bishop cannot go further than refusing to raise the interdict, and there is no human force that would be able to oblige him to do it."[59] The viscount of Inhomerim felt that coercive measures should

---

[55] ". . . 1) Porque o processo criminal deverá affectar gravemente a dignidade e a força moral do Episcopado; 2) Porque os tribunaes hesitarão perante a questão de consciencia que motivara o conflicto, e essa questão difficilmente será elevada á categoria de crime; 3) Porque a presença do Bispo dará azo a novos conflictos, alimentando a guerra religiosa; 4) Porque, sendo os dois Poderes, temporal e espiritual, independentes e distinctos, a expulsão do territorio será uma analogia do modo como uma Soberania procede para com o representante de outra, quando a presença della se torna incompativel com a paz publica; 5) Porque nem-um outra meio occurre mais efficaz e conforme as reclamações da paz publica, desde que o Bispo insistir em não reconhecer as instituições do paiz, e os Poderes do Estado." *Ibid.*, pp. 50-51.

[56] See p. 145, note 40, above.

[57] *Relatório do Ministério dos Negócios do Império, 1874*, p. 52.

[58] Filgueiras, *op. cit.*, p. 101, Art. 96—"Obstar ou impedir de qualquer maneira o effeito das determinações dos poderes moderador e executivo, conforme a Constituição e as leis."

[59] *Relatório do Ministério dos Negócios do Império, 1874*, p. 52.

be used if needed, but he hoped that such measures would not be necessary. He had confidence "in the good intentions, intelligence, and patriotism of the Reverend Prelate, who has the obligation as a Brazilian to recognize and respect the Constitution and the laws of the Empire."[60] The viscount of Jaguari agreed that a civil tribunal might be appealed to, but only after the higher ecclesiastical authority had been consulted. The bishops "in the fervor of their apostolic zeal,"[61] he declared, might have committed excesses, but they did not act in the hostile spirit attributed to them. Jaguari thought that the conflict would be quickly terminated through "the wisdom of the Civil Power and the prudence of the Bishops, who will not cease to respect the Constitution and the laws of the State of which they are subjects."[62] The viscount of Niterói, the last councilor to speak, took the opposite view from Jaguari relative to the possible length of the conflict. The controversy between the civil and spiritual authorities, according to his prediction, would be long and serious. He did not regard the Supreme Tribunal of Justice as qualified to handle such a case, for there was nothing criminal, he said, in the act of the bishop, since his excesses stemmed from religious zeal and were committed in obedience to the precepts of the Supreme Pontiff. He suggested that the bishop's action be submitted to a synod for consideration.

Summarizing the opinions of the members of the Council of State, we find that all except Abaeté were in favor of accepting the recourse of the brotherhood. The majority of the members (São Vicente, Sousa Franco, Inhomerim, Bom Retiro,[63] and Caxias[64]) agreed that legal processes should be invoked in the event that the bishop refused to fulfill the order of the crown and did not lift the interdict imposed on the brotherhood. Even

---

[60] *Ibid.*, p. 53.

[61] *Ibid.*, p. 59.

[62] *Ibid.*

[63] The viscount of Bom Retiro delivered a long discourse that was a reiteration of all that had been said in the report of the committee, whose secretary he had been, and to whose principles and conclusions he fully subscribed.

[64] The duke of Caxias agreed with the committee, of which he had been a member, both in its principles and in its conclusions.

Abaeté supported the theory that legal action should be taken against the prelate if the recourse was accepted and he refused to comply with the order of the crown. Muritiba, Niterói, Sapucaí, and Jaguari were opposed to the application of force; Nabuco, who objected to legal proceedings, alone favored the revival of the old penalty of deportation which had not been in force since the imperial government had passed the decrees of 1838 and 1857 relative to the recourse.[65]

When the emperor had been apprised of the decision of the Council of State, he directed the imperial minister, João Alfredo Corrêa de Oliveira, to notify Bishop Dom Vital, and to order him to lift within a month the interdict he had placed on the Brotherhood of the Most Holy Sacrament of Recife. This command, which the American minister in Rio de Janeiro described as "not unlike a command to a charitable society of the Established Church to admit Dissenters to its ranks,"[66] was to have serious consequences for the empire. The government, in its apparent determination to keep the Church subservient to the State, allowed itself to be drawn into this quarrel with the Catholic Church, in support of Freemasonry; yet it was not ready to subscribe to a strictly Masonic policy in dealing with the bishops. As a result, the course pursued by the imperial government caused it to lose the support of both Catholics and Freemasons, and contributed in an important way, as will be pointed out later, to the ultimate overthrow of the monarchical system in Brazil.

---

[65] *Relatório do Ministério dos Negócios do Império, 1874*, p. 63. Resolution of the Council of State: "Como parece á maioria do Conselho d'Estado, para se dar provimento ao recurso e ser o reverendo Bispo sujeito a processo criminal. Como parece ao Conselheiro d'Estado Nabuco de Araujo na parte em que considera em vigôr as temporalidades. Paço, 12 de junho de 1873—Com a rubrica de Sua Magestade o Imperador.—João Alfredo Corrêa de Oliveira."

[66] National Archives, Department of State, Purrington to Fish, No. 288, September 20, 1875.

# CHAPTER VI

## TRIAL AND IMPRISONMENT OF THE BISHOPS OF OLINDA AND PARÁ

In his letter to João Alfredo Corrêa de Oliveira relative to the imperial order to raise the interdict, the bishop of Olinda called attention to the fact that from time immemorial the Church has found it necessary to remind the temporal authority that it was not the latter's mission to act as judge in religious matters. No one could deny, the prelate said, that the matter now under consideration was a religious matter. The official communication itself "confesses to treat of a *spiritual penalty* directed by the ecclesiastical authority against a religious corporation . . . ."[1] The official organ of the government published an account of the controversy under the headline: "Ministry of the Interior — Religious Question." Apparently the government admitted that the question was a religious one; yet according to Vital, it assumed the right "to define, to legislate, and to order."[2] The *aviso* of June 12, 1873, said that the matter under discussion was not purely religious, but religious and civil at the same time. If this was true, Dom Vital maintained, it belonged to neither power to decide the issue, but to both. The government, however, had assumed sole competence in the matter.

> The Brotherhoods, [which are] religious associations, established for the purpose of attaining eternal salvation more easily and more conveniently, promoting and aiding external worship, are not a purely spiritual matter, but rather a mixture of the spiritual and the

---

[1] *Relatorio apresentado á Assembléa Geral na terceira sessão da decima quinta legislatura pelo Ministro e Secretario d'Estado dos Negocios do Imperio, Dr. João Alfredo Corrêa de Oliveira* (Rio de Janeiro, 1874), appendix D, p. 65. This work will hereafter be cited as *Relatório do Ministério dos Negócios do Império, 1874.*

[2] *Ibid.*, p. 65.

temporal. Therefore it is of the exclusive jurisdiction of the Civil Power to decide whether the excommunicated person, who for that reason does not belong to the Church of Jesus Christ, outside of which no one can be saved, is permitted or not to be a member of those Brotherhoods.[3]

If the ordinary could not act alone in deciding the case of the brotherhood, the bishop asked, could the temporal power do so? Actually it could not: only the pope had the authority to question the spiritual activity of a bishop. The Supreme Pontiff could act through the metropolitan, the archbishop of Baía, but never through the State. Vital's position was plain: he would obey the emperor in temporal matters; the pope, in spiritual ones.

The prelate then proceeded to enumerate the four basic principles of João Alfredo's argument, viz., 1) without the *placet* of the civil power, the laws of the Church could not be enforced; 2) it was possible to have recourse from an ecclesiastical tribunal to the crown; 3) the brotherhoods were of a mixed nature; and 4) Masonry was an inoffensive society. The source of these principles was clear to the bishop and so also was the position of the Church regarding them. To João Alfredo he wrote:

> I assure Your Excellency that all that the illustrious Council of State explained to His Majesty the Emperor, and was communicated to me, is faithfully laid down in the works of all the Jansenists, of all the Gallicans, and of all ancient and modern Regalists; all this has already been completely refuted by orthodox Theologians and Canonists; all this has already been expressly condemned by the Holy Apostolic See,

---

[3] "As Irmandades, corporações religiosas, estabelecidas no intuito de mais facil e comodamente alcançar a eterna salvação, promover e auxiliar o culto externo, não são materia puramente espiritual; porem mixta de espiritual e temporal. Logo, é de exclusiva competencia do Poder Civil decidir se ao excomungado, que por isso não pertence á Igreja de Jesús Cristo, fora da qual ninguem pode salvar-se, é permitido ou não fazer parte dessas Irmandades." *Ibid.*

infallible teacher of truth and indefectible judge of Catholic teaching.[4]

The bishop's surprise that a Catholic government was so little conversant with Catholic teaching was couched in a rhetorical question:

> What value in the eyes of a Catholic Bishop can the personal opinions have of Borges Carneiro, Coelho Sampaio, Melo Freire, Pereira e Sousa, Vivien, Portalis, Dupins, Beugnot, and others who sustain the necessity of the *placet* and of recourse to the Crown, when the Church of God, infallible teacher and doctor of Catholic teaching, anathematizes such doctrines and declares them contrary to revealed truth?[5]

Dom Vital acknowledged that the constitution sanctioned the *placet*, but he did not approve the privilege. ". . . either this disposition of our constitution has not the meaning which political interpreters popularly assign to it, or then it [the right of *placet*] is incomprehensible and contrary to faith."[6] Equally incomprehensible is it that article 14 of the constitution which confers on the emperor the right of *placet* should contradict article 5 which establishes Roman Catholicism as the religion of the empire. Nor is it conceivable that a truth of faith could at the same time be and not be a dogma of faith; that a truth of faith declared by the Sovereign Pontiff could be dogma in

---

[4] "Asseguro a V. Ex. que tudo aquillo que o illustrado Conselho d'Estado ponderou a Sua Magestado o Imperador, e me foi communicado, está fielmente consignado nas obras de todos os Jansenistas, de todos os Gallicanos e de todos os Regalistas antigos e modernos; tudo já foi cabalmente confutado pelos Theologos e Canonistas orthodoxos; tudo já foi expressamente condemnado pela Santa Sé Apostolica, mestra infallivel da verdade e juiz indefectivel do ensino Catholico." *Ibid.*, p. 66.

[5] "Que valor podem ter aos olhos de um Bispo catholico as opiniões particulares de Borges Carneiro, Coelho, Sampaio, Mello Freire, Pereira e Souza, Vivien, Portalís, Dupins, Beugnot e outros que sustentam a necessidade do beneplacito e do recurso à Coroa, quando a Igreja de Deus, mestra e doutora infallivel do ensino catholico, anathematiza tais doutrinas e declara-as contrarias à verdade revelada? *Ibid.*

[6] *Ibid.*, p. 69.

some countries but not necessarily in Brazil. Quoting St. Robert Bellarmine, Dom Vital wrote:

> We live in a time . . . in which it is very difficult to defend ecclesiastical liberty without incurring the indignation of the secular power. On the other hand, if we are negligent and timid, we offend God and his glorious Vicar. It is necessary to show the Princes and their Ministers, by our mode of proceeding, that we do not seek to quarrel with them, but that only the fear of God, only the love of his Holy Name determines us to fight for the liberty of the Church.[7]

Turning then to the nature of the brotherhoods, the second principle on which the imperial minister had based his arguments, the bishop asserted that if these religious associations were of a mixed nature, then the bishop had no right to enter into the domain of the temporal, nor the temporal authority the domain of the spiritual. The prelate emphasized the fact that he had restricted his penalty to the spiritual aspect of the brotherhood in question, when he placed it under interdict. The fraternity, he pointed out, still existed as a civil society that could possess temporal goods and enjoy purely temporal privileges. But, he asserted, when it was a matter of deciding who could continue to be a member of a religious society, notwithstanding formal disobedience to the laws of the Church, who could assist at religious rites, who could celebrate them in their chapels, the Church alone was competent to act. The civil power, by acknowledging that these were the matters under consideration, tacitly admitted that it had invaded the realm of the spiritual. The imperial government, said the bishop, would have him recognize the civil power as supreme in the matter of religion. This principle, he maintained, was the principle of Protestant socie-

---

[7] "Vivemos em um tempo . . . em que é mui difícil defender a liberdade eclesiastica sem incorrer na indignação do poder secular. Do outro lado, se somos negligentes e timidos, ofendemos a Deus e a seu glorioso Vigario. Cumpre mostrar aos Principes e aos seus Ministros, pelo nosso modo de proceder, que não procuramos lutar como eles; mas que só o temor de Deus, só o amor de seu Santo Nome nos determina a pugnar pela liberdade da Igreja." *Ibid.*

ties, which held that all authority, be it religious or civil, derived from the crown. Such a principle, said Dom Vital, prevailed in England, but he continued:

> It is to be presumed that the wise Imperial Govern-
> ment, Catholic as it confesses itself to be, does not
> desire, does not hope, or pretend that a Catholic
> Bishop, unfaithful to the most sacred vows, taken at
> his baptism, at his ordination, and principally at his
> consecration, may have the misfortune of accepting a
> Protestant principle for the sole purpose of not in-
> curring the displeasure of the Government of his
> country.[8]

The bishop considered whether or not the brotherhoods were
of a mixed nature. He was careful to point out that he was considering them *in se*, since he was not concerned with any ex-
traneous additions foreign to the nature of the original institution. His conclusion was that they were not mixed but purely
spiritual,[9] since the ultimate end of the association was to facilitate the winning of eternal salvation, while the proximate end,
or the means, was concerned with religious acts and practices.
The bishop maintained that the government could certainly take
preventive measures to deter a brotherhood from degenerating
into a clandestine society of revolutionaries which under the
specious mantle of religious practices conspired against the legitimate constitutional authority. The prelate expressed surprise
that the imperial government defended Masonic activity in such
societies, where it was able "to scheme with impunity against

---

[8] "É de presumir que o sabio Governo Imperial, catholico, como se confessa,
não deseje, não espere, nem pretenda que um Bispo catholico, faltando aos mais
sagrados juramentos, prestados no seu baptismo, na sua ordenação e principalmente na sua sagração tenha a desventura de aceitar um principio protestante,
só no intuito de não incorrer no desagrado do Governo de seu paiz." *Ibid.*,
p. 70.

[9] See F. Deshayes, *Memento Juris ecclesiastici publici et privati* (Pariis,
1902), titulus II, ss. 62-63, p. 22. [This gives a good brief discussion of
the object of ecclesiastical power and of the relations which should exist between the spiritual and the temporal.]

the altar, the throne, and society in general . . ."[10]

Calling attention to the fact that the monarch and the ministers in Brazil were supposed to be Catholic, the bishop reminded them that they were Catholic not only as *individuals* but also as *a government*. A government, he concluded, might be either Catholic or non-Catholic. If Catholic, it had to follow the teachings of the Church; if non-Catholic, it should not interfere in the affairs of the Church.[11] The government seemed to reason, the prelate said, that because it nominated bishops, gave them an allowance, and conceded civil honors to them, they were *ipso facto* public officials. The right of a government to recommend a candidate for a see did not make the bishop subordinate to that government. His jurisdiction and his power came from the pope and from his episcopal consecration.[12] Concerning the matter of allowance, Vital reminded the imperial government that "the allowance given to bishops is only a small compensation for the ecclesiastical property which the government incorporated into the patrimony of the nation, and of the tithes which it engaged itself to receive directly from the hands of the faithful on the condition of transmitting them to the Bishops and Pastors."[13] The government, therefore, had con-

---

[10] *Relatório do Ministério dos Negócios do Império, 1874*, p. 71.

[11] *Ibid.* The bishop, having remarked that in England the government regulates the Anglican Church, but does not meddle in the affairs of the Catholic Church, recounts the following incident: "Ainda ha pouca, Exm. Sr., o Conego O Keef, suspenso e privado do seu beneficio pelo Eminentissimo Cardeal Cullen [archbishop of Dublin, primate of Ireland] seu legitimo superior, recorreu ao Tribunal da Rainha; mas o juiz protestante de religião, depois de condemnal-o, disse-lhe publicamente: 'Não promettestes obediencia ao vosso Bispo quando vos ordenastes? Não foi o Bispo quem vos confiou este emprego? O que pretendeis pois? O Bispo que vol-o deu, vol-o tira, por conseguinte, obedecei.' "

[12] *Ibid.*, p. 73. Bishop Dom Vital distinguishes a canonical nomination from a civil nomination. He writes: "Quanto á nomeação dos Bispos feita pelo Governo Imperial, todos sabem, em primeiro logar, que não é nomeação canonica, mas simples proposta, que a Santa Sé Apostolica, *por mera condescendencia*, aceita; em segundo logar, que tal nomeação não confere ao Governo Imperial direito algum sobre os Bispos, além dos que tem elle sobre qualquer cidadão brazileiro."

[13] "Todos sabem igualmente que a congrua dada aos Bispos é apenas uma

stituted itself a sort of procurator for the bishops, but "the procurator, by the simple fact of being procurator, was not above those whose rents he collects."[14] The bishop added that if the meager sum paid to the bishops was to be the price of their perfidy to the sacred and inalienable rights of the Church, the imperial government should immediately withdraw the allowance. He said further that he could not understand why the civil honors which the government conferred on bishops should be a title to authority over them. If acceptance of these honors meant subservience,

> . . . then we renounce most willingly the flag that flies
> from the mast of ships when we sail; we renounce the
> roll of drums; we renounce the sounding of trumpets;
> we renounce the salvos of artillery; in a word, we re-
> nounce all the civil honors that the Government of
> His Majesty gives us, on condition that it restore to
> us the liberty of being able to direct and govern in
> conformity with the teaching of Holy Mother Church
> and the dictates of our conscience the portion of the
> flock of Our Lord Jesus Christ which the Holy Spirit
> confided to our care and solicitude.[15]

As regards Freemasonry the bishop said that he had always considered it proscribed by the laws that prohibited secret societies.[16] He was surprised to learn from the imperial order

pequena compensação dos bens ecclesiasticos que o Governo incorporou aos bens da Nação, e dos dizimos que elle comprometteu-se a receber directamente das mãos dos fieis, com a condição de transmittil-os aos Bispos e Vigarios." *Ibid.*

[14] *Ibid.*

[15] "Então renunciamos de muito bom grado a bandeira que tremúla no mastro dos paquetes, quando embarcamos; renunciamos o rufar dos tambores; renunciamos o toque de clarim; renunciamos as salvas de artilharia; em uma palavra, renunciamos todas as honras civis que nos dá o Governo de Sua Magestade, comtanto que nos restitúam a liberdade de poder dirigir e governar a porção do rebanho de Nosso Senhor Jesus Christo, que o Espirito Santo, confiou aos nossos cuidados e solicitudes, segundo o ensino de Santa Madre Igreja, e os dictames de nossa consciencia." *Ibid.*

[16] *Ibid.*, 74. Dom Vital writes: "Baseando-me sobre o Decreto de 24 de maio de 1818, sobre o art. 3 da Lei de 20 de outubro de 1823 e sobre o art

of June 12 that, by virtue of these very laws, Masonry, as a secret society, was permitted. Then he proceeded to a brief exposition of Catholic teaching and of the incompatibility of Freemasonry with it. He closed his remarks with a recapitulation of all that he had said, and a statement of his position.

It is not lawful for me to give any reply to the Government of His Majesty, which may not be entirely in accord with the sacrosanct oaths which I took to God particularly on the occasion in which I was consecrated bishop of the Church of Olinda. I vowed to observe the Constitution of the Empire of Brazil, but only in so far as it was not in opposition to the laws of God, which are those of the Holy Catholic Church. To act otherwise would be to promise not to obey God, which, besides being impious, would be ridiculous. This appears to me more than clear. In things purely civil and of the jurisdiction of the Civil Power, I recognize the full and entire competence of the Government of His Majesty, and like each and every Brazilian citizen, I should submit myself with all humility to its decision. In this regard, I shall always be prompt to cherish, esteem, and execute faithfully and joyfully the orders of the Civil Power, even though the latter should be committed to unworthy persons, because thus Holy Mother Church orders us: *obedite praepositis vestris, etiam discolis.*[17]

---

282 do nosso Codigo Criminal, suppunha eu que as sociedades secretas no Brasil estivessem prohibidas não só pelas disposições da Igreja universal como até pelas leis do Imperio."

[17] ". . . nenhuma resposta me é licito dar ao Governo de Sua Magestade, que não esteja inteiramente de acordo com os juramentos sacrosantos que prestei a Deus, particularmente na ocasião em que fui sagrado Bispo da Igreja Olindense. Jurei observar a Constituição do Imperio do Brasil, mas tão somente emquanto esta não fôr de encontro ás leis de Deus, que são as da Santa Igreja catolica. Do contrario, seria jurar não obedecer a Deus o que, alem de impio seria ridiculo. Isto parece-me claro de mais. Em cousas puramente civis e da alçada do Poder Civil, reconheço a plena e inteira competencia do Governo de Sua Magestade e como todo e qualquer cidadão brasileiro submeter-me-ia com toda a humildade á sua decisão. Neste elemento, sempre estarei pronto para acatar, venerar e executar fiel e alegremente as ordens do Poder Civil, ainda quando este porventura estivesse cometido a pessoas indignas, porquanto assim nos

Vital held that one could not recognize in the civil power the *jus cavendi*, whence it pretended to derive the rights of imperial *placet* and of recourse to the crown. But, he continued, one could recognize not only the right of the government, but also the right of any subject to appeal from the judgment of the diocesan authority to that of the archbishop or in more serious cases to the Supreme Pontiff.

The bishop made the government aware that he had not acted without the approbation of the Holy See.

> From the beginning of that lamentable question, I brought to the knowledge of the Holy Father Pius IX, as was my duty, a faithful account of what, in the performance of the arduous duties of my holy mission, I had done and intended to do; and I solicited humbly his irrefragable judgment concerning it, entirely resolved to take pen in hand and by a single stroke undo all that was done, if the Vicar of Jesus Christ should thus counsel me. But, Excellency, on the same day, at the same hour, at the same instant in which the order of Your Excellency, accompanied by the resolution of the Council of State, reached me, I received, and by the same bearer, the resolution of the infallible Vicar of Jesus Christ. I have in one hand the order of Your Excellency through whose intermediation His Majesty the Emperor says to me: 'You erred, recede [from your position]'; and in the other the autograph of the immortal Vicar of the Infinite Majesty of Heaven and earth, by means of whom the incorruptible Judge of our souls says to me: 'You have acted wisely, continue. We cannot refrain from commending the zeal with which you have striven and are striving to resist so great an evil. We commit full power to you, of proceeding in accordance with the severity of Canon law against those spiritual societies which through this impiety have so basely vitiated their nature, of dissolving some at once and uniting others which may correspond with their own natural arrangement'."[18]

---

mando a Santa Madre Igreja:—*obedíte prepósitis vestris, etiam discolis."* Ibid., pp. 74-75.

[18] "Desde o principio dessa lamentável questão, levei ao conhecimento do

The prelate, having said that he was convinced that he was doing God's will in the matter at hand, and therefore, could not carry out the order of the imperial government, added boldly: "We ought to obey God, rather than men."[19]

## II

Before surveying the steps which led the bishops of Olinda and of Pará to the Supreme Tribunal of Justice, where they were tried and found guilty of having violated the law, it will be useful to investigate the report on ecclesiastical affairs given in 1874 by the minister of the empire, João Alfredo Corrêa de Oliveira.[20] This report, presented to the imperial legislature on May 12, undertook to show that the stand taken by the two bishops against Masonry was only part of a wider movement of the Brazilian episcopacy to nullify the authority of the State in ecclesiastical affairs. In this connection João Alfredo wrote:

> Without speaking of older disputes settled without diminution of temporal authority and in accord with the common interest of State and Church, some Bish-

---

Santo Padre Pio IX, como era dever meu, uma fiel relação do que, em desempenho das árduas obrigações de minha santa missão, eu havia feito e tencionava fazer; e solicitei humildemente o seu juizo irrefragável a respeito, inteiramente resoluto a lançar mão da pena, para de um só traço desmanchar tudo que estava feito, se assim m'o aconselhasse o Vigário de Jesús Christo. Mas, Exm. Sr., no mesmo dia, na mesma hora, no mesmo instante, em que ás minhas mãos chegava o aviso de V. Ex. companhado da resolução do Conselho de Estado, recebia eu, e pelo mesmo portador, a resolução do infallivel Vigário de Jesús Christo. Tenho em uma mão o aviso de V. Ex., por cujo intermédio Sua Magestade o Imperador me diz: 'Erraste, retrocede'; e na outra o autógrafo do imortal Vigário de nossas almas me diz: andaste avisado, continúa! *Nequimus non commendare . . . zelum, quo tanto malo studuisti et studes occurrere . . . . Plenam tibi potestatem facimus procedenti juxta canonicarum legum severitatem in ea spiritualia sodalitia, quae per hanc impietatem indolem suam tam foede viciarunt, illaque prorsus dissolvendi, aliasque consociando, quae nativae suae institutioni respondeant'.* Ibid., p. 75.

[19] "Obedire oportet Deo magis quam hominibus." *Acts* 5, 29, quoted in *Ibid.*

[20] *Relatório do Ministério dos Negócios do Império, 1874*, pp. 67-75.

ops have manifested, for some years past, the preten-
sion of increasing their attributions to the prejudice of
those of the Civil Power.[21]

As an instance of this he cited the case of a bishop "otherwise
deserving of respect for his virtue and for the mildness with
which he governs his Diocese,"[22] who in 1857 refused to accept
a candidate designated by the imperial government for canonical
appointment. Of the two ecclesiastics in line for the vacancy,
the one rejected by the government, the bishop asserted, was
the better candidate. Acting on the recommendation of the
Council of State, the imperial government affirmed that the bishop had no right to make such a decision.[23] If a bishop could so
act, the power of bestowing ecclesiastical benefices, which was the
prerogative of the executive power, as a right inherent in patronage and expressly conferred by the imperial constitution,[24] would
be annulled. To the bishops would accrue this constitutional
prerogative if, instead of acting freely, the government should
take upon itself the task of ratifying the preference of the ordinary, or should allow him the right of absolute veto.

In 1863 a number of bishops, continued the report, opposed an imperial decree which dealt with the administration of
diocesan seminaries subsidized by the imperial government.[25]
These bishops, said the imperial minister, "did not wish to admit
that the imperial government should prescribe rules for the filling of chairs [in the diocesan seminaries], and for the supervision
of the public funds with which they are maintained."[26] The

---

[21] "Sem fallar de questões mais antigas, resolvidas sem quebra da autoridade
temporal e segundo o interesse commum do Estado e da Igreja, tinham alguns
Bispos manifestado, ha annos e esta parte, a pretenção de dilatar suas attribuições em prejuizo das do Poder civil." *Ibid.*, pp. 67-68.

[22] *Ibid.*, p. 68.

[23] *Ibid.* The imperial minister writes: "Mas o Govêrno Imperial manteve
por Aviso de 4 de agosto de 1857, depois de ter ouvido o Conselho d'Estado,
a doutrina de que não é livre, e sim necessaria, a collação dos sacerdotes apre-
sentados para os beneficios ecclesiasticos, escolhidos d'entre os que se habilitarem
em concurso e forem propostos."

[24] Article 102, section 2.

[25] Decree 3073 of April 22, 1863.

[26] *Relatório do Ministério dos Negócios do Império, 1874*, p. 68. On this

ministerial report enumerated the details of supervision of these seminaries that remained in the hands of the bishops, but did not deny that the supreme control rested with the State.

A third complaint against diocesan prelates, according to João Alfredo, concerned parish vacancies. The policy followed by some bishops, he maintained, practically abolished the right of presentation. He asserted that grave evils were likely to follow upon this innovation. Not only was patronage being disregarded, but vicars were also entirely dependent on their bishops, "without guarantee against the excesses of episcopal authority . . . ."[27] João Alfredo questioned any excuse offered by a bishop in justification of such policy, because he felt that this excuse hid the underlying reason for the irregularity: the bishop's desire to evade patronage. To give a basis for his suspicion, he cited the case of one bishop who so acted, "having denied before his nomination the Patronage of Brazil and the rights inherent in it."[28]

"From this exposition, to which many other instances symptomatic of resistance to the civil power, may be added,"[29] the minister concluded that the question raised by the bishops of Olinda and Pará did not suggest that the government had given the Church new causes for conflict, but that it was only

> the continuation of a preconceived plan, according to which the State ought to subordinate itself to the Church, model itself on its laws, accept those [Church laws] that are contrary to the civil ones, and admit submissively that commands, pastoral instructions, and other acts of the ecclesiastical authority produce all external effects by their own force, free of inspection, *placet*, and recourse.[30]

---

controversy see *Correspondencia entre o governo imperial e os bispos do Rio Grande do Sul, Maranhão, e Pará, ácerca do Decreto nº 3.073 de 22 de Abril de 1863, que uniformisa os estudos das cadeiras dos seminarios episcopaes que são subsidiadas pelo estado* (n. p., n. d.).

[27] *Ibid.*, p. 69.

[28] *Ibid.*

[29] *Ibid.*

[30] ". . . a continuação de um plano preconcebido, segundo o qual deve o

Only by such pretensions, said João Alfredo, could the quarrel now beginning be explained. Masonry, he declared, was only a pretext: ". . . in truth, the question is one of principles approved and consecrated in our law, and invariably respected by many Bishops who honored the country and are pointed out as luminaries of the Roman Catholic Apostolic Church."[31] The minister admitted that Masonry had been anathematized by various popes, but he contended that no one would think of imputing to Brazilian Masonry "ends and acts contrary to the religion of the Empire,"[32] nor would any bishop "aware of our law"[33] wish to give effect to the bulls of condemnation. After summarizing what had happened between the bishops of Olinda and Pará and the brotherhoods, the imperial minister concluded his report with these words:

> As a Brazilian and a Catholic, I most sincerely hope for the re-establishment of the desired harmony between State and Church. I hope that Brazilian Bishops, so full of virtues and so notable for their erudition, will become aware at last of the great convenience and common interest there is in maintaining the good relations which existed, paying to the civil authority and to the laws of the country the respect and obedience which they owe, as the State has invariably respected the spiritual authority in the sphere of its just action and has aided its divine mission. In order that this may happen, the Government will employ all the means at its command, with the moderation of which it has given proof, but with the firm determination of one who neither can nor ought to yield.[34]

---

Estado subordinar-se á Igreja, modelar-se pelas suas leis, aceitar estas no que têm de contrario ás civis, e admittir submissamente que mandamentos, instrucções pastoraes e outros actos da autoridade ecclesiastica produzem todos os effeitos externos pela sua propria força, livres de inspecção, beneplacito e recurso." *Ibid.*

[31] *Ibid.*

[32] *Ibid.*

[33] *Ibid.*

[34] "Faço os mais sinceros votos, de brazileiro e catholico, para que se restabeleça a desejada harmonia entre o Estado e a Igreja. Espero que Bispos bra-

Attention has been called to the fact that the imperial minister opened his report with the assertion that there was a concerted movement on the part of some bishops to invade the rights of the civil power. Investigation undertaken to discover what bishops the minister had in mind when he made this remark revealed that, during the interval referred to in the report, the bishops in question occupied the foremost sees and were recognizd as leaders of the Brazilian hierarchy. João Alfredo cited three instances in his report which he regarded as typical of episcopal opposition to the civil power. The details of a clash between the bishop of Mariana (Minas-Gerais) and the imperial government in 1855 are identical with the first controversy mentioned by the minister; only the discrepancy of date — João Alfredo assigns the quarrel to 1857 — prevents identifying the two occasions with certainty. Dom Antônio Ferreira Viçosa, bishop of Mariana,[35] proposed Father Joaquim Antônio de Andrade Benfica for a vacancy in the chapter of the cathedral of Mariana, and excluded another candidate from consideration because he judged him unworthy of the office. "In addition to his proud disposition," the prelate wrote to the imperial government, "all know of the lack of decency of his habits."[36] Ignoring the testimony of Bishop Viçosa, a man advanced in years and universally esteemed for his prudence and integrity, the imperial government decided "in virtue of the patronage which it exercised over the Church,"[37] to appoint the priest

---

zileiros, tão cheios de virtudes e tão notaveis por seu saber, se compenetrarão emfim da alta conveniencia e interesse commum que ha em mantar as boas relações que existiam, prestando á autoridade civil e ás leis patrias o respeito e obediencia que devem, como o Estado tem invariavelmente respeitado a auttoridade espiritual no circulo de sua justa efficiencia, e ajudado a sua missão divina. Para que isto aconteça empregará o Govêrno, com a moderação de que tem dado prova, mas com a firme decisão de quem não póde nem deve ceder, todos os meios a seu alcance." *Ibid.*, p. 72.

[35] On Bishop Viçosa, see Raimundo Trindade, *Archidiocese de Marianna*
[35] On Bishop Viçosa, see Raimundo Trindade, *Archidiocese de Marianna* wards made count of Conceição.

[36] See Américo Jacobina Lacombe, "O aspecto religioso da questão dos bispos," *Verbum*, I (December, 1944), 335.

[37] *Ibid.*, p. 335.

whom the bishop had described as unworthy of the office. Viçosa appealed to the emperor, entreating him to hold up the execution of such an unjust decree. The sovereign submitted the case to the committee on justice of the Council of State, which decided that "it belongs only to the emperor to decide whether or not any of the candidates deserves presentation."[38] When the emperor convoked the Council of State for a full session on January 23, 1857, the Council affirmed the conclusion of the committee on justice and made clear that "the royal right relative to the filling of benefices passed through the constitution to the emperor . . . . The question," it added, "is today entirely temporal."[39]

In support of this decision, the emperor instructed the ordinary to execute the order of presentation previously dispatched. The bishop, however, remained adamant. "If the government of His Majesty decides that I am disobedient," he wrote, "let it do with me what it will, for I trust in the mercy of God that will give me courage to suffer prisons, banishment, and the rest; remembering that it was always the lot of the Church of God to suffer in silence."[40] When the committee on justice reviewed the bishop's statement, Councilor Eusébio de Queiroz observed that "presentation of an ecclesiastic to the bishop by the patron to be instituted in a benefice was and is necessary among us; installation is involved, and therefore the bishop cannot say that he will disobey without exposing himself to just admonition, and, depending on circumstances, to legal proceedings."[41] The committee on justice concluded its investigation on December 3, 1858, but no further action was taken by the imperial government; it did not force the bishop to accept the candidate he deemed unworthy. The supposition is that the imperial government feared the repercussion that would follow a contest with a venerable prelate revered for his virtue and learning.[42]

---

[38] *Consultas do Conselho de Estado sôbre Negócios Eclesiásticos* (Rio de Janeiro, 1870), II, 76, quoted in *ibid.*, p. 336.

[39] *Ibid.*

[40] *Ibid.*

[41] *Ibid.*

[42] Lacombe, "O aspecto religioso da questão dos bispos," *loc. cit.*, p. 336,

Bishop Viçosa was not unique in his firm opposition to the appointment by the imperial government of unworthy candidates for ecclesiastical offices. In 1862 the bishop of Olinda, Dom João da Purificação, marquis of Perdigão, refused to make effective the presentation of a benefice to a candidate nominated by the imperial government. The majority of the Council of State judged the remonstrance of the bishop not worthy of notice, but the marquis of Olinda, who was prime minister at the time, proposed a compromise: the bishop should again declare the parish vacant and open for candidacy.[43] Because of these conflicts, the government consulted the Council of State as to measures to be employed to exact obedience from prelates who resisted imperial commands. The Council was of the opinion that the crown could "entrust to any other bishop or ecclesiastical dignitary of any diocese the faculty of installing the nominee, in spite of the obstinacy of the diocesan prelate."[44] The instances just cited help to clarify what the imperial minister had in mind when he said in his report that some bishops tried to render the right of patronage useless.

In the same ministerial report, João Alfredo called attention to the opposition offered by a number of bishops to imperial legislation regulating diocesan seminaries.[45] Among such bishops was Dom Antônio de Macedo Costa of Pará, who led the opposition. In protest against the decree which provided for uniform courses of study in diocesan seminaries subsidized by the imperial government, the bishop wrote his famous *Memória* of July 28,

---

says: "Êste voto [of the Section], datado de 3 de dezembro de 1858 é a ultima peça do processo que se interrompeu. não tendo o govêrno insistido na colação do candidato julgado indigno pelo Ordinário, provàvelmente temendo a repercussão que teria uma luta com um prelado carregado de virtudes, prestigiado pela ciência e pela provecta idade."

[43] *Ibid.*, p. 337.

[44] *Consultas do Conselho de Estado sôbre Negócios Eclesiásticos*, II, 120, quoted in *ibid.* ". . . cometer a qualquer outro bispo ou dignidade eclesiástica de qualquer diocese a faculdade de colar o apresentado, apesar da obstinação do diocesano."

[45] The bishop, according to the ministerial report, opposed particularly decree 3073 of April 22, 1863.

1863, presented to the emperor in September of the same year.[46] The document contained an analysis of the decree and gave the reasons for episcopal opposition to it. The decree, the bishop wrote, was "without doubt inspired by most pure desires to be of assistance to the Church . . . ."[47] Yet in his opinion it made a new breach in ecclesiastical discipline, inflicted new humiliations on the Church, and bound more tightly the chains with which the Church in the empire was shackled. The bishops of Brazil were grieved, he continued, by the regulations and decrees which restricted the liberty and independence of their ministry:

> We note with sadness the ominous tendency of the government to meddle in the economy of the Church, as if it would seek to reduce it little by little to the condition of a human establishment, to a mere branch of civil administration. The Bishops of Brazil appear to be no more than public servants, subject to the Council of State, which, in imitation of the celebrated Board of Conscience and Orders, decides in the last instance the gravest questions of canon law and of ecclesiastical administration, only deigning at times to consult the Bishops as mere informants.[48]

The imperial government, according to the bishop, had subjected to state control even such concerns of spiritual jurisdiction as religious instruction; residences of pastors; the length of the novitiate in convents; the administration of churches; the organization and laws of, and even the names assigned to, cathe-

---

[46] For the *Memória*, see Dom Antônio de Almeida Lustosa, *Dom Macedo Costa* (Rio de Janeiro, 1939), pp. 50-78.

[47] *Ibid.*, p. 51.

[48] ". . . notamos com magoa a funesta tendencia do governo a ingerir-se na economia da Igreja como se se procurasse reduzí-la pouco a pouco à condição de um estabelecimento humano, a um mero ramo de administração civil. Parecem não ser mais os Bispos do Brasil que funcionarios publicos, sujeitos a conselho de Estado, que, a imitação da celebre Mesa de Consciencia e Ordens, decide em ultima instancia as questões mais graves do direito canonico e da administração eclesiástica, apenas dignando-se às vezes consultar os Prelados como meros informantes." *Ibid.*, pp. 51-52. The Board of Conscience and Orders [Mesa de Consciência e Ordens] was at one time the principal governing agency in Portugal for matters of ecclesiastical administration.

drals and seminaries; the requirements to be met by candidates for Holy Orders. These and other matters the State judged to be within its jurisdiction.[49]

The imperial government, said Dom Antônio, acted on the supposition that the civil power had the right to legislate for seminaries without reference to the ecclesiastical authority and even without its knowledge. The government, the decree supposed, had the right to establish and reform seminaries and limit their program of studies. The imperial government claimed further the right to stipulate conditions for the appointment of professors, which implied the right to dismiss them at pleasure. Even the textbooks used in the classes had to be approved by the State. All this, argued the prelate, was equivalent to secularizing these establishments and subjecting them entirely to the supervision and direction of the civil power.

That the sovereign should exercise the right of inspection over schools whose work it was to prepare candidates for the priesthood, the bishop readily acknowledged. The ruler should employ necessary vigilance to prevent transgressions of the law, to maintain the rights and honors of the sovereign, and to reform abuses in the interest of civil order. In his position as patron of the Church (bispo do exterior), he should be able to bring about reforms in the spiritual order and should add the strength of the secular arm to insure the enforcement of canonical regulations. But diocesan prelates, maintained Macedo Costa, had certain inalienable rights. The civil power could not reform seminaries; it could only furnish to the bishops the material means for these reforms. The government could not without doing

---

[49] Ibid., p. 52. Dom Antônio writes: "A catequese, as residências dos Párocos, o noviciado dos Conventos, a administração das Igrejas deles, os estatutos das Catedrais e dos Seminários, a organização que se deve dar a êstes últimos estabelecimentos e até os nomes que lhes competem, as condições que se devem exigir para admissão às Ordens, tudo isto julga o Govêrno sêr de sua alçada, sobre tudo isto se crê com direito de decidir, decretar e legislar, e, se um Bispo do Império promove esmolas em favor das pias obras da Propagação da Fé e da Santa Infância, é porque dois Decretos lhe concedem para isso uma autorização que aí se declara necessária; e, enfim, para podermos assistir ao exame dos nossos lentes do Seminário, é mister que o Decreto de 22 de Abril último declare que os Bispos poderão assistir a êste exame."

grave injury to the dignity and honor of the episcopacy, subject the regulations of seminaries to the supervision of its officials. Neither could it deprive prelates of the right to nominate freely professors who were to teach in diocesan seminaries.[50]

The imperial government, continued the prelate, had repeatedly drawn attention to the fact that candidates for the priesthood needed to be given a broader education in conformity with the exigencies of the times. Yet the decree in question, instead of furnishing bishops with convenient means for enlarging the program of study in the major and minor seminaries, suppressed a number of courses. The minor seminaries henceforth would teach only Latin, French, rhetoric, and philosophy. Mathematics, science, history, and other essential branches of learning were to be ignored. The government, realizing that the course of study could not be reduced if the seminaries were to give adequate training to clerical students, suggested that bishops create additional chairs and support them from episcopal revenues (*rendas da mitra*). This suggestion elicited a frank rebuttal from the bishop.

> I do not know, Sir, whether, with the insufficient allowance of 300 *milréis* a month which the bishops of Brazil have, an allowance inferior to the salaries and emoluments of many subalterns of the government offices, I do not know whether with this parsimonious and shameful allowance, together with some insignificant revenue from the chancery office, the Bishops could fill these lacunae left by the Government in Seminary education. Moreover every day they have so many poor to aid, so many pious works to support, and so many commitments to satisfy. The income of the see! Sir, for my part I confess frankly to Your Majesty that I do not know what this is . . . . If the government seriously wants the Bishops to create the necessary chairs, let it commence by endowing the Seminaries decently.[51]

---

[50] The regulation that the bishop is opposing at this point seems to have been made in an effort to keep Jesuit professors out of diocesan seminaries. See p. 176 below.

[51] "Eu não sei, Senhor, se com a minguada côngrua de 300$ por mês que

By its legislation, said the bishop, the imperial government wronged and humiliated the clergy. It treated seminary professors, chosen by the bishops from the foremost ranks of the clergy, as mere public servants subject to dismissal at the whim of the government. Besides, the imperial government by this new decree deprived religious teaching of the liberty and independence which it ought to have in a Catholic country. He pointed out the evil latent in this encroachment of the civil authority. The present ministry, he granted, might never interfere with the subject matter taught by professors in diocesan seminaries, but what assurance had the government that in the future civil officials who had deviated from orthodoxy might not use their power to dismiss professors and otherwise to interfere with orthdox teaching in seminaries?

Dom Antônio stressed the fact that in degrading and humiliating the clergy, the imperial government endangered the religion of the empire. The clergy, the prelate continued, had for a long time been inured to poverty, and if it were necessary it could accustom itself to penury, but he continued,

we shall never cease protesting against the doctrine discernible in these and other acts of the government, which consists in regarding simply as salaries these allowances and subsidies given to ecclesiastical officials as restitution for the tithes and other revenues of the Church of which the State took possession under the condition solemnly stipulated of furnishing all the necessities of worship.[52]

---

têm os Bispos do Brasil, côngrua inferior aos ordenados e emolumentos de muitos empregados subalternos das Repartições do Estado; eu não sei se com essa mesquinha e vergonhosa côngrua, unida a alguns rendimentos insignificantes do cartório eclesiástico, poderão os Bispos preencher essas lacunas deixadas pelo Govêrno no ensino do Seminário, tendo eles aliás todos os dias tantos pobres que socorrer, tantas pias obras que alimentar e tantos encargos inevitaveis que satisfazer. As rendas da mitra! Senhor, pela minha parte confesso ingenuamente a Vossa Majestade Imperial que não sei o que isto seja . . . . Se o govêrno quer seriamente que os Bispos criem as cadeiras necessárias, comece por dotar convenientemente os Seminários." Lustosa, op. cit., p. 68.

---

[52] ". . . não cessaremos de reclamar contra a doutrina que transparece nestes

Instead of curbing the action of the Church, the government could very profitably employ itself in furthering its cause. It could create new episcopal sees in the vast territory of the empire. These sees would insure the unity, both religious and political, of the nation. The government could establish and endow in each diocese major and minor seminaries provided with classical and theological curricula, and well enough financed to allow for the gratuitous admission, or the admission on the payment of a small tuition, of students in sufficient numbers to supply the needs of the Church in Brazil. Directing a final plea to the emperor, who, he said, could do a great work in restoring Catholicity to the country, Macedo Costa concluded his *Memória* with the petition that the execution of the decree of April 22, 1863, be suspended.

Although strongly supported by the hierarchy and clergy, the *Memória* did not win favor with the government. The prime minister, the marquis of Olinda, attempted in his reply of October 24, 1863, to refute the charges made by the bishop of Pará. His letter evoked a second communication from Dom Antônio in which he undertook once more to clarify the position of the Church, and to list the reasons why conscientious bishops must oppose all decrees interfering with ecclesiastical liberty.[53] The prime minister insists, wrote Dom Antônio, that "the government does not wish to interfere in the administration of seminaries!"[54] But, continued the prelate, "all that beautiful theory so laboriously constructed is undermined, destroyed, and overthrown by the right of governmental inspection, to which Your Excellency gives, if I am not mistaken, excessive latitude."[55] He reminded the marquis, further, of how much this right of

---

e noutros piocedimentos do Governo, a qual consiste em considerar como simples ordenados estas côngruas e subsídios dados aos empregados eclesiásticos, em restituição dos dízimos e outros reditos da Igreja de que se apoderou o Estado, debaixo da condição solenemente estipulada de prover a todas as necessidades do culto." *Ibid.,* pp. 72-74.

[53] For the reply of the bishop of Pará to the marquis of Olinda, see Lustosa, *op. cit.,* pp. 88-106.

[54] *Ibid.,* p. 97.

[55] *Ibid.*

inspection had been abused in the past.

Parliamentarian Jansenism, Febronianism or Josephism constantly covered its aggressive tendencies under
the specious name of *jus inspectionis circa sacra* and
even under another still more specious *jus protectionis*
all of which can well be reduced in the last analysis
to this brief and more expressive formula: *jus in
sacra*.[56]

Having reiterated the rights of the State and of the Church in
the supervision of seminaries, the prelate concluded his second
letter with the unqualified assertion that the episcopacy could not
subscribe to any civil law that infringed on the free action of the
Church in Brazil. Moreover, he emphasized the fact that the
testimonials which he had received from all his colleagues in the
episcopacy[57] confirmed what he had set forth in his *Memória*.[58]
The bishop observes that "the Brazilian Episcopacy is unanimous in lamenting with me those invasions that have been made,
that are being made each day into the domains of the Church."[59]
To substantiate his position further, he quoted at length from
the writings of the metropolitan of Baía, Dom Romualdo de
Seixas, who retained throughout a long episcopacy the reputation of champion of the rights of the Church that he had won as
a young prelate in his encounters with Feijó.[60]

---

[56] "O Jansenismo parlamentar, o Febronianismo ou Josefismo acobertaram
constantemente suas tendências invasoras sob esse especioso nome de—*jus inspectionis circa sacra*—e até sob outro ainda mais especioso de—*jus protectionis*—o que tudo bem se póde reduzir em última análise a esta fórmula mais
breve e mais expressiva:—*jus in sacra*.—Precisemos bem o sentido daquela
palavra." *Ibid.*

[57] There were in Brazil at this time eleven suffragan sees and one metropolitan see.

[58] Lustosa, *op. cit.*, p. 92, Dom Antônio writes: "Os testemunhos e os fatos
aí estão altamente confirmando as tristes verdades que eu avancei na minha
'Memoria.' Os testemunhos. Tenho por mim os de todos os meus Veneráveis
Colegas no Episcopado."

[59] *Ibid.*

[60] See pp. 73-82 above. Dom Antônio de' Macedo Costa writes of Dom
Romualdo (*ibid.*, p. 93): "E em . . . suas obras [Dom Romualdo] assinala
o espírito de 'rivalidade, ciume e receio de que em grande parte eivada a nossa

From these investigations it appears that João Alfredo's assertion that the Brazilian episcopacy was attempting to increase its spiritual jurisdiction was well founded. Besides the four bishops already mentioned who openly opposed State interference in spiritual affairs, four others were to qualify as intransigent before the publication of the report under consideration. In the Masonic pamphlet, *Ponto Negro,* published in 1872,[61] the bishops of Pará, Rio Grande do Sul, Ceará, and Rio de Janeiro were accused of dominating the Brazilian Church. All four were assailed by the author of the pamphlet as ultramontanes. All were condemned for their favorable attitude toward the Jesuits, and particularly for preferring these priests as professors in their diocesan seminaries.[62] Another Masonic pamphlet added the name of the bishop of São Paulo, Dom Antônio Joaquim de Melo, to the list of prelates who were introducing Jesuitical and ultramontane ideas into Brazil.[63] In the period covered by the minister's report at least eight members of the Brazilian hierarchy expressed their disapproval in one way or another of government policies toward the Church. The bishop of Pará testified that all the members of the hierarchy were united in their opposition to governmental interference; the conclusion can be

---

legislação, que sob diversos pretextos estorva a ação do Episcopado e o submete ao poder civil, ou pelas suas multiplicadas e muitas vezes antinômicas disposições restritivas, ou pela arbitrária interpretação de seus executores; mostra o clero pobre, mendicante, humilhado que, debaixo do império de uma carta que proclamou solenemente a religião católica, apostólica romana, ouve ressoar até no recinto do santuário os cânticos de uma liberdade cujos benefícios ainda não pôde saborear . . . .' "

[61] See p. 102 above.

[62] *Ponto Negro,* p. 7. "Quatro bispos dominam hoje na egreja brasileira; o do Pará, o do Rio Grande, o do Ceará, e o do Rio de Janeiro.

"Com elles vieram membros esparsos da Companhia." These bishops were Dom Antônio de Macedo Costa, Dom Sebastião Dias Laranjeira, Dom Antônio dos Santos, and Dom Pedro Maria de Lacerda. In passing, it may be recalled that Dom Antônio de Macedo Costa's predecessor in the see of Pará, Dom Romualdo de Sousa Coelho, was accused of propagating doctrines "subversive of public order." See p. 140 above.

[63] X [pseud. of Cônego Dr. Joaquim do Monte Carmelo], *Questão Religiosa. O Arcipreste da Sé de S. Paulo Joaquim Anselmo de Oliveira e o cléro do Brasil. Artigos publicados no jornal 'A Reforma'* (Rio de Janeiro, 1873).

drawn, therefore, that those bishops who were not publicly embroiled with the Brazilian government were of the same mind as those who openly challenged it.[64]

That the outstanding bishops of Brazil openly contested imperial policies toward the Church is established, but João Alfredo's avowal that their opposition constituted an invasion of the civil power must be disputed. He begged the question when he assumed that the fact of opposition was proof of guilt. Furthermore, while characterizing the Episcopal-Masonic controversy as another manifestation of aggression prejudicial to the civil power, João Alfredo refused to consider the possibility of civil aggression against the Church. Similar implications appear in his statement that Masonry was used by the bishops as a pretext for the quarrel. As can be seen from their pastorals, the bishops were absolutely serious in their opposition to Masonic infiltration into Catholic society. It was rather the government, it seems, that used Masonry as a pretext for its quarrel with the bishops. In its apparent eagerness to take advantage of the Episcopal-Masonic crisis so that the power of the State over the Church could be publicly attested, it circumvented one technicality after another that might have prevented the matter from coming to issue.

## III

The government, we have said, was determined to make a test case of its differences with the bishops of Olinda and Pará.

---

[64] In one of the first despatches in which the American minister mentioned the Episcopal-Masonic controversy, we find the following comment: ". . . the opponents of the Clerical party, in the Legislature, in the journals, and in private, declare that this question of masonry is only a pretext with those bishops who have not heretofore disturbed them, on that account; but now, under its cover, attempt to establish the supremacy of their church regulations over the civil laws of the Empire . . . . In this connection, may be noticed, also, the reply of the bishop of Rio Grande do Sul to an inquiry, in respectful language, addressed to him, by the Provincial Assembly, as to the number of Jesuits employed in his diocese. His answer was that they had no right to address such inquiries to him, as the matter was exclusively of ecclesiastical jurisdiction and discipline." National Archives, Department of State, Purrington to Fish, No. 113, May 23, 1873.

When, therefore, João Alfredo received letters from Dom Vital and Dom Antônio, stating that they would not lift the interdicts they had imposed, he ordered[65] the procurator of the crown to send to the Supreme Tribunal of Justice the accusations against them in the name of the emperor. The Supreme Tribunal would determine whether or not a true bill existed against the prelates, and, if it did, on what articles of the criminal code the bishops should be indicted.[66] The Tribunal of Justice announced on December 12 that it had found a true bill, and charged Dom Vital with violation of article 96 of the criminal code;[67] on March 24, 1874, it reached the same decision in the case of Dom Antônio. Since this offense did not permit of bail, the court ordered that each prelate be immediately imprisoned preparatory to trial.

When, on December 22, Vital was presented with the formal order for imprisonment, he said that he could not accept the decision of the imperial government in a matter which he had consistently maintained belonged to the spiritual jurisdiction. If the order was to be carried out, it must be done forcibly and without his consent.[68] The official who presented the order petitioned the president of the province of Pernambuco for assistance, and this was granted. When Dom Vital was later told that officers had arrived to carry out the sentence, he submitted and was conducted to the naval arsenal in Recife. From there he was sent to Baía, then to Rio de Janeiro, where he arrived on the evening of January 13. At Baía he was met by a large group of the clergy and laity headed by the archbishop, Dom

---

[65] By *avisos* of September and November, 1873.

[66] *Relatório do Ministério dos Negócios do Império, 1874*, pp. 82-83. See also National Archives, Department of State, Shannon to Fish, No. 157, March 1, 1874.

[67] José Antônio de Araújo Filgueiras Júnior, *Codigo Criminal do Imperio do Brasil* (Rio de Janeiro, 1876), p. 101: Art. 96—"Obstar ou impedir de qualquer maneira o effeito das determinações dos poderes moderador e executivo, conforme a Constituição e as leis: Penas: No gráo maximo—seis annos de prisão com trabalho. No gráo medio—quatro annos *idem*. No gráo minimo—dous annos *idem*."

[68] *Relatório do Ministério dos Negócios do Império, 1874*, pp. 89-90.

Manuel Joaquim da Silveira.[69] The archbishop asked the government to allow Vital to reside at the archiepiscopal palace during his stay in Baía, but the request was refused.[70] On his arrival in Rio de Janeiro, Dom Vital was lodged in the naval arsenal, his temporary prison, where he was presented on February 5, 1874, with the official bill of complaint. After listing his asserted transgressions, the order concluded:

> [It] will be proved that the defendant by such behavior violated the Political Constitution of the Empire and the legislation regulating it, and finally he is found to have incurred the sanctions of article 96 of the Criminal Code, whose penalties ought to be imposed on him to a maximum degree because the aggravating circumstances of Sections 3, 4, 8, and 10 of article 16 of the same code were present; therefore he should be condemned on all counts.[71]

---

[69] D. Manuel Joaquim da Silveira, count of São Salvador, was appointed to the metropolitan see of Baía, June 27, 1861, succeeding Dom Romualdo de Seixas, who died December 27, 1860.

[70] *Diario da Bahia* quoted in João Dornas Filho, *O padroado e a igreja brasileira* (São Paulo [1938]), p. 159. "Pelas 11 horas da manhã S. Ex. o sr. conde de S. Salvador, bem como differentes membros da associação actholica se dirigiram n'um vapor com o fim de cumprimentar o prelado olindense; mas apenas foi permittido o ingresso a S. Ex. o sr. arcebispo, a seu secretario e ao religioso franciscano sr. frei Raymundo; visto uma ordem terminante do governo vedando a admissão perante o sr. D. Vital de quasquer outras pessoas . . . . Tambem nos consta que o sr arcebispo fez um protesto contra o acto do governo e se dirigira ao sr presidente da provincia afim de obter a permissão de desembarque para o sr. D. Vital, a cuja disposição punha o palacio archiepiscopal durante a demora do *Recife* neste porto, que será de quatro dias, até que chegue o transporte *Bonifacio* que deve conduzil-o ao Rio de Janeiro; mas que o sr. presidente respondera não poder annuir ao pedido de S. Ex. Revma.; visto as ordens que tinha recebido da côrte."

[71] "Provará que o réo com similhante procedimento infringiu a Constituição Politica do Imperio e a legislação reguladora de tal materia, e por fim acha-se incurso na disposição do artigo 96 do Codigo Criminal, cujas penas lhe devem ser impostas no grau maximo, por se darem as circumstancias aggravantes dos SS 3º, 4º, 8º, 10 do artigo 16 do mesmo Codigo, sendo tambem condenmado em todas as custas." Augusto Olímpio Viveiros de Castro. "Contribuições para a biographia de D. Pedro," Parte 1ª, *Revista do Instituto Histórico e Geográfico Brasileiro*, tomo especial (1925), p. 501.

Dom Vital answered this charge with the phrase: *Jesus autem tacebat.*[72]

On the morning of February 18, when he appeared before the Supreme Tribunal of Justice for the first session of his trial, Vital was accompanied by Bishop Lacerda, who had visited him previously in prison and had conferred on him the honor of full jurisdiction over the diocese of Rio de Janeiro.[73] On the second day, February 21, Dom Vital was attended by Bishop Lacerda and Bishop John B. Miège, vicar apostolic of Kansas and the Indian territory, who happened to be in the Brazilian capital at the time.[74] The trial was a routine procedure. At the second session Councilor Zacarias de Góis e Vasconcelos and Senator

---

[72] *Ibid.*

[73] Dornas, *op. cit.*, pp. 159-160.

[74] Bishop Miège, in a letter to his brother written from the College of St. Louis in Itú, Brazil, and dated January 15, 1874, gives the following summary of the Episcopal-Masonic controversy: "Le Brésil est un pays de confréries innombrables, de beaucoup de processions; c'est aussi un pays de très peu d'instruction religieuse, et encore moins de pratique de religion. Sous le titre de bienfaisance, la Maçonnerie a réussi à faire beaucoup d'adeptes et à s'introduire dans les dites confréries, qui sont presque toutes gouvernées par elle; et cependant les beaux messieurs qui, après avoir passé la soirée à la loge, vont le lendemain à la procession en pénitents blancs, se permettent les plus horribles blasphêmes contre l'Immaculée-Conception, contre l'infaillibilité du Pape et contre tout ce qui leur déplaît. Les Evéques, généralement bons et forts, se sont déterminés à mettre fin à ces abus, et soutenus par le Saint-Père, ils ont publié que la franc-maçonnerie du Brésil, ne valait pas plus que celle des autres pays. L'Evêque de Pernambuco a ordonné aux confréries de chasser les francs-maçons, sous peine d'interdiction pour leurs chapelles; elles ont refusé! il les a interdités. Figurez-vous la fureur et les grincements de dents . . . L'affaire a été portée au Congrès, et le Président du Conseil des ministres, qui est Grand-Orient, a plaidé la cause des francs-maçons. Le Congrès, presque tout composé de cette secte, a décidé que l'Evêque annullerait son ordre ou serait traduit devant les tribunaux. L'Evêque, bien entendu, a refusé de retirer son ordre et a déclaré le tribunal incompétent. Alors le gouvernement l'a fait accuser d'obéir à un pouvoir étranger, le Pape, contre la constitution de l'Empire. C'est le point sur lequel il aura à se défendre; mais ne reconnaissant pas la compétence du tribunal, il ne se défenda pas. La peine du délit est de quatre à seize ans de prison. Le véritable motif d'accusation vient de ce que l'Evêque a publié un bref du Saint-Père contre la franc-maçonnerie Brésilienne sans le placet du gouvernement." J. Garin, *Notices Biographiques sur Mgr. J.-B. Miège Premier Vicaire Apostolique du Kansas et sur les prêtres de de la paroisse Chevron (Savoie)* (Moutiers, 1886), pp. 191-192.

Cândido Mendes de Almeida presented a carefully prepared and sound defense, using arguments already familiar to us from the writings of the two bishops.[75] Nevertheless, following this session, the court, deliberating in secret, decided that the bishop had violated article 96 of the criminal code and should be given the penalty of four years in prison at hard labor. Of the seven members participating in this deliberation, five concurred in the majority opinion. Of the two who dissented, one declared that the bishop had incurred only the crime of disobedience; the other, that the accused should be acquitted because the Supreme Tribunal was not competent to judge in spiritual matters.[76] On March 12, the sentence was commuted by the emperor to simple imprisonment, and Vital was confined in the Fortress of São João in Guanabara Bay.[77]

Dom Antônio de Macedo Costa was tried on June 27 and July 1. Despite the able defense offered by Councilor Zacarias de Góis e Vasconcelos and Deputy Antônio Ferreira Viana,[78]

[75] See *Discursos proferidos no Supremo Tribunal de Justiça na Sessão de 21 de Fevereiro de 1874 pelos Exms. Srs. Conselheiro Zacarias de Goes e Vasconcellos e Senador Candido Mendes de Almeida por occasião do julgamento do Exm. e Revm. Sr. D. Fr. Vital Maria Gonçalves de Oliveira, Bispo de Olinda* (Rio de Janeiro, 1874).

[76] *Relatório de Ministério dos Negócios do Império, 1874,* pp. 91-93.

[77] Basílio de Magalhães, *Estudos de história do Brasil* (São Paulo, 1940), pp. 128, 135. In a letter to his brother written from Puerto Rico, April 4, 1874, Bishop Miège describes the trial and imprisonment of Bishop Dom Vital: "Il [a Capuchin Father who had accompanied Miège from São Paulo to Rio de Janeiro] allait visiter et conforter son confrère l'Evêque de Pernambuco, au jugement duquel j'ai assisté, ainsi que l'Evêque de Rio. Il fut condamné à quatre ans de travaux forcés pour n'avoir pas voulu lever l'interdit qu'il avait lancé contre les chapelles qui étaient sous le contrôle des francmaçons . . . .

"L'empereur a commué cette peine en quatre ans de réclusion dans une forteresse du port. Il y a dans toute cette affaire des détails si revoltants d'iniquités, une telle prostitution de la justice et de l'équité, qu'on ne peut s'empêcher de trembler pour un pays où le gouvernement lui-même est le promoteur et l'exécuteur de si criantes injustices." Garin, *op. cit.*, p. 193.

[78] Lídia Besouchet, *José Ma. Paranhos, Vizconde Do Río Branco* (Buenos Aires [1944]), pp. 246-247, says of this defense: "La defensa de D. Macedo, espontáneamente asumida por Zacarías de Gois y Ferreira Viana, contiene tópicos para comprender los choques de mentalidad entre las clases

the decision of the court was that Dom Antônio had also violated article 96 of the criminal code and should likewise suffer
the penalty of four years' imprisonment at hard labor.[79] The
sentence was again commuted by the emperor to simple imprisonment. Dom Antônio was jailed in the Fortress of Ilha das
Cobras.[80]

---

dirigentes del Imperio. Revela la contradicción fundamental en materia religiosa, de existir dentro de las Confraternidades, masones convictos: caso *sui
generis* tanto en la historia de la Iglesia Católica como en la de la masonería.
Es por ello que, cuando se invoca la diferencia de calidad en la composición
de las Hermandades brasilenas, Zacarías de Gois clama con justa razón diciendo:
'¡ Señores! Consta que en Europa no existe ese rigor de parte de las autoridades
eclesiásticas; ¿mas por qué? Porque allá, quien es católico no va a la masonería
y quien es masón no va a una Hermandad . . . .' La argumentación de Zacarías
es de una lógica poderosa, delimitando perfectamente los poderes del Estado en
los asuntos de conciencia."

[79] In his letter to his brother written from Itú, January 15, 1874, and
referred to above, Bishop Miège says of Dom Antônio's entrance into the controversy: "L'Evêque de Para aura le même sort et d'autres le suivront. Le
pauvre Brésil va au schisme, si le bon Dieu n'y met une forte main." Garin,
*op. cit.*, p. 192.

[80] Castro, *op. cit.*, pp. 505-506, note 1; Lustosa, *op. cit.*, pp. 243-251.

# CHAPTER VII

## REPERCUSSION OF THE IMPRISONMENT OF THE BISHOPS

If the imperial government expected its prompt and decisive action against the bishops of Olinda and Pará to put an end to the Religious Question, it was destined to be disappointed. The year and a half that the bishops were in prison[1] was for Brazil a period of intense political, religious, and social ferment.[2] The American minister[3] wrote in his despatch of April 22, 1874, that "since the condemnation and imprisonment of the Bishop of Olinda which caused such rejoicing among the Liberal party and the Masonic Fraternity, things have taken another turn.

---

[1] Only the bishop of Olinda was in prison a full year and a half after conviction (March 12, 1874-September 17, 1875). The bishop of Pará was convicted on July 1, 1874; with the commutation of his sentence on July 23, the period of his official imprisonment began. The bishop of Olinda was in prison awaiting trial from January 13, 1874; the bishop of Pará, from April 28, 1874.

[2] An investigation of trends during this interval will complement the survey previously made of the relations of Church and State, and will contribute to a more correct orientation of all the factors in the Episcopal-Masonic controversy. This survey will not be based on the controversial writings of the period (see Basílio de Magalhães, *Estudos de história do Brasil* [São Paulo, 1940]), pp. 140-151, *Verbum,* I [December, 1944], 351-380, and *A Ordem* xxxvi [December, 1944], 451-461, for bibliographies), since such an approach would be too complicated and of questionable value in view of the purpose the examination is to serve; rather, it will be founded on the reports of the American ministers in Brazil. These reports have a twofold value: they are the accounts of a third party, and they represent the attempts of men who are themselves exponents of Protestantism to analyze the relations of Church and State in a society that is, traditionally and numerically, overwhelmingly Catholic. Frequently their observations will throw into relief the very inconsistencies that make the Religious Question so difficult to interpret.

[3] James R. Partridge was envoy extraordinary and minister plenipotentiary to Brazil at this time; Richard Cutts Shannon was secretary of legation until 1875, when he was replaced by William A. Purrington. Hamilton Fish was secretary of state.

The victorious party are now the complainants."[4] They claim, continues the despatch, that the government has not had the courage to execute the sentence of the bishop, for they contend that

> instead of undergoing imprisonment, in any house of detention or jail (*cadea*) — according to law, in such cases, — the Bishop has been provided for by the Government in a sumptuous manner, by the seaside, in the house of the Commandant of the fort, which was expressly papered and painted for his sojourn, — with a retinue of servants paid by the Government, — whose officers await the Bishop's commands, whose Commandant in an Order of the Day, requires the officers and garrison 'to pay the most reverent respect and attention to their illustrious guest' — and whose guards present arms to him, as he passes freely in and out.[5]

The American minister appears to have been correctly informed, for, while the description is slightly exaggerated, the facts are true.[6] The inference is that, while there were many regalists in the Brazilian government who would side with their more Liberal colleagues in defending the rights of the State over the Church, and would even go so far as to indict and condemn bishops who challenged these rights, they recoiled from treating the prelates as common criminals. That the ultra-Liberal faction maintained a vindictive attitude toward the bishops, and especially toward the papacy, is attested in the same despatch:

> All this, and more, is shown forth in some remarkably well-written articles over the signature of 'Ganga-

---

[4] National Archives, Department of State, Brazil Despatches, vol. 40, Partridge to Fish, no. 168, April 22, 1874. Hereafter cited as National Archives, Department of State.

[5] *Ibid.*

[6] João Dornas Filho, *O padroado e a igreja brasileira* (São Paulo [1938]), pp. 176-177.

nelli,'[7] by the Councillor Saldanha Marinho,[8] formerly a Deputy, one of the leaders of the extreme wing of the Liberal party, and now Grand Master of the Brazilian Orient. In these, he contrasts the course of the Government now, with a prisoner convicted by the highest court, without hesitation, upon his own confession of a treasonable offense in attempting to set up a foreign authority over the Constitution of the Empire, with the course pursued in 1848, with certain persons, — many still living and now in high positions — who then took part in the movement at Pernambuco (Olinda) in a mere political opposition to the then Ministry, whom they thus attempted to force into compliance with the Constitution, without undertaking themselves to subvert or supplant it.[9]

That aspect of the controversy which may be called the struggle for spiritual supremacy between disaffected and orthodox Catholics[10] was entirely lost on the American minister. Interpreting the situation in terms of his own experience, he readily gave credence to the assertions of the ultra-Liberals that the pope, in an attempt to regain his temporal authority, was about to transform Brazil into a veritable theocracy.[11] The extreme Liberals

---

[7] "Ganganelli," the pseudonym used by Saldanha Marinho, has a significant derivation. Ganganelli was the family name of Pope Clement XIV, who suppressed the Jesuits in 1773. On Masonic opposition to the Society of Jesus, see p. 8, note 22, above.

[8] For a list of the large number of articles published by Saldanha Marinho, most of them under the pseudonym "Ganganelli," see Verbum, I (December, 1944), 359-360, 372. The most important work and the one most sought during the Episcopal-Masonic controversy was his A Egreja e o Estado (4 v., Rio de Janeiro, 1873-1876), since placed on the Index of prohibited books.

[9] National Archives, Department of State, vol. 40, Partridge to Fish, no. 168, April 22, 1874.

[10] Lídia Besouchet, José Ma. Paranhos, Vizconde Do Río Branco (Buenos Aires [1944], p. 198. "La 'cuestión religiosa' fué . . . una cuestión entre católicos masones y católicos ortodoxos por la supremacía espiritual, por el derecho a dirigir al pueblo, moral y políticamente."

[11] The recent unification of Italy gave currency to this propaganda. Actually it was rooted in the antagonism of Liberals 'for Pius IX, whose Syllabus of Errors and whose triumph in the Vatican Council had aroused their displeasure. On this assertion, see pp. 190, 225-226 below. See also Partridge to

who, under the domination of Freemasonry, were eager to control the Church, found propaganda suggesting the threat of ultramontanism amazingly effective. Moderate Liberals refused to acknowledge that Brazilian Masonry was hostile to the Church; they seem never to have suspected that the fraternity had manufactured the ultramontane scare.[12] In the best regalistic tradition, they proceeded to a defense of civil authority allegedly endangered by ecclesiastical aggression.

The Religious Question had not failed to arouse the anxiety of the emperor and the members of the royal family. In the despatch just referred to, the minister commented that "all this gives great anxiety at the Palace. The Empress — who is very charitable and a most devout Catholic — looks at it, of course, in but one way. The Emperor is much concerned. He is determined to vindicate the national supremacy, yet he is anxious not to offend."[13] The attitude of Pedro II toward the Catholic religion, discussed in a previous chapter,[14] doubtless influenced his position in the present crisis; yet the meager appeal which revealed religion had for him was not alone accountable for his stand on the present ecclesiastical problem. Pedro, like his ministers, was strongly regalistic in his ideology. Lídia Besouchet analyzes his political attitudes in these words:

> . . . the right to rule over the people without interference of any other power was profoundly rooted in his mentality; his regalism was the more sincere since it continued the immediate tradition bequeathed by Feijó, the most legitimate representative of regalism

---

Fish, no. 223, January 20, 1875: ". . . the conditions of this same conflict, in other countries — not only in Europe, but in South America — in Chile, Mexico and Peru — and even in Venezuela, where the Ultramontanes have been beaten in their attempt to establish their 'higher law' — assists the resolution of this ministry. It even warms up the courage of those who wished to see the national supremacy vindicated; but feared that dire things must result from an attempt to impose mere civil law on sacred persons."

[12] See pp. 100-101 above.

[13] National Archives, Department of State, vol. 40, Partridge to Fish, no. 168, April 22, 1874.

[14] See pp. 90-92 above.

on Brazilian soil. Moreover, the regalism of Pedro II was intrinsic, fundamental, since it came to him 'through family tradition, through personal conviction, and through the exercise of power.'[15]

The emperor's attitude will be further clarified when the rôle of the prime minister, Rio Branco, is discussed, but it should be observed in passing that Pedro II was aware that the religious crisis of the empire might well have serious political implications. He saw, as Oliveira Lima puts it, that it might be necessary "for the Imperial Government to go to Canossa";[16] yet he refused, as long as possible, to recede from the position which he had chosen,[17] and it was he who held out longest against granting the amnesty.[18] Even after he was forced by political necessity to exonerate the two prelates, he continued his animosity toward them.[19] In the opinion of the emperor, wrote Joaquim Nabuco,

[15] ". . . estaba profundamente enraizada en su mentalidad el derecho a reinar sobre el pueblo sin interferencias de ningún otro poder; su regalismo era tanto más sincero cuanto continuaba la tradición inmediata dejada por Feijó, el más legítimo representante del regalismo en tierra brasileña. También el regalismo de Pedro II era intrínseco, fundamental, pues le venía, por tradición de familia, por convicción personal y por el ejercicio del poder'." Besouchet, *op. cit.*, pp. 188-189.

[16] Manuel de Oliveira Lima, *O imperio brazileiro 1822-1889* (São Paulo, 1927), p. 174.

[17] Magalhães, *op. cit.*, p. 136, cites the following incident to illustrate the attitude of the emperor: "Quando Pio IX, em carta autógrafa ao imperador do Brasil, a êste pediu pusesse em liberdade os diocesanos de Pernambuco e do Pará, então recolhidos presos nas fortalezas da baía de Guanabara, o nosso derradeiro soberano, dando conta da solicitação papal ao gabinete, declarou alto e bom som: — 'O poder moderador não transige'." Joaquim Nabuco, *Um estadista do imperio Nabuco de Araujo, sua vida, suas opiniões, sua época* (Rio de Janeiro, 1897-1899), III, 388-389, writes: "Ha um tanto da dignidade imperial offendida na attitude do Imperador; elle sente pessoalmente a offensa, recebe o desafio, e desde logo avoca a si a questão. A submissão dos Bispos, *per fas et nefas*, como a guerra do Paraguay, como a emancipação dos escravos, torna-se um caso reservado á Corôa." See particularly Wanderley Pinho, ed., *Cartas do Imperador D. Pedro II ao Barão de Cotegipe* (São Paulo, 1933), pp. 239-240.

[18] Magalhães, *op. cit.*, pp. 128, 137; Pinho, *op. cit.*, p. 474.

[19] Magalhães, *op. cit.*, p. 137.

the recalcitrant bishops are two high strung individuals [*exaltados*], who come to alarm and disturb consciences, to perturb the peace in which the Church and the Episcopacy had always lived with it [the State]; they are two well-known, ambitious persons who want to be talked about, and for that purpose revolt against the Sovereign who nominated them, and against the Constitution, thanks to which they were bishops, because, without imperial presentation, the apostolic succession would probably have fallen on others.[20]

According to the American minister, the imperial cabinet, no less than the emperor, was deeply concerned about the agitation which attended the trial and imprisonment of the bishops. It had to consider, he writes, what effect the Episcopal-Masonic controversy would have on its majority in the chambers when the May session convened.[21] The minister repeatedly called attention to the fact that the clerical party, as he called it, might upset the ministerial majority.[22] From the entrance of the gov-

---

[20] ". . . os Bispos recalcitrantes são dois exaltados que vêm alarmar e transtornar as consciencias, perturbar a paz em que a Igreja e o Episcopado sempre viveo com elle; são dois ambiciosos de nomeada, que querem fazer fallar de si, e para isso revoltam-se contra o Soberano que os nomeou e contra a Constituição, graças á qual elles eram Bispos, porque sem a apresentação imperial a successão apostolica teria talvez recahido em outros." Nabuco, *op. cit.*, III, 388.

[21] National Archives, Department of State, vol. 40, Partridge to Fish, no. 168, April 22, 1874.

[22] A typical example occurs in Partridge to Fish, no. 117, June 23, 1873: "Sir: In my No. 113, I mentioned the question which had arisen here and which has since been debated in the Chambers, in consequence of the publication and attempted enforcement by the bishop of Pernambuco of the papal bulls of excommunication against the Free-Masons and the (irmandades) brotherhoods. The matter has occasioned a great deal of excitement, and the petition of the Free-Masons, *etc.*, claiming that such publication was illegal were referred to the department of State. This body had decided, and advised the Emperor, that the bishop had infringed the Brazilian constitution and laws by his proceedings . . . . The daily papers are filled with articles and communications growing out of this affair . . . . The clerical party have thus met with a signal defeat, but it is still strong in the Chambers, and will throw itself on either side to defeat the other, whose measures may have displeased it." National Archives, Department of State, vol. 40.

ernment into the controversy, the cause of the prelates had vigorous defenders in the two chambers; yet it is not to be inferred that the national legislature was thoroughly aroused in the cause of the bishops. The contrary seems nearer the truth. Basílio de Magalhães, whose thesis is that the nation was not moved to support the bishops, calls attention to the fact that of the five priests in the Chamber of Deputies, not one spoke in defense of them.[23] Other authors, who stress the fact that the cause of religion had valiant and brilliant defenders in parliament, do not neglect to say that the Brazilian Church suffered because of "the spirit of servility that unhappily animated not a few representatives of the Catholic people . . . ."[24] It is true, however, that the episcopal cause was defended by some statesmen of superior ability and unimpeachable integrity. Oliveira Lima brings this out when he speaks of parliamentary reactions to the social and religious unrest of the period:

> These tumults were the reflections of the many discussions in the press and also in Parliament, where pure conservatives like Ferreira Viana, Cândido Mendes, and Paulino de Sousa, and moderate Liberals like Zacarias, declared themselves champions of the orthodox doctrines of the persecuted prelates, and pronounced themselves against a government that, in the words of those orators, practiced a veritable abuse of authority by attempting to institute criminal action against high and worthy ministers of the Church who in nothing offended the civil law by their defense of ecclesiastical rights which referred exclusively to spiritual matters and were agitated round a question of religious beliefs.[25]

---

[23] Magalhães, op. cit., pp. 130-131. "Na assembléia geral, tinham então assento cinco sacerdotes católicos: o padre Manuel José de Siqueira Mendes, deputado pelo Pará; o padre Tomás de Morais Rego, do Piauí; o padre João Manuel de Carvalho, do Rio-Grande-do-Norte; o padre Francisco Pinto Pessôa, da Paraíba; monsenhor Joaquim Pinto de Campos, de Pernambuco; e o protonotário Ernesto Camilo Barreto, de Máto-Grosso."

[24] Antônio de Almeida Lustosa, Dom Macedo Costa (Rio, 1939), p. 219. See also Oliveira Lima, O imperio brazileiro, p. 180.

[25] "Eram estes motins o reflexo das multiplas discussões na imprensa e tam-

On the other hand, a large but inarticulate group in both chambers firmly supported the ministry. Members of this group found it impossible to believe that Freemasonry in Brazil was other than a beneficent society engaged in charitable works, and readily gave credence to the regalistic theory that the bishops were not attacking Masonry, but were trying to foist upon Brazil the doctrines enunciated by Pius IX in the *Syllabus of Errors*. Speaking in the Senate on May 17, 1873, José Maria Paranhos, viscount of Rio Branco, said that Brazilian Masonry was not concerned either with politics or with religion; its mission, he affirmed, was purely moral and beneficent; hence it was European, not Brazilian Masonry that was condemned by the Church.[26] With like conviction, Alencar Araripe, speaking in the Chamber of Deputies on May 24, 1873, placed emphasis on the anti-Liberal aspect of the action taken by the bishops against Freemasonry. He described graphically what in his opinion would happen if the ultramontane group was to have its way. There would be a resurrection, he said, of the temporal power of the pope and of the bishops, together with the application of the anti-Liberal doctrines of the *Syllabus*, which would restrain all human liberty.[27] These two ideas, which had been popular-

bem no Parlamento, onde conservadores puros como Ferreira Vianna, Candido Mendes e Paulino de Souza, e liberaes moderados, como Zacharias, se declararam campeões das doutrinas orthodoxas dos prelados perseguidos, pronunciando-se contra um governo que, no dizer d'aquelles oradores, praticava um verdadeiro abuso de auctoridade intentando acção criminal contra altos e dignos ministros da Egreja que em nada offendiam as leis civis com sua defesa dos direitos ecclesiasticos, os quaes se referiam exclusivamente a assumptos espirituaes e eram agitados em redor de uma questão de crenças religiosas." Oliveira Lima, *O imperio brazileiro*, pp. 172-173. See also Lustosa, *op. cit.*, p. 251. "No parlamento brasileiro, distinctos oradores defenderam a causa dos Bispos, estreitamente vinculada aos interesses gerais dos católicos. Zacarias, Figueira de Melo, Mendes de Almeida, Rodrigues Silva, Abaeté e principalmente Silveira Lobo, fulminaram no Senado a prepotência do governo, neste memoravel conflito, com eloquência máscula e ciência profunda. Na câmara temporária, Paulino de Souza, Ferreira Viana, Tarquínio de Souza, Diogo de Vasconcelos, Araújo Lima, Duque Estrada Teixeira, Leandro Bezerra, Carlos da Luz e outros esmagaram o ministério perseguidor."

[26] *Anais do Senado*, 1873, I, 105-107.

[27] *Anais da Câmara dos Deputados*, 1873, I, 163-164. Alencar Araripe

ized by Freemasonry, were accepted by many honest, patriotic men who believed themselves to be perfectly orthodox Catholics.[28]

In connection with the ministerial reaction, the American minister gives an interesting estimate of the Rio Branco ministry:

> The present Ministry (Rio Branco) has lasted an uncommonly long time and this is due as much to the tact and dexterity, as to the undoubted ability and capacity of its chief. He has certainly more of all these than any other I have seen here, and has known well how to avail himself of the changes and shades in public opinion. He offended some of his own party, the extreme Conservatives (slaveholders and planters) when he supported and established the Emancipation Bill;[29] and yet he has disarmed, at least a part of their resentment by relieving their products from taxation. By his course in this ecclesiastical affair he has compelled the Liberals to support him. So although he has, on one or two occasions, modified the Cabinet 'of the 7 [of] March'[30] it still remains in power. Yet no one knows better than himself that it is still quite uncertain how far he can rely upon his majority in the Deputies when they shall meet in May.
>
> He is probably wise enough to be satisfied with the judgment of the Court which secured his victory, and does not wish to create sympathy for the defeated

---

admitted that Brazilian Masonry followed the dictates (*dictames*) and principles of universal Masonry. He therefore had to admit the existence of the bulls condemning Masonry. For him as for all regalists these bulls had no value in Brazil without the imperial *placet*.

[28] Lúcio José dos Santos, "A maçonaria no Brasil," *A Ordem*, XII (July, 1932), p. 23, writes: "Resulta desses discursos a convicção dominante, convicção que nos custa crer fosse sincera, de que a Maçonaria no Brasil era apenas uma sociedade beneficente, em nada contrariando a religião, e si condemnação houvera, referia-se apenas á Maçonaria europea." These two discourses were printed by the Masonic fraternity and dispersed throughout the empire. (*Ibid.*, n. 1.)

[29] See p. 99 above.

[30] The Rio Branco ministry came into power on March 7, 1870. Ministries during the empire were frequently distinguished in this fashion.

party by a vigorous execution of the sentence. For
there are some among the Deputies of the Liberal party
in politics who are still extreme Conservatives on this
ecclesiastical question.[31]

This report calls attention to a fact that must not be overlooked in an interpretation of the Religious Question. Undoubtedly many statesmen had purely political reasons for the
stand they took in the controversy. It would be rash to assume
that every man was intellectually committed to one side or the
other. The passage, however, intimates that the position of the
viscount of Rio Branco was determined largely by political
interests, which probably was not true. He was intensely loyal
to the emperor, and he was convinced, moreover, that it was the
duty of the State to preserve its integrity and to prevent the
infringement of its rights. A recent biography of Rio Branco
stresses these points:

> For Pedro II 'the resistance of the bishops was a triple
> offense: against national sovereignty, against the
> majesty of the Empire, and against the dignity of the
> Emperor.' This deeply rooted opinion was shared by
> many, inasmuch as Paranhos [the viscount of Rio
> Branco], as well as Sousa Franco, João Alfredo,
> Pimenta Bueno, Sapucaí, Bom Retiro, and the Baron
> of Lucena (President of the province of Pernambuco),
> all partners of the great religious-masonic drama, were
> convinced of the rights of the monarchy to act against
> the interference of the Vatican and moreover [they
> were convinced] that it was obliged to act in this man-
> ner in defense of the nation.[32]

---

[31] National Archives, Department of State, vol. 40, Partridge to Fish, no.
168, April 22, 1874.

[32] "Para Pedro II 'la resistencia de los obispos era una triple ofensa: contra
la soberanía nacional, contra la magestad del Imperio y contra la dignidad del
Emperador.' Esta opinión, muy arraigada, era compartida por muchos, pues
tanto Paranhos como Souza Franco, João Alfredo, Pimenta Bueno, Sapucaí,
Bom Retiro, y el Barón de Lucena (Presidente de la provincia de Pernambuco), comparsas todos del gran drama religioso-masón, estaban convencidos
de los derechos de la monarquía para actuar contra la ingerencia del Vaticano y

The same biographer says that the Episcopal-Masonic controversy served to demonstrate the fact that during the entire second reign, Paranhos rallied to the side of Pedro II in the gravest moments of the nation. "Paranhos is always the providential man, the one called to support the throne when the latter is at the point of being destroyed in its moral or political structure."[33]

The accumulation of evidence points more and more to regalism as the force behind the government in the Episcopal-Masonic controversy. Men like Rio Branco and João Alfredo were so committed to a regalistic position in political affairs that they did not discern that many of the current rumors about re-establishing the temporal power of the pope and of the bishops were nothing more nor less than Masonic propaganda. To most Brazilian statesmen, the Masonic fraternity was the symbol of national autonomy, but they failed to recognize that Brazilian Masonry had changed since the time of Dom Pedro I. Lúcio José dos Santos describes the change, and suggests reasons for it.

> Until the fall of the first emperor, in 1831, Masonry in Brazil was a society almost exclusively political and patriotic, endeavoring to secure by all means, not always licit, the independence of the country. Its goal was a Republic; it accommodated itself, however, to a Constitutional representative monarchy, as more consistent with the conditions of the moment.

> From that time forward, whether because it became more intimate and more affective in its union with European Masonry; whether because until then, it had had more urgent business to take care of . . . the fact is that during the second empire Brazilian Masonry could show all its hostility against the Church.[34]

---

por otra parte estaba obligada a actuar así en defensa de la nacionalidad." Besouchet, *op. cit.*, pp. 185-186.

[33] *Ibid.*, p. 187.

[34] "Até a queda do primeiro imperador, em 1831, foi a Maçonaria no Brasil uma sociedade quasi exclusivamente politica e patriotica, procurando por todos os meios, nem sempre licitos, a libertação da patria. O seu objectivo era a republica; accomodou-se, porém, á monarchia constitucional representativa, como mais consentanea com as condições do momento.

Later in the same article Santos says, "We owe especially to Saldanha Marinho, to the indefatigable Ganganelli, the inestimable service of having unmasked the Masonic plans."[35]

If the imperial government was determined to assert its right to regulate the activity of the Church within the empire, the spiritual authority was no less determined to maintain its claim to exercise spiritual jurisdiction free from governmental supervision. These conflicting objectives had led to the trial and imprisonment of the two prelates; they were presently to provoke juridical action against the vicars general who had been appointed by the bishops of Olinda and Pará to administer their dioceses during the period of the bishops' imprisonment. In November, 1874, the American minister reported that the Religious Question had altered.

> The conflict (*questão religiosa*) between the civil power and the ecclesiastical party has come into a new phase.

> The bishops (of Olinda and of Pará) are still undergoing their nominal imprisonment; yet, through their Vicars General they govern their dioceses, and exhort the faithful, politically as well as spiritually, by 'Private' letters which are immediately published in the newspapers. The administration has allowed this to go on quietly, but has now addressed positive orders to the Presidents of the Provinces (Pará and Pernambuco) to require the Vicars General to recall or withdraw the Episcopal interdicts (the issue of which caused the bishops' trials) against the fraternities which admitted to membership those belonging to the Masonic order.[36] This withdrawal is to take place

---

"Dessa epocha em deante, seja porque a sua ligação com a Maçonaria europea se tornou mais intima e mais affectiva, seja porque até então, tivera cousas mais urgentes em que cuidar . . . o certo é que, no segundo imperio, pôde a Maçonaria brasileira demonstrar toda a sua hostilidade contra a Igreja." Santos, "A maçonaria no Brasil," *loc. cit.*, p. 23.

[35] *Ibid.*, p. 24.

[36] Augusto Olímpio Viveiros de Castro, "Contribuções para a biographia de D. Pedro II," Parte Iª, *Revista do Instituto Histórico e Geográfico Brasileiro,*

within eight days thereafter under penalty of the said Vicars General being held (as the bishops were) to answer criminally for infraction of the law.[37]

The clergy of these dioceses met, says the despatch, and submitted a protest to the government; they maintained that it was not within their power to lift the interdicts which were canonically imposed sanctions. The clergy asserted, continues the minister,

> that in the instrument by which powers to govern *ad interim* were conferred by the imprisoned bishops on them, there was an express reservation and public withholding of any power to suspend, relieve, recall, withdraw, or annul in any way those interdicts and suspensions; so that they could not if they would, — after having first said that they would not if they could.[38]

Each bishop, foreseeing that the government would bring pressure on his vicar general, and that the latter's refusal to lift the interdict would, in all probability, condemn him to trial and imprisonment, had left a long list of ecclesiastics, each of whom in his turn would succeed as vicar.[39] The American minister observed that enough alternates were provided to occupy the

tomo especial (1925), 506-507. This work will hereafter be cited as Castro. The inconsistency in the procedure of the imperial government is apparent in the speech delivered by the minister of justice on September 21, 1874: "Encontramos responsabilizados, presos e condemnados, ou em via de sê-lo não só os respectivos bispos, como tambem os governadores por elles nomeados, cuja auctoridade fôra reconhecida pelo Govêrno, mas que a seu turno recusaram levantar os interdictos. Dahi resultara ficar a diocese do Pará sem regime regular, porquanto, condemnado o governador, e deliberando o Govêrno Imperial não reconhecer mais a autoridade dos prepostos nomeados pelos bispos, ordenou que o Cabido elegesse vigario capitulár. Ora, essa ordem não foi cumprida; entretanto que a governador, apesar de preso, continuava a exercer a jurisdicção espiritual." *Ibid.*

[37] National Archives, Department of State, vol. 41, Partridge to Fish, no. 211, November 20, 1874.

[38] *Ibid.*

[39] Dom Vital and Dom Antônio both wrote to the prime minister to explain that the assertions of their respective vicars general to the effect that they

imperial ministry for a long time.[40]

In January, 1875, Partridge informed the Department of State that the Brazilian government "still follows up its determination to punish the refractory Ecclesiastics who persist in violating the laws of their own country in order to comply with the mandates from Rome."[41] He did not conceal the fact that his sympathies were with the ministry, which he viewed as commendably liberal and progressive. In his message of November 20, 1874, he had written:

> It will be interesting to know the results of all this; and to see whether Brazil is going still forward in these matters, or whether, just at this moment, the pendulum which regulates all progress, must have another swing backwards for the moment, only to come up higher on the other side, at the next movement that is sure to follow.[42]

This observation is typical of the point of view of the American diplomatic representative toward the whole Religious Question.[43]

The so-called Conservative ministry of Rio Branco[44] was re-

---

had not the authority to lift the interdict were entirely correct. For these letters see Lustosa, *op. cit.*, pp. 254-256.

[40] National Archives, Department of State, vol. 41, Partridge to Fish, no. 211, November 20, 1874.

[41] *Ibid.*, no. 223, January 20, 1875.

[42] *Ibid.*, no. 211, November 20, 1874.

[43] For other examples, see Partridge to Fish, no. 121, July 22, 1873: "From these two decisions [to punish the bishops and to recognize Protestant marriages] of the Council of State, if the Government shall have the courage to enforce them, there may begin a new era of toleration and liberality in this Empire." National Archives, Department of State, vol. 40, Partridge to Fish, no. 223, January 20, 1875: "There seems no reason to fear that the Government here will not triumph in the great struggle." *Ibid.*, Vol. 41.

[44] Joaquim Nabuco, *Minha formação* (Rio de Janeiro, 1900), pp. 28-29, has this to say of the Rio Branco Ministry: "Nesses annos o partido liberal leva o ministerio Rio-Branco para onde quer. Seguramente a opinião liberal teve muito mais poder sobre aquelle ministerio do que sobre o ministerio Sinimbú ou qualquer outro do seu proprio partido, — excepto o ministerio Dantas, porque neste o Presidente do Conselho era impressionavel á menor

placed on June 25, 1875, by another ministry of the same party under the presidency of the duke of Caxias. Although the ecclesiastical question was not responsible for the downfall of the viscount of Rio Branco,[45] the new prime minister recognized the seriousness of the religious problem, and immediately approached the emperor on the matter of amnesty. The emperor was reluctant to recede from the position which the imperial government had taken relative to the bishops, but Caxias succeeded in impressing him with the fact that the present situation was untenable. On September 17, 1875, the emperor granted amnesty to the two bishops, and to all vicars general who had been imprisoned for refusing to lift the interdicts. Many historians have asserted incorrectly that it was the Princess Elizabeth, heiress presumptive to the throne, who signed the amnesty.[46] Equally inaccurate appears the inference that the princess was responsible for bringing about the exoneration of the two pre-

censura do liberalismo. A verdade é que o ministerio Rio-Branco foi um ministerio reformista como desde o gabinete Paraná não se tinha visto outro e não se viu nenhum depois. O governo tinha o prurido das reformas, não talvez por inclinação propria, mas para desarmar a opposição liberal. Em dois pontos sómente elle mostrou-se conservador, á moda antiga: na sua prevenção contra a eleição directa, que provavelmente era tambem do Imperador, e em relação ao equilibrio do Prata . . . . Em tudo mais foi um ministerio innovador como o partido liberal não teria egual. O panno das reformas era fornecido pelos liberaes; era todo de padrão liberal; mas o mestre conservador talhava nelle com um largueza de tesoura que faria chorar no poder toda a alfaiataria contraria. Na questão religiosa, principalmente, á attitude de Rio-Branco só se poderia chamar conservadora por ser Pombalina, ultra regalista. O partido liberal em vez de exultar dizia-se roubado, pleiteava as suas patentes de invenção, suas marcas de fabrica." Lima, O imperio brazileiro, p. 173, refers to the Rio Branco ministry as "do ministerio de rotulo conservador e de facto anti-clerical."

[45] Financial reasons appear to have been foremost in the opposition to the Viscount of Rio Branco. Besouchet, op. cit., p. 251, has this to say: "El gabinete del 7 marzo sufre los violentos ataques de los Liberales por las reformas que intenta realizar: 'El gabinete de Río Branco ha sido acusado de causar el aumento de los gastos publicos. . . .'"

[46] Heitor Lyra, Historia de Dom Pedro II 1825-1891 (São Paulo, 1938-1940), II, 358, note 332. Lyra says the mistake was first made by Oliveira Lima, who erred in chronology.

198      *The Church and Freemasonry in Brazil*

lates,[47] for, as Nabuco says, the amnesty was a political necessity.[48] The government in taking civil action against the bishops had proceeded "by a road that did not offer any outlet."[49] The cabinet, the councilors of state, and even the emperor were forced to acknowledge that "the wiser procedure would have been to avoid the policy of coercion, to appeal to Rome."[50] Even the American diplomatic agents, who had no feeling for the Church, and who accepted unquestioningly the assertion of the imperial government that the two bishops had obstructed the moderative power of the emperor, found it difficult to see why religion was subject to temporal jurisdiction. In a review of the Episcopal-Masonic controversy, the American chargé d'affaires described the brotherhoods, the reason for their conflict with their ordinaries, the way the government became embroiled in the quarrel, and the refusal of the bishops to lift the interdict. He wrote:

> The Church persisted, and held that in matters spiritual she would look only to Rome for guidance. The State also remained firm. Then came the condemnation and imprisonment first of the Bishops, and later on of the governors, or rectors, appointed by them in their absence, who also refused to remove the interdicts. By this step all hope of an amicable settlement at Rome, was dispelled; and nothing was left but that

---

[47] While the princess was eager to have the bishops exonerated and certainly urged her father to grant amnesty, it is most improbable that the emperor would have acquiesced had not the political situation demanded the action.

[48] Nabuco, *Um estadista*, III, 385; Lyra, *op. cit.*, pp. 358-359: "A anistia não foi, como se disse, uma inspiração do sentimento catolico da Princeza Imperial. Foi uma medida de exclusiva iniciativa do Ministerio, que fazia dela, como declarou Cotegipe no Senado, uma *questão sua*. 'Conscienciosa e livremente' — acentuaria o ministro da Justiça desse Gabinete, conselheiro Diogo Velho, — ela foi submetida á aprovação do Imperador. O Ministerio estava persuadido de que a prisão dos Bispos era a unica razão pela qual a Santa-Sé negava-se a consentir nos levantamentos dos interditos; atendendo, portanto, a esta consideração, e tendo em conta tambem que os prelados já haviam sofrido, moral e fisicamente, o devido castigo, êle solicitou do Imperador a concessão da anistia."

[49] Castro, p. 506.

[50] ". . . mais acertado teria sido evitar a politica de coerção, appellar para

the Bishops should be punished or that one party should abandon its position, and the alternative has been at last chosen by the State.

As to the rights of both parties to the controversy; the Bishops doubtless violated the law that forbids any obstruction of the Acts of the Moderative Power, at the same time the order against the interdicts was one such as would not have been issued either in the United States or in England, an order that can only be regarded as tolerable in the light of the intimate relations between Church and State in Brazil; and one not unlike a command to a charitable society of the established church to admit Dissenters to its ranks.[51]

## II

After the amnesty was granted, the old question of the interdicts remained to be settled. Almost immediately the Holy See took action; in a letter dated September 30, 1875, Cardinal Antonelli, papal secretary of state, commissioned the chargé d'affaires, Monsignor Bruschetti,[52] to order the interdicts lifted.[53]

Roma." *Ibid.* W. A. Purrington reported some unofficial observations made to him by the representative of the Vatican (Purrington to Fish, no. 288, September 30, 1875) : "In a conversation yesterday with the Chargé d'Affaires of the Holy See, he told me that the Cabinet had been unanimous for the measure, the Minister of Marine Dr. Luis Antonio Pereira Franco being the only one who hesitated in his opinion. In the Council of State there were but three opponents to it, two of them members of the Last Ministry [Rio Branco's] and he represented Baron de Cotegipe as saying that it was a measure founded on public policy solely and with a view to quiet the agitation of the country which might culminate in serious outbreaks during the coming election." National Archives, Department of State, vol. 42.

[51] National Archives, Department of State, vol. 42, Purrington to Fish, no. 288, September 30, 1875.

[52] Luigi Bruschetti arrived on March 30 to replace Ferrini, who died on January 13, 1875. See *Relatorio da Repartição dos Negocios Estrangeiros apresentado á Assembléa Geral Legislativa na quarta sessão da decima-quinta legislatura pelo Ministro e Secretario de Estado Visconde de Caravellas* (Rio de Janeiro, 1875), p. 30. See also Partridge to Fish, no. 213, November 23, 1874. ". . . we hear, from Rome, that the Pope is so dissatisfied with hostility shown by Brazil, to the just rights of the Church, that he will maintain here only a Charge d'Affaires in place of the late Internunzio [*sic*] Sanguigni, now sent as nunzio to Lisbon." National Archives, Department of State, vol. 41.

[53] This letter is given in Antônio Manuel dos Reis, *O Bispo de Olinda*

telegram from the Holy See that the pope had removed the interdicts. In the light of what had happened, these communications
occasioned considerable surprise. Purrington reflected the current
reaction in his despatch of October 12, 1875:

> Color would seem to be given to the statement that
> the Amnesty would restore concord between Church
> and State, by the receipt of a telegram announcing that
> the Pope had removed the interdicts laid on the
> Masons.[54] But the despatch itself does not gain uni-
> versal credence. It is hard to conceive how the Pope,
> even for the sake of policy, could, in the face of his
> own Bull, grant such a concession to a body of men,
> whom the Church of Rome had denounced; and who
> have expelled from their ranks the head of that
> Church. Add to this that the Bishop of Olinda, in a
> pastoral letter, had denounced the Masons as the Arch-
> Enemies of the Church, as profane men scoffing at all
> the mysteries that lie at the bottom of the Roman
> faith, and it will appear more incredible that the Pope
> should assume an attitude at once illogical and re-
> flecting on the course of the 'martyred' bishops. Up to
> this time the telegram has not been officially con-
> firmed.[55]

The papal order to lift the interdicts was not an unqualified act
of clemency on the part of the Holy See. Almost immediately
the Supreme Pontiff notified the imperial government that an
internuncio would be sent to arrange a concordat. The Liberals
were alarmed, because they knew that the question of the Masonic affiliation of Catholics would be reopened. The political

---

*Perante a Historia* (Recife 1940-1942), II, 319-320.

[54] *Ibid.*, p. 320, note 51, comments: "O levantamento dos interditos . . .
foram objéto de discussões pró e contra; apesar de tudo pensamos que a sua
publicação fosse providencial para indicar aos Prelados que não ficavam desobri-
gados de limpar as irmandades do virus maçonico." See Félix de Olívola, *Um
Grande Brasileiro, D. Frei Vital Maria Gonçalves Oliveira* (2d. ed., Recife,
1936), p. 212.

[55] National Archives, Department of State, vol. 42, Purrington to Fish,
no. 289, October 12, 1875.

tension in Brazil at this time is remarked by Partridge, who indicated the forces that were being marshalled against the empire.

> We have news (by telegram) from Rome, that Monsignor Roncetti will be sent here as Internunzio, and for the purpose of arranging the still unsettled 'ecclesiastical question' by insisting on the exclusion of the Masonic order from the religious brotherhoods; and with intention, also, of making a *Concordat* upon this and other points involved in that question. This announcement has aroused the Press and political pamphleteers; and a series of articles have been published by Counsellor Saldanha Marina [*sic*] speaking in very plain language, and declaring that if during this (the Princess') Regency the present government should yield at all to the pretensions and exactions of the Roman Curia, the Brazilian people will know how to resist any such surrender of their liberties and sovereignty, and will themselves do the work that is necessary to remedy the evil already done and prevent in future all priestly influence, through females, for the subverting of the Constitution.
>
> In short, it is plainly said, and by men who mean what they say — that any repetition of what has been done in this matter, and any sign of further yielding will be met by revolution.[56]

Oliveira Lima, referring to the Religious Question, remarked that the regalism of the imperial constitution was more powerful than the Catholic sentiment of Brazil,[57] and in the light of the political situation just reviewed, this statement by one of the foremost historians of nineteenth century Brazil is easily accepted. Yet, when we marshal all the evidence, we find that among the surprisingly large number of regalistically-inclined statesmen who wanted the Church subservient to the State, only a very small number were hostile to the Catholic faith.[58] The cleavage

---

[56] National Archives, Department of State, vol. 42, Partridge to Fish, no. 336, July 10, 1876.

[57] Lima, *O imperio brazileiro*, p. 180.

[58] Besouchet, *op. cit.*, pp. 199-200. ". . . desde las logias masónicas, la *elite* liberal brasileña combatió al clero ortodoxo [those supporting Rome],

between the regalist and the Freemason is discernible at this point.[59] Men like Nabuco de Araújo, João Alfredo, Rio Branco, and a host of others wanted to dominate the Church under the pretext of protecting it, but they did not want to destroy the Catholic faith. Young radicals like Rui Barbosa and Joaquim Nabuco were for a time avowedly hostile to the Church; yet even with them antipathy for the Church was fundamentally a rebellion against papal supremacy, which they felt infringed on national autonomy. What Joaquim Nabuco writes of himself might be applied to many of the ultra-Liberals of his era:

> At that time and during some years, radicalism carried me; I am, for example, among those who take a more active part in the Masonic campaign of 1873 against the bishops and against the Church. I even toy with the idea of Feijó, of a National Church, independent of Roman discipline . . .[60]

## III

When the imperial government began its action against Dom Vital and Dom Antônio, the archbishop of Baía, Dom Manuel Joaquim da Silveira, was among the first of the Brazilian hierarchy to support openly the policy of his suffragans. Early in 1873, the archbishop issued two pastoral letters against Mason-

---

mas no a la Iglesia. Los hombres más avanzados y progresistas de la época — Ottoni, Teixeira Leite, Mauá, Paranhos, todos aquellos que formaban la vanguardia en las iniciativas nacionales —, continuaban fieles al catolicismo, mandaban sua hijos a colegios de curas, exigían la disciplina religiosa hasta en la familia de sus esclavos, obligando a rezar el rosario en los cuarteles, en las *senzalas*, en las *fazendas* . . . . El casamiento era el eclesiástico tanto como las actas de bautismo, nacimiento y defunción; se desconocía aún la independencia y separación de facultades entre Iglesia y Estado; recién es la cuestión religiosa la que provocará la clarificación de estos valores hasta entonces confusos."

[59] The propaganda against Catholic dogma which appeared in certain Masonic publications was not endorsed by statesmen. They opposed the dogma of infallibility, it is true, but for political reasons, and even in the campaign against the papacy, only a few public figures, like Saldanha Marinho, resorted to abusive and unbecoming language.

[60] Nabuco, *Minha formação*, pp. 29-30.

ry,[61] and in November of the same year published the papal brief
*Quamquam dolores.*[62] On January 8, 1874, he sent a remonstrance to the emperor against the trial of the bishop of Olinda,[63]
and on March 2, 1874, he directed a circular to his suffragans
on the condemnation of the bishop. In his circular, he urged
the bishops to offer passive resistance to what he considered to
be the despotism of imperial Masonry.[64] An added manifestation of the attitude of the Brazilian metropolitan is seen in the
fact that he kept in touch by letter with his imprisoned suffragan, Dom Vital.[65] Dom Manuel, who died before the bishop
of Pará was convicted, was prevented from carrying his activities
to a decisive conclusion, yet his conduct during the opening stages
of the Episcopal-Masonic controversy shows that he supported
the position taken by the two bishops. The objection might be
raised that while the archbishop gave public approbation to the
actions of these bishops after they launched their campaign
against the Masonic infiltration of Catholic associations, he did
not initiate any movement against such infiltration. The Masonic fraternity had not, however, challenged the archbishop.
It will be recalled that Dom Vital stated explicitly in his first
letter to João Alfredo that he would not have attacked Masonry
if it had not first attacked him.[66]

Every bishop in Brazil published the papal brief *Quamquam
dolores,* even though it had not received the imperial *placet,*[67]
and every bishop replied to the archbishop's circular.[68] The ven-

[61] Reis, *op. cit.,* II, 322.
[62] *Ibid.,* p. 323. This brief, it will be recalled, was received by Dom Vital
on the same day that he received the imperial order to lift the interdicts placed
on the recalcitrant brotherhoods (see p. 161 above). The Pope ordered the
bishop of Olinda to communicate his message to all the bishops of Brazil.
[63] *Ibid.,* p. 324.
[64] Ibid., p. 325; Magalhães, *op. cit.,* p. 130, quotes from this circular:
"Um bispo de calceta, por desempenhar os seus sagrados deveres! . . . E' triste,
é bem triste, é consternador, é degradante, desce até á última escala da abjeção
um procedimento de tão degenerada natureza!"
[65] Reis, *op. cit.,* II, 326.
[66] See p. 132 above.
[67] Reis, *op. cit.,* II, 323-328, *passim.*
[68] *Ibid.,* p. 326-329.

erable bishop of Mariana, Dom Antônio Ferreira Viçosa, who during his long episcopacy had been uncompromising in his defense of the liberty of the Church,[69] directed to the emperor a remonstrance against Masonry,[70] and on April 30, 1874, he sent a circular to the pastors of his diocese recommending that they expel Freemasons from the religious brotherhoods.[71] In the spring of 1874, Dom João Antônio dos Santos, bishop of Diamantina (Minas-Gerais), issued a pastoral condemning Masonry.[72] In the fall of the same year, the bishop of Rio Grande do Sul, Dom Sebastião Dias Laranjeira, issued a pastoral ordering public prayers for the Church in her time of persecution.[73] In June of the following year the same prelate issued a pastoral announcing the jubilee year; in this he confirmed his adherence to the acts of the bishops of Olinda and Pará.[74]

The weakness displayed by Bishop Lacerda of Rio de Janeiro in not sustaining the position he took against Freemasonry in the spring of 1872 was not to characterize him during the Episcopal-Masonic controversy. One of the first Brazilian prelates to publish the papal brief *Quamquam dolores*, Bishop Lacerda prefaced it with an introduction in which he considered the attitude of popes and bishops toward Freemasonry. He stated unequivocally that Brazilian Masonry was under the same censure as European Masonry. Fourteen Brazilian prelates, he said,

---

[69] See Cônego Raimundo Trinidade, *Archidiocese de Marianna* (São Paulo, 1928), I, 433-438.

[70] *Ibid.*, p. 434.

[71] *Ibid.*, pp. 434-437. Canon Raimundo Trinidade writes (*ibid.*, pp. 434-435) : ". . . sahiu-se D. Viçosa com a seguinte circular . . . tão corajosa, tão franca, tão nos moldes das do Bispo de Olinda, que o ministerio maçonico tremeu, e receando haver-se com o Bispo de Marianna — da altiva e catholica Minas — determinou ás lojas da provincia que não se movessem nem fizessem o menor acto de provocação ao prelado mariannense."

[72] Reis, *op. cit.*, II, 327. This was not Dom João's first public condemnation of Freemasonry. See Pedro Maria de Lacerda, *Carta pastoral do Bispo de S. Sebastião do Rio de Janeiro publicando as Letras Apostolicas do Summo Pontifice e Santo Padre Pio IX de 29 de Maio de 1873* . . . . (Rio de Janeiro, 1873), p. 6.

[74] *Ibid.*, p. 335.

condemned it.[75] Lacerda cited the pastoral against Masonry published not long before by the archbishop of Baía, and urged his people to heed its warning. He concluded his introduction with the assertion:

> In Brazil there is no law which obliges anyone to join Masonry, and which prohibits leaving it. Therefore, Brazilian Catholics who in order to obey their Prelates and the Pope should not wish to be Masons or wish to leave Masonry, will be able to do it without disobeying the laws. In this fashion they would give to God what is God's, without taking away from Caesar what is Caesar's.[76]

The trial of Dom Vital prompted Lacerda to direct to the emperor a remonstrance condemning the civil action against his Olinda colleague.[77] These public testimonials, together with his visiting Vital in prison, his conferring on him the honor of full episcopal jurisdiction in the diocese of Rio de Janeiro, and his accompanying him on both days of the trial are indicative of his sympathy and support. In short, Bishop Lacerda was in full accord with the action taken by the bishops of Olinda and Pará against the Masonic infiltration of Catholic society.

In the course of the Episcopal-Masonic controversy, the Catholic journal, *Apóstolo,* of Rio de Janeiro, published letters from

---

[75] Lacerda, *op. cit.*, pp. 5-6.

[76] "No Brazil não ha lei nenhuma que obrigue a entrar para a maçonaria, e que prohiba sahir della. Portanto, os Catholicos Brazileiros que para obedecerem a seus Prelados e ao Papa, não quizerem ser maçons, ou quizerem deixar a maçonaria, bem o poderão fazer sem desobedecerem ás leis. Deste modo darão a Deus o que é de Deus, sem tirarem de Cesar o que é de Cesar." *Ibid.*, p. 8.

[77] *Representação que á S. M. o Imperador dirige o Bispo de S. Sebastião do Rio de Janeiro sobre a prisão e processo do Exmo. e Revmo. Sr. Bispo de Olinda e aderindo á representação do Exmo. Sr. Arcebispo da Baía* (Rio de Janeiro, 1874), cited in Reis, *op. cit.*, II, 344.

the bishops of Mariana,[78] Rio Grande do Sul,[79] São Paulo,[80] Baía,[81] and Goiaz,[82] in which these prelates declared themselves in sympathy with the action of Dom Vital. In April, 1874, the bishop of Diamantina (Minas-Gerais) directed a letter to the imperial government protesting its action in the Episcopal-Masonic controversy,[83] and in May of the same year, the bishop of Goiaz sent a remonstrance to the emperor on the same matter.[84] These manifestations of approval[85] given to the two prelates who openly attacked Masonry support the assertions made by the American chargé d'affaires:

> After the receipt of the papal Bull of the 29 of May last, applauding the course of the Bishop of Olinda in interdicting the various religious brotherhoods of his diocese, — because they declined to expel, upon his order, those of their members who were Free Masons, — all the other bishops announced it as their resolute purpose to faithfully obey any and all instructions which His Holiness might send them, being firmly convinced that, though Brazilians, their first allegiance

[78] "Carta que o Bispo de Mariana dirigiu ao Bispo de Olinda, aderindo à resolução tomada por este Prelado contra as Irmandades," *Apóstolo* (Rio de Janeiro), May 11, 1873, cited in Reis, *op. cit.*, p. 322.

[79] "Carta do Bispo de S. Pedro do Rio Grande do Sul, aderindo aos átos do Bispo de Olinda contra a Maçonaria do Brasil," *Apóstolo*, November 20, 1873, cited in *ibid.*, p. 324; "Carta do Bispo de S. Pedro do Rio Grande do Sul sobre a prisão do Bispo de Olinda," *Apóstolo*, February 18, 1874, cited in *ibid.*, p. 325.

[80] "Carta do Bispo de S. Paulo sobre a prisão do Bispo do Olinda," *Apóstolo*, February 6, 1874, cited in *ibid.*, p. 325.

[81] "Carta do Arcebispo da Baía ao Bispo de Olinda," *Apóstolo*, March 21, 1874, cited in *ibid.*, p. 326.

[82] "Carta do Bispo de Goiás ao Bispo de Olinda." *Apóstolo*, April 12, 1874, cited in *ibid.*, p. 326.

[83] "Ofício do Bispo da Diamantina ao Ministro do Imperio," *Apóstolo*, April 3, 1874, cited in *ibid.*, p. 326.

[84] "Representação do Bispo do Goiás a S. M. o Imperador," *Apóstolo*, May 3, 1874, cited in *ibid.*, p. 327.

[85] See G. Bezerra de Meneses, "O Episcopado Brasileiro e a Questão Religiosa," *Vozes de Petrópolis*, N. S. III (January and February, 1945), 105-109.

was due to Rome. Thus the Government was forced to the adoption of extreme measures; and since the opposition of the Bishop of Olinda had been more vigorous — and even defiant — than that of his colleagues, — he having persistently refused to obey the Resolution of the Council of State of the 12 of June,[86] it was finally resolved to bring that prelate to trial.[87]

## IV

Anyone who attempts to gauge popular reactions to the Episcopal-Masonic controversy is confronted with two conflicting opinions. One school of thought deduces from the evidence that the Brazilian people were passive; the other, that there was a general and articulate movement in support of the bishops. Basílio de Magalhães, who belongs to the first group, says: "The unconcealed truth is that the nation was not stirred in favor of the martyred bishops, and there was not the least attempt made to liberate them from prison."[88] His position is opposed by historians like Eugênio Vilhena de Morais, who refers to "the clamor of the Brazilian people for the liberation of the bishops."[89] An examination of the facts shows that the position taken by Vilhena de Morais is the more tenable, although something can be said for Magalhães' assertion. He is certainly right in his statement that the five clerics who were members of the Chamber of Deputies did not champion the cause of the episcopacy.[90] In fact, one of them sided so completely with the ministry that his speech in the session of June 17, 1874, elicited a protest from the clergy of Recife.[91] The failure of this group of

---

[86] See pp. 154-163 above.

[87] National Archives, Department of State, vol. 40, Shannon to Fish, no. 157, March 1, 1874.

[88] "A verdade insofismavel é que a nação não se movementou em prol dos bispos mártires, e não houve a menor tentativa para libertá-los do cárcere." Magalhães, op. cit., p. 131.

[89] Ibid., p. 131.

[90] See p. 189, note 23, above.

[91] Reis, op. cit., p. 330. "Protesto do Clero do Recife contra o discurso pronunciado pelo Padre João Manoel, na sessão de 17 de Junho, na Câmara dos Deputados." Apóstolo, August 19, 1874. For the speech, see Anais da

ecclesiastics to support the bishops is not, however, so significant as the fact that there was a scanty representation of clerics in the Chamber. It will be recalled that twenty-two priests were elected to the first Chamber of Deputies, in 1824.[92] The comparison becomes really significant when one recalls a statement made by Badaró in his *L'Église au Brésil* that priests friendly to Rome had no hope of election.[93] It ought not be difficult to predict, therefore, the stand that priests who were elected would take on the issue.

While one does not contest the fact that there were priests who failed to support the episcopacy in its concerted action against the infiltration of Freemasonry into Catholic society, yet one cannot overlook the abundance of evidence proving that a great many priests were in sympathy with the bishops. Magalhães leaves the reader with a false impression when he confines his comments on the clergy to the five priests in the Chamber of Deputies. A wider investigation will give a different picture. There were many ecclesiastics who remained silent during the Episcopal-Masonic controversy; among these were undoubtedly some who felt sympathetic with Masonry, and some who believed that the prelates were following the right course. The number in neither of these groups can be determined. In contrast to these, however, there were priests who openly took sides. A few who were very articulate created the impression of a concerted movement of opposition. These sought to justify the regalistic doctrines of the imperial *placet* and right of recourse, and they undertook to popularize the idea that Brazilian Masonry was not condemned by the Church. An example of this type of cleric was Joaquim do Monte Carmelo, whose prolific writings were a bulwark of the imperial position.[94] There were

---

Câmara dos Deputados, 1874, I, 186-194.

[92] See p. 64 above.

[93] P. 37. "Quant à ceux qui étaient amis de Rome, leur élection était impossible." See also Magalhães, *op. cit.*, p. 92.

[94] Most of Joaquim do Monte Carmelo's works were published anonymously. Among the most important is *O Brasil mystificado na Questão Religiosa* (Rio de Janeiro, 1875): this work was condemned by the Sacred Congregation of the Index by the decree of March 6, 1876; *A Luz e as Trevas,*

other priests who tried to maintain a *via media* between the attitude of the bishops and that of the government. Monsignor Pinto de Campos exemplifies this group. His address of June 15, 1873, in the Chamber of Deputies, is typical. He defended the action of the bishops and showed why it was perfectly valid; at the same time, he intimated that these prelates were making too much ado over the dangers of Masonry.[95] He did not repudiate the government; in fact, he eulogized Rio Branco, whose policies, he said, he would support because he knew that the prime minister would act in the interests of the Church.[96] Opposed to such an attempt to compromise were priests who by word and act supported wholeheartedly the action of the bishops against Freemasonry. At the very beginning of the controversy, on the order of Bishop Dom Vital, all the priests of the diocese of Olinda, except two, abjured Masonry.[97] Later, after the bishops were imprisoned, the clergy of the dioceses of Olinda and Pará agreed unanimously to defy the order of the government to raise the interdicts. Their opposition was shared by many priests of other dioceses, who sent messages to the imprisoned bishops,

---

*Sermão do Espirito Santo* (Rio de Janeiro, 1876), placed on the Index by decree of September 4, 1876 [cited in Reis, *op. cit.*, II, 346]; *Questão Religiosa, Carta á Serenissima Princesa Regente* (Rio de Janeiro, 1876): only the first part of this work seems to have been published. Another work by the same author, published under the pseudonym "Canonista," is *O Brasil e a Cúria Romana. Apreciação das exigencias que podem ser concedidas e das que devem ser recusadas — ou — Análise e refutação do Direito contra Direito do Sr. D. Antônio de Macedo Costa, Bispo do Pará* (Rio de Janeiro, 1876) [cited in *Verbum*, I (December, 1944), p. 354.] Articles published in the magazine *Reforma* later appeared in pamphlet. See *Questão Religiosa, O Arcipreste da Sé de S. Paulo Joaquim Anselmo de Oliveira e o cléro do Brazil por X . . .* (Rio de Janeiro, 1873).

[95] Attention has already been called to the fact that Monsignor Pinto de Campos said that if the sensible element in Masonry did not subscribe to the virulent attacks on Catholic dogma, common in Masonic journals, it should openly repudiate such propaganda. See p. 118, note 63, above.

[96] Joaquim Pinto de Campos, *Discurso pronunciado na sessão de 15 de Julho de 1873 por . . . deputado á Assembléa Geral pelo 5º. districto eleitoral da Provincia de Pernambuco* (Rio de Janeiro, 1873), p. 19.

[97] The two priests who refused to abjure were Father Francisco João de Azevedo and Dean Joaquim Francisco de Faria.

assuring them of their allegiance.[98] Moreover, some of the clergy, like João Silvério Esberard and Father Gomes Pimenta, met the attack of their disaffected colleagues with articles and pamphlets in which the episcopal position was defended.[99]

Magalhães asserts that the cause of the bishops created little excitement in the Chamber of Deputies, and alleges that what clamor there was, derived from political interest rather than ardor of faith.[100] He cites, by way of example, the denunciation presented by Deputy Leandro Bezerra de Meneses against the ministry of Rio Branco, and then observes that this denunciation was rejected. The account in the proceedings of the Chamber of Deputies makes the incident appear less simple than one might infer from Magalhães' observation. On September 2, 1874, Deputy Meneses presented a formal denunciation of the prime minister, the viscount of Rio Branco; the minister of the interior, João Alfredo Corrêa de Oliveira; and the minister of foreign affairs, the viscount of Caravelas. The deputy asserted that his denunciation was the echo of 100,000 citizens who had already sent complaints to the Chamber.[101] His testimonial of accusation[102] was assigned to a special commission for consider-

---

[98] Reis, *op. cit.*, pp. 321-339, lists all the letters and protests that were published in *Apóstolo*, the Catholic journal of Rio de Janeiro. In this tabulation, which gives indication of popular feeling, the clergy is well represented.

[99] See Dupanloup, bishop of Orléans, *Estudo sôbre a Maçonaria, Traduzido, oferecido e dedicado pelo Padre João Esberard aos venerandos Confessores da Fé, o Exmo. e Revm. Sr. D. Antônio de Macedo Costa, Bispo do Pará* (Rio de Janeiro, 1874) ; João Esberard, *A Igreja Católica, o Sr. Bispo Diocesano e o Maçonismo* (Rio de Janeiro, 1872) ; Father João Filippo, *Justificação da crença Católica contra o "Brasil Mistificado"* (São Paulo, 1880) ; S. G. P. [Father Silvério Gomes Pimenta] *Resposta ao Discurso do Sr. Conselheiro Saldanha Marinho proferido na Assembléa Maçônica a 27 de abril de 1872* (Rio de Janeiro, 1872). [Father Silvério Gomes Pimenta was vicar general of the diocese of Mariana following the death of Bishop Viçosa (d. 1875), and was later appointed first archbishop of that diocese.] Under his own name, Father Gomes Pimenta published *O papa e as Revoluções ou as obrigações dos fiéis para com o Sumo Pontífice* (Rio de Janeiro, 1879). All of these works are cited in *Verbum*, I (December, 1944), 351-380.

[100] Magalhães, *op. cit.*, p. 131.

[101] *Anais da Câmara dos Deputados*, 1874, V, 28.

[102] Signed by Monsignor Joaquim Pinto de Campos, Canon Tomás Rego.

ation. No action was taken against the three ministers, but the public denunciation accomplished exactly what its author had in view: it brought before the nation the fact that these ministers, in persecuting the two prelates, were in reality only fighting the cause of Masonry when they thought they were safeguarding civil authority.[103] But Magalhães says further that even if 100,000 citziens petitioned the government, nearly 10,000,000 did not.[104] One answer to this conclusion is that 100,000 more persons signed petitions asking for redress for the two prelates than signed testimonials commending the government for action against them.

The weakest of Magalhães' arguments is his contention that, had the Catholic faith of Brazil been sincere and ardent, it would have produced an armed revolt throughout the nation.[105] It is highly probable that such a revolt would have indicated not

---

Father Francisco Pinto Pessoa, Dr. Fernando Alves de Carvalho, and the prothonotary, Ernesto Camilo Barreto.

[103] Lustosa, op. cit., pp. 285-286. "Leandro Bezerra Monteiro, como cidadão brasileiro, usando do direito conferido pelo § 30 do artigo 169º da constituição do Império e pelo art. 8º do decreto de 15 de Outubro de 1827, e como deputado tambem servindo-se de outra disposição desta mesma lei, vem perante esta augusta câmara denunciar do conselheiro visconde do Rio Branco, atual presidente do Conselho de Ministros, do Conselheiro João Alfredo Correia de Oliveira, ministro e secretário de negócios do Império, do Conselheiro visconde de Caravelas, ministro e secretário de negócios estrangeiros, pelo crime de maquinar destruir a religião do Estado, adotada pelo pacto fundamental, e pelo crime de suborno.

"Os fatos criminosos são: perseguição a Dom Vital Maria Gonçalves de Oliveira, Bispo de Olinda, e Dom Antônio de Macedo Costa, Bispo do Pará, presos e mártires em satisfação à vontade e caprichos da maçonaria, seita muitas vezes condenada por diversos santíssimos padres, a cujo preceito queriam esses ministros obedecessem os referidos Prelados; e porque mais por intermédio de seu delegado, presidente de Pernambuco, empregaram peditório e influência para que os vigários da cidade do Recife fizessem o que não deviam, desobedecer ao Prelado, seu chefe e superior legítimo."

[104] Magalhães, op. cit., p. 132, note.

[105] Ibid., p. 133, note. "Si houvesse no Brasil uma fé cristã sincera e ardorosa, não apenas de palavras estilizadas, porém que inflamasse realmente o coração e o espírito dos que receberam a água lustral da Igreja, — a questão espíscopo-maçônica devera ter produzido, fatalmente, uma revolta armada em todo o país, em defesa dos dois bispos mártires."

faith, but an instigated reaction. The bishops could very likely have aroused the people to armed rebellion if they had wished to do so; instead, they advocated passive resistance.[106] This last fact is significant, for it lends weight to the assertion made repeatedly by members of the Brazilian episcopacy that at no time was the act of challenging the right of the government to interfere in ecclesiastical affairs an act of rebellion against the imperial government.

There is one instance of such rebellion, but, instead of undermining the assertion just made, it tends rather to strengthen it. The Episcopal-Masonic controversy coincided in time with the establishment in Brazil of the metric system. The new measures were very unpopular in certain regions, notably in Paraíba, Pernambuco, Rio Grande do Norte, Minas-Gerais, Pará, and Rio Grande do Sul. The opposition coalesced into distinct groups who called themselves *Rasga-listas* or *Quebra-quilos*.[107] In the northern districts, groups from the hinterland came into the cities and destroyed the new measures, to the cry of "Down with the Portuguese, Down with the Freemasons!"[108] Undoubtedly the country folk associated the economic innovation with the Masonic-Portuguese agitation rife in the urban centers of that section at the time. In the report of the minister of justice for 1875 are repeated references to the popular action against the Freemasons in Paraíba and Pernambuco,[109] and against the Portuguese, especially in the province of Pará.[110] The inference

---

[106] See p. 203 above.

[107] *Besouchet, op. cit.*, p. 241.

[108] *Ibid.*

[109] *Relatorio apresentado á Assembléa Geral Legislativa na quarta sessão da decima quinta legislatura pelo Ministro e Secretario de Estado dos Negocios da Justiça Dr. Manoel Antonio Duarte de Azevedo* (Rio de Janeiro, 1875), pp. 3-4.

[110] *Ibid.*, pp. 7-8. See also Teodoro Braga, *Historia do Pará* (São Paulo, n. d.), p. 117. "Mal começavam a serenar os animos eis que a *Tribuna* [periodical published in Pará, 1870-1876], allegando que os bispos e padres perseguidos eram brasileiros e que o grosso da maçonaria se compunha de estrangeiros, mudou de alvo e começou violentamente a atacar os portuguezes. No fundo, a allegação não passava de pretexto; a verdade é que o sopro das paixões sacudira as cinzas sob que jazia mal extincto o braseiro do antigo incendio:

throughout the whole report is that these movements were instigated by the Jesuits.[111] But the Jesuits were the constant target of Masonic propaganda; therefore, it is not hard to conjecture the origin of the assertion.

These sporadic attacks were primarily social and economic, and the links that bind them to the Religious Question are tenuous. Yet the promptness with which the organs of Masonic propaganda picked up such instances of rebellion and associated them with the clergy, indicates how anxious the forces of opposition were to find evidence that the movement of the bishops in defense of ecclesiastical freedom was a rebellion against civil authority. When the American minister described the turmoil, he made the assertion that the disturbances were sponsored by what he called the ecclesiastical party, but neither in his despatches nor in the report of the minister of justice is any priest named who participated in these uprisings, nor is any evidence cited to prove that the insurrections had ecclesiastical approbation. The minister wrote:

A serious disturbance and outbreak which has even assumed the form of rebellion has occurred in the Northern provinces of Parahyba and Pernambuco.

Numbers of half-savage inhabitants of the inner districts of these provinces — known as *Sertejos* [sic; i.e., *Sertanejos*] . . . have assembled and attacked some of the smaller towns and even threatened the chief town (Parahyba) of the province. These armed mobs have, in every instance, attacked the authorities, sacked the public buildings, burnt the archives, and especially destroyed the newly sent standards for measures and weights (decimal system) while, in many cases also,

---

era a ultima phase da reacção anti-lusitana, gerada pelo movimento da independencia, que se manifestava tão extemporanea quão ameaçadora."

[111] *Relatorio* . . . *pelo Ministro e Secretario de Estado dos Negocios da Justiça Dr. Manoel Antonio Duarte de Azevedo*, p. 3. "Na opinião do chefe de policia, como consta do seu relatorio, foi o jesuitismo quem promoveu a sedição com mão occulta." *Ibid.*, p. 5. ". . . os jesuitas tiveram grande parte no conflicto episcopal, e não foram estranhos aos movimentos sediciosos: o que os factos vieram confirmar."

they have pillaged private property, and attacked and wounded peaceable inhabitants.

In all cases their cry has been 'Down with the freemasons! Down with the Government! Long live religion!'

This cry shows both the origin and leadership of this movement; which, in fact, is secretly directed by the ecclesiastical party, and in many cases the mobs are headed by padres. The cause declared, or avowed, is that the government is 'attempting to cheat the people by the introduction of new and false weights and measures'; but all the facts ascertained go to show that it is a preconcerted movement and rebellion directed against the present Ministry, under which the bishops of Pará and Olinda (Pernambuco) were convicted and are now undergoing a modified imprisonment.

This insurrection, from its real cause, as well as its locality (the northern provinces being generally in a nearly constant state of disaffection and suspected of 'republicanism') have given the government great concern.[112]

Granting that individual priests may have participated in these movements, there is no evidence to support the assertion that they represented, officially or unofficially, the so-called ecclesiastical party. Since no evidence proves that these sporadic uprisings were instigated by the ecclesiastical authority, and since their connection with the Religious Question is superficial, the public declaration of the clergy of Pará deserves to be recognized as a valid repudiation of the statement that the ecclesiastical party sponsored rebellion. When they unanimously resolved to continue the resistance initiated by their bishop, and to defy the order of the government to lift the interdict, the clergy of Pará declared: "We do not engage in or counsel revolution, but we engage in and advise passive resistance, that is to say, resistance by word and by suffering."[113] This statement reflects the advice

---

[112] National Archives, Department of State, Partridge to Fish, vol. 41, no. 216, December 14, 1874.

[113] D. Antônio de Macedo Costa, *Direito contra o direito ou o estado sobre*

given by the archbishop of Baía to the bishops of Brazil in his circular of 1874.[114] They could not in conscience recognize as just the infringement of the temporal power on the domain of the spiritual, yet neither could they rebel against legitimately constituted authority.

In view of the religious and political reactions produced by the Episcopal-Masonic controversy, it is evident that the impact was not an unmixed evil for the Church. It is, in fact, easy to see why Vital referred to the conflict as providential. The bishops of Brazil were strengthened and purified by the contest they were forced to wage in defense of spiritual freedom. They emerged from it with a new prestige which made it possible for them to command the respect of the clergy and laity; under their leadership a resurgence of religious fervor took place. In government circles the right of the Church to operate as a free institution was defended publicly against the principles of regalism. The controversy made it clear that the government must either recognize the Roman Catholic religion for what it was or delete from the constitution the clause declaring it to be the religion of the empire.

---

tudo refutação da theoria dos politicos na Questão Religiosa seguida da resposta ao Supremo Tribunal de Justiça pelo Bispo do Pará (Rio de Janeiro, 1874), p. 230.

[114] See p. 203 above.

# CHAPTER VIII

## THE DEFEAT OF THE GOVERNMENT

When viewed in perspective, the Religious Question is seen to be but the climax in the long struggle of the Church in Brazil to free herself from the domination exerted by regalistic statesmen under the pretext of protection. The imperial constitution of 1824 had not only given juridical foundation for civil jurisdiction in ecclesiastical affairs, but it had also set a precedent which was followed by subsequent lawmakers.[1] With each new encroachment on the domain of the spiritual power, the regalism of imperial policy became more firmly entrenched; gradually privileges came to be looked upon as rights, and as such were often exercised to the detriment of the Church. The danger in this situation was augmented by the fact that priests and even bishops, adherents of the ideology of Liberalism on which Brazilian regalism was founded, aided the State in gaining control over the Church. The policy of restrictive supervision had been firmly established when, in the period of the Regency, Dom Romualdo de Seixas, archbishop of Baía, began to oppose civil interference; by the last years of the empire, the movement that he started had gained for the Church a recognition of her right to act as a free institution. Dom Romualdo's successful opposition to the efforts of Father Feijó to establish a national church in Brazil marked the beginning of systematic episcopal opposition to regalism.[2] Two decades passed before the contest between Church and State reached a climax, but during this interval a series of minor impacts between the imperial govern-

---

[1] As we have already seen, the imperial constitution conferred the right of royal patronage on the emperor, and established the right of imperial *placet*. The *Ato Adicional* further curtailed the right of the Church to operate freely, and reduced the clergy to the category of civil servants. Later imperial legislation tended to reduce the Church to a mere department of the State. See pp. 92-93 above.

[2] See pp. 68-88 above.

216

ment and individual bishops showed that the Brazilian episcopacy was a force to be conjured with. This continuous opposition has long been ignored, with the result that the Religious
Question of the seventies has been viewed as an isolated instance
of episcopal revolt, one that contrasted rudely with the peaceful
and harmonious relations which had up to that moment prevailed between Church and State.

Equally unfortunate is the assumption that after the Episcopal-Masonic question was settled, perfect understanding prevailed
between Church and State in Brazil. Periodically during the
next decade, individual bishops had to stand firm against imperial interference in ecclesiastical affairs.[3] In all of these con-
tests the issue was essentially the same: the right of the ecclesiastical authority to publish pontifical acts which had not received
the imperial *placet*. The continued insistence of the episcopacy
led in 1879 to an acknowledgment by Saldanha Marinho, the
highly vocal Ganganelli, that the right of *placet* was a wornout
institution in Brazil. This admission, a delayed triumph for
Bishops Dom Vital and Dom Antônio, indicates the persistence
with which the episcopacy had followed up the victory won for
the Church by those two prelates. In a speech on September 3,
1879, in the Chamber of Deputies, Saldanha Marinho, referring
to the intransigence of the bishops, reviewed conflicts between
the civil power and the ecclesiastical authorities of Mariana, São
Paulo, Maranhão, Pará, and Rio de Janeiro.[4] Pontifical acts, he
said, were executed without the *placet*; bishops, ignoring the
laws of the empire, acted as they pleased. But his protest was
useless: the Church in Brazil had by then freed itself from

---

[3] See Américo Jacobina Lacombe, "Ecos da questão religiosa no parlamento
imperial," *A Ordem*, XXXII (December, 1944), 429-450.

[4] *Anais da Câmara dos Deputados*, 1879, V, 2. "Em Mariana há agora
sérios distúrbios porque o novo prelado obstava casamentos e batizados quando
os padrinhos eram maçons. 'Reaparecem pois, as bulas não placitadas' . . . .
Também do Maranhão chegavam más notícias—o novo bispo, D. Antônio
Cândido de Alvarenga, empossado no ano anterior, entendera-se com o que
êle chamava de 'general em chefe da cruzada ultramontana' (Macedo Costa)
—e já andava perturbando a paz das famílias, perseguindo maçons. E até em
S. Paulo lhe diziam ter o bispo tomado atitudes suspeitas." Lacombe, "Ecos
da questão religiosa no parlamento imperial," *loc. cit.*, pp. 442-443.

regalistic control.[5]

The fundamental element in the struggle between Church and State was the resolution of the former to operate as a free institution in opposition to the determination of the latter to be supreme arbiter in religious matters. Besides, certain fluctuating elements were always present, but not always in the same degree; foremost among these were the influences of Freemasonry, of the papacy, of personalities, and of contemporary politics. While attention was given to each of these at the time the various phases of the struggle were examined, it is essential that they be viewed now in relation to the whole. In this way their importance can be emphasized without any one of them assuming an unwarranted prominence.

## II

The secret character of Masonry as well as its system of degrees made it possible to unite heterogeneous groups of people and to exhibit different aspects of the fraternity to each. The social and philanthropic aspects of Brazilian Masonry were so apparent that many lodge members honestly believed that they constituted the whole of Masonry. Others who recognized the esoteric character of its higher degrees, and who knew, or at least suspected, that its inner circles sponsored a strongly anti-Catholic program, chose to overlook this feature in order that they might enjoy the social, economic, and political advantages accruing to members of the fraternity. To Brazilians in general, Freemasonry was a social and philanthropic society, whose charitable and political activities after the empire was established followed upon its revolutionary and political activities in the earlier epoch of revolution and independence.[6] Special emphasis must be placed

---

[5] Lacombe, "O aspecto religioso da questão dos bispos," *loc. cit.*, p. 335. "A situação era falsa, e era visível a tendência das autoridades eclesiásticas para libertarem-se da situação 'de aviltante subordinação' como se exprimiu o próprio D. Antônio de Macedo Costa, 'Que fazia do Estado o árbitro supremo de tôdas as questões religiosas, e considerava o sacerdócio em tôda a sua escala hierárquica, desde o minorista até o Bispo, —até o Papa! — como subalternos de um ministro civil dos cultos e dependentes das decisões de sua secretaria!'"

[6] Its revolutionary activities after independence were confined largely to

on the fact that Freemasonry in Brazil stood as the symbol of national autonomy, and as such permeated all aspects of national life. For somewhat the same reason that a nation's flag merits a place of honor at governmental, religious, and social functions, the emblems of Masonry were sacred to many patriotic Brazilians. This symbolism insured to the Masonic fraternity ready access into all phases of Brazilian life, and after religion, it came to be the strongest social force in the empire. It follows then that the supreme triumph of Masonry was its infiltration into the religious associations, for when this was achieved the two strongest social forces of the empire were united under a single Masonic leadership.

Exactly when Brazilian Masonry became openly hostile to the Church cannot be said with certainty, but indications of change can be pointed out. Attention has already been called to the fact that Brazilian regalists, among them many priests, joined Freemasonry because the fraternity aided them in their efforts to separate the Brazilian Church from papal supervision.[7] This group, which was out of sympathy with Rome, would of necessity oppose any member of the hierarchy who attempted to disrupt its plan for a national Church, or who dared to oppose Freemasonry because the fraternity was condemned by Rome. The existence of this latent hostility to the Brazilian episcopacy is attested by the contest of 1834-1835 between Dom Romualdo de Sousa Coelho, bishop of Pará, and the Masonic fraternity of that province. Dom Romualdo, in a pastoral letter of May 28, 1834, warned his people against Freemasonry.[8] The Masons prevented the publication of the pastoral, and in their journal *Pelicano* the bishop was described as a troublemaker who disturbed public order through incendiary pastorals and subversive doctrines.[9]

Masonic hostility seems to have become more open as well as

Pernambuco. See Mário Melo, *A Maçonaria e a revolução republicana de 1817* (Recife, 1912).

[7] See pp. 64-65 above.

[8] Macedo Costa, *A Maçonaria em opposição á moral, á Igreja, e ao Estado* (Recife, 1875), pp. 69-71.

[9] *Pelicano*, no 65, quoted in *ibid.*, p. 69, n. 130. See also p. 140 above.

more general following the change in 1852 to the so-called Scottish rite.[10] Mário Melo, who tells of the shift, says that it stimulated Masonic activity.[11] Cooper's observation that "the rise of the Scottish Rite in France . . . brought into the order the spirit of aggressive antagonism to Christian beliefs,"[12] lends weight to the supposition that hostility to the Church spread among Brazilian Freemasons after the more general adoption of this rite. Close affiliation with the Scottish rite fraternity of France introduced, moreover, into the ideology of Brazilian Masonry a new positivistic element that of necessity made it more and more inimical to revealed religion.[13] It is reasonable to conclude, therefore, that the Brazilian fraternity[14] which showed such hatred for the Church around 1870 had been latently hostile for some time before it came out into the open with its denunciations.

One of the reasons why many statesmen failed to perceive the

---

[10] The Scottish rite seems to have been introduced into Brazil as early as 1822. Sérgio Corrêa da Costa, *As quatro coroas de D. Pedro I* (2d ed., Rio de Janeiro, 1942), p. 42, n. 44, writes: "A primeira loja de Rito Escocês no Brasil foi a de nome 'Educação e Moral,' fundada pelo marechal João Paulo dos Santos Barreto autorizado por carta-patente passada pelo Consist.: do Gr.: Or.: de França em 29 de agosto de 1822 . . . ."

[11] Mário Melo, *A Maçonaria no Brazil pioridade de Pernambuco* (Recife, 1909), p. 26. "Pela indolencia de seus obreiros, pela falta de uma luta externa que os fortificasse no seio da loja e os encorajasse, ou por outro qualquer motivo que escapa á investigação, a oficina a que pertencemos adormeceu ainda uma vêz para novamente surjir em 1852, rezolvendo seus obreiros a permuta de rito do francêz para o escossêz, no qual ainda hoje se conserva."

[12] John M. Cooper, "Freemasonry and Modern Life," *The Ecclesiastical Review*, LVII (July, 1917), 172.

[13] Cooper, "Freemasonry's Two Hundredth Birthday," *ibid.*, LVI (June, 1917), 607, writes: "Atheism penetrated the ranks of French Masonry [Scottish rite] in the second half of the eighteenth century under the influence of the Encyclopedists, and in the nineteenth century, materialism and the positivist philosophy of Comte largely dominated the craft not only in France but throughout the greater part of the rest of Latin Masonry . . . ."

[14] See p. 101, note 9, above. William Scully, who visited Brazil in the second half of the nineteenth century, describes the break in Brazilian Masonry and the radical nature of one sector. *Brazil; Its Provinces and Chief Cities; the Manners and Customs of the People* (London, 1866), pp. 158-159.

increasingly anti-Catholic tenor of Brazilian Freemasonry was that when it began its open campaign against the Church in 1870, its activities reflected the reaction of Liberals the world over to Pius IX's denunciation of Liberalism and to the promulgation by the Vatican Council of the dogma of papal infallibility. The declaration of this dogma challenged the assertion of the Liberals that by his illiberal policies Pius IX had deprived the papacy of all prestige. In Brazil, the regalists were so absorbed in justifying Liberalism and in warding off the supposed pretensions of the Holy See that without investigating Freemasonry they welcomed all the help it could give. They were willing to overlook the fact that many Masonic journals, while assailing the papacy, were also making scurrilous attacks on the Brazilian episcopacy and on Catholic dogma.[15]

The attack of the Freemasons on the Brazilian episcopacy is significant. Apparently the opposition which the bishops had for some years been showing to State domination in spiritual affairs was meeting with sufficient success to alarm them.[16] The efforts of the bishops to reorganize diocesan seminaries seem to

---

[15] Santos says that some men were honestly unaware of the true character of Masonry, others refused to recognize it: "Até 1872, portanto, soube a Maçonaria disfarçar mais ou menos os seus intuitos, no Brasil; e espalhar-se entre nós adquirindo prestigio, attrahindo ao seu gremio muitos catholicos até membros do Clero. Muito frequentemente eram maçons, e maçons graduados, os presidentes do conselho, ministros e representantes do povo. Alguns destes, certamente, assim procediam, para abrirem caminho e chegarem até as mais altas posições, na politica e na administração, ignorando ou fingindo ignorar quaes os verdadeiros intentos da ordem maçonica." Lúcio José dos Santos, "A Maçonaria no Brasil," A Ordem, XII (July, 1932), 24.

[16] In this connection see Joaquim Nabuco, O Partido ultramontano suas invasões, seus orgãos, e seu futuro (Rio de Janeiro, 1873), pp. 12-13: "O perigo é imminente; quando muito os actuaes bispos educados entre nós continuarão a reger com prudencia as suas dioceses, indifferentes á satyra do Sr. Mendes de Almeida [Nabuco is very hostile to the so-called ultramontane doctrines enunciated by Almeida] sensiveis somente ao bem que espalham e á confiança que encontram em todas as almas; mas os futuros bispos, sobretudo si elles forem tirados dos seminarios de Roma, juntar-se-hão ao partido da reacção, a menos que o estado reivindique todos os seus direitos ou que um novo pontifice queira sinceramente conciliar o catholicismo e o seculo, a fé e a liberdade. Si não póde o executivo apoiar-se nos bispos, apoie-se nos parochos."

have been recognized as the supreme threat to Masonic interests. Attention has already been called to the contest between the bishop of Pará and the imperial government over legislation relative to seminaries subsidized by the State, and to that prelate's repeated assertion that all the bishops of Brazil were deeply concerned over governmental policies in this regard.[17] According to Dom Vital, laxity among the clergy was not the greatest threat to the Church in Brazil, for this could have been remedied by the bishops if it were not cynically favored by the government.[18] The great danger, he added, was Freemasonry, which dominated in the capital and in the other great commercial cities and which inoculated with its virus not only the lay brotherhoods but the clergy as well.[19] The inference is that Masonry would have lost its hold on the clergy and ultimately on Catholic society had the bishops been able to reform the seminaries.[20] This inference is strengthened by appeal to Masonic sources. The pamphlet *Ponto Negro*[21] observed that the four leading bishops of Brazil — Pará, Rio Grande do Sul, Ceará, and Rio de Janeiro — were ultramontane and dangerous because they sponsored Jesuit professors in their diocesan seminaries.[22] Such professors could hardly be counted upon to train seminarians to

---

Mas aqui a decepção é maior. Os parochos são hoje da privativa confianca dos Ordinarios, cuja tendencia é destruir a perpetuidade do beneficio que constitue a independencia do funccionario. A jurisdicção dos prelados torna-se assim sem limites, e a mais bella das instituições catholicas, a mais cheia de grandeza e de poesia, a parochia não é sinão uma divisão administrativa regida por um empregado de confiança, amovivel *ad nutum.*"

[17] See pp. 169-175, 194-207 above.

[18] In a letter to one of his former seminary professors Vital describes conditions as he found them in the Brazilian Church at the time of his episcopal consecration. For this letter see Félix de Olívola, "Alma Franciscana," *Verbum*, I (December, 1944), 341.

[19] *Ibid.*

[20] Eurico [pseud. for Francisco Ramos Paz], *O ponto negro considerações a proposito do recente acto do bispo do Rio de Janeiro* (Rio de Janeiro, 1872), p. 22, discusses the increasing importance of Jesuits in education in Brazil.

[21] See p. 176 above.

[22] Eurico, *op. cit.*, pp. 7-8. "Foi assim que a um e um começaram os seus emissarios [of Jesuitism] a occupar as sédes episcopaes do Brasil. Quatro

have due respect for the philosophy of Liberalism; yet a Liberal clergy was absolutely essential if Freemasonry was to succeed in its attempt to dominate in Brazil. Throughout the pamphlet, fear was manifested that the diocesan clergy might be slipping from the control of the government.[23] This would mean, in effect, from the control of Freemasonry. Proof of the integrity of the Brazilian episcopacy of this time can be adduced from the virulence of the attacks made by the Masonic press upon its members.

The quarrel between the bishops and the Masonic fraternity would never have become a governmental issue without the existence of the regalistic tradition in Brazil. In its origin the contest was between the Church and Masonry and it was viewed in this light by the bishops and by the fraternity.[24] For regalistic statesmen, however, the quarrel constituted a test case for civil supremacy; they maintained that the fraternity could not be condemned in the empire by appeal to papal bulls that had never received the imperial *placet*. Obvious as it seems in retrospect, contemporary regalists appear not to have seen the dangers inherent in such a test. If Freemasonry could be proved to be hostile to the Church the regalist's assertion that the *placet* was a justifiable right never exercised to the detriment of the Church would be in jeopardy. Statesmen tried to justify the exercise of the *placet* in this instance by alleging that Brazilian Masonry was different from European Masonry, was not hostile to the

---

bispos dominam hoje na egreja brasileira . . . . Com elles vieram membros esparsos da Companhia. Havia no Rio de Janeiro um seminario episcopal, onde a instrucção era dada por meio de professores habeis e nacionaes. O prelado fluminense expulsou-os todos e substituiu-os por gente sua, queremos dizer adeptos de Gesú."

[23] *Ibid.*, p. 10. "O clero—o baixo clero, como se diz na linguagem ecclesiástica — é hoje, mais que nunca, um instrumento nas mãos dos superiores. A egreja passou a ser um regimento; e Loyola é o seu Conde de Lippe." The author speaks of Jesuit schools in Sobral, Ceará, and Rio Grande do Sul, and of Jesuits as professors in the seminary at São Paulo where Bishop Dom Vital was entertained after his consecration in the local cathedral.

[24] Melo, *A Maçonaria no Brazil*, p. 26, writes: "Durante a grande campanha da Maçonaria com a igreja católica, luta conhecida pelo titulo de *questão relijioza* . . . ."

Church, and was, therefore, not condemned by the pontifical decrees. These assertions were untenable, since Masonic journals in Brazil were openly attacking Catholic dogma, and publicly attesting to the affiliation of Brazilian Masonry with the European fraternity.[25] The issue of the contest endangered the regalistic position of the imperial government, and placed it in the embarrassing political dilemma of having to choose between a break with Rome, that would certainly be followed by a strong protest within the nation,[26] and a retraction, that would be utilized against it by the Republican party. If Freemasonry had dominated political circles the first alternative would in all probability have been chosen; the fact that it was not chosen seems to justify the assertion that Masonry in Brazil was not a dominant force in Brazilian politics, but only a tool of regalistic statesmen.[27]

### III

The doctrine of regalism, that provided many Brazilian statesmen with an apology for civil encroachments into the domain of the spiritual power, encountered in the papacy the greatest threat to its effective realization. A consistent regalist would have openly denounced the possibility of recognizing a jurisdiction superior to that of the State, and would have established a national church, but Brazilian regalists who wanted affiliation

---

[25] See pp. 117-120 above.

[26] In spite of civil decrees the interdicts remained in force, and religious activities in the dioceses of Pará and Olinda remained in a state of suspended animation. Rome refused to act while the bishops were in prison. The establishment of a national church would have been the only solution, if the imperial government had persisted in its intransigence.

[27] Freemasonry lost prestige as a result of its public contest with the Church, because its hostility to religion was revealed and thereafter it could not openly demand a place of honor in Catholic society. The episcopacy could fight its infiltration into the ranks of the clergy and into religious associations without at the same time appearing to challenge a revered symbol of national autonomy. The significant aspect of the change is not that many people left the society (Melo, *A Maçonaria no Brazil*, p. 26, says that many did), nor that many continued their affiliations, but that the true nature of the fraternity was revealed.

with the papacy without obligation to it, did not let fear of inconsistency hamper them. This attitude is exemplified in the statesmen of the First Empire (1822-1831); they sought recognition from the Holy See, but they refused to acknowledge that royal patronage was not a right inherent in sovereignty. This orientation prepared the way for the doctrines of royal *placet* and right of recourse to the crown, prerogatives which the Holy See would never sanction, but which could be educed from a right of patronage constitutionally established.[28] All these prerogatives of sovereignty, guaranteed by the imperial constitution and later legislation to safeguard Brazil from so-called papal aggression, were threatened when the bishop of Olinda ignored the imperial *placet* and denied the validity of recourse to the crown.[29] Dom Vital's independence of action appeared especially threatening to Brazilian statesmen, because it was judged to be part of a universal movement inaugurated by Pius IX to

[28] Joaquim Nabuco, *O Partido Ultramontano*, p. 9. "O pensamento dos autores da constituição foi fundar entre nós uma igreja nacional, que vivendo na unidade catholica tivesse certa independencia da centralisação romana, que sujeita ao papa nos pontos de doutrina não o fosse nas decisões contrarias ao espirito do christianismo, aos canones recebidos e aos *costumes dos nossos pais*, esse privilegio da igreja gallicana. Para isso o legislador constituiu o imperador a primeira autoridade ecclesiastica do paiz, n'este sentido — que lhe pertence não só a escolha do pessoal, a formação da hierarchia da igreja, como o julgamento supremo de todas as leis e decretos dos papas e dos concilios."

[29] *Ibid.*, pp. 10-11. Nabuco writes: ". . . si o primeiro pensamento do legislador foi esse, a saber, dar á relgião catholica o privilegio de religião do estado, o segundo foi crear uma igreja nacional, desligada em seu movimento politico da sé romana, adequada ao regimen democratico, feita para a America. Não se póde d'isso duvidar, vendo que direitos deu elle ao poder executivo sobre o pessoal e sobre a doutrina da igreja brazileira. Foi esse principio que constituiu a alma do decreto de 28 de março de 1857, quando admittiu o recurso á corôa 'por notoria violencia no exercicio da jurisdicção e poder espiritual, *postergando a lei natural* e os canones recebidos na *igreja brazileira!*' Pois bem; essa igreja brazileira vai desapparecendo, e em breve não haverá d'ella sinão poucos vestigios! Enganaram-se os autores da constituição pensando que a igreja catholica se contentaria com a situação que elles lhe deram de serva do estado; que os seus bispos se sujeitariam a ver as bullas e os canones julgados em ultima instancia pelo ministro do imperio, por um leigo!; que o espirito de resistencia não havia de quebrar logo esse cordão sanitario entre a sé de Roma e a sociedade dos feis, chamado o beneplacito."

enforce his illiberal doctrines throughout the world, and especially among nations where a union of Church and State existed. The alleged threat was given various names: clericalism, ultramontanism, Jesuitism, but it was considered by Liberals to be in its essence simply a reactionary movement designed to destroy liberty and hamper progress. This is the point of view from which the radical wing of Masonry viewed the action of Dom Vital. The notion was publicized by Joaquim Saldanha Marinho, and was endorsed for a time by extreme Liberals,[30] most of whom were members of the new Republican party.[31] Speaking in the United Grand Orient of July 21, 1876, Rui Barbosa said that the reform which certain Brazilian bishops were sponsoring was part of a secret universal movement inaugurated by Pius IX for the sole purpose of retarding progress toward greater human freedom.[32] Nabuco made a similar charge when he alleged that democracy was incompatible with the Syllabus, which denied human liberty and the dignity of reason, and when he claimed that the bishops who were relinquishing their power to an in-

---

[30] As young men Joaquim Nabuco and Rui Barbosa headed this group of extreme Liberals, yet both as mature statesmen regretted their attacks on the Church and became her staunch supporters. See Américo Jacobina Lacombe, "Ecos da questão religiosa no parlamento imperial," A Ordem, XXXII (December, 1944), 435; Hélio Viana, "Bibliografia da 'Questão Vitalista,'" ibid., pp. 458-459.

[31] See p. 2, note 2, above.

[32] Rui Barbosa, "A igreja e o estado," Novos discursos e conferencias colligidos e revistos por Homero Pires (São Paulo, 1933), pp. 7-64. This address, which Barbosa gave in the United Grand Orient of Brazil on July 21, 1876, makes repeated allusions to the so-called secret movement inaugurated by Pius IX. On p. 13 is a defense of Barbosa's own position: "Não é uma rebelia contra o verbo divino: é a defesa da vossa integridade moral contra as incursões do clericalismo. Não é a capa da confraria o que os maçons disputam: são as garantias constitucionaes. Não são as insignias da Ordem o que açula contra elles a raiva dos anathemas: é a civilisação hodierna, a independencia do pensamento individual, a precedencia temporal do Estado na administração da sociedade visivel." On p. 15 he says: "O dogma da infallibilidade pontificia não é senão a supremacia perenne, incontrovertivel, omnipotente do papa sobre a autoridade temporal. Não é uma crença religiosa é um estratagema politico."

fallible pope were doing so because they feared the progress of democracy.[33]

The strongest argument against this alleged secret movement sponsored by Pius IX is found in the reception which the pope accorded to the baron of Penêdo when the latter was sent on a special mission to Rome in 1873 to urge the pope to put an end to the Episcopal-Masonic controversy. An examination of the situation shows that the papacy pursued in this diplomatic crisis the same policy it had followed in all its previous relations with the imperial government.[34] It was ready to accept a compromise to preserve harmony between the spiritual and the temporal authorities, but it was determined to safeguard its inalienable moral and religious prerogatives.[35] In examining the Penêdo mission,

---

[33] Nabuco, *O Partido Ultramontano*, pp. 41-42. "A igreja, em sua longa historia que se confunde com a da civilisacão, passou da aristocracia á democracia, voltou depois áquella e afinal chegou ao despotismo. O pontificado actual marca o auge da centralização na igreja. Nunca o papado teve sobre a sociedade religiosa o poder que tem hoje. No tempo em que elle dominava os reis a consciencia era mais livre. A infallibilidade pessoal decretada pelo ultimo concilio do Vaticano annos depois da proclamação de um novo dogma por autoridade exclusiva do pontifice, veiu pôr nas mãos d'este o dominio absoluto da igreja. De onde provem esse temor e essa fraqueza que faz o episcopado renunciar ás suas prerogativas seculares e abdicar em um poder historicamente mais recente do que elle e comprometido em uma grave crise politica? A razão d'esse temor é o progresso incessante da democracia. Em vez de alliar-se a ella a igreja latina quer destruil-a; ora esse combate é desigual." Elsewhere (*ibid.*, p. 41) Nabuco writes: "O partido ultramontano não mediu bem os seus recursos ao empenhar a lucta religiosa que ameaça a igreja de um schisma. Os seus orgãos não são sufficientes para a reacção que elle quer operar . . . . N'essas condicões a luta é impossivel, e a sociedade catholica, em vez de perder com ella, poderia até ganhar o direito de eleger os seus parochos e os seus prelados, como outr'ora."

[34] See pp. 64-68, 76-88 above.

[35] In nations where the union of Church and State exists, the Holy See does not expect ideal conditions to prevail, but assumes that, accepting conditions as they are, the hierarchy will safeguard the interests of the Church at the same time that it maintains, as far as possible, harmonious relations with the State. The problem is national, and ordinarily best handled by the hierarchy of the nation; however, in the event that a government feels that the policies of the hierarchy are incompatible with the national policy, yet can not win the hierarchy to this conviction, that government has a perfect right to appeal to Rome. This appeal to a higher ecclesiastical authority is a recognized protec-

one must bear in mind two facts: it is possible for a situation to be misrepresented without the evidence being explicitly tampered with, and it is also possible for interested groups to exercise undue pressure on Vatican decisions as on the decisions of other deliberative bodies.

The government had begun legal process against the bishop of Olinda because he had published without imperial *placet* the brief *Quamquam dolores* in which the Holy Father had commended his action against the disaffected brotherhoods, had authorized him to continue, and had directed him to advise the other bishops of Brazil to take similar measures.[36] The imperial government realized, when other bishops began to publish this brief, that it could not prosecute the whole episcopacy. It decided then to appeal to the Holy See: if by diplomacy it could persuade the Vatican to add ecclesiastical censure to its own civil action against the bishop of Olinda, there would be little likelihood that the remaining prelates would continue to rally to his support.[37] The baron of Penêdo, who had discharged a successful diplomatic mission to the Holy See in 1858, and who was now Brazilian minister in London, was chosen as envoy extraordinary and minister plenipotentiary to the Vatican. According to the instruction[38] from the minister of foreign affairs, the viscount of Caravelas, Penêdo was to acquaint the Holy Father and the cardinal secretary of state with what had happened in Brazil, and was to impress upon them the evils that would ensue if these acts of episcopal irregularity and disobedi-

tion for both powers.

[36] Joaquim Saldanha Marinho stated the issue succinctly when he said: "Mas a questão da qual resultaram os interditos às irmandades, consistiu em terem ou não, execução no Brasil as bulas do pontificado, independente de beneplácito." *Jornal do Comércio*, October 22, 1875, quoted by Lacombe, "O aspecto religioso da questão dos bispos," *loc. cit.*, p. 338.

[37] This was not a vain speculation. Olívola, *Um grande brasileiro, D. Frei Vital Maria Gonçalves Oliveira* (2d ed., Recife, 1936), p. 153, observes that episcopal and clerical support did drop off when it was rumored early in 1874 that the pope had censured Bishops Dom Vital and Dom Antônio and had ordered the interdicts lifted.

[38] Barão de Penêdo, *Missão especial a Roma em 1873* (London, 1881), pp. 3-6. The instruction is given in full.

ence continued. The envoy, the minister indicated, was to persuade the Holy Father that, instead of encouraging the bishops
in their disobedience, he ought to counsel them to conform to the
precepts of the constitution and the laws of the empire. While
the envoy was given full authority to act in the name of the imperial government, he was told explicitly that he was to inform
the Holy Father that, no matter what the result of the mission,
the imperial government might have to take legal measures
against the bishop of Olinda, whose trial had already been ordered. The undiplomatic nature of the instruction reflects the
intransigence of the ministry; it did not seem aware of the fact
that, even though its approach to the Holy See was motivated
by necessity rather than by deference, it would have to make
some concessions. It was preposterous to suppose that the papacy would comply with imperial demands without having first
been given the assurance that the Brazilian government would
drop its prosecution of the bishop; yet from the instruction it
is clear that this was what the government expected the Penêdo
mission to accomplish. The instruction concluded with the order
that in all his conferences and communications with Cardinal
Antonelli, the envoy was to use "moderate but firm language,"[39]
because the imperial government did not ask a favor or solicit
any agreement, but wished only to reclaim what was its due.
José Nabuco de Araújo's opinion that these instructions were
directions not for a negotiation but for an ultimatum[40] may be
taken as a criterion of how moderate regalists viewed them. It
is not difficult, therefore, to predict that the baron of Penêdo,
a consummate diplomat, would modify their spirit even if he
fulfilled their precept.

In a confidential communication sent to Penêdo on the same
day,[41] the minister of foreign affairs laid special emphasis on the
necessity of influencing the Holy Father who, said the minister,

---

[39] *Ibid.*

[40] Nabuco, *Um estadista do imperio Nabuco de Araujo, sua vida, suas
opiniões, sua época* (Rio de Janeiro [1898-1899]), III, 376. "Eram instrucções, como se vê, não para uma negociação, mas para um ultimatum,
porque a prisão dos Bispos era como que represalias espirituaes contra o Papa."

[41] Penêdo, *Missão especial a Roma*, pp. 6-7. The letter is given in full.

could with a word put an end to the conflict. The minister next directed the attention of the envoy to the question of Masonry.

> Your Excellency well knows that the Masons in Brazil, *even though there may be among them some and even many who think with certain liberty in matters of religion, are in general good Catholics,*[42] and do not diverge from the purpose of their institution, which is entirely charitable. If the Masonic lodges can cause apprehension, it is relative to politics, and this tendency, which is not even constant, ought not to preoccupy the Roman Curia.[43]

The minister warned Penêdo to make this point clear to the Holy Father, who appeared not to have been well informed on it.[44] Commenting on these instructions, the baron of Penêdo said that it was obvious he was not going to Rome to discuss the imperial *placet* or to obtain from the pope the recognition of this prerogative of the crown of Brazil, or to display before the Holy Father the triumph of the imperial government in the indictment and imprisonment of the bishop. Neither these nor similar ends were the purpose of his mission: he was going to persuade the Holy Father to put an end to the conflict.[45]

[42] The author of the Masonic pamphlet *Ponto negro* (p. 11) gives some idea of this "liberty in matters of religion" when he says: "A maçonaria é perseguida porque é uma reunião de todas as religiões e crenças, isto é, porque praticamente exerce a tolerancia e o respeito da consciencia humana. Uma associação que não pergunta ao protestante, nem ao catholico, nem ao musulmano se estão de acordo na efficacia da graça ou na naturesa das penas eternas, que os recebe taes quaes são, taes quaes a naturesa os poz sobre a terra, que os recebe emfim como homens, pedindo-lhes apenas que amem a Deus e ao proximo, tal associação deve ser, era natural que fosse condemnada."

[43] "V. Ex. bem sabe que os maçons no Brasil, *embora possa haver entre elles alguns e mesmo muitos que pensem com certa liberdade em materia de religião, são em geral bons catholicos,* e não se apartão do fim da sua instituição, que é toda de caridade. Se as lojas maçonicas podem causar receios é em relação á politica, e esta tendencia, que nem é constante, não deve preoccupar a Curia Romana." (Italics mine). Penêdo, *Missão especial a Roma,* p. 7.

[44] In the instructions to Penêdo Caravelas writes: "E conveniente que V. Ex., quando for admittido a fallar a Sua Santidade, se não olvide de esclarecer este ponto, em que elle parece não estar bem informado." *Ibid.*

[45] *Ibid.,* pp. 8-10.

In spite of the tone of the instruction, the baron of Penêdo showed himself eager to interpret his mission as a mark of deference paid by the government of Brazil to the Holy See. Writing to the minister of foreign affairs shortly after he had received his assignment, Penêdo said: ". . . a special mission sent to the Holy See on the occasion of such grave and extraordinary occurrences, when the Government has in its laws the means of action, does honor to the spirit of moderation and respect of a Catholic Government for the Supreme Head of the Church."[46] In his answer, the Brazilian minister made a similar reference, but his gesture of respect for the Supreme Pontiff was lacking in enthusiasm: "We are ready for a *non possumus*; but it shall not be said that we did not attempt that means, which at least is a deference toward the Visible Head of the Church."[47] If Penêdo had executed his mission in the spirit of his superiors it would never have succeeded.[48] In defending his procedure later, he maintained that he did not violate his instructions; that he did not give the Holy Father any assurance that civil action would not be taken against the bishop in the event that the Holy See stepped in and put an end to the conflict. But from the situation itself,[49] from his own account of his conduct, and from his subsequent placing of the blame for the failure of his mission on the fact that civil action was taken in regard to the bishops, it can be safely inferred that Penêdo, even though he did not make any explicit statement to that effect, allowed the impression to be created that the im-

---

[46] *Ibid.*, p. 13.

[47] *Ibid.*, p. 14.

[48] The Penêdo mission can profitably be compared with the mission of the Brazilian minister to Rome during the Regency, when the question of Father Moura's nomination for the see of Rio de Janeiro was under consideration. Then the Brazilian minister followed the directions of the home office, with the result that the Pope did respond *"Non possumus."*

[49] Penêdo thus describes the situation: "Um conflicto entre o Estado e a Igreja; uma revolta quasi geral do nosso episcopado; um dos Bispos processado, outro em vesperas de o ser; interdictos lançados em varios templos; o Governo sitiado pelas exigencias dos partidos extremos, ancioso por ver terminada a luta, receando do futuro, e recorrendo ao mesmo tempo ás suas leis e á Santa Sé; tal era o transumpto do estado da causa quando foi entregue á acção da diplomacia." Penêdo, *Missão especial a Roma*, p. 33.

perial government would drop the issue as soon as the interdicts were lifted.

The baron of Penêdo had his first interview with the Holy Father on October 26, 1873. Pius IX immediately turned to the question of Masonry in Brazil. Penêdo hastened to impress upon him that no one in Brazil believed that Masonry was in any way hostile to religion; to pretend the contrary, he asserted, would be to injure the public conscience of the country. He went on to say that some of the most notable persons in Brazil, among them the president of the Council, were Freemasons; that a large number of the members of the fraternity were active in the religious brotherhoods, and contributed generously to the splendor and magnificence of the Catholic cult. After assuring the Holy Father that all Brazilians knew that Freemasonry was not hostile to the Church, the envoy expressed his surprise that bishops and representatives of the Holy See should never have been rightly informed about a fact so generally known.[50] Penêdo wrote in his report that since he had not come to defend Masonry, he did not go beyond these first observations, but endeavored to enter into an exposition of principle. He directed the discussion so that it would center on the fact that this controversy between the bishops and the Freemasons was the first quarrel to occur in Brazil on a matter of religion. In his first as in all subsequent conferences with the Holy Father, and also with the cardinal secretary of state, the Brazilian envoy made every effort to concentrate attention on the allegation that harmonious relations between Church and State in Brazil were now disrupted for the first time in the history of the empire.[51]

> For more than half a century, I said to the Holy Father, we have lived in peace with the Holy See. This is the first time that a serious quarrel on a religious question arises between us, and it was necessary

---

[50] *Ibid.*, pp. 19-20. The reply of the Holy Father (*ibid.*, p. 20) was far from reassuring: "Mas disso não podeis saber, retorquio-me o Santo Padre, porque não estais nos arcanos, visto não seres maçon."

[51] *Ibid.*, p. 21.

for the Bishop of Olinda to have provoked it, for a
reason tolerated until that time by all our bishops
since the independence of the Empire! To suppose
that all those venerable Prelates may have neglected
their duties, or may have been ignorant of what was
passing in Brazil, is so absurd that one cannot admit
it.[52]

Clearly, these observations were diplomatically useful; but they
were not true. In making the assertion that this was the first
time that a serious quarrel on a religious question had occurred
in Brazil, Penêdo prescinded from the fact that during the Regency (1831-1840) relations with the Holy See were so strained
that schism was imminent.[53] In saying that the bishop of Olinda
provoked the present quarrel, Penêdo overlooked the facts that
Masonic propaganda had begun openly to attack the Church long
before Dom Vital was consecrated bishop of Olinda in 1872;
that the first open conflict between the fraternity and the episcopacy occurred, not in Olinda but in Rio de Janeiro, and involved
not Dom Vital but Bishop Lacerda; and that the Masonic press
had been attacking Dom Vital for some months before he took
any measures against the fraternity. Furthermore, the baron of
Penêdo, in affirming that all Brazilian prelates had tolerated
Masonry until Vital took action against it, implied that no other
member of the episcopacy in Brazil had until then challenged its
infiltration into Catholic society. But Lacerda, in his pastoral
of November 1, 1873, named fourteen Brazilian prelates who
condemned Brazilian Freemasonry,[54] and Bishop Dom Antônio
de Macedo Costa, in his pastoral of March 25, 1873, told how
Bishop Dom Romualdo de Sousa Coelho, his predecessor in the

---

[52] "Ha mais de meio seculo, disse eu ao Santo Padre, que temos vivido em
paz com a Santa Sé. He esta a primeira vez que apparece entre nós uma luta
séria em materia religiosa, e foi preciso vir o Bispo de Olinda provoca-la por
um motivo tolerado até então por todos os nossos diocesanos desde a independencia do Imperio! Suppor-se que todos esses Prelados venerandos houves-
sem esquecido os seus deveres, ou ignorassem o que se passava no Brasil, he
tão absurdo que não se pode admittir." *Ibid.*

[53] See pp. 76-88 above.

[54] See pp. 204-205 above.

diocese of Pará, had warned the people against it.[55] Moreover, when Penêdo said that it was inadmissible that the bishops should not have known what was going on in Brazil, he contradicted his previous expression of surprise over their lack of information on the question. It is equally difficult to reconcile Penêdo's assertions about the pope's attitude toward Masonry with his avowal that the Holy Father condemned severely the action of Vital. The baron said that "no one would be able to convince the Holy Father . . . that Masonry in Brazil does not conspire against religion";[56] yet he maintained that when he described the Brazilian crisis to the Holy Father, His Holiness said to him, in apparent disapproval of the excesses of the bishop, "*Che volete? È una testa calda!* It was not in Rome that he studied, but in France; I had many scruples in nominating him Bishop so young; but the Government insisted, and I did it in order to be agreeable to the Emperor."[57] If the Holy Father reacted as vehemently as Penêdo seemed to think, he must have been convinced that Dom Vital had culpably disrupted the harmony between Church and State. But Pius IX would never grant that challenging the right of Freemasons to membership in religious associations was a culpable act. He must, therefore, have been given some false impressions.[58] The alternate conjecture is that the pope's remark — if true at all — was, in context, not a severe condemnation, but only a mild expression of regret over the possibility that the young prelate had acted hastily, as well as a gentle reminder that Dom Vital owed his ap-

---

[55] See p. 219 above.

[56] Penêdo, *Missão especial a Roma*, p. 21.

[57] Cited in *ibid.*, p. 22.

[58] Penêdo admits that he kept the question of Masonry in the background. Writing to Rio Branco on December 20, he says (*ibid.*, p. 53) : "Não quiz redigir o *memorandum* . . . antes de sondar o espirito deste Governo sobre o objecto da missão. Logo na primeira entrevista com o Cardeal, bem como na audiencia de apresentação ao Santo Padre, pude ver a direcção que devia dar á questão e o modo por que convinha apresenta-la. Assim verá V. Ex. que fallei da maçonaria com reserva e parcimonia: *o que não foi senão occasião e pretexto para os excessos commettidos pelo Bispo de Olinda, reconheci para logo ser aqui considerado como objecto principal de toda a questão.*" (Italics mine).

pointment to the insistence of the emperor himself.[59]

The Holy Father asked Penêdo to prepare a memorandum[60] which could be presented to a commission that His Holiness would appoint to consider the Brazilian situation.[61] In this memorandum, sent to Cardinal Antonelli on October 29, 1873, Penêdo described the brotherhoods, placed special emphasis on their dual character, indicated that action had been taken against them by the bishop without reference to the civil authority, stressed the point that Masonry was not condemned by the imperial government, and called attention to the fact that the bishop, in his intransigence, had denied the validity of recourse to the crown and the right of imperial *placet*. Having described the events that disturbed the harmony "which had always existed"[62] between Church and State, and having suggested the evils that would follow if peace were not quickly restored, the envoy concluded his testimony with a plea to the Supreme Pontiff:

---

[59] The baron of Penêdo's explanation and defense of his mission to Rome evoked from D. Antônio de Macedo Costa in 1886 one of the most famous works connected with the Religious Question, *A Questão Religiosa a Santa Sé, ou a Missão Especial a Roma em 1873, á luz de documentos publicados e ineditos* (São Luiz do Maranhão, 1886). In this work, the bishop of Pará charged Penêdo with assuring the Holy Father that civil action would not be taken against the bishop of Olinda if His Holiness ordered the interdicts lifted and peace restored to Brazil. This and many other charges were leveled against Penêdo, who in 1887 published a second work, *Bispo do Pará e a Missão especial a Roma* (Lisboa, 1887), in which he attempted a refutation of the charges. The following year, the bishop of Pará published his *O Barão de Penedo e a sua missão a Roma* (Rio de Janeiro, 1888). In this work (p. 5) Macedo Costa makes the following comment on Penêdo's *missão especial*: "O seu novo opusculo é a verdadeira oração funebre da Missão, e todos vão dizer comigo o *sit illi terra levis*, com que o antigo gentilismo se despedia de seus mortos antes de entrarem no eterno repouso."

[60] Penêdo, *Missão especial a Roma*, pp. 24-30. This memorandum is given in full.

[61] *Ibid.*, p. 31. Penêdo, writing to the viscount of Caravelas, says: "Sobre esse *memorandum*, por ordem do Santo Padre, e como he de costume em questões de certa gravidade, tem de ser ouvida uma congregação de Cardeaes nomeados *ad hoc* e cuja decisão, ainda que consultiva serve quasi sempre de base á resolução da questão."

[62] *Ibid.*, p. 30.

The Imperial Government hopes, therefore, that the
Supreme Head of the Church will find in his high
wisdom and in his paternal affection for an Empire
destined to be the greatest representative of Catholicism in America, a means of putting an end to such
conflicts, and of preventing them from multiplying
and taking on even greater proportions.[63]

Penêdo conceded that, when he talked with Cardinal Antonelli,
the latter said that except for the point of harmonious relations
between the two powers, everything else in the memorandum
was contrary to what the Holy See sanctioned. The cardinal
referred to the *placet* as not acknowledged by the Holy See, but
only tolerated by it; it had never been recognized by the Church
in Brazil or in any other country. Penêdo quickly assured the
cardinal that the matter to be investigated was not the right of
*placet*, but the disruption of the long-continued harmonious relations between Church and State, through the action of the
bishops, "without the least provocation of the Civil Power . . . ."
He impressed on the cardinal and on the Holy Father as well
that, in order to restore harmony, the interdicts placed by the
bishops of Olinda and Pará had to be lifted. For this purpose
he petitioned not only the secretary of state, but also Cardinal
di Pietro and Cardinal Berardi, members of the commission,
who knew him from his earlier mission.[64]

In a letter of December 18, Cardinal Antonelli informed the
Brazilian envoy that the Holy Father had decided to accede to
his entreaties and to end the quarrel between Church and State
in Brazil. The cardinal secretary remarked that the Holy Father
deplored the grave conflict, regretted the circumstances that provoked it, and feared the fatal consequences that might follow it.
His Holiness, continued Antonelli, was gratified by the deference
paid the Holy See by the imperial government, when it invoked

---

[63] "Espera, pois, o Governo Imperial que o Chefe Supremo da Igreja achará,
na sua alta sabedoria e paternal affeição para com um Imperio destinado a ser
o maior representante do catholicismo na America, um meio de pôr termo a
semelhantes conflictos, e impedir que se reproduzam e tomem ainda maiores
proporções." *Ibid.*, p. 30.

[64] *Ibid.*, pp. 34-37.

papal authority to bring peace, and declared its desire to maintain harmony between the two powers.[65] The tenor of this letter testified to the tact and finesse with which Penêdo had presented his case; there is every indication that he did not allow the intransigent attitude of the home government to be discerned either by the Holy Father or by his secretary of state. The cardinal, after expressing the Holy Father's willingness to co-operate with the imperial government, indicated that the pontiff hoped "that the Imperial Government on its side will help to remove all the obstacles that could hamper the prompt re-establishment of the desired harmony and will assent in this fashion to the benign dispositions of the Holy See." The cardinal secretary added that it would be superfluous to make any observations on the right of *placet* or of recourse to the crown, because the attitude of the Holy See toward them was well known.[66]

In describing his mission to Rome and in accounting for its failure, Penêdo observed that the imperial government did not want merely the restoration of religious tranquility; if it had, this could have been achieved by diplomacy.[67] The government wanted to discipline the bishops for challenging its supreme authority over the Church, and, at the same time, persuade the pope to lift the interdicts so that the Brazilian clergy and laity might be led to believe that the bishops had acted without the approval of the Holy See.[68] When Penêdo reported to his gov-

---

[65] *Ibid.*, pp. 57-58. The entire text of this letter is given.

[66] *Ibid.*

[67] *Ibid.*, p. 50. Penêdo writes: "No Brasil, como explicou na Camara dos Deputados o Ministro dos Negocios Estrangeiros, sessão de 2 de Junho de 1874, 'preferio o Governo dar desde logo execução á lei, e mandou a Roma sómente solicitar o apoio moral, a influencia santa que podia pôr termo aos excessos dos Bispos.' "

[68] Olívola, *Um grande brasileiro*, p. 153. See also Antônio Manuel dos Reis, *O Bispo de Olinda perante a história* (rev. ed., Recife, 1940), I, 139. "O plano do Governo, enviando aquela missão á Roma, era, me parece, esmagar logo os Bispos do Pará e de Olinda, sob o peso de duas condenações, uma civil e outra eclesiástica. Depois queria se justificar perante o país de seu modo de obrar para com os dois Bispos e de sufocar o movimento católico, a reação religiosa que a perseguição fizera nacer no Brasil."

ernment that the Holy Father had directed Cardinal Antonelli to write a letter to the bishop of Olinda[69] censuring his conduct and ordering him to lift the interdict,[70] the imperial government believed that it was about to achieve its goal. Penêdo said that the content of the letter the cardinal had showed him was "rather severe."[71] It opened, Penêdo informed the minister, with the phrase, "we do not praise your action,"[72] indicating that the bishop, who had acted with severity, had understood badly the pope's letter of May 29, 1873,[73] in which His Holiness had recommended moderation and clemency. His Holiness ordered, continued the envoy, still quoting the letter as he remembered it, that the bishop restore to its "former state, *ad pristinum statum adducas*, the peace of the Church which he had disturbed."[74] Penêdo informed the minister that this letter was being sent to the internuncio, Sanguigni, to be delivered to Dom Vital, and

---

[69] The letter was addressed to the bishop of Olinda, but a copy was to be sent to the bishop of Pará. The bishop of Olinda was considered the instigator of the conflict. Penêdo, *op. cit.*, p. 29.

[70] *Ibid.*, pp. 52-56. The letter is given in full.

[71] *Ibid.*, p. 53.

[72] *Ibid.* The bishop of Olinda denied that this phrase appeared in the letter he received from Cardinal Antonelli. See Reis, *op. cit.*, I, 141, note 86. "Refere-se á célebre carta que se dizia conter as palavras *Gesta tua*, etc., *non laudantur*, etc., as quais o ilustre Bispo de Olinda afirmou de viva voz a diversas pessôas, entre elas, ao autor deste livro, não existirem nem no principio nem no meio e nem no fim da tal carta." Joaquim Nabuco, *Um estadista*, III, 378-379, note 3, writes: "Carta do Bispo de Olinda ao Arcebispo de Buenos Ayres, negando a verdade da affirmação de Penedo. A carta Antonelli não continha a expressão *gesta tua non laudantur*, que Penedo affirmara ter ouvido; no principio ha as palavras 'Quae jam ab integro fere anno a Te *isthic gesta sunt* adversus quasdam pias sodalitates . . . .'palavras (*isthic gesta sunt*) que podiam ter dado logar á confusão. A affirmação de que não existia o documento, a que se referira Penedo, por ter havido má apprehensão, á leitura, das palavras com que elle procurava designal-o e authentical-o, é o que se chama em Casuistica uma *oequivocatio*, para a qual os Bispos acreditavam ter *justa causa*." For the letter of Dom Vital to Archbishop Federico Aneiros, see Reis, *op. cit.*, I, 105-117.

[73] See p. 162 above.

[74] "Pelo que o Santo Padre lhe ordenava que restabelecesse ao antigo estado, *ad pristinum statum adducas*, a paz da Igreja que se havia perturbado." Penêdo, *Missão especial a Roma*, p. 53.

that it should arrive at the same time as his (Penêdo's) despatch.[75] When the internuncio received this letter,[76] he commissioned Bishop Lacerda to deliver it to Dom Vital, who was then in Rio de Janeiro, a prisoner in the naval arsenal. Dom Vital, certain that the Supreme Pontiff would never have ordered the lifting of the interdicts had he known that the government intended to continue its action against him and his colleague, realized the disastrous results that would follow if he were to carry out the papal command. After he had tried unsuccessfully to get advice from the internuncio,[77] Vital decided not to carry out the order of the Holy See until he had sent an envoy to the Vatican to explain the true situation to the Holy Father.[78]

---

[75] *Ibid.*, p. 39. Penêdo admits that he tried unsuccessfully to secure a copy of this letter at the time that Cardinal Antonelli read it to him. He says in his account of his mission to Rome: "Pedi, he verdade, instantemente ao Cardeal uma copia dessa carta, não para proclamar esse resultado como victoria diplomatica, e demoralisar o Bispo tirando-lhe o prestigio necessario a um alto dignitario da Igreja; esse assomo de inutil vaidade, confesso sinceramente, não entrou no meu espirito, nem na minha longa vida official fui jamais adepto da diplomacia de praça publica; mas por mera satisfação de certas exigencias, a que tem de acceder os governos parlamentares com a discrição inherente á alta administração . . . . Para recusar-me essa copia oppunha-me o Cardeal taes motivos de conveniencia, escrupulos a tradições, que tive de ceder e desistir da instancia, como referi ao Governo no meu officio de 20 de Dezembro."

[76] For the text of this letter as translated by the bishop of Pará and published in his work *A questão religiosa perante a Santa Sé*, see Augusto Olímpio Viveiros de Castro, "Contribuções para a biographia de D. Pedro II," Parte I, *Revista do Instituto Histórico e Geográfico Brasileiro*, tomo especial (1925), 511, note 1. This work will hereafter be cited as Castro. [Macedo Costa's book is out of print and I have been unable to secure a copy].

[77] Cardinal Antonelli's letter, dated Dec. 18, 1873, was delivered to Bishop Vital on January 21, 1874. Reis, *op. cit.*, I, 140-141, writes: "No dia seguinte o Bispo de Olinda mandou rogar a Monsenhor Internuncio que lhe concedesse uma palavra. O Bispo disse-lhe que estava pronto a dar execução á Carta de S. Emcia. o Cardial Antonelli; mas rogava a S. Excia. que lhe désse primeiramente alguns esclarecimentos necessarios sobre certas dificuldades mui graves que encontrava na pratica. Monsenhor Internuncio respondeu que êle não as podia dar de nenhuma maneira, porque não tinha recebido instruções alguma a este respeito. Entretanto aconselhou o Bispo a publicar a carta logo, e a pedir instruções depois a S. Emcia. o Cardial d'Estado."

[78] Olívola, *op. cit.*, p. 154. Bishop Dom Vital sent his secretary, Father José de Lima e Sá, to Rome. The author adds: "E teve rasão. O Papa

When the pope heard that the bishop of Olinda had been tried and condemned by the supreme tribunal of justice, he realized that the bishop had been victimized by Brazilian diplomacy.[79] He immediately notified the internuncio to instruct the two prelates to destroy Cardinal Antonelli's letter; the prelates did as they were directed; the interdicts were not lifted, and in time the very existence of the famous letter was questioned.[80]

Vital's resolution not to carry out the papal order until he had communicated with the Holy Father annulled the triumph of the much-acclaimed Penêdo mission.[81] Masonic journals that had exulted over the defeat of ultramontanism and the victory of Freemasonry[82] discovered that people who at first believed their accounts were beginning to suspect that these accounts were part of a campaign to draw support away from the bishops.[83] Members of parliament began to press the ministry for tangible evidence that the papacy had actually ordered the interdicts lifted.[84] The minister of foreign affairs urged the minister in Rome

---

mandou destruir a carta do Cardeal Antonelli."

[79] Reis, *op. cit.*, II, 288-292, gives the texts of two letters written by Pius IX on March 4, 1874, the first to Monsignor Joaquim Camelo de Andrade, vicar of the diocese of Olinda, the second to Bishop Dom Vital; *ibid.*, pp. 296-298, gives the text of the letter written by Cardinal Antonelli on March 30, 1874, to the baron of Alhandra. Cardinal Antonelli writes (p. 297): "O Sr. Barão de Penêdo assegurou ao abaixo assinado que o seu Governo não tomaria medida alguma desagradavel contra o Bispo de Pernambuco; e era muito natural que assim acontecesse achando-se pendentes as negociações entre a Santa Sé e o Governo Imperial."

[80] Nabuco, *Um estadista*, III, 378-381.

[81] Olívola, *op. cit.*, p. 154. "Essa resolução de d. Frei Vital anulou a tão afamada missão Penêdo, e todas as esperanças do governo numa condemnação do Papa aos Bispos de Olinda e do Pará."

[82] *Ibid.*, p. 155. ". . . os jornais anunciaram a carta em que o Papa não louvava o Bispo (*gesta tua non laudantur*), e dava ordem para levantar o interdito. Disseram que esta vitória tinha custado ao governo dois mil contos, que Roma (a antiga Babilônia) tudo vendia por dinheiro e que a maçonaria tinha vencido, e D. Frei Vital era mais catolico do que o Papa! . . . ." See also Reis, *op. cit.*, I, 141-143, for a fuller account of Masonic propaganda.

[83] Reis, *op. cit.*, I, 144; Olívola, *op. cit.*, p. 156; Penêdo, *Missão especial a Roma*, pp. 100-102.

[84] Penêdo, *Missão especial a Roma*, pp. 74-75. Penêdo writes (*ibid.*, p. 74): "Vencida a luta episcopal nos conselhos do Vaticano, e chamado o Dio-

to try to secure a copy of the letter from the cardinal secretary of state, and at the same time informed the baron of Penêdo that his mission must be judged a failure if specific evidence could not be obtained to substantiate his assertion that the Holy Father had censured the bishops and had ordered harmonious relations reestablished between Church and State in Brazil.[85] When no evidence was secured,[86] the government was confronted with an untenable situation. In August, 1874, the viscount of Araguaia

[85] cesano aos seus deveres, os agoureiros da missão, desconcertados pelo seu exito, mudaram de tactica na opposição ao Governo e ao negociador. Negar a existencia da carta, era contestar *prima facie* o resultado da missão; e d'ahi a duvida engendrada acerca da entrega desse documento, logo que fora annunciada pelo *Diario Official*. Uma Alliança singular de elementos os mais oppostos, no Parlamento e na imprensa, apoderou-se dessa duvida, como expediente de occasião, para adiar o golpe ou fazer naufragar a missão dentro do porto."

[85] On February 11, 1874, Rio Branco informed Penêdo (*ibid.*, p. 101) that "O resultado da missão está sendo discutido com lamentavel má fé. . . . Procura-se evidentemente demover o Bispo de Olinda do cumprimento immediato das recommendações do Papa, a pretexto de que a prisão do Prelado não era caso previsto em Roma." On February 18, 1874, Caravelas wrote (*ibid.*, 100): "Devo aqui dizer a V. Ex. que o procedimento do Bispo tende a annullar o resultado da sua missão; e que para isso contribue de certo a circumstancia de não haver o Cardeal Antonelli dado a V. Ex. copia da carta que lhe mostrou. Isto obriga-me a dirigir ao Barão de Alhandra [Brazilian minister in Rome] o despacho constante da inclusa copia, recommendando-lhe que peça o dito documento, e dizendo-lhe que não será publicado salvo o caso de accordo prévio com a Santa Sé."

[86] *Ibid.*, p. 60, Penêdo explains why no evidence was available. "Na nota official do Secretario de Estado não se diz, como eu desejava, que seria o Bispo censurado e advertido, e que o Santo Padre mandaria levantar os interdictos. Isso porêm não admittio Sua Santidade: não quiz por cousa alguma reprehender publicamente n'um documento diplomatico o Bispo de Olinda." See also *ibid.*, pp. 52-56, for Penêdo's letter to the minister of foreign affairs. Further on, when commenting on the baron of Alhandra's failure to secure a copy of the letter, Penêdo says (*ibid.*, pp. 100-101): "O documento que devia restabelecer a paz na Igreja do Brasil não podia ser um documento publico. As relações entre a Santa Sé e o episcopado em casos desta natureza são de ordem muito particular e delicada; e o Summo Pontifice he o primeiro interessado em manter o prestigio, a força moral dos Bispos, e em acatar-lhes a autoridade como Altos Dignitarios da Igreja. Não foram por mera complacencia diplomatica respeitados os escrupulos do Secretario de Estado em dar uma copia da carta ao negociador. Não lh'a podia dar então, nem nunca a pôde conseguir o Barão de Alhandra a pezar das repetidas instancias por ordem

was sent as envoy to the Holy Father in the hope that he could improve relations with the Vatican.[87] He was not successful, however, for in November the American minister reported that the word from Rome is "that the Pope is so dissatisfied with the hostility shown by Brazil to the just rights of the Church, that he will maintain here only a Chargé D'Affaires, in place of the late Internunzio, now sent as nunzio to Lisbon . . . . the mission of . . . Magalhaens (Baron Araguaya) has not been, as yet, successful."[88] Not until February of the following year did the Brazilian envoy succeed in persuading the Holy Father to communicate with the emperor. In this letter, the pope indicated that the Holy See would continue to consider ways of restoring peaceful relations between Church and State, but that it would expect the imperial government to remove the Freemasons from the religious brotherhoods. The Holy Father stated explicitly that if the bishops were released the interdicts would be lifted. The pope wrote:[89]

> Your Majesty's Minister to this Holy See suggested that I should write to Your Majesty on the case of the

---

do Governo, e da reserva promettida, salvo o accordo prévio para a sua publicação."

[87] National Archives, Department of State, Partridge to Fish, vol. 41, no. 196, August 24, 1874.

[88] Ibid., Partridge to Fish, vol. 41, no. 213, November 23, 1874. Magalhaens was viscount of Araguaia, not baron.

[89] "Insinuou-me o Ministro de V. Majestade junto a esta Santa Sé, que escrevesse a V. M. sobre o caso dos Bispos súditos seus e dos mações que igualmente o são.

"Não posso, entretanto, escrever no sentido insinuado pelo Sr. Ministro, uma vez que os Bispos, ainda pelos mais recentes relatórios que tenho á vista conduziram-se perfeitamente bem, de conformidade com as leis canônicas; como todavia, não estão de acôrdo as leis civis com as leis canônicas, não podia deixar de surgir um dissidio. Em substancia pede o Ministro a reabertura das igrejas interditas e semelhante ordem não creio eu possa dá-la enquanto não virem restituidos á antiga liberdade os Bispos que, de acordo com as leis canônicas, se acham injustamente encarcerados. Aliás a soberana prerogativa de conceder indulto está sempre ao arbítrio de V. M. que póde fazer o que lhe apraz.

"Concedida essa graça, é certo que as igrejas, ora em parte fechadas, serão imediatamente abertas, comtanto, porém, que se afastem os mações dos cargos

Bishops, your subjects, and of the Masons, who are equally so.

I cannot, however, write in the tenor suggested by the Minister, since the bishops, according to the most recent reports that I have before me, conducted themselves perfectly well, in conformity with canon law; yet inasmuch as civil law is not in accord with Canon law, a conflict was bound to arise. In substance, the Minister asks the reopening of the interdicted Churches, and I do not believe that I can give such an order as long as the Bishops, who according to Canon law are unjustly incarcerated, are not restored to their former liberty. Besides, the sovereign prerogative of conceding pardon is always at the will of Your Majesty who can do what pleases you.

This favor granted, it is certain that the Churches, now partly closed, shall be immediately reopened, on condition, however, that the Masons be removed from the offices that they hold in the brotherhoods. The Masons of Brazil — the Minister will say — are different from the Masons of Europe. I know well, however, that they absolutely do not differ from those that exist here, and that they have the same tendencies, the same rules, the same objective: and as the Masons

---

*que exercem nas irmandades.* Os mações do Brasil — dirá o Sr. Ministro — são diferentes dos mações da Europa. Bem sei, porém, que absolutamente não diferem dos que cá existem, e que têm as mesmas tendências, as mesmas regras, o mesmo objetivo: e assim como estão condemnados pela igreja os mações da Europa, não resta duvida que incidam os mações da America na mesma condemnação.

Magestade! Rogo-lhe que reflita que devemos todos comparecer perante o tribunal de Deus e que quanto mais alto estiver alguem, mais severo ha de ser o ajuste de contas, rasão pela qual enquanto vivos peregrinarmos por este mundo, é mister que façamos tudo quanto se acha ao nosso alcance para prevenirmos um juizo severo e sem appelação.

"Oro por V. M., supplicando humildemente a Deus queira conceder-lhe, pela intercessão da Virgem S. S. salutares conselhos e a graça necessária para traduzí-los em obra. *Liberte os Bispos e ponha termo a essa dolorosa historia.* E' o que espero do generoso coração de V. M. a quem concedo bem como á Augusta Familia a Benção Apostólica." Olívola, *Um grande brasileiro,* pp. 193-195. [Since it is likely that the italics did not appear in the original letter, we are omitting them from the translation.]

of Europe are condemned by the Church, therefore no doubt remains that the Masons of America fall under the same condemnation.

Your Majesty! I beg of you to reflect that we must all appear before the Tribunal of God and that the higher one has been, the more serious shall be the settling of accounts, for which reason while we, the living, journey through this world, we must do all in our power to prevent a severe judgment and one without appeal.

I pray for Your Majesty, humbly supplicating that God may be willing to concede to you, through the intercession of the Most Holy Virgin, wholesome counsels and the grace necessary to translate them into deeds. Free the Bishops and put an end to that sad history. This is what I hope from the generous heart of Your Majesty to whom I concede, as well as to your August Family, the Apostolic Benediction.

The Holy Father was obviously giving Pedro II, allegedly a staunch Catholic and a personal friend,[90] an opportunity to step gracefully out of the embarrassment into which the Religious Question had necessarily thrust the monarchy. Pedro's regalism was unfortunately more deeply rooted than his faith; and the appeal of the Sovereign Pontiff was unavailing.[91]

Basílio de Magalhães thinks that Pius IX lacked courage in his handling of the Religious Question, and he cites three instances of papal vacillation.[92] On February 22, 1874 (the day following the condemnation of Vital), the internuncio Mon-

---

[90] Nabuco, *Um estadista*, III, 376. In speaking of the Penêdo mission, Nabuco refers to the fact that one year before, the emperor "like a son," had visited Pius IX at the Vatican.

[91] When João Dornas, *O padroado e a igreja brasileira* (São Paulo [1938]), p. 261, writes that "A alma de toda a campanha foi o Imperador, cujo regalismo não admittia e não perdoava a altaneria dos bispos, que se sobrepunham á dignidade da Corôa, suppostamente offendida pela sua rebeldia," he expresses the common opinion of those who have studied the Religious Question.

[92] See Basílio de Magalhães, *Estudos de história do Brasil* (São Paulo, 1940), pp. 132-134.

signor Sanguigni, wrote to the minister of foreign affairs, the viscount of Caravelas, protesting the government's disregard of ecclesiastical immunity in subjecting the bishop to a civil tribunal.[93] On March 1, Caravelas replied by characterizing Sanguigni's protest as "impertinent and null."[94] According to Magalhães, the Holy Father should have withdrawn his representative from Brazil at this juncture.[95] Considering that many regalistically-inclined statesmen were seeking an excuse to break relations with Rome and to establish a national church,[96] and considering the disastrous spiritual effects on Brazil if schism occurred, one may rightly question whether at this time such a breaking of diplomatic relations would have been either prudent or courageous. Later, when the full import of the situation had had time to impress itself on the people, and when they were in a position to view the Episcopal-Masonic question in its full significance,[97] the Holy See did withdraw its internuncio, and refused to maintain more than a chargé d'affaires in the imperial capital.

Magalhães refers to a note written by Cardinal Antonelli to the Brazilian minister at Rome, the baron of Alhandra, in which the cardinal said that "the unexpected and sad event [the imprisonment of the bishops], producing an irremovable obstacle to the execution of the benign resolutions of the Supreme Pontiff toward the imperial government, had grieved excessively the heart of the Holy Father."[98] This note showed, according to

---

[93] Castro, p. 524.

[94] *Ibid.*, pp. 524-525. The minister wrote in part: "O protesto do snr. internuncio apostolico, permitta s. exa. que o diga, é, portanto impertinente e nullo, e, como tal, não pode produzir effeito algum."

[95] Magalhães, *op. cit.*, pp. 132-133.

[96] See p. 202 above.

[97] Reis, *op. cit.*, I, 150, writes: "A questão [Episcopal-Masonic question] tem sido providencial; ela ha despertado o sentimento católico no Brasil, ha reacendido aí o fogo da fé que se extinguia todos os dias pouco a pouco; e, se houve algum áto de fraqueza, houve tambem exemplos mui numerosos de devotamento e fidelidade que fazem honra aos sacerdotes e aos fiéis de meu país, sobretudo quando se pensa que é sómente agora que se começa alí a ter um verdadeiro conhecimento da Religião."

[98] Magalhães, *op. cit.*, p. 133.

Magalhães, that the pope did not expect Dom Pedro to carry the Religious Question to its ultimate consequence.[99] His observation is undoubtedly correct; yet the Holy Father had two valid reasons for thinking that the emperor would not proceed against the bishops: 1) the fact that the imperial government had sent Penêdo to negotiate for peace, and 2) the fact that while at the Vatican, Penêdo avoided discussion of all matters likely to arouse opposition, and threw the burden of his discourse on the eagerness of the imperial government to restore harmony. Antonelli was justified in saying in his letter to Alhandra that the pope was grieved because the imperial government had made it impossible for him to restore tranquility between Church and State in Brazil. Pius IX, interested above all in establishing and maintaining amicable relations without sacrifice of principle, could only regret that the imperial government had put itself into a position wherein it must choose between two undesirable alternatives. That the government would have to decide between mounting popular hostility and retraction was apparent by the summer of 1874.[100]

Finally, Magalhães is of the opinion that, in his letter of February 5, Pius IX confined himself to consoling the prelates without assuming, as was his duty, a complete defense of their acts: "In order to be logical the pope ought not to have begged from the emperor the pardon of the bishops, but ought to have used energy and ought even to have excommunicated the Brazilian monarch".[101] That Pius IX did none of these things is proof enough that he was not trying to establish a theocracy in Brazil; neither was he instigating a secret ultramontane movement by means of which he could superimpose his will on secular

---

[99] *Ibid.*

[100] Penêdo, *op. cit.*, p. 103, writes: "No 1o de Julho de 1874 estava igualmente condemnado o Rev. Bispo do Pará, e assim completado o quadro de martyrio, qual teria naturalmente de figurar-se aos olhos daquelle que he o Primaz de todos os Bispos na jerarchia da Igreja. De facto e bem depressa os protestos e queixas da Santa Sé precedidos pelos do seu representante no Brasil, se fizerão ouvir por toda parte; e a causa dos Bispos tornou-se então claramente a causa do Papa."

[101] Magalhães, *op. cit.*, p. 134.

princes. The pope's behavior in this situation was amazingly tolerant. When the imperial government wanted to arbitrate — or appeared to want to arbitrate — the Vatican was ready; when the imperial government wanted to act alone, the Vatican withdrew and left it to act and to reap the consequences of its actions. The pope did not, however, assume an attitude of intransigence because the imperial government had treated two prelates contumeliously; as the letter of February 5 showed, the Supreme Pontiff still hoped that the emperor would save his nation from the disaster of schism.[102]

When, on September 17, 1875, Dom Pedro conceded amnesty to the two bishops, the imperial government immediately petitioned the Holy See to lift the interdicts. The Supreme Pontiff, in conformity with the promise he had given the emperor in his letter of February 5, directed that the bishops be instructed to do so. In spite of the fact that the Holy Father was simply fulfilling his pledge to the emperor, the order caused much comment.[103] Masonry viewed the papal order as an ultimate victory

---

[102] Reis, *op. cit.*, II, 319, says that the notice of the amnesty reached Rome more quickly than news of the imprisonment of the bishops. On September 30, 1876, Cardinal Antonelli wrote to Monsignor Bruschetti, agent of the Holy See in Rio de Janeiro, ordering him to communicate to the two bishops the Holy Father's order that the interdicts be lifted.

[103] See p. 200 above. See also Reis, *op. cit.*, I, 151-152. "A' este áto da Santa Sé se deu entre nós, como se vê pelos jornais, duas interpretações bem diferentes uma da outra.

"Os católicos, guiados pelos sentimentos da Fé, o interpretam segundo o espírito dos sagrados Cánones e das admiráveis Letras, que Nosso Santíssimo Padre o Papa se dignou escrever aos Bispos do Pará e de Olinda depois do começo da questão, sobre a mesma materia. D'ai concluem que, se a Santa Sé fez levantar os interditos, sem dúvida ela terá posto por condição que os mações sairão das Confrarias, e que estas, em logar de remanecer lojas maçonicas nas Igrejas, tornar-se-ão realmente verdadeiras Confrarias religiosas, fiéis ao fim para o qual elas têm sido criadas. E êles estão com a verdade. A condição foi posta formalmente: nós o sabemos, nós os Bispos, por documentos que temos recebido.

"Os mações ao contrario dizem e escrevem que o Soberano Pontifice fez levantar os interditos sem nenhuma condição, e que, além disto êle tem justificado a Maçonaria, a tem inocentado, declarado isenta das censuras e das excomunhões lançadas sobre ela em outros paises; e fazem por isso festas de regosijo."

for the fraternity; it failed to realize that the Holy Father was merely providing an armistice, and that full peace would come only after the Freemasons had been eliminated from the religious associations. But since the interdicts had been raised by pontifical act, only a papal pronouncement would make it clear to all that Brazilian Masonry was condemned by the Church and that those affiliated with the fraternity could not hold membership in religious associations. One reason for Dom Vital's departure for Rome, on October 5, was the urgency of this need.[104] The prelate knew that many false impressions had been created among the cardinals about the Brazilian situation; consequently, he was eager to present his case in person. It was not, however, until after he had left Rome and gone to France that Dom Vital learned that his mission had succeeded.[105] On May 3, 1876, he received from Pius IX a copy of the encyclical *Exortae in ista ditione*, and a reassuring message, "I approve as long ago I approved all that you have done."[106] In the encyclical, directed to the hierarchy of Brazil, the Supreme Pontiff ordered the reform of the Brazilian brotherhoods, and the elimination of Masons from them. Some of these associations were slow to offer their submission,[107] but after the papal order was promulgated, none could any longer deny that members of the Masonic fraternity were illicitly admitted to any society that claimed to be Catholic.

---

[104] Olívola, "Alma franciscana," *loc. cit.*, pp. 344-345.

[105] *Ibid.*, p. 345.

[106] *Ibid.*

[107] The submission of the Third Order of St. Francis of Penitence (Ordem Terceira de S. Francisco da Penitência) and the Third Order of Our Lady of Mount Carmel (Ordem de N. S. do Monte Carmelo) of the diocese of Pará, in 1880, was extremely important. These were the religious associations that had been most obstinate in their refusal to remove members affiliated with Masonry, and that had presented recourse to the crown against the bishop of Pará. (On their submission see Lustosa, *op. cit.*, pp. 486-489).

# CONCLUSION

In the first chapter of this study, it was shown that modern Masonry underwent a significant evolution in its relation to Catholicism. At the outset, the fathers of modern Masonry viewed their new society as heir to Christianity without regard to individual Christian beliefs. Shortly, however, it developed that Freemasonry was not to be the heir of Christianity as such, but the rival of Roman Catholicism. Ultimately it became apparent that the Masonic fraternity was not only the rival of Roman Catholicism, but also the protagonist of all those who for any reason had grievances against the papacy. This final development was supremely important in countries where a union of the Catholic Church and the State existed. In some instances, Freemasonry gained full control of the disaffected groups and dictated a strongly anti-Catholic policy which was acquiesced in by Liberal Catholic statesmen. The result eventually was open persecution of the Church through the instrumentality of the government. This situation was exemplified in Portugal in 1910 and in Mexico in 1856. In other instances, regalistically-inclined statesmen never yielded the reins of government to Freemasonry, but contrariwise used the fraternity as a rallying point for party loyalties. This was the case in Brazil.

Throughout the period of the empire, Freemasonry in Brazil had great political importance; nevertheless it never supplanted regalism as the dominant force in shaping imperial policy. The foremost statesmen seem to have been regalists first, Freemasons second. When the interest of the fraternity conflicted with the interests of the regalistic state, Masonry was sacrificed. This policy, examination has shown, carried through the whole imperial period. When the First Empire was created, José Bonifácio de Andrada e Silva, as we have seen, persuaded Dom Pedro I to disband the fraternity because it threatened the monarchy. Vasconcelos de Drummond says that José Bonifácio used Freemasonry as a means of uniting men for a given purpose, but that the patriarch of independence, although the first grand master of the Brazilian Grand Orient, would not permit Masonry to become a state within a state.[1] Later, in the Constitutional Convention (1823), the Masonic group sought persistently to effect a radical separation of Church and State,[2] but were unsuccessful; yet the regalists in the first legislature were powerful enough to establish a royal patronage which from its very nature must inevitably bring the Church under the domination of the State.[3] During the period of the Regency, Father Diogo Antônio Feijó used Masonry to insure party loyalty, but his policies were fundamentally regalistic, not Masonic. Feijó, like Joseph II of Austria, was ready to play the sacristan or to usurp the functions of the Holy See and for essentially the same reason: to curtail the jurisdiction of the papacy. In the Second Empire a number of notable statesmen like Joaquim Nabuco, João Alfredo, and the viscount of Sousa Franco avowed publicly that they had left the fraternity; yet when the Religious Question arose, they defended tenaciously the rights of Freemasonry because as regalists they would not admit that papal bulls condemning it could be promulgated in the empire without having first received the imperial *placet*. Finally, it is a generally acknowledged fact that the person who held out longest against granting amnesty to the bishops was the emperor. Dom Pedro II was not a Mason, neither was he fighting the cause of Masonry as such; he was simply defending the philosophy of regalism on which rested his theory of Church-State relations. He resented the fact that the right of the State to supervise the Church was challenged by the bishops. The imperial government

---

[1] "Projecto de constituição no 'Apostolado' e sua auctoria," *Revista do Instituto Histórico e Geográfico Brasileiro,* LXX (1914), ii, 45.

[2] The separation that was sought by the Masonic group in the Constitutional Convention would have been the type of separation that Bishop Macedo Costa condemned in the collective pastoral of March 19, 1890, see p. 53, note 95, above.

[3] The ultra regalists, who rejected the right of patronage conferred on the Brazilian emperor by the Holy See and established patronage as a right inherent in sovereignty, were in many cases members of the Masonic fraternity. They used the fraternity to insure political cohesion, but their political theories derived not from Masonry, but from Portuguese regalists.

was, in fact, so preoccupied with defending its regalistic claims to full jurisdiction over the Church that many of its statesmen refused to believe that Bishop Dom Vital and Bishop Dom Antônio de Macedo Costa were essentially interested in fighting the infiltration of Freemasonry into Catholic society. They insisted on believing that this quarrel was ostensibly over Freemasonry, but that in reality Masonry was only a pretext by means of which the episcopacy hoped to make new inroads into the sphere of civil jurisdiction.

Brazilian regalists, attracted to Freemasonry largely because it was a useful political tool, chose to ignore the fact that a radical element was developing in the Brazilian fraternity. They chose also to ignore the hostility to religion which this group showed, and prescinding from it, they found justification in their own minds for withholding the *placet* from papal bulls that condemned the international fraternity as inimical to Catholicism. So it came about that imperial statesmen found justification for their regalistic policy and at the same time persuaded themselves that anyone who rejected this policy was attacking not the Masonry that it sought to justify, but the civil authority that formulated it. For this reason the Episcopal-Masonic controversy was transformed from a conflict between two social forces into a contest between the spiritual and temporal powers. The bishops knew they must free the Church in Brazil from the domination of Freemasonry if they were to retrieve her ebbing right to operate as a free institution; the imperial statesmen knew that such an episcopal achievement would destroy the regalist's claim to full jurisdiction in spiritual affairs. In order to place the Episcopal-Masonic controversy in proper perspective it must, therefore, be viewed not as an isolated conflict, but as the most serious, as well as the most spectacular, in a series of altercations between the Church and the State during the period of the empire in Brazil.

# APPENDIX A

## DOCUMENT I

"Consistory of the Brotherhood of
the Most Holy Sacrament of St.
Anthony's Parish,
Recife,
January 19, 1873.

"Most Illustrious and Most Reverend Sir:

"The letters of Your Reverence, dated the 12th and 13th of the current month, were submitted to the consideration of the Governing Board. These [letters] accompanied the circulars of His Excellency the very worthy and virtuous Prelate of this Diocese, who, in the first one of the 9th of the present month, determines that Your Reverence demand the reconsideration of the reply which with all respect the Governing Board unanimously gave to the order of our virtuous Bishop dated December 28, 1872, in which he ordered the expulsion from the membership of our Brotherhood of Dr. Antônio José da Costa Ribeiro, who is known notoriously to be a Mason, and of others who do not wish to abjure this sect; and in the second one [*i.e.*, circular], written on the 13th of the present [month], our illustrious Ordinary determines that Your Reverence demand from the Governing Board a reconsideration within the space of four days, beginning from the 13th, under pain of the reply's being considered as negative in the event of not doing it.

---

"Consistorio da Irmandade do Santissimo Sacramento da freguesia de Santo Antonio do Recife, 19 de janeiro de 1873 — Illm., e Revm. Sr. —

"Foram submettidos á consideração da Mesa Regedora os officios de V. S. Revm. datados de 12 e 13 do corrente, os quaes acompanharam as circulares de S. Ex. Revma., mui digno e virtuoso Prelado desta Diocese, que na primeira 9 do corrente, determina a V. S. Revm. que exija a reconsideração da resposta que com todo respeito deu a Mesa Regedora por unanimidade de votos á ordem do nosso virtuoso Bispo datada de 28 de desembro de 1872, pela qual mandava expulsar do gremio da nossa Irmandade ao Dr. Antonio José da Costa Ribeiro, que consta notoriamente ser Maçon, e outros que não querem abjurar esta seita; e na segunda, lavrada de 13 do presente, determina o nosso illustrado Diocesano que V. S. Revm. exija da Mesa Regedora a reconsideração no praso de quatro dias contados de 13, sob pena de na falta, ser considerada como negativa a resposta.

"May Your Reverence know that the letters were delivered to me on the 12th and 13th and that I endeavored to convoke the Governing Board which was able to meet only today. It is, then, evident that I did not try to delay the meeting; on the contrary, it [the meeting] was the earliest possible, seeing that only twenty-four hours had intervened from the reception of the last letter of Your Reverence. And the motive which impelled me was to remove from me the tremendous responsibility of appearing disrespectful to our illustrious Prelate, delaying an answer which had to be considered by others.

"Thus justifying my personal behavior, and manifesting the respect and esteem which the orders of our illustrious Bishop deserve from me, may Your Reverence permit me with the greatest attention to give you the opinion of the Governing Board in regard to the order of Your Reverence as the delegate of His Excellency.

"The Governing Board read with the most attentive consideration and in the most profound silence the letters and orders of our illustrious Bishop, the Most Excellent and Most Reverend Friar Dom Vital, and after mature reflection, compatible with the haste ordered by our renowned Bishop who with all due consideration indicated so short a period of time that it does not permit it [the Governing Board] to consult and hear third parties, nor even to consider the suggestion alluded to in your letter of December 21, replies [sic]

"In these sad and constrained circumstances, the Governing Board, benumbed

---

"Saiba V. S. Revm. que os officios me foram entregues nos dias 12 e 13, pelo que tractei de fazer a convocação de Mesa Regedora, que só hoje pôde reunir-se. É pois evidente que não procurei demorar a reunião, e ao contrario foi a mais proxima possivel, visto como só mediaram 24 horas do recebimento do ultimo officio de V. S. Revm. E o motivo que me impelliu foi arredar de sobre mim a tremenda responsabilidade de parecer desrespeitador ao nosso illustrado Diocesano, demorando uma resposta, que por outros devia ser considerada.

"Assim justificando o meu procedimento pessoal, e manifestando o respeito e acatamento que me merecem as ordens do nosso illustrado Bispo, consinta V. S. Revm. que com a maior attenção leve o sentir da Mesa Regedora ácêrca da ordem de V. S. Revm. como delegado de S. Ex. Revm.

"A Mesa Regedora leu com a mais subida consideração e no mais profundo silencio os officios e ordens do nosso illustrado Bispo, o Exm. e Revm. Sr. D. Frei Vital; e depois de madura reflexão, compatível com a brevidade ordenada pelo nosso preclaro Bispo, que com a devida venia marcou um praso tão exiguo, que não permitte-lhe consultar e ouvir a terceiros mais competentes, nem mesmo opinar pelo alvitre lembrado por V. S. Revm. em seu officio de 12, responde.

"Nestas tristes e apertadas circumstancias a Mesa Regedora, transida de

by affliction, oppressed by the most intimate sorrow, confesses to Your Reverence, with the greatest humility, that it cannot change its conviction relative to the order of our illustrious and virtuous Bishop.

It is perhaps a mistake; but Your Reverence knows that until the light of truth produces a change of mind, it [the Governing Board] must be sincere in the manifestation of its thought; the contrary would be of the empire of hypocrisy, which is prejudicial to society, and condemned by Our Father and Creator Jesus Christ.

"The Governing Board has no ulterior motive which might determine it not to execute the orders of our worthy and respected Bishop, but does so because it feels it is also fulfilling a sacred duty.

"Thus it solicits Your Reverence, whose knowledge and religious zeal cannot be gainsaid, to be good enough to implore pardon for the Governing Board, which, with the greatest sorrow of heart is not able to give faithful execution to the determinations of our virtuous Prelate, who will not interpret this resolution as a lack of humility and of respect for his high and worthy person, noble and venerable under whatever circumstance. And certain that inspiration is the appanage of benevolence and that charity is a characteristic virtue of our illustrious Pastor, it [*i. e.*, Governing Board] is confident that its supplication will be well received.

"I take advantage of the occasion to assure Your Reverence, . . .

Galdino Antônio Alves Ferreira, Judge."

---

afflicção, acabrunhada pela mais intima dôr, vem com a maior humildade confessar a V. S. Revma. que não pode mudar de convicção acêrca da ordem de nosso illustrado e virtuoso Bispo. E' talvez um erro; mas sabe V. S. Revm. que, emquanto a luz da verdade não operar no espirito outro facto, deve ella ser verdadeira na manifestação do seu pensamento; do contrario seria o imperio da hypocrisia, prejudicial á sociedade, e condemnada por nosso Pae e Creador Jesus Christo.

"A Mesa Regedora não tem motivos alheios que a determinem a não executar as ordens do nosso digno e respeitavel Bispo, mas o faz porque pensa cumprir tambem um sagrado dever.

"Assim solicita a V. S. Revm., cuja illustração e zêlo religioso não podem soffrer contradicção, que se digne implorar perdão para a Mesa Regedora, que com a maior mágua no seu coração não póde dar fiel execução ás determinações de nosso virtuoso Prelado, que não possa traduzir esta resolução como falta qualquer relação. E certa de que a illustração é o apanagio de benevolencia e que a caridade é uma virtude caracteristica de nosso illustrado Pastor, confia que sua supplica será bem acolhida.

"Aproveito a occasião para asigurar a V. S. Revm. . . .

Galdino Antonio Alves Ferreira, Juiz."

*Relatório do Ministério dos Negócios do Império, 1874*, pp. 18-19.

## DOCUMENT II

Rio de Janeiro,
June 12, 1873.

"Most Excellent and Reverend Bishop:

"The recourse interposed by the Brotherhood of the Most Holy Sacrament of the mother church of the parish of St. Anthony, of the city of Recife, in conformity with Decree no. 1,911, of March 28, 1857, against the sentence by which Your Excellency judged it interdicted, was brought to the attention of His Majesty the Emperor; and,

"Having heard the Committee of the Affairs of the Empire of the Council of State, which gave the enclosed opinion;

"Having heard the full Council of State which accepted the doctrine and the conclusions of the same opinion;

"Considering that the decrees of the Councils and apostolic letters, as well as any other ecclesiastical constitutions, depend for their execution on the *placet* of the Government, or on the approval of the General Legislative Assembly, if they should contain any general disposition: art. 102, sec. 14 of the Political Constitution of the Empire;

"Considering that the bulls which fulminate excommunication against the Masonic Societies did not have the *placet*;

---

## AVISO DE 12 DE JUNHO DE 1873

"4ª Secção — Ministerio dos Negocios do Imperio — Rio de Janeiro em 12 de Junho de 1873.

Exm. e Revm. Sr. — Foi presente a Sua Magestade O Imperador o recurso interposto pela Irmandade do S. Sacramento da igreja matriz da parochia de Santo Antonio, da cidade do Recife, de conformidade com o Dec. n. 1.911, de 28 de março de 1857, contra a sentença pela qual V. Ex. Revma. a julgou interdicta; e

"Ouvida a Secção dos Negocios do Imperio do Conselho d'Estado, que deu o parecer junto;

"Ouvido o Conselho d'Estado pleno, que acceitou a doutrina e as conclusões do mesmo parecer:

"Considerando que os decretos dos Concilios e letras apostolicas, assim como quaesquer outras constituições ecclesiasticas, dependem, para sua execução, do beneplacito do Governo, ou da approvação da Assembléa Geral Legislativa, si contiverem disposição geral — art. 102, sec. 14 da Constituição Politica do Imperio;

"Considerando que não tiveram beneplacito as bullas que fulminam excommunhão contra as Sociedades Maçonicas;

"Considering that Masonry, as a secret society, is permitted by the civil law, does not have religious ends, and does not conspire against the Catholic Religion, and that consequently it lacks the character and purposes that subject it to ecclesiastical jurisdiction, to condemnation without the form and figure of a legal decision;

"Considering that the organic constitution of the Brotherhoods in Brazil belongs principally to the civil Power, and that the diocesan Prelate, whose business it is to approve the respective statutes in the purely religious part, has authority limited to the duties of that nature which the members contract;

"Considering that the petitioning Brotherhood did not neglect those duties, such as are found defined in its charter with force of law, nor was this alleged;

"Considering that the Brotherhood itself had not the power to expel from its membership the members who might belong to Masonry, a contingency which was not considered in the charter approved by the Ordinary, and consequently that punishable disobedience toward the ecclesiastical authority was not committed, when it declared itself unable to comply with an exorbitant order of the attributes of the same authority;

"Considering that even if Masons were subject to the penalty of expulsion and loss of rights which the civil law guarantees to them as members of the Brotherhoods, a personal motive of censure and punishment could not extend itself to all the confraternity, for the purpose of declaring it interdicted for not

---

"Considerando que a Maçonaria, como sociedade secreta, é permittida pela lei civil, não tem fins religiosos, nem conspira contra a Religião Catholica, e que portanto faltam-lhe caracter e intuitos que a sujeitem á jurisdicção ecclesiastica á condemnação sem fórma e figura de juiso;

"Considerando que a constituição organica das Irmandades no Brasil compete principalmente ao Poder civil, e que o Prelado diocesano, a quem cabe approvar os respectivos estatutos na parte puramente religiosa, tem autoridade limitada aos deveres dessa naturesa, que os associados contrahem;

"Considerando que a Irmandade recorrente não faltou a esses deveres, taes como se acham definidos em seu compromisso com força de lei, nem isto foi allegado;

"Considerando que a mesma Irmandade não tinha poder para expellir do seu gremio os membros que pertencessem á Maçonaria, caso de que não cogitou o compromisso approvado pelo Ordinario, e consequentemente que não commetteu para com a autoridade ecclesiastica desobediencia punivel, quando se declarou impossibilitada de cumprir uma ordem exhorbitante das attribuições da mesma autoridade;

"Considerando que, ainda quando os maçons estivessem sujeitos á pena de expulsão e perda dos direitos que a lei civil lhes garante como membros de Irmandades, não podia um motivo pessoal de censura e punição estender-se a toda a Confraria, para o effeito de ser declarada interdicta, por não querer

wishing to take the responsibility of an act which in view of its charter it judged violent and illegal:

"The same Imperial Master approved the opinion that the recourse should be accepted, and he orders that in the period of one month this decision shall be fulfilled, the effects of the action from which the aforesaid Brotherhood had recourse, ceasing as if it [the act] had not existed.

"Transmitting to Your Excellency this resolution of the Imperial Government, grounded in the Constitution and in the laws until now respected by the Brazilian Bishops, I must observe that the words and acts that oppose the legitimacy of the recourse to the Crown, as well as the *placet* which nearly all Catholic States use, and which in Brazil was and must always be cherished, incur just and serious admonition.

"It therefore behooves Your Excellency, realizing the great convenience of the most perfect agreement and harmony between the spiritual and temporal powers, each maintaining itself in the sphere of action which is limited by its laws and character, to accept and observe in accordance with the purpose and duty which prompted it, the Resolution of the Imperial Government inasmuch as this act in no wise diminishes the esteem which the person of Your Excellency deserves and the respect owed to the Episcopacy, on whose holy ministry the peace of the faithful and the splendor of the Brazilian church so much depends."

---

tomar a responsabilidade de um acto que em face do seu compromisso reputava violento e illegal:

"Houve por bem o mesmo Augusto Senhor conformar-se com o parecer de se dar provimento ao recurso, e manda que no praso de um mez seja cumprido esta decisão, cessando os effeitos do acto de que a mencionada Irmandade recorreu, como se não houvesse existido.

"Transmittindo a V. Ex. Revm. esta Resolução do Governo Imperial, fundada na Constituição e nas leis até hoje respeitadas pelos Bispos brasileiros, devo observar que incorrem em justo e serio reparo palavras e actos que se oppõem á legitimidade do recurso á Corôa, assim como ao beneplacito de que usam quasi todos os Estados catholicos, e que no Brasil foi e deve ser sempre acatado.

"Cumpre, pois, que V. Ex. Revma., compenetrado da alta conveniencia do mais perfeito accôrdo e harmonia entre os Poderes espiritual e temporal, mantendo-se cada um na esphera de acção que é limitada por suas leis e indole, receba e observe a Resolução do Governo Imperial conforme a intenção e o dever que a dictaram, sem que este acto em nada diminúa a consideração que merece a pessoa de V. Ex. Revma. e o respeito devido ao Episcopado, de cujo santo ministerio tanto depende a paz dos fieis e o esplendor da igreja brasileira."

*Relatório do Ministério dos Negócios do Império, 1874,* pp. 63-64.

# APPENDIX B

## DOCUMENT I

Rio de Janeiro, 15 de Febereiro de 1873.

"Exmo. e Revmo. Sr. Bispo.

"Permitta V. Exa. Revma. que eu lhe falle com a franqueza que nos devemos como amigos e que as circumstancias exigem.

"Estou muito inquieto com a questão maçonica, e infelizmente vejo que a acção do tempo não a tem modificado.

"Receio que as manifestações de resistencia á resolução que V. Exa. Revma. tomou prosigam e perturbam a ordem publica nessa provincia. Receio tambem que V. Exa. Revma. seja levado pela coherencia a estender a todas as irmandades a providencia que já deu a respeito de muitas, e quando isto acontecer, Deus sabe o que será.

"Prevejo que V. Exa. Revma. terá contra si quasi toda a população de Recife, animada pelas adhesões que vão chegando de outras provincias e incitada a outros meios de opposição.

"Respeito os motivos de consciencia que V. Exa. Revma. tem para praticar os actos que têm levantado tantos clamores, e tenho o mais firme desejo de não me achar em disaccordo com V. Exa. Revma. em providencias *que me sejam pedidas e que eu deva dar,* mas a minha posição é difficilima desde que, segundo o nosso direito, não podem ter execução no Imperio as bullas que não estão placitadas.

"Tenho ouvido a opinião de pessoas insuspeitas, de bispos e de sacerdotes respeitaveis; elles reconhecem que V. Exa. Revm. *está na regra canonica, mas intendem que podia ser differente a applicação e até dispensada.*

"Os jornaes têm publicado que sou maçon e, não dizem a verdade, porque fui iniciado, sim, ha quinze annos, mas compareci sómente a tres ou quatro sessões, e logo depois fiz quanto me parece sufficiente para tranquillizar a minha consciencia de catholico. Não sou, portanto, suspeito, quando penso, como quasi todos pensam, que a Maçonaria entre nós e innocente e até benefica a certos respeitos.

"Ora, sociedades que estão neste caso, e que de facto contam em seu gremio as pessoas notaveis do paiz e mais influentes, bem podem deixar de ser tractadas com rigor, que, sem proveito para a religião, traz perigos de desacatos e desordens. Estas sociedades existem em todas as nações catholicas, toleradas pelo Estado, e deixadas em paz pelos bispos, apesar da prohibição da Egreja.

"A nossa Constituição permitte todas as religiões com o seu culto domestico ou particular. Organizam-se aqui sociedades compostas de extrangeiros para fins religiosos differentes dos nossos, com auctorização do poder civil e funccionam livremente.

"Quando isto acontece, não sei somo poderia o Govêrno prohibir as sociedades maçonicas que se compõem de catholicos que não têm fins contrarios á religião do Imperio, e que, dado que os tivessem, trabalham a portas fechadas.

"O que V. Exa. Revma. diz a respeito das irmandades é em parte exacto, mas desde que compete ao poder civil legislar a respeito de sua organização, e ellas regem-se por compromissos em que intervêm os dous poderes, temporal e espiritual, *duvidam quasi todas as pessoas que tenho consultado, e negam muitas, que seja legitimo o acto de V. Exa. Revma., mandando eliminar os membros maçons.*

"Ainda não ha resolução tomada pelo Govêrno Imperial; eu tenho evitado toma-la em respeito a V. Exa. Revma. pela muita consideração que merece, e que eu devo á authoridade ecclesiastica; mas não sei até quando poderei esquivar-me *á intervenção que é solicitada, e que os podem tornar urgente e indispensavel.*

"Nestas circumstancias, e cheio de verdadeira afflicção, venho rogar a V. Exa. Revma., que cogite meios de nada adeantar na questão e de moderar a opposição, até que, pelo tempo, pela reflexão ou por meio de providencias mais opportunas, cesse para o Govêrno a obrigação de conjurar os perigos de ordem publica, e se offereça a V. Exa. Revma., occasião de conseguir de suas ovelhas pacificamente, pela auctoridade moral da Egreja, que lhe acceitem os conselhos e determinações. O tempo é um grande remedio, e o que em certas occasiões e circumstancias levanta resistencias e clamores geraes, em outras faz-se com grande facilidade, com um só acto, com uma só palavra.

"Fallo a V. Exa. Revma. como filho obediente, como amigo dedicado; e, creia nos meus mais puros sentimentos; é levado por elles que eu lhe endereço a supplica constante desta carta, e confio sua efficacia da prudencia e do patriotismo de V. Exa. Revma.

"Sou com o maior respeito a V. Ex. Revm., amigo fiel e obediente criado.

*João Alfredo Corrêa d'Oliveira."*

Castro, pp. 481-483.

## DOCUMENT II

"Recife, 27 de Febereiro de 1873.

"Exm. Sr. Conselheiro.

"Apresso-me a responder á carta de V. Exa. datada de 15 do corrente. Agradecendo do intimo d'alma a franqueza e delicadeza com que V. Exa. se dignou de escrever-me, peço licenca a V. Exa. para apresentar-lhe, com igual lhaneza e abertura de coração, algumas breves reflexões, mais no intuito de fazer patentes a V. Exa. os meus sentimentos que de advogar a causa propria.

"Nunca me restou duvida acerca dos embaraços e serias difficuldades em que ia a questão maçonica collocar a V. Exa. Comprehendi-os e medi-os, desde que attendi para a circunstancia de, sendo V. Exa. catholico, fazer parte de um Ministerio, cujo presidente é grão-mestre de uma das fracções maçonicas do Imperio. De antemão senti profunda e vivamente as affilicções que V. Exa. ia experimentar. Mas que fazer deante do dever?

"Desde que aqui cheguei, Exa. Sr., que a Maçonaria me offereceu dilemma terrivel, ou acceitar a lucta, cumprindo os deveres de bispo catholico e passar por *imprudente, precipitado e temerario,* o que é muito consentaneo com a minha edade; ou então fechar os olhos a tudo, transigir com a consciencia, resignar-me a ser um bispo negligente, pusilanime e culpado (isto foi confessado pelos proprios maçons).

"Eu tinha de admittir inevitavelmente um dos dous principios, e d'ahi fazer dimanar todo o meu Episcopado.

"Enquanto me foi possivel, sem culpabilidade perante Deus, declinei de pronunciar-me. Mas afinal, vi-me na dura necessidade de escolher, e não hesitei em optar, como era dever, pela primeira parte do dilemma.

"Quando mesmo já fosse eu bispo octogenario, tendo apenas alguns dias de vida, não trahiria os deveres da minha missão; quanto mais tendo ainda talvez uma longa peregrinação a fazer.

"Que terrivel perspectiva, Exa. Sr., um longo Episcopado inglorio e criminoso perante Deus, si bem que glorioso aos olhos dos homens pela condescendencia e frouxidão!

"Demais estou certo que V. Exa., referendando o decreto da minha nomeação, persuadiu-se de que o eleito seria um bispo catholico e cumpridor dos seus deveres, sem o que, por certo, não teria feito.

"Si a Maçonaria se tivesse contentado com trabalhar em suas lojas, *de portas fechadas,* com diz V. Exa., nada teria havido. Mas, para provocar o prelado diocesano, ella creou um periodico; começou a atacar, insultar e negar os dogmas de nossa Sancta Religião, como provo em minha Pastoral de 2 de Fevereiro com documentos irrefragaveis; mostrou-se enfim de viseira alçada, publicando o nome de seus adeptos, tomando cantas á Egreja, e formando no seio das Irmandades mesas á maçonica.

"Não fui perturbar os maçons em suas officinas, Exm. Sr., não saï do recincto da Egreja, da qual sou chefe. Não questiono directamente com os maçons porêm sim com as Irmandades. Não pretendo exterminar a Maçonaria; infelizmente nem os proprios monarchas já hoje o podem: só Deus. Desejo tão sómente que as Irmandades realizem o fim para que foram creadas. Entretanto parece-me que a Maçonaria devia ser um pouco mais consequente. Já que ella não reconhece a auctoridade da Egreja, brade muito embora contra a Egreja, mas abandone-a, deixe-a áquelles que se prezam de filhos obedientes.

"É verdade, Exm. Sr., que as Irmandades se regem por compromissos approvados pelos dous poderes, temporal e espiritual; porêm o que lhes confere o character religioso é tão sómente a sancção deste, sem a qual, como todos bem sabem, não são ellas mais do que sociedades méramente civis. E desculpe-me

V. Exa. a franqueza de dizer-lhe que, na parte religiosa, o poder temporal não é juiz competente.

"Peço licença a V. Exa. para não dizer cousa alguma ácerca do opinião dos *bispos e sacerdotes*, que julgam *dispensavel* a *applicação* das bullas condemnando a Maçonaria.

"Apesar da negação do beneplacito, a Maçonaria entre nós está realmente condemnada por muitas razões, que de outra occasião poderei expender, si V. Exa. assim julgar conveniente. Por ora limito-me a dizer a V. Exa., que na Allocução de 25 de Setembro de 1865, o Smo Padre declarou formalmente condemnada a Maçonaria, *até mesmo nos paizes em que é tolerada pelo poder secular*. E isto basta para o catholico.

"A Maçonaria, Exmo. Snr., tem movido ceu e terra, tem feito protestos e appellações, tem finalmente envidado todos os meios para desauctorar-me. Eu, pelo contrario, com quanto tenha recebido muitos actos de adhesão com milhares de assignaturas de leigos, e tenha a melhor gente desta cidade a meu favor, confiado na justiça da causa que defendo e nos sentimentos religiosos de V. Exa., até o presente me hei conservado em silenço. Mas já vou conhecendo que este silencio é prejudicial á causa da Egreja.

"A carta de V. Exa., me deixa entrever, a menos que eu não a tenha comprehendido devidamente, que si eu continuar na resolução tomada, talvez a decisão do Govêrno imperial me seja desfavoravel.

"Muito me custa a crer, Exm. Sr., que o mesmo punho que, ha tão pouco tempo, assignou o decreto da minha nomeação, lavre agora a sentença de minha desauctoração. Todavia si tal acontecer, rogo encarecidamente a V. Exa. como bom amigo, lavre antes o meu decreto de prisão ou de ostracismo, porque o apoio prestado á Maçonaria pelo Govêrno imperial, não me fazendo de modo algum ceder, dará infallivelmente occasião a conflictos lamentaveis.

"Comprehende V. Exa., que esta questão é de vida ou de morte para a Egreja brasileira; cumpre-me antes arcar com os maiores sacrificios, que afrouxar. Procederei sempre com muita calma, prudencia e vagar; porêm ceder ou não ir avante, é impossivel. Não vejo o meio termo. Si V. Exa. prevê que não póde apoiar-me, e que a minha resistencia vai dar logar a scenas tristes, conjuremos a tempestade emquanto é tempo E para isto só conheço um meio: peça o Govêrno imperial á Sancta Sé que me mande para o meu convento quanto antes. Porém, esta medida pouco adeanta ao Govêrno. Si eu fosse politico ou de mais edade, diria que sérias perturbações de ordem publica estão imminentes em quasi todo o Brasil, e são inevitaveis, apesar da maior prudencia; a causa reservo-me para dize-la a V. Exa. pessoalmente, quando tiver ensejo.

"Peço a V. Exa. que não se admire de minha excessiva franqueza. Na occasião presente não escrevo ao Exm. Sr. ministro do Imperio, escrevo *confidencialmente* a um amigo, e a um amigo diz-se a verdade inteira, sem rebuço.

Em questão deste alcance e magnitude, toda a franqueza entre amigos não é demais.

"Não desanimo; pelo contrario, muito espero da amizade e dos sentimentos religiosos de V. Exa., depois do auxilio divino.

"Creia V. Exa. na sincera amizade e inteira dedicação de quem é.

"De V. Exa., etc.

etc.

Castro, pp. 483-485.                                    (✠ *Fr. Vital*, bispo de Olinda.)"

## DOCUMENT III

"Exm. e Revm. Sr.

"Depois da minha carta responsiva á prezadissima de v. exa. revma., de 1° de Janeiro p.p., relativa á bomba que fez arrebentar, muito me foi agradavel vêr que os negocios tomaram melhor andamento. É consolante na verdade o comportamento favoravel do Clero, e de todos que conservam em sua consciencia os principios da Religião e da justiça.

"Ainda assim precisa todavia muita prudencia, muitissima moderação e paciencia, sendo  onegocio por si melindroso e achando-se o inferno inteiro com todo o mundo manobrando contra o bem.

"Aqui se trabalhou e se trabalha com todo empenho. Alem do exm. sr. ministro, ha bastantes deputados empenhados e pessoas gradas. Muito, porém, precisa do auxilio da divina Providencia.

"Isto posto, me vêm uma idéa que lhe manifesto, e na esperança de que achará na sua muita penetração conveniente, e por isso não deixará de adopta--la. Eis a idéa.

"A medida da qual se falla teve já a sua execução, produziu o seu effeito, e os ermãos (maçons) dirigiram ás Camaras as suas queixas e reclamações.

"O que agora me parece util é que v. exa. revma. escolhesse algum logar de sua diocese que melhor conhece, e levando em sua companhia alguns sacerdotes de confiança, fosse para lá fazer e inaugurar a visita pastoral. O revm. vigario geral, já práctico, poderia ficar no govêrno da diocese.

"Esta resolução levaria consigo tres vantagens:

"1ª. Cumpriria uma parte do seu dever episcopal;

"2ª. Seria recebido, estou certo, em triumpho verdadeiro, e este facto lhe augmentaria toda a força moral;

"3ª. Deixaria os inimigos e incredulos consumir-se entre si, e resfriar-se no vacuo.

"Quando v. exa. revma. encontrasse difficuldade na approximação da Quaresma, attenta á lei da Residencia, eu lhe concedo desde já a competente auctorização e dispensa, podendo voltar á sua cathedral para fazer as funcções da Semana Sancta. E, no caso de verificar util e proficua esta diversão, poderia novamente continuar a visita.

"Previ tambem um outro obstaculo, a necessidade de levar consigo algum dinheiro em occasião da visita, tanto para occorrer aos pobres, como por outras extraordinarias occorrencias. E como tivesse longa conferencia sôbre este negocio com o exm. sr. ministro, e assim me acho no caso de dar-lhe certeza que *está prompto tambem a dar-lhe um auxilio de dinheiro*.

"Eis o meu pensamento, e as medidas que o facilitam com toda conveniencia e decoro, e eu espero que o adoptará sem muita demora.

"Aqui juncta achará a resposta que com muito atrazo me remetteu o revm. sr. d. abbade de S. Bento, ácerca de obter uma parte do Mosteiro para abrir o pequeno Seminario. Elle pediu informações. Veremos.

"O exm. sr. bispo Lacerda esteve bem doente com a febre amarella, mas com auxilio de Deus N. S. e a protecção da Virgem S. S. Immaculada, está hoje restabelecido, mas ainda fraquissimo.

"Queira conserva-se na mais perfeita saúde, e acceite a confirmação da minha mais distincta obsequiosa estima e consideração.

"De v. exa. revma. muito Atto. venr. obseqm° servo.

"Petropolis, II de Fevereiro de 1873".

(*D. Sanguigni*, Int° Aplico.)"

Castro, pp. 486-487.

## DOCUMENT IV

"Exm. Sr. Internuncio

"Apresso-me em responder á preciosa carta de v. exa., datada de 11 do corrente.

"Não acho termo para agredecer o interesse que v. exa. tem tomado nesta questão vital para a Egreja Brasileira, cujo futuro, si a impiedade levar agora a palma, será deploravel e tristissimo.

"Exm. sr., ponderei e pesei muito a idéa que v. exa. teve a bondade de communicar-me em relação á visita pastoral, e achei-a com effeito excellente porém, irrealizavel actualmente, permitta-me v. exa. que lh'o diga com franqueza. A sua execução nas circunstancias actuaes produziria um effeito diametralmente opposto ao que v. exa. se propõe. Os inimigos da Egreja, exm. sr., têm-se esforçado para me arredar daqui para fóra, quando mesmo fosse para Olinda, afim de clamarem victoria. É justamente o que elles querem.

"Da leitura da carta de v. exa., deprehendi que v. exa. me suppõe sem força moral. Não, exm. sr., não ha tal. Felizmente tenho por mim um grande partido composto da melhor gente, tanto na capital como fóra della. Todos os dias me chegam actos de adhesão dos leigos com milhares de assignaturas; saio todos os dias, percorro as ruas mais populosas e frequentadas da cidade, e, mercê de Deus, ainda não recebi o menor insulto; antes, pelo contrario, todos me comprimentam. Sem força moral ficaria eu, si agora cedesse. Está me parecendo que as noticias chegam lá muito adulteradas. O que se ha de fazer? Muitos daquelles, que por justiça e caridade deviam ajudar o prelado, são os que mais procuram embaraça-lo e compremette-lo. Custa a crêr: entretanto é a pura verdade, exm. senhor.

"Estou inteiramente compenetrado da necessidade de uma visita pastoral na diocese. E creia v. exa. que, depois da reforma e da fundação dos dous Seminarios, é ella a idéa que mais me preoccupa. Mas sou obrigado a deferi-la até Agosto:

"1°, porque estou cuidando do Seminario pequeno, cujos interesses não podem prescindir da minha presença;

"2°, porque está a abrir-se o Seminario de Theologia, e tendo eu feito nelle algumas mudanças, devo estar presente para ver como correm as cousas;

"3°, porque não tendo as irmandades todas respondido, e variando o seu modo de obrar a cada momento, torna-se absolutamente necessaria não só a minha presença na capital, sinão tambem muita attenção de minha parte.

"Pelo que muito sinto não poder utilizar-me da faculdade que v. exa. se dignou de conceder-me, e sobremodo agradeço o recurso pecuniario que me offereceu por parte do exm. sr. ministro do Imperio.

"Quando mesmo, exm. sr., eu tivesse de saïr agora em visita, dispensa-lo-ia; porquanto, tendo feito voto de pobreza, tenho-me acostumado a distribuir com os pobres o que não me é absolutamente necessario, e na qualidade do pobre. Capuchinho com pouco me contento, e os meus diocesanos não me deixariam fazer um real de despesa. Todavia, já que o exm. sr. ministro se acha tão bem disposto para com a Egreja de Jesus Christo e para com esta desditosa diocese, v. exa. tenha a bondade de pedir-lhe o favor de applicar a quantia que me destinava ao acabamento e mobiliamento do Seminario pequeno, que muitissima necessidade tem, e de apoiar o meu acto: é este c maior serviço que póde elle prestar á minha diocese e á Egreja.

"Agora outra cousa.

"Os macons daqui, exm. sr., tripudiam de prazer desde que chegou o vapor de 22; porque, dizem elles, o Govêrno imperial deu-lhes ganho de causa, e v. ex. e o sr. ministro do Imperio me reprehenderam. Dizem mais que pessoa bem informada (dão até um nome que ambos conhecemos) communicou-lhes da Côrte que v. ex. de accôrdo como o sr. ministro me querem obrigar a ceder.

"Coitados! Como se illudem.

"Ignoram que v. ex. além de ser o mui digno delegado do immortal Pio IX, que tantas vezes condemnou a Maçonaria, fez-me jurar antes da minha confirmação, que nunca havia sido maçon, que sempre condemnei as hereticas doutrinas maçonicas e contra ellas premuniria as ovelhas confiadas á minha vigilancia.

"Estão convencidos de que v. ex. não só reprovou muito o meu acto, como até reprehendeu-me amargamente.

"Deixa-los em sua doce illusão. E eu irei meu caminho, andando com prudencia e vagar, como v. revma. me recommenda, porêm, ao mesmo tempo disposto a morrer mil vezes, si possivel fosse, do que ceder uma só, a menos que o vigario de Jesns Christo me ordene, o que não é provavel nem mesmo admissivel.

"Implorando de v. ex. desculpa por não poder actualmente pôr em practica o bom conselho de v. ex., peço se digne de lembrar-se em suas orações de quem dellas tem muita necessidade e é com respeito e veneração.

"De V. Exa. servo humilde.

(✠ *Fr. Vital*, bispo de Olinda.)"

Castro, pp. 487-489.

# SELECT BIBLIOGRAPHY

(Additional References are cited in the Footnotes)

## I. WORKS OF BIBLIOGRAPHY AND REFERENCE

Attwater, Donald. *A Catholic Dictionary.* New York, 1943.

Blake, Augusto Vitorino Alves Sacramento. *Diccionario bibliographico brazileiro.* 7 vols. Rio de Janeiro, 1883-1902.

Campos, Raúl Adalberto de. *Relações diplomaticas do Brasil contendo os nomes dos representantes diplomaticos do Brasil no estrangeiro . . . de 1808 a 1909.* Rio de Janeiro, 1913.

Galvão, Sebastião de Vasconcelos. *Diccionario chorographico, historico e estatistico de Pernambuco.* 2 vols. Rio de Janeiro, 1913.

Machado, Diogo Barbosa. *Bibliotheca lusitana.* 4 vols. Lisboa, 1741-1759.

Silva, Inocêncio Francisco da. *Diccionario bibliographico portuguez.* 21 vols. Lisboa, 1858-1914.

## II. PRIMARY SOURCES

### A. MANUSCRIPT SOURCES

National Archives. Washington, D. C. Division of Department of State Archives. Despatches, Brazil. Vols. 40, 41, 42.

Sousa Correia Papers. The Oliveira Lima Library, The Catholic University of America. Washington, D. C.

### B. PRINTED SOURCES

#### 1. GOVERNMENT PUBLICATIONS

Brazil. Ministério das Relações Exteriores. *Archivo diplomatico da independencia.* Vol. 3. Rio de Janeiro, 1922.

Brazil. Assembléia Geral. *Annaes da Camara dos Deputados do Imperio do Brasil.* 1826, 1827, 1832, 1834, 1836, 1837, 1873, 1874, 1875, 1879, 1880.

Brazil. Assembléia Geral. *Annaes do Senado do Imperio do Brasil.* 1870, 1873, 1874, 1879.

Brazil. Repartição dos Negócios da Justiça. *Relatorio apresentado á Assembléa Geral Legislativa na terceira sessão da decima quinta legislatura pelo Ministro e Secretario de Estado dos Negocios da Justica Dr. Manoel Antonio Duarte de Azevedo.* Rio de Janeiro, 1875.

Brazil. Repartição dos Negócios Estrangeiros. *Relatorio da Repartição dos Negocios Estrangeiros apresentado á Assembléa Geral Legislativa na sessão ordinaria de 1834, pelo respectivo Ministro e Secretario de Estado Aureliano de Souza e Oliveira Coutinho.* Rio de Janeiro, 1834.

Brazil. Repartição dos Negócios Estrangeiros. *Relatorio da Repartição dos Negocios Estrangeiros apresentado á Assembléa Geral Legislativa na sessão ordinaria de 1835, pelo respectivo Ministro e Secretario de Estado Manoel Alves Branco.* Rio de Janeiro, 1835.

Brazil. Repartição dos Negócios Estrangeiros. *Relatorio da Repartição dos Negocios Estrangeiros apresentado á Assembléa Geral Legislativa na quarta sessão da decima-quinta legislatura pelo Ministro e Secretario de Estado Visconde de Caravellas.* Rio de Janeiro, 1875.

Brazil. Repartição dos Negócios do Império. *Relatorio apresentado a Assembléa Geral na terceira sessão da decima quinta legislatura pelo ministro e Secretario d'Estado dos Negocios do Imperio Dr. João Alfredo Corrêa de Oliveira.* Rio de Janeiro, 1874.

*Collecção das leis do imperio do Brazil.* Rio de Janeiro, 1828, 1834, 1857, 1860.

*Constitutição politica do imperio do Brazil.* Lisboa, 1826.

## 2. OTHER PUBLICATIONS

### a. Books.

*Acta es iis decerpta quae apud Sanctam Sedam geruntur in compendium opportune redacta.* Vol. 4. Romae, 1868.

Agassiz, Prof. and Mrs. Louis. *A Journey in Brazil.* Boston, 1868.

Almeida, Tito Franco de. *A Igreja no Estado.* Rio de Janeiro, 187–.

Araújo, José de Sousa Azevedo Pizarro e. *Memorias historicas do Rio de Janeiro e das provincias annexas a jurisdicção do vice-rei do estado do Brasil, dedicadas a el-rei nosso senhor D. João VI.* 9 vols. Rio de Janeiro, 1820-1822.

Areias, Antônio Francisco. *O Evangelho de Christo perante a egreja dos papas.* Recife, 1875.

Barbosa, Rui. "A Igreja e o estado," *Novos discursos e conferencias colligidos e revistos por Hermero Pires.* São Paulo, 1933. pp. 7-64.

———. *O papa e o concilio por Janus, versão e introdução de Rui Barbosa.* 2d ed. São Paulo, 1930.

*Bullarii Romani continuati: Benedictii XIV pont. opt. max. olim Prosperi Cardinalis de Lambertinis Bullarum, tom. III in quo continentur constitutiones.* Pragae, 1884.

*Bullarium diplomatum et privilegiorum sanctorum Romanorum pontificum.* Taurinorum, 1857.

Campos, Joaquim Pinto de. *Discurso pronunciado na sessão de 15 de julho de 1873 por . . . deputado á Assembléa Geral pelo 5° districto eleitoral da Provincia de Pernambuco.* Rio de Janeiro, 1873.

Castro, Augusto Olímpio Viveiros de. "Contribuções para a biographia de D. Pedro II," Parte 1ª. *Revista do Instituto Histórico e Geográfico Brasileiro.* Tomo especial (1925), 477-534.

*Causa da religão e disciplina ecclesiastica do celibato clerical defendida da inconstitucional tentativa do Padre Diogo Antonio Feijó.* Rio de Janeiro, 1828.

*Correspondencia entre o Governo Imperial e os Bispos do Rio Grande do Sul, Maranhão, e Pará, ácerca do Decreto n.° 3.073 de 22 de Abril de 1863, que uniformisa os estudos das cadeiras dos Seminarios Episcopaes que são subsidiadas pelo Estado,* n. p., n. d.

Costa, Dom Antônio de Macedo. *O Barão de Penedo e a sua missão a Roma.* Rio de Janeiro, 1888.

————. *Carta pastoral do excellentissimo e reverendissimo Bispo do Pará publicando as constituições dogmaticas do sacrosancto concilio geral do Vaticano.* São Luiz do Maranhão, 1871.

————. *Direito contra o direito ou o Estado sobre tudo refutação da theoria dos politicos na Questão Religiosa seguida da resposta ao Supremo Tribunal de Justiça pelo Bispo do Pará.* Rio de Janeiro, 1874.

————. *A Maçonaria em opposição á moral, á igreja, e ao estado pastoral de S. Exc. Revm. o sr. D. Antonio de Macedo Costa, Bispo do Pará.* Recife, 1875.

————. *A questão religiosa perante a Santa Sé, ou a Missão especial em Roma em 1873, á luz dos documentos publicados e ineditos.* São Luiz do Maranhão, 1886.

Davenport, Frances F. *European Treaties Bearing on the History of the United States and Her Dependencies to 1648.* Vol. I. Carnegie Institution of Washington, publication No. 254. Washington, D. C., 1917.

Denzinger, Henricus. *Enchiridion symbolorum definitionum et declarationum de rebus fidei et morum.* Friburgi, 1837.

*Discursos proferidos no Supremo Tribunal de Justiça na sessão de 21 de Fevereiro de 1874 pelos Exms. Srs.* Conselheiro Zacarias de Góes e Vasconcellos e Senador Candido Mendes de Almeida por occasião do julgamento do Exm. e Revm. Sr. D. Fr. Vital Maria Gonçalves de Oliveira, Bispo de Olinda. Rio de Janeiro, 1874.

Donoso Cortés, Juan. *Obras escogidas de Don Juan Donoso Cortés.* 2 vols. Madrid, 1932.

Eurico [pseud. for Francisco Ramos Paz]. *O Ponto negro considerações a proposito do recente acto do bispo do Rio de Janeiro.* Rio de Janeiro, 1872.

Ewbank, Thomas. *Life in Brazil.* New York, 1856.

*Fallas do throno desde o anno de 1823 até o anno de 1872.* Rio de Janeiro, 1872.

Filgueiras Júnior, José Antônio de Araújo. *Codigo criminal do imperio do Brasil annotado com os actos dos poderes legislativo, executivo, e judiciario que tem alterado e interpretado suas disposições desde que foi publicado, e com o calculo das penas em todas as suas applicações.* 2d. ed. Rio de Janeiro, 1876.

Freirii, Paschalis Josephi Mellii [Freire, Pascual José de Melo]. *Institutionum juris civilis lusitani.* Olisipone, 1794.

Freitas, Ernesto Adolfo de. *Considerações sobre o opusculo publicado no Rio de Janeiro com o Titulo de Considerações relativas ao Beneplacito, e Recurso á Coroa em materias do culto, pelo conselheiro d'estado Marquez de S. Vicente.* Lisboa, 1874.

Ganganelli [pseud. for Joaquim Saldanha Marinho]. *A Egreja e o Estado.* 4 vols. Rio de Janeiro, 1873-1876.

Gardner, George. *Travels in the Interior of Brazil.* 2d. ed. London, 1849.

[Joaquim do Monte Carmelo]. *O Brasil mystificado na Questão Religiosa.* Rio de Janeiro, 1875.

———. *Questão Religiosa, carta á serenissima Princesa Regente.* Primeira Parte. Rio de Janeiro, 1876.

Kidder, D. P., and Fletcher, J. C. *Brazil and the Brazilians.* Philadelphia, 1857.

Koster, Henry. *Travels in Brazil.* London, 1816.

Lacerda, Dom Pedro Maria de. *Carta pastoral do Bispo de S. Sebastião do Rio de Janeiro publicando as letras apostolicas do Summo Pontifice e Santo Padre Pio IX de 29 de maio de 1873 sobre a absolvição dos Maçons.* Rio de Janeiro, 1873.

Meneses, Manuel Joaquim de. *Exposição historica da maçonaria no Brasil particularmente na provincia do Rio de Janeiro em relação com a independencia e integridade do imperio.* Rio de Janeiro, 1857.

Nabuco, Joaquim. *Minha formação.* Rio de Janeiro, 1900.

———. *O Partido ultramontano suas invasões, seus orgãos, e seu futuro, artigos publicados na "Reforma."* Rio de Janeiro, 1873.

[Oliveira, Dom Vital Maria Gonçalves de.]. *Carta pastoral do Bispo de Olinda premunindo os seus diocesanos contra as ciladas e maquinações da Maçonaria.* Recife, 1873.

———. *O Bispo de Olinda e os seos accusadores no Tribunal do Bom Senso.* Recife, 1873.

Penêdo, Barão de. *O bispo do Pará e a missão especial a Roma.* Lisboa, 1887.
———. *Missão especial a Roma em 1873.* London, 1881.

Pinho, Wanderley (ed.). *Cartas do Imperador D. Pedro II ao Barão de Cotegipe.* São Paulo, 1933.

*Reflexões imparciaes sobre a falla do trono e as respostas das camaras legislativas de 1836, na parte relativo ao bispo eleito d'esta diocese e á Santa Sé Apostolica.* Rio de Janeiro, 1837.

Reis, Antônio Manuel dos. *O Bispo de Olinda perante a história.* 3 vols. New edition, revised and enlarged, edited by Félix de Olívola. Recife, 1940-1944.

Santos, Luiz Gonçalves dos. *Memorias para servir á historia do reino do Brazil, divididas em tres epocas da felicidade, honra, e gloria; escriptas na corte do Rio de Janeiro no anno de 1821, e offerecidas a s. magestade elrei nosso senhor D. João VI.* 2 vols. Lisboa, 1825.

São Vicente, Marquês de. *Considerações relativas ao beneplacito, e recurso á corôa em materias do culto.* Rio de Janeiro, 1873.

Schroeder, H. J. *Canons and Decrees of the Council of Trent.* St. Louis, 1941.

Scully, William. *Brazil; Its Provinces and Chief Cities; the Manners and Customs of the People.* London, 1866.

Seixas, Dom Romualdo Antônio de. *Memorias do Marquez de Santa Cruz, Arcebispo da Bahia.* Rio de Janeiro, 1861.

Spix, Johann Baptist von and Martius, Carl Friedrich Philipp von. *Reise in Brasilien auf Befehl Sr. Majestät Maximilian Joseph I. Königs von Baiern in den Jahren 1817 bis 1820.* 3 vols. München, 1823-1831.

Tavares, Francisco Muniz. *Historia da Revolução de Pernambuco em 1817.* 3d. ed. Revised and annotated by Manuel de Oliveira Lima. Recife, 1917.

Tollenare, L. F. de. *Notas dominicaes Tomadas durante uma residencia em Portugal e no Brasil nos annos de 1816, 1817, e 1818, parte relativa a Pernambuco traduzida do manuscripto francez inedito por Alfredo de Carvalho Com um prefacio de M. de Oliveira Lima.* Recife, 1905.

Walsh, R. *Notices of Brazil in 1828 and 1829.* 2 vols. London, 1830.

X [pseud. for Joaquim do Monte Carmelo]. *Questão religiosa O Arcipreste da Sé de S. Paulo Joaquim Anselmo de Oliveira e o cléro do Brazil. Artigos publicados na "Reforma."* Rio de Janeiro, 1873.


b. *Newspapers and Periodicals.*


Drummond, Antônio de Meneses Vasconcelos de. "Annotações de A. M. V. de Drummond á sua biographia publicada em 1836 na *Biographie Universelle et Portative des Contemporains." Anais da Biblioteca Nacional do Rio de Janeiro,* XIII (1885-86), ii, 1-149.

*Jornal dos Debates.* Rio de Janeiro, May 20, 1837.

Olívola, Félix de. "Alma Franciscana," *Verbum* [Rio de Janeiro]. I (December, 1944), 339-345.

*O Sete d'Abril.* Rio de Janeiro, May 27, 1837.

III. SECONDARY AUTHORITIES

Almeida, Bartolomeu de. "A Maçonaria no Brasil," *A Ordem* [Rio de Janeiro], XXII (March-April, 1933), 236-241.

Almeida, Cândido Mendes de. *Direito civil ecclesiastico Brasileiro antigo e moderno em suas relações com o direito canonico.* Vol. I. Rio de Janeiro, 1866.

Almeida, Fortunato de. *História da igreja em Portugal.* 4 vols. Coimbra, 1910-1926.

Aluísio de Almeida. *Arevolução liberal de 1842* (Rio de Janeiro, 1944).

Alves, José Luiz. "Os Claustros e o Clero no Brazil," *Revista do Instituto Histórico e Geográfico Brasileiro.* LVII (1894), ii, 1-257.

André, Michel. *Cours alphabétique et méthodique de droit canon dans ses rapports avec le droit civil ecclésiastique.* 5 vols. Paris, 1852-1853.

Armitage, John. *The history of Brazil, from the period of the arrival of the Braganza family in 1808, to the abdication of Don Pedro the first in 1831. Compiled from State Documents and Other Original Sources. Forming a continuation to Southey's history of that country.* 2 vols. London, 1836.

Ataíde, Tristão de [pseud. for Alceu Amoroso Lima]. "Formação do Brasil," *Estudos.* Fifth series, Rio de Janeiro, 1933.

"Authority of the Holy See in South America," *Dublin Review,* V (July, 1838), 239-242.

Azevedo, J. Lúcio de. *O Marquês de Pombal e a sua epoca.* 2d. ed. Lisboa, 1922.

Badaró, F. *Les Couvents au Brésil.* Florence, 1897.

———. *L'Église au Brésil pendant l'Empire et pendant la République.* Rome, 1895.

Besouchet, Lídia. *José Ma. Paranhos, Vizconde Do Río Branco ensayo histórico-biográfico.* Buenos Aires, 1944.

Bord, Gustave. *La Franc-maçonnerie en France des origines à 1815.* Vol. I. Paris [1909].

Braga, Teodoro. *Historia do Pará.* São Paulo, n. d.

Brandão, Mário and Almeida, M. Lopes de. *A Universidade de Coimbra esbôço da sua história.* Coimbra, 1937.

Burnichon, Joseph. *Le Brésil d'aujourd'hui.* Paris, 1910.

Butler, E. C. *The Vatican Council.* London, 1930.

Calógeras, João Pandiá. *Da Regencia á quéda de Rozas.* São Paulo, 1933.

Cardozo, Manoel S. "The Lay Brotherhoods of Colonial Bahia," *The Catholic Historical Review*, XXXIII (April, 1947), 12-30.

Castro, [Augusto Olímpio] Viveiros de. *Accordams e votos (Commentados)*. Rio de Janeiro, 1925.

Cavalcanti, Manuel Tavares. "Relações entre o estado e a igreja," *Revista do Instituto Histórico e Geográfico Brasileiro*. Tomo especial, VI (1922), 301-318.

Constantin, C. "Libéralisme catholique," *Dictionnaire de théologie catholique*. Paris, 1909-1934. IX, 506-628.

Cooper, John M. "Freemasonry and Modern Life, *The Ecclesiastical Review*, LVII (July, 1917), 43-65.

———. "Freemasonry, State and Church," *The Ecclesiastical Review*, LVII (July, 1917), 43-65.

———. "Freemasonry's Two Hundredth Birthday," *The Ecclesiastical Review*, LVI (June, 1917), 590-616.

Correia, Manuel Francisco. "Memoria apresentada ao Instituto Histórico e Geográfico Brasileiro em 10 de Outubro de 1890 para ser lida depois da morte de Imperador o Sr. D. Pedro II," *Revista do Instituto Histórico e Geográfico Brasileiro*. LV (1892), ii, 1-13.

Corrigan, Raymond. *The Church in the Nineteenth Century*. Milwaukee, 1938.

Costa, Sérgio Correia da. *As quatro coroas de D. Pedro I*. 2d. ed., rev. Rio de Janeiro, 1941.

Cunha, Francisco. *Reminiscencias, propaganda contra o imperio na imprensa e na diplomacia 1870 a 1910*. Rio de Janeiro, 1914.

Debidour, Antonin. *Histoire des rapports de l'église et de l'état en France de 1789 à 1905*. Paris, 1898-1906.

Degert, A. "Gallicanism," *The Catholic Encyclopedia*. New York, c 1907-1922. VI, 351-356.

Deshayes, F. *Memento juris ecclesiastici publici et privati*. Parisiis, 1902.

Dornas Filho, João. *O padroado e a igreja brasileira*. São Paulo [1938].

Egas, Eugênio. *Diogo Antonio Feijó*. 2 vols. São Paulo, 1912.

Faÿ, Bernard. *Revolution and Freemasonry (1680-1800)*. Boston, 1935.

Ferraris, F. Lucii. "Juspatronatus," *Bibliotheca canonica iuridica moralis theologica nec non ascetica polemica rubricistica historica*. Vol. IV. Romae, 1888. Pp. 662-699.

Findel, J. G. *History of Freemasonry*. 2d. ed. rev. London, 1871.

Galanti, Rafael M. *Compendio da historia do Brazil*. 4 vols. São Paulo, 1896-1905.

Gomes, Francisco Luiz. *Le Marquis de Pombal, esquisse de sa vie politique*. Lisbonne, 1869.

Gould, Robert F. *A Concise History of Freemasonry*. New York, 1924.

Grainha, Manuel Borges. *Histoire de la franc-maçonnerie en Portugal, 1733-1912*. Lisbonne, 1913.

Granderath, Theodore. *Histoire du Concile du Vatican depuis sa première annonce jusqu'à sa prorogation d'après les documents authentiques édité par Le P. Conrad Kirch, S.J., et traduit de l'allemand par des religieux de la même Compagnie*. 3 t. in 4. Bruxelles, 1907-1913.

Gruber, Hermann. "Liberalism," *The Catholic Encyclopedia*. New York, c1907-1922. IX, 212-214.

———. "Masonry," *The Catholic Encyclopedia*. New York, c1907-1922. IX, 771-788.

Halévy, Élie. *Le Radicalisme philosophique*. Paris, 1904.

Hergenröther, Joseph. *Anti-Janus: an Historico-Theological criticism of the work entitled "The Pope and the Council" by Janus*. Trans. from the German by J. B. Robertson. Dublin, 1870.

Hettner, Hermann. *Geschichte de englischen Literatur*. Vol. I, *Literaturgeschichte des achtzehnten Jahrhunderts*. Braunschweig, 1894.

Hilgenreiner, K. "Liberalismus," *Lexikon für Theologie und Kirche*. Freiburg in Breisgau, 1930-1938. VI, 542-546.

Hughes, Emmet John. *The Church and the Liberal Society*. Princeton, New Jersey, 1944.

Hull, Robert. *The Syllabus of Errors of Pius IX*. Huntington, Indiana, 1926.

Jemolo, Arturo Carlo. "Giurisdizionalismo," *Enciclopedia Italiana*. Roma, 1929-39. XVII, 366-367.

Lacombe, Américo Jacobina. "O aspecto religioso da questão dos bispos," *Verbum* [Rio de Janeiro], I (December, 1944), 333-338.

———. "Ecos da questão religiosa no parlamento imperial," *A Ordem* [Rio de Janeiro], XXXII (December, 1944), 439-450.

Leite, Serafim. *História da Companhia de Jesus no Brasil*. 1- vols. Lisboa, Rio de Janeiro. 1938-.

Leroy-Beaulieu, Anatole. *Les Catholiques libéraux, l'église et le Libéralisme de 1830 à nos jours*. Paris, 1885.

Lima, Manuel de Oliveira. *O imperio brazileiro 1822-1889*. São Paulo, 1927.

———. *O movimento da independencia 1821-1822*. São Paulo, 1922.

———. *Pernambuco seu desenvolvimento historico*. Leipzig, 1895.

Luzio, Salvatore. "Exequatur," *The Catholic Encyclopedia*. New York, c1907-1922. V, 707-708.

Lyra, Heitor. *Historia de Dom Pedro II*. 3 vols. São Paulo, 1938-1940.

Machado Filho, Aires da Mata. *Arraial do Tijuco Cidade de Diamantina*. Rio de Janeiro, 1944.

Mackey, Albert G. *The Encyclopedia of Freemasonry.* Chicago, 1927.

Magalhães, Basílio de. *Estudos de historia do Brasil.* São Paulo, 1940.

Maistre, Joseph de. *Du Pape.* De l'église gallicane dans son rapport avec le souverain Pontife.* Paris, 1821.

Maria, Júlio. "A Religião, ordens religiosas, instituições pias e beneficentes no Brazil," *Livro do Centenario: 1500-1900.* Rio de Janeiro, 1900. I, ii, 3-134.

Maritain, Jacques. *The Angelic Doctor: The Life and Thought of St. Thomas Aquinas.* New York, 1931.

———. *The Things That Are Not Caesar's.* New York, 1930.

Martin, Percy A. "Causes of the Collapse of the Brazilian Empire," *The Hispanic American Historical Review,* IV (February, 1921), 4-48.

Meisel, Henri-Auguste. *Cours de style diplomatique.* 2 vols. Paris, 1826.

Melo, Mário [Carneiro do Rêgo]. *Frei Caneca.* Recife, 1933.

———. *A Maçonaria e a Revolução Republicana de 1817.* Recife, 1912.

———. *A Maçonaria no Brazil prioridade de Pernambuco.* Recife, 1909.

Mendes, Oscar. "O liberalismo no Brasil sob o ponto de vista catholico," *A Ordem,* XI (January, 1932), 31-45.

Meneses, G. Bezerra de. "O Episcopado brasileiro e a questão religiosa," *Vozes de Petrópolis,* Nova Série, III (January and February, 1945), 105-109.

Morais, Eugênio Vilhena de. "O Patriotismo e o clero no Brasil," *Revista do Instituto Histórico e Geográfico Brasileiro.* XCIX (1926), 113-168.

Mourret, Fernand Roman. *L'Église et la Révolution,* Vol. VII of *Histoire générale de l'église.* Paris, 1914.

Nabuco, Joaquim. *Um Estadista do imperio Nabuco de Araujo, sua vida, suas opiniões, sua época.* 3 vols. Rio de Janeiro [1897-1899].

Nys, Ernest. *Idés modernes, droit international et franc-maçonnerie.* Bruxelles, 1908.

Oliveira, Oscar de. *Os dízimos eclesiásticos do Brasil nos períodos da Colônia e do Império.* Juiz de Fóra, Minas Gerais, 1940.

Olívola, Félix de. *Um Grande Brasileiro, D. Frei Vital Maria Gonçalves Oliveira.* 2d. ed. Recife, 1936.

Pallen, Condé B. *What is Liberalism?* Englished and adapted from the Spanish of Félix Sardá y Salvany. St. Louis, Missouri, 1899.

Pereira, [Antônio] Baptista. *A formação espiritual do Brasil.* São Paulo, 1930.

Pinheiro, J. C. Fernandes. "D. Manoel do Monte Rodrigues de Araujo," *Revista do Instituto Histórico e Geográfico Brasileiro,* XXVII (1864) ii, 194-227.

——. "Os Padres do Patrocinio ou o Porto Real de Itú," *Revista do Instituto Histórico e Geográfico Brasileiro*, XXXIII (1870), ii, 137-148.

Portela, Joaquim Pires Machado. *Constituição politica do imperio do Brazil confrontadas com outras constituições* (Rio de Janeiro, 1876).

"Projecto de constituição no 'Apostolado' e sua auctoria," *Revista do Instituto Histórico e Geográfico Brasileiro*, LXXVII (1914), ii, 3-19.

Primério, Fidélis de. *Capuchinhos em terras de Santa Cruz nos séculos XVII, XVIII e XIX.* [São Paulo] 1942.

Renaut, F. P. "Le Brésil et l'Europe," *Revue d'histoire diplomatique*, XXXVI (1922), 50-95.

——. "L'Émancipation du Brésil," *Revue d'histoire diplomatique*, XXXII (1918), 541-599.

——. "L'Organisation constitutionnelle du Brésil, les débuts de la politique personnelle de Dom Pedro," *Revue d'histoire diplomatique*, XXXIII (1919), 39-89.

Ruggiero, Guido de. *The History of European Liberalism.* Trans. by R. G. Collingwood. London, 1927.

Ribeiro, Manuel Braga. "Historia religiosa," *Diccionario historico, geographico e ethnographico do Brasil.* Rio de Janeiro, 1922. II, 223-229.

Sägmüller, Johannes Baptist. "Patron and Patronage," *The Catholic Encyclopedia.* New York, c1907-22, XI, 560-562.

Santini, Cândido. *De Regio Jure Patronatus in Brasilia perquisitio historicojuridica in praefati Iuris originem et specificam naturam (1514-1890) accedit Historica exposito conflictus Sanctam Sedem inter et Gubernium Brasiliense ob Iuris Patronatus exercitium exorti.* Pôrto Alegre, 1934.

Santos, Lúcio José dos. *A Inconfidencia mineira, papel de Tiradentes na inconfidencia mineira.* São Paulo, 1927.

——. "A Maçonaria no Brasil," *A Ordem* [Rio de Janeiro], XII (July and August, 1932), 10-24, 86-94.

Sardá y Salvany, Félix. *El Liberalismo es pecado.* Barcelona, 1887.

Schmidlin, Josef. *Papstgeschichte der Neuesten Zeit.* Vol. 2. München, 1934.

Schneider, L. *A guerra da triplice alliança (Imperio do Brazil, Republica Argentina e Republica Oriental do Uruguay) contra o governo da Republica do Paraguay (1864-1870) com Cartas e planos.* Trans. by Manoel Tomaz Alves Nogueira. Rio de Janeiro, 1875-1876.

Séché, Léon. *Les derniers Jansénistes et leur rôle dans l'histoire de France depuis la ruine de Port-Royal jusqu'à nos jours (1710-1870).* 3 vols. Paris [1891].

Silva, João António dos Santos e. *Revista historico-politica de Portugal desde o ministerio do Marques de Pombal até 1842. Precedida d'uma rapida exposição dos factos principaes da revolução franceza em 1789 até á invasão dos francezes em Portugal.* Coimbra, 1852.

Smith, John. *Memoirs of the Marquis of Pombal.* 2 vols. London, 1843.

Sousa, Octávio Tarquínio de. *Diogo Antônio Feijó.* Rio de Janeiro, 1942.

Stillson, Henry L. (ed). *History of the Ancient and Honorable Fraternity of Free and Accepted Masons and Concordant Orders written by a Board of Editors.* Boston, 1906.

Taunay, Visconde de [Taunay, Alfredo d' Escragnolle]. *O Visconde do Rio Branco.* 2d. ed. São Paulo [1930].

Trindade, Raimundo. *Archidiocese de Marianna.* 3 vols. São Paulo, 1928-1929.

Ursel, Charles d'. *Sud-Amérique.* Paris, 1879.

Varnhagen, Francisco Adolfo de. *História da independência do Brasil.* Rio de Janeiro [1940].

Waite, Arthur E. *A New Encyclopaedia of Freemasonry.* 2 vols. London, 1921.

Ward, John S. M. *Freemasonry and the Ancient Gods.* London, 1921.

Weill, Georges J. *L'Éveil des nationalités et le mouvement libéral 1815-1848.* Paris, 1930.

———. *Histoire du Catholicisme libéral en France 1828-1908.* Paris, 1909.

# INDEX